A BRIEF HISTORY
OF
PHYSICAL EDUCATION

EMMETT A. RICE
LATE, NORMAL COLLEGE OF THE
AMERICAN GYMNASTIC UNION

JOHN L. HUTCHINSON, Ed.D.
PROFESSOR OF EDUCATION
TEACHERS COLLEGE, COLUMBIA UNIVERSITY

MABEL LEE, LL.D., D.P.E.
EMERITUS PROFESSOR OF PHYSICAL EDUCATION
UNIVERSITY OF NEBRASKA

FOURTH EDITION

THE RONALD PRESS COMPANY · NEW YORK

2

Library of Congress Catalog Card Number: 58-6058

PREFACE

The history of any subject may be taken as a means of measuring its progress. It provides data for comparison of past and present with respect to the importance and influence of the subject. It constitutes a record of experiments and achievements and demonstrates the relationship existing between certain elements in civilization and the status of the subject in a particular society. Only through the study of history can a broad and appreciative view of the subject be obtained.

This book is a history of physical education from early times to the present. Its purpose is to give the undergraduate student an overview of the position physical education has occupied throughout the years in civilized society. It discusses those political, social, and religious situations which determine the character of a given society and which reflect the physical activities of its people. For example, the book explains why one religious group promoted the development of physical power while another stifled it and why certain countries under the influence of a dominating political power supported a vigorous physical training program while others under similar influence had no program of any consequence. The theories and methods of the leaders, the heritages from early movements, as well as the relationship which physical education has borne to general education, receive attention.

The material of the book is organized in three parts. Part I highlights the beginnings of physical education in ancient oriental cultures, in Greece, and in Rome. Part II reviews the place physical education held in the Dark Ages, the Age of Chivalry, the Renaissance, the Age of Realism, and the Age of Enlightenment; and then it presents the background of physical education in various modern European countries and other selected countries of the world. Part III treats the history of physical education in the United States from colonial times to the present.

The history of the physical education movement in the United States is of considerable importance because the program is more highly organized than those in other countries. For this reason, the devotion of one half of the text to the development of the United States program seems warranted. The heritages from early movements, combined with the knowledge of current activities, afford the student of physical education a sound basis not only for understanding the present status of physical education but also for judging the trends which may occur in the years ahead.

Since the objective of this book is to give the beginning student an overview of the status of physical education, past and present, we have not prepared an exacting, detailed reference work, nor have we attempted to cover every country. Also, we have felt it unnecessary to include an elaborate bibliography. We have included, however, a chapter-by-chapter list of those important publications in the history of physical education which have been used as sources of information in the preparation of this fourth edition. In addition, many of the old books and foreign publications cited by Emmett A. Rice, who wrote the original edition in 1926, have been retained for their historical value.

The Appendix lists the many organizations which have played a part in the development of physical education in the United States, the names of their officers through 1957, and those persons honored for their service to the profession. In addition, the biographical sketches in Part III accord recognition to those whose contribution has been of major significance. Sketches of leaders still living have not been included, since these persons have not yet made their total contribution to the profession. Two exceptions are Elizabeth Burchenal and Ethel Perrin, whose contributions have been of great significance from the very opening of the twentieth century.

We express our appreciation to those who cooperated in supplying information and photographs. In particular we wish to acknowledge our indebtedness to *Mind and Body* and the *American Physical Education Review*, which through their many years of publication offer rich sources of historical material; to the valuable historical research work of Dorothy Ainsworth, Ruth Elliott, Edward Mussey Hartwell, Ruth E. Houston, A. G. Kindervater, Frederick E. Leonard, and Frederick Leuhring; and to the national offices of the National Recreation Association, the Young Men's Christian Association, and the Young Women's Christian Association, for their kindness in furnishing historical data on their organization work. For illustrative material we wish to thank Oberlin College for the photograph of Delphine Hanna; Wellesley College for permission to reproduce the portrait of Amy Morris Homans; the University of Pennsylvania for permission to reproduce the portrait of Robert Tait McKenzie; Lea and Febiger, Publishers, for illustrations of Edward Mussey Hartwell and Harvard University's Hemenway Gymnasium; and the American Association for Health, Physical Education, and Recreation for illustrations of Edward Hitchcock, Dudley A. Sargent, Luther Halsey Gulick, and Thomas D. Wood.

John L. Hutchinson
Mabel Lee

January, 1958

EMMETT A. RICE

It was while teaching at the Normal College of the American Gymnastic Union in Indianapolis, Indiana, that my father was inspired to write a textbook concerned with the history of physical education. Through his classroom experiences he became aware of the fact that a brief, authentic study of physical education, its growth and its relationship to general education through the ages, was needed for a broader and more appreciative understanding of this subject and its place in the field of education.

He saw the progress of physical education as "a great movement with many undercurrents, co-existent with civilization itself and as a part of general education." With this concept in mind he undertook the writing of *A Brief History of Physical Education*, which was first published in 1926.

Shortly after my father was born in Cuba, Indiana, February 2, 1893, his family moved to the nearby town of Spencer. Here he attended grade school and was graduated from high school in 1911. While a student at Indiana University, he spent his summers teaching, first in a rural school near Spencer, then in the high schools of Bloomington, Worthington, and Brazil.

In 1916 he received an A.B. degree from Indiana University and in 1919 an M.A. degree. In that same year he became an instructor in the history department of Shortridge High

School in Indianapolis and in 1920 met and married Lillie Gally, a physical education teacher in the same school. During the next few years his teaching activities took him into the Normal College of the American Gymnastic Union where, with my mother's devoted assistance, the research and writing of his book was begun.

In 1926 he was appointed vice-principal of Shortridge High School and held that position until 1943, when he was made director of special youth services. In this capacity he headed the summer high school program, evening high school, and an afternoon recreation and activities program in areas of the city unserved by any other agency. In 1946 he became director of physical education and health for the Indianapolis public schools and remained in this position until his death, December 23, 1947.

As an educator my father was intensely interested in youth, in the trends of modern education, and in the problems of the world about him; as an historian he strove to enlighten, interpret, and evaluate in the light of past experience and knowledge.

Patricia Rice McArdle

Highland Park, Ill.
January, 1958

CONTENTS

ix

Part I

Physical Education in Ancient Cultures

1

PHYSICAL EDUCATION
IN ANCIENT ORIENTAL NATIONS

Instinct and the opportunity to play are more pronounced among primitive people than among those of civilized nations. Foot racing as a competitive sport is as widespread as the human family. Wrestling and boxing are hardly less so. Throwing at a target with weapons, stones, or other objects occurs among nearly all peoples. With some it takes the form of bowling, with others hurling the spear, and with the Canadian Indians sliding the spear over the ice. Swimming is engaged in by nearly all. Ball playing with a bat or racket is less common but was well known among the American Indians. Lacrosse was invented by them. Fencing with sticks or spears, too, is widespread.

Labor, searching for food, dancing, games, and the outdoor life of primitive man are all conducive to the development of sound bodies. Civilization took from some the body building labor of primitive man and gave to others far too great a burden. The machine, requiring little skill, accuracy, or strength, had supplanted the crude tool of the savage. The search for food passed long ago; today it is delivered to the home. Until recent times, for the great majority, games were put aside with childhood. The primitive hut gave way to the airtight house, and the outdoor life, to indoor life. Many shortcomings known to all have followed in the wake of these changes and have given rise to the necessity for conscious purposive physical education.

No one geographical area receives recognition by all authorities as the birthplace of civilization. The development of a sequential approach to early education and physical education depends, therefore, upon an arbitrary selection of the earliest civilization. Some contend present records show that the first civilized people lived in Mesopotamia, "the land between the rivers," while others hold that Egypt deserves this distinction. The authors of this text feel that these two civilizations probably paralleled each other and so, without unchallengeable authorities to rely upon, have decided to begin with the Egyptians.

EGYPT

Although Egyptian civilization reached its peak in approximately 1500 B.C., the oldest records relating to Egypt go back nearly to 5000 B.C. As Egypt transformed from a primitive to a civilized existence, formal education received much attention. Eventually, a trend toward the inclusion of physical education activities as an important aspect of the total culture became evident.

These physical activities included gymnastic exercises and wrestling, both performed to honor the gods. Wrestling became a favorite entertainment; children's games were plentiful, as excavations have revealed; lifting and swinging weights, swimming, ball games of men, women, and children (including racquets), and bull fighting represent other physical activities peculiar to this early civilization. The common people, when their work was finished, also participated in these activities. Wrestling, swimming, and gymnastics, along with other sports, became a part of vigorous training for war. Interestingly, the participation of women in many physical activities was a common rather than exceptional occurrence.

Dancing held a prominent place for all Egyptian people. While the upper class participated only in religious dances, the common people engaged in folk dancing, and professionals, both men and women, performed at royal festive occasions and dinners. Drums, the lyre, the flute, castanets, and other instruments often accompanied the many forms of dancing that were practiced so extensively in Egypt. The dancing of civilized people since that time often has been traced to these early Egyptians.

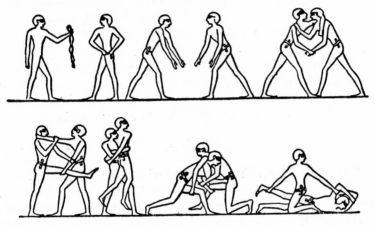

Fig. 1. Wrestling in Ancient Egypt. (Taken from drawings in Egyptian tombs.)

SUMER

Although others undoubtedly occupied lower Mesopotamia earlier, the Sumerians are usually recognized as the forerunners of the Babylonians. No concrete evidence seems available that indicates the Sumerians developed a system of physical fitness. However, their interest in wrestling and fishing and advocation of hunting as a means for keeping the upper class physically fit during peace time gives evidence of this people's viewpoint toward physical activity. The heroic tales of Gilgamesh tend to emphasize the importance of physical prowess, and the stories about this famed hunter, the first of the Paul Bunyan stories, stress the importance of physical strength, skill, and endurance.

BABYLONIA AND ASSYRIA

These nations perhaps never gave sports and games as much emphasis as the Egyptians. However, these people that dwelled between the rivers did participate in dancing and singing as they related both to religion and to the amusement of the common people. Like the Sumerians, they hunted not only for food but also as preparation for war.

Ancient reliefs indicate that boxing and wrestling as physical contests occurred. Games and bow-shooting, too, had their place. Swimming was emphasized to a great extent. Although some swimming for pleasure perhaps did exist, most evidence uncovered shows that swimming formed a basic part of the training of warriors. Inflated skins were and still are used in Mesopotamia to aid the swimmer.

CHINA

The Chinese civilization is one of the oldest in the world. It is composed of people who are industrious and frugal. Until recently they also exhibited peaceful and docile characteristics throughout their long history. Very early they adopted a policy of isolation, and when the Himalaya Mountains proved an insufficient barrier, the Great Wall was built. When that failed, laws were passed forbidding foreigners to enter China. This nonintercourse with other nations tended to crystallize the social order and prevent change. Chinese have had great reverence for their ancestors and the teachings of the past; these ideals are also partly responsible for the static society. The difficulty of writing or reading the Chinese language made universal education almost impossible.

Schools in China were private. Boys of the upper class paid tuition; girls were not educated. The aim of the school was to teach the sacred books of Confucius in such a way that pupils could repeat them or write them from memory. In higher schools the style and content of books were studied until pupils could imitate the ancient sacred literature. Officers for the nation were chosen by competitive examinations among students of the highest schools. Nothing was taught to develop individual capacity; on the other hand, everything was done to obliterate the personality and individuality of the students and make them fit into the static social order.

Very early Chinese history indicates a stress on physical activities. Archery, charioteering, and physical exercises apparently had a place in the very early Chinese civilization. With the advent of religions like Confucianism and Buddhism, intellectualism was stressed at the expense of physical education.

In the fifth century A.D., a priest made note of a series of medical exercises called Cong Fu which had been practiced in China since 2600 B.C. Diseases were thought to result from organic inactivity. Certain bodily movements combined with breathing exercises were intended to keep the organs functioning and to prolong life and insure immortality of the soul. The Swedish system of medical gymnastics has no connection with this but arose quite independently.

Boxing in China can be traced back to nearly 700 B.C., while its counterpart, wrestling, evidently started, according to modern records, much later or between 300 and 250 B.C. Wrestling became a familiar exercise for conditioning soldiers. Various forms of football or kicking games began to appear between the third and second centuries B.C.

As in all ancient cultures, dancing was stressed. Various forms of dance evolved—aggressive action, defensive action, worship, and agriculture were symbolized in some of these dances. Music as usual was combined with the dance in China, with both men and women participating individually and together. Some danced for pleasure; others were paid. Dancing became so important in the ancient feudal society that a man's prestige often depended on his prowess as a dancer.

INDIA

The civilization of India is as ancient as China's. While the warm climate in certain parts has made the inhabitants a dreamy and speculative people, this condition does not hold true for the entire country. India is a land of religious and mystic philosophies. The dominant teachings are Hinduism, Mohammedanism, and Christianity. The theory of Hinduism reduces the multiplicity of things in the universe to unity. That unity is Brahma. The aim of religion is to unite in Brahma. Meantime, man's soul immigrates from body to body through thousands of reincarnations. Ambitions, desires, and individuality combine to increase the reincarnations and postpone the time of self-liberation and absorption in Brahma. The surest way to attain that is to refrain from activity and the enjoyments of this life.

Brahmins were the only teachers, and the sons of Brahmins were the pupils. The sacred books were the texts, and memorization followed by a study of content and meaning was the learning process. Although India was attacked many times by enemies, the stable society, coupled with the prevalent philosophy, was undisturbed until relatively recent times.

The children of India did play games of their own invention and in imitation of the elders. Adults undoubtedly participated in hunting the elephant, archery, boxing, riding, running, and the like because it is known that Buddha specifically prohibited such activities. And it has been noted that during peacetime those in the military pursued sports as a means of entertainment and diversion from the regular mode of living. Centuries later the game of polo evolved from the high military personnel.

IRAN

In the seventh century B.C. the Persians and their kinsmen the Medes formed the greatest nation of the Indo-European branch of the white race. At the dawn of history these people were living in a tribal and nomadic state, tending their sheep on the hillsides and valleys of Iran. They were a rugged, industrious, serious, religious, and progressive people. From early times the Medes and Persians were noted as intrepid hunters, expert horsemen, and brave warriors.

The Persian Empire began its separate independent existence when King Cyrus the Great revolted from Media in 558 B.C. and in turn subjected the Medes to his power. With the wealth of his conquered kinsmen and the valor of his own victorious army, Cyrus incorporated nation after nation into his rapidly expanding empire; the Bactrians, the Lydians, the Asia Minor Greeks, tribes along the Caspian Sea, and finally the powerful state of Babylonia. At the end of the reign of Cyrus, 529 B.C., Persia extended from the Indus River to the Aegean Sea. The astonishing success of these conquests was due in large measure to the education of the Persian boy and young man.

Persian education was primarily moral and physical. The three classes of society were composed of farmers, tradespeople, and mechanics. Intellectual training was not thought useful and was therefore neglected. Boys were taught to shoot with the bow, to ride, and to speak the truth. Education began in infancy in the home. The mother demanded obedience and truth from her sons and instructed them in the teachings of Zoroaster. According to that religion, Ahuramazda, the god of light, truth, beauty, and goodness, is in constant conflict with Ahriman, the leader of the forces of evil, darkness, disease, and sorrow. All good Persians should take their stand with Ahuramazda, and the evils of the world will be eradicated. The truthfulness of the Persians was referred to frequently by the Greeks; their abhorrence of falsehood partly accounts for their reluctance to engage in trade to any great extent.

At about the age of six, boys were taken over by the state for physical and military training. The Persian lad was expected to rise before dawn and appear at a designated field where he exercised with other boys in running, slinging, shooting the bow, and throwing javelins. In about one year, his instruction in riding began. In addition to ordinary horsemanship, he practiced jumping on and off while in full gallop and shooting and throwing with accuracy while the mount was at top speed. After gaining some skill in these sports, the boy was allowed to participate in the hunt, which was also conducted by state officials. While on the hunt, boys were made to endure extremes of heat and cold, to make forced marches day after day, to cross streams without wetting their weapons, to eat very little food, perhaps one meal in two days, to support themselves by foraging, and to stalk and kill wild animals, such as the lion, leopard, wild boar, and antelope.

When not on the hunt, boys continued regular training in archery, riding, and athletic sports. Some time was passed in the manufacture of weapons, shields, and traps and in the pursuits of agriculture. From the age of six to twenty this training continued, although from fifteen to fifty the individual was subject to active military service. The educational system of the Persians produced the finest army in Asia. Nearly every able-bodied man must have remained in the service until the age of fifty, for Persians not only protected their own native land but also garrisoned and patroled conquered neighbors as well.

In addition, Persian history reveals that dance for men and women was discouraged or suppressed by religion but flourished as an exhibition by professional dancers. Wrestling, feats of strength, acrobatics, hunting, and polo comprise other sports practiced in Persia.

The character of Persian education was determined by what the rulers might have called "manifest destiny," namely, to conquer and hold in subjection the alien races about them. To accomplish that aim, physical, military, and moral training was thought necessary. Intellectual, cultural, and industrial training and pursuits were neglected. The Egyptians, Phoenicians, Babylonians, and other subject nations surpassed the Persians in those activities and furnished the enormous empire with the products of their labor. When the high tide of Persian conquests had been reached, a period of stagnation ensued. Wealth, tyranny, vice, and corruption, foes which the Persians were unable to withstand, so weakened the army and destroyed the stamina of the nation that when the great Alexander invaded Persia in 334 B.C. he found it to be like a hollow shell. The Persians failed to take into account the values of intellectual, industrial, and scientific training, and education of the masses as a means of building and preserving a mighty empire.

2

PHYSICAL EDUCATION
IN GREECE

The Greeks were the first people in Europe to attain a high degree of civilization. So advanced did they become that the modern world has received a rich heritage in literature, government, art, and architecture from them. Physical education held a more important place among the Greeks than in any society since that time.

The mountains of Greece served to divide the inhabitants into independent political groups called city-states which were, a great part of the time, more or less hostile to each other. The rugged coast line and the proximity of the sea lured the Greeks to maritime enterprise and colonization. A mild climate, beautiful mountain ranges, the quiet sea, and the blue sky kindled the inherent sense of beauty, proportion, delicacy, and refinement so abundant in Athenian achievement.

EARLY PERIOD AND THE HOMERIC AGE

Aegean Age. Excavations at Mycenae and Tiryns, by Schliemann, revealed that as early as 2500 B.C. the mainland of Greece and adjacent islands were inhabited by a short, dark people who were well along in civilization. Knossos and other sites in Crete, laid bare by Sir Arthur Evans, gave up remains of a splendid civilization and mighty government. Judging from the excavations, Aegeans kept written records, had enormous palaces, powerful governments, houses with plumbing, wall paintings, great varieties of art, and a thriving commerce with foreign nations. Popular gymnastics, such as the Greeks later practiced, seemed to be lacking. A painting of three acrobats and a bull was found in the Knossos palace. One performer hangs on the bull's horns, another leaps over his back, and another stands behind the animal to catch his partner who is in mid-air. Other vigorous physical activities in which the people of Crete engaged were grappling the bull as a hunting activity, acrobatics, hunting deer with the bow and arrow, hunting lions with the hunters armed like soldiers, swimming with some evidence of the refinement of certain strokes, and boxing and wrestling with indications of these activities being closely related to both religious affairs and physical conditioning for soldiers.

Women played a prominent part in dancing, especially those forms associated with religion. Also, dance depicting peasant life, war, and acrobatics received considerable attention.

Homeric Age. During the century preceding 1000 B.C. great numbers of tall, fair-haired immigrants came into the peninsula of Greece from the north. These invaders mingled with the comparatively few native Aegeans and formed the Greeks of the Homeric Age and of later times. Migrations continued until the islands of the Aegean Sea and the coast of Asia Minor were occupied. The Homeric Age continued from the migrations until about 750 B.C. and is a distinct period of Greek history though origins of later institutions can be recognized at this time.

When the reader distinguishes between myth and fact, which is not difficult to do, the great epics, the *Iliad* and *Odyssey*, said to have been written by the blind bard Homer, give a complete and accurate account of the life of this period. The Homerics lived a simple, rustic life; wealth

consisted in flocks and herds. Labor, even among the nobility, was not despised. Gold, silver, iron, tin, lead, and
copper were known and used in a crude way in manufacturing weapons and tools. Very few laws existed. A crime was
avenged by the injured one or by his kinsmen; piracy was
common and not considered as dishonorable. Women were
considered inferior, and a double standard existed. Although
the wives had certain rights denied the slave women, both
were treated as if they were property. The men were brave
and hospitable to strangers. Each small community had its
king and nobility. The religion of the Greeks had its origin
in this period.

Zeus was the supreme god of all things, Apollo the god
of light and truth, Ares of war, Hermes a messenger and the
god of commerce, Poseidon the god of the sea, and Hephaes-
tus of fire. Hera was the wife of Zeus, Athena the goddess
of wisdom, Artemis of the chase, Aphrodite of love and
beauty, Demeter of the harvest, and Hestia of the hearth.
These twelve major deities formed the Olympic Council and
resided on or near Mount Olympus from whence they guided
the destinies of the Hellenic individual and political groups.
Besides these, scores of minor spirits inhabited the earth,
sky, and sea. The gods had all the faults and passions of
humans but were immortal and endowed with miraculous
powers. The Greek approached his deities with a friendly
human understanding, seeking help for which he made
proper sacrifice and offering. In their honor, temples were
erected and festivals celebrated.

Importance of Sports and Exercises. The *Iliad* and the
Odyssey reveal the prominent place which athletic sports
held in Homeric society. Sacrifices to the gods, funerals,
entertainments for guests, and even less formal occasions
called for chariot races and tests in manly strength and skill.
The *Iliad* is the story of the war of the Homeric Greeks
against the Trojans. Agamemnon, the commander of the
Greeks, quarrels with his great warrior, Achilles. The latter
sulks in his tent and will not fight; consequently, the Trojans

are victorious, and the Greeks sustain severe losses. Finally
Hector, a Trojan prince, kills Patroclus, the friend of Achilles.
The latter then seeks revenge, and by his hand Hector is
slain.

The funeral of Patroclus related in the twenty-third book
should attract attention. After much lamenting and mourn-
ing and after many oxen and prisoners have been slain and
sacrificed, the funeral games, presided over by Achilles,
begin. First comes the chariot race. There being no race
course, they drive over the rough plain to a designated spot
and return. Phoenix is placed at that turn "that he may
note the running and tell the truth thereof." First prize
consists of a "woman skilled in fine handiwork" and a tripod;
second place receives a six-year-old mare; third prize is a
large bright caldron; fourth place gets two talents of gold;
and fifth, a two-handled urn. Five nobles enter their teams
and cast lots for starting positions. The race is on; the gods
interfere, helping some drivers and hindering others; spectators argue on who leads the race; finally Diomedes wins,
closely followed by the other four. All entrants received
prizes.

Next came the boxing match—a sturdy mule for the winner and a two-handled cup for the loser. Epeios, a famous
boxer, arose and said, "The mule I say none other of the
Achaians shall take for victory with his fists, for I claim
to be the best man here." Euryalos answered the challenge.
Friends girded them with belts and bound their hands in
thongs, and they fell to. Euryalos was so completely knocked
out that some of his comrades "led him through the ring
with trailing feet . . . drooping his head awry, and they set
him down in a swoon . . . and themselves went forth and
fetched the two-handled cup."

For the wrestling match two prizes were offered: a tripod
valued at twelve oxen and a woman, skilled in all kinds of
work, valued at four oxen. The contestants were Aias, of
great strength, and Odysseus, "of many wiles." Upright
wrestling was used, in which one must throw the other
down. Two attempts were made, and they were starting the

third when Achilles stopped the affair and awarded them equal prizes. They seemed to be too well matched.

Three prizes were offered for the foot race. A rare and beautiful silver mixing-bowl, an ox, and a half talent of gold. Aias the son of Oileus, Odysseus, and Antilochos were the entrants. It was a close race, but the goddess Athena caused Aias to slip in the blood where the oxen had been killed, and Odysseus won the race. Aias was second, and Antilochos came in third. The races closed the games, and the assembly broke up.

The *Odyssey* is the story of the adventures of Odysseus in his wanderings from Troy to his home in Ithaca. During his long absence, Penelope, his faithful wife, is beset with numerous unwelcome suitors who frequently amuse themselves before the palace in "casting weights and spears on a leveled place" (Book IV). These trials are the predecessors of the discus and javelin throws.

During his wanderings, Odysseus comes to the land of the Phaeacians who entertain him with feasting and minstrelsy. After the banquet, King Alcinous says, "Let us go forth anon and make trial of divers games, that the stranger may tell his friends when he home returneth how greatly we excel all men in boxing and wrestling and leaping and speed of foot." Odysseus is challenged to participate in any sport, but he, being sorrowful and longing for home, does not wish to compete with them. One of the boldest begins to chide and mock him, whereupon he catches up a weight much heavier than those that were being thrown and casts it far beyond their farthest mark and then challenges them to boxing, wrestling, or a foot race, "for I am no weakling in all sports." No competitor is found, and so the Phaeacians boast of their skill in dancing and give an exhibition with which Odysseus is pleased (Book VIII).

When Odysseus returns home dressed as a beggar and unknown to all, he is provoked to quarrel with another vagabond before his own palace gates. The suitors, joyed at the prospect of a fight, urge them on offering choice dishes of food to the winner. Their rags are girded up, and, when the thighs and arms of Odysseus are seen, the outcome of the match is known to all, even to Irus, the opposing beggar. The common fist fights of this time were raised to the dignity of a boxing match by the sportsmanship of bystanders.

A company of Homeric Greeks were ever ready to test their strength and skill in sports and material activities; it was their recreation and amusement. No record exists of a gymnasium or even a permanent athletic field in this period. The place of meeting was determined by convenience, and contests were impromptu and not preceded by special training. In funeral games of the Homerics, athletic sports took on a religious aspect and gave rise to the custom of celebrating great festivals by means of gymnastic competitions.

Boys and girls participated in many games together that resemble some modern activities. As they grew older, boys participated in a great variety of sports and physical exercises. Hunting for sport, as well as food, thrived, and dogs were bred and trained to further this sport. Although physical activities of all kinds were fostered to a high degree, the Homeric contests were informal as contrasted with the Great Games that followed later in Greece.

Place of Dance. Dancing was an activity participated in by all Greeks from earliest times. Homer, in the first book of the *Odyssey*, in speaking of the suitors of Penelope, says, "Now the wooers turned them to the dance and delightsome song and made merry and waited until evening should come on." When Odysseus was being entertained by the Phaeacians, the king, Alcinous, ordered the dancers, "the best in the land," to make sport. "So they leveled the place for the dance and made a fair ring and a wide. And the henchmen drew near bearing the loud lyre to Demodocus who got him into the midst, and round him stood boys in their first bloom, skilled in the dance and they smote the good floor with their feet. And Odysseus gazed at the twinkling of the feet and marveled in spirit." From this evidence it appears that dancing was cultivated and enjoyed but that exhibitions were frequently as impromptu as athletic contests.

PHYSICAL EDUCATION IN SPARTA

The growth of wealth, increase in population, intercourse with Oriental civilizations, and natural progress and achievements caused the primitive, simple, and rustic age of Homer to pass into the brilliant and productive period of Greek history, the fifth and fourth centuries B.C. By the fifth century B.C. the city-states had democratic governments, public education, and considerable wealth and prosperity. The orators, sculptors, architects, legislators, and dramatists of this century equalled those of any subsequent period of the world's history. The political groups varied in many respects, but in one they were very similar, namely, their attitude toward physical and military training. Greeks excelled all people in the extent of national participation in gymnastics, in the importance attached to physical education, and in honors conferred on the victors. The words gymnastic, athletic, agonistic, antagonist, hippodrome, and stadium are of Greek origin as well as the activities to which they refer. In this work, space permits only a study of the two leading city-states, Sparta and Athens.

The Spartans were, from the beginning of their history, a very patriotic and warlike people. Their victorious armies reduced almost every city-state in southern Greece to submission. This warlike spirit and successful hegemony over her neighbors shaped Sparta's social and educational institutions, her military policy, and her philosophy. Every freeborn Spartan gave his life to the state.

At birth the child was examined by state authorities and if found to be physically deficient it was exposed in some remote place to die; if strong and healthy the parents were permitted to rear it. The mother cared for the training and rearing of the children from birth to the age of seven. Her aim was to give the child a well-disciplined character and a hardy, rugged constitution. The Spartan child had to learn obedience, respect for elders, bravery, resourcefulness, self-restraint, and the endurance of pain and discomfort. The stories he heard, the songs he sang, and the life about him were conducive to that end. The hardiness of body was attained through the simple and scanty food, little or no clothing regardless of weather or season, rough and dangerous games, and fatiguing sports.

Methods of Physical and Moral Training. In Sparta moral and physical training had the same end in view and differed only slightly in methods. At the age of seven boys left the roof of their mother and entered the public barracks, which became their school and home. There they were grouped into companies, and the boys who showed the most native leadership were made the captains. The training was supervised by elders. Each company had its own quarters and mess table. The barracks offered the rudest accommodation; the boys slept on the ground or on their own improvised pallets. One garment sufficed the year round. The daily activities consisted in free play, throwing the javelin and weights, jumping, wrestling, running, making long hikes, and swimming.

At about the age of twelve the companies were reorganized, and a closer supervision of training began. The elders attended the place of exercise daily, and instruction, encouragement, and chastisement were never lacking. A youth about twenty years of age took command of the company. In addition to a more intensive and varied training, the boys were now compelled to secure some of the food for the mess; usually it had to be obtained by theft from peasants, the market, or the dwellings. Thieving was not a crime, but if the thief were detected he was severely punished. The aim was to teach craftiness and courage. Plutarch says that scanty food made them grow tall. The story of the boy who stole the fox and concealed it under his shirt and, rather than be detected, permitted it to gnaw his entrails until he fell dead, may or may not be true, but it reveals the ideal Spartan character. During the festival of Artemis, boys were lashed before the altar of that goddess that they might learn to withstand pain; some are said to have died without uttering a cry.

The moral training in citizenship was also of great importance. Everything was done to teach by example and precept that the state of Sparta was all important and that the individual and his likes and dislikes amounted to nothing. Self was to be totally subordinated, and Sparta exalted. The captain frequently tested his company on moral questions. The question "Who is a good citizen?" is asked. The boy is to give an accurate but very short answer; the Spartans always aimed at laconic and pointed speech. All that needed to be said on whether Sparta should be fortified was "that city is well fortified which has a wall of men instead of brick." The whole of Spartan philosophy was couched in terse maxims and proverbs which were learned by all. These tests of morality and speech were attended by the elders, and if the captain did not give rewards and punishments justly he himself was chastised when the boys were gone.

At the age of twenty the youth was a trained soldier and ready for war. War was welcomed as a relief from the strenuous discipline of peace. At the age of thirty he was compelled to marry to produce children for the state. He still continued in the army, however, only seeing his wife when he visited her clandestinely. Spartan men remained in the service of the city until they reached sixty years of age. They remained in service even longer if the government had need of them.

Information concerning Spartan women and girls is not so abundant, however. They were not secluded, and they held a very honorable and important place in society. The girls were given physical training somewhat comparable to that of the boys but under the supervision of women. They exercised publicly in running, jumping, throwing the weights and the javelin, and in wrestling. The aim was to develop robust, healthy mothers of sturdy children. It is thought that physical training for girls began at about the age of seven and continued until the age of twenty unless there was an earlier marriage. The Athenian women recognized the superiority of the Spartans in beauty, strength, and social position.

Labor, commerce, and handicrafts were despised by all Spartans; Lycurgus, who is said to have originated all important Spartan institutions, is supposed to have made the coins of great pieces of iron to purposely hamper commerce. The necessary labor was done by the Helots, who were conquered neighbors reduced to serfdom; certain other subjugated cities paid tribute to the Spartans.

The Spartan system of physical and military training obtained the desired results: the army was the best in the world. Spartans never made the mistake of substituting specialization in athletics for the ultimate goal of specialization for war. For this pre-eminent military position they sacrificed personal liberty, individualism, home life, and the achievements of peace. Sparta did not contribute great drama, immortal verse, models of architecture, and inimitable sculpture but left such accomplishments to her more cultured neighbor, Athens.

Place of Dance. In Sparta dancing was a more serious affair than in most lands and was usually one of three kinds, gymnastic, festive, or military. The Bibasis, engaged in by both men and women, consisted in springing from the ground and striking the feet behind. Prizes were given to those who could do it the greatest number of times. Another dance was participated in by youths and maidens together. The youth led with steps and gestures of a military nature followed by the maiden who approximately imitated him but gave a feminine interpretation. The most widespread military dance was the Pyrrhic, supposed to have been originated in Sparta. It was danced by naked youths armed with sword and shield; the steps and gestures imitated the charge, the retreat, and the thrust and parry of real battle, all in rhythm to the music of the flute.

PHYSICAL EDUCATION IN ATHENS

The Athenian father—not the state—decided whether his offspring was to be reared. Deformed, weak, or sickly babies, as in Sparta, were exposed and let die. The children, boys and girls, spent the first seven years under the charge and instruction of the mother and nurses. They learned to obey and respect the elders and became acquainted with the stories of the heroes and gods. The life of the children of Athens was not far different from that of America; they had balls, hoops, swings, carts, and jackstones and played hide-and-seek, blind-man's-buff, and hopping games.

At the age of seven the boy began a more serious education, but the girl remained in the home. The aim of Athenian education was to fit the boy for social, political, military, and religious life in Athens; this demanded a training of mind, morals, spirit, and body to their highest capacities. Three main studies were pursued: gymnastics, grammar, and music. The pedagogue, a male slave, accompanied the boys to and from school daily, protecting them from harm and giving instruction concerning interesting things about the city. In addition, the slave oversaw much of the boy's social life, such as eating habits, behavioral conduct, dressing, attitude toward elders, and the like. He carried the boy's books, music, and whatever else was needed.

Methods of Physical and Military Training. The school of gymnastics was called the palestra, which originally and literally meant a wrestling ground. The palestrae, of which there were many in Athens, were usually located on the banks of a stream where facilities for bathing and swimming might be had. As the importance of these institutions increased, more and more conveniences and accommodations were secured. First of all, a room for dressing and undressing was erected because all exercises were performed without clothing; then a room where the body could be properly oiled was provided; then a sand room, where conveniences for sprinkling sand on the body were maintained; need was also found for quarters equipped with bathing facilities. Last of all, rooms for recreation with punching bags and balls of varying weights and sizes were added. The entire structure formed a hollow square; a court in the middle where jumping, boxing, and wrestling might be practiced was open to the sky. Running and throwing the discus and javelin usually took place in the open field outside the building if the interior court was too small.

Nearly all the palestrae, open to boys, were owned by private individuals who conducted them for profit, but like all other Athenian schools they were regulated by the government officials. Expert teachers in all varieties of wrestling, boxing, running, jumping, and the discus and javelin throw were employed. These sports were so universally taught in Athens that it was easy to arrange a track meet among boys at any time. The festival of Hermes was largely an exhibition of boys' gymnastic accomplishments. Many boys trained in the palestra for the great national games. At the age of eighteen the youth deserted the palestra and found recreation and amusement in the gymnasium.

Along with physical education the boy attended the grammar school (didascaleum) where he very early learned to read and write and to calculate simple arithmetic problems. In the latter part of his schooling he not only studied and memorized the *Iliad* and *Odyssey* and other selections of the national literature but also practiced public speaking and oratory. In addition to these studies, moral lessons and instruction for citizenship were not lacking; the father and the pedagogue were constantly guiding and correcting his manners and conduct.

At about ten years of age musical education began; it was presumed that every educated man could play the lyre and sing the songs of Greece.

When eighteen years of age the youth became a man. He was enrolled as a cadet or ephebus, and with the other young men he took the famous Athenian oath.

I will never disgrace these sacred arms or desert my companions in the ranks. I will fight for temples and public property, both alone and with many. I will transmit my fatherland, not only not less, but greater and better than it was transmitted to me. I will obey the magistrates who may at any time be in power. I will observe both the existing laws and those which the people may unanimously hereafter make, and if any person seek to annul the laws or to set them at nought, I will do my best to prevent him, and will defend them both alone and with many. I will honor the religion of my fathers. And I call to witness Agraulos, Enyalious, Ares, Zeus, Thallo, Auxo, and Hegemone.

Then began an intensive military training lasting for two years. The first year was occupied by considerable time in guard duty in and about Athens and, at the same time, practicing warlike exercises and sham battles. At the end of the year a great exhibition in athletic and military sports was held. The second year was spent in more training and actual military service in some outlying province. If no war was in progress the young man was freed at the end of his training and might become a philosopher, poet, dramatist, historian, sculptor, merchant, politician, or any one of the many callings to which the cosmopolitan life of Athens invited one. But whether he specialized in any one activity or not he remained always a gymnast; for gymnastics meant pleasure, sport, health, a handsome body, amusement, social intercourse, moral training and complete development, and even honor and fame.

This compulsory ephebic training as designed by the state indicated a lack of faith in the previous method of developing strength and loyalty through individual freedom, creativeness, and voluntary choice. This preparation became a paternalistic state effort to insure military security and efficiency.

Importance of the Gymnasia. To serve the men of Athens the three great gymnasia, the Academy, the Lyceum, and the Cynasargus were established and maintained by the state. The earliest gymnasium was merely an athletic field usually located near a stream. When buildings were needed the architectural form resembled that of the palestra, and the hollow square building in a gymnasium is frequently called a palestra. The information concerning the arrangements of these Athenian gymnasia is very scanty; there is just an allusion to them here and there in the literature. The excavations at Delphi and Olympia tell more about the gymnasia of those cities.

The Lyceum building consisted of the great hollow-squared palestra. Near the entrance was the large undressing room (apodyterion). Seats and benches were around the room, and there were hooks on the walls for hanging up clothing. Also some gymnasium equipment was kept in this room: perhaps strigils, halteres, and a discus. Around the inside of the entire structure was a colonnade connecting the different rooms. From the apodyterion the athlete might go to the oil room where he or the attendants oiled the body thoroughly. The youth was then ready for exercises or contests. Along one side of the colonnade was a covered running track (zystos) suitable for short sprints or running in bad weather. If he chose to wrestle or jump or hurl the discus, opponents could be found in the open court. If he preferred to exercise alone he might go to the punching bag room where bags of various sizes and weights were suspended. Outside the palestra young men engaged in long runs and received lessons in riding.

After the youth had finished his exercises he proceeded to the bath. In the gymnasia of the fifth century, the bath was very simple. To remove the oil, perspiration, and perhaps dust, he used a scraper called a strigil. Large tubs and troughs of water were provided from which the athlete washed himself. Some gymnasia seem to have had cold plunge baths. All three Athenian gymnasia were on small streams where plenty of water was available. After dressing, the youth had, as further recreation, walks along the river or conversations with poets, authors, and sculptors in or about the gymnasium. The Lyceum was a place of recreation and amusement for the idle youth, a place of training for the gymnast who wished to enter the Pan-Hellenic games, and a place of exercise for the elderly gentlemen who gave thought to their physical welfare.

During the fourth and third centuries B.C. the Greek gymnasia became much more elaborate and magnificent as a result of the increase in wealth and luxury and, later, the Roman influence. Particularly there were added more at-

Fig. 2. Scenes from the Greek Pentathlon, 500 B.C. Upper: Discus, javelin, and wrestling events. Center: Discus and javelin events. Lower: A javelin thrower, a jumper, an athlete, and a javelin thrower. Note the picks, disci, strigils, halteres, and javelin thongs.

tendants, beautiful interiors, several bathing pools of various temperatures, rooms for a sport similar to hand ball and other games of recreation, and commodious lounging quarters for poets, philosophers, and musicians. Aristotle conducted his philosophic teachings at the Lyceum, Plato at the Academy; so famous became these gymnasia as intellectual centers that both names have come to refer to places of mental rather than physical culture. The Cynasargus became the home of the Cynic philosophers.

Position of Women. The social position of women in Athens was similar to that in the Oriental nations, one of semiseclusion. Consequently no provision was made for their education. The girl was reared by her mother and nurses in the duties of the housewife. She was taught to spin and weave, sew, cook, and care for the home. If she learned to read or write it was only through her mother's teachings. No provision was made for physical education other than the simple games of childhood. Athenians were superior to their warlike neighbors the Spartans in all the arts of peace except in the education and the social position of women.

PAN-HELLENIC GAMES

The individual city-states of Greece celebrated the festivals of the deities in dances, songs, and games. Among these were the Panathenaea, the Dionysia, and the Eleusinia in honor of Athena, Dionysus, and Demeter respectively. More important than these, however, were the four great Pan-Hellenic festivals, the Olympian, Pythian, Nemean, and Isthmian.

Olympian Games. Olympia, in Elis on the River Alpheus, was a sacred spot where religious ceremonies and athletic contests were given long before the Olympian games were organized. The first recorded Pan-Hellenic celebration at Olympia was held in 776 B.C. and thereafter every fourth year in late summer until abolished by the Roman Emperor Theodosius in 394 A.D. As the games became more and more varied and attracted more visitors and competitors, the site of Olympia became adorned with many magnificent buildings such as the Temple of Zeus, the great stadium, and the palestra. Their remains and the descriptions left to us afford means of locating them with accuracy.

Before the festival, heralds journeyed through Greece announcing a sacred truce among all the people, the visitors and contestants might go to and from Olympia unmolested. Zeus, who was being so honored, would punish the one who

failed to heed the warning. The entire management was controlled by ten magistrates who lived in Elis. All entrants
for the games had to undergo examination; they must be of
Greek blood, must never have committed crime, must take
an oath to compete fairly, must have been in training for
ten months before the games, and the last month must have
been spent at Olympia. Ritual and ceremony marked the
opening and every important stage of the games. Women
were not permitted to be present.

Events. The foot races were among the oldest and most-
honored events. The actual distances depended on the
length of the stadium. A stade race, one length of the
stadium, was about 200 yards, the diaulos was double the
distance, and the dolichos was any number of stades, perhaps as many as twenty-four. Boys were not expected to
run quite so far; Plato says they should run only one-half
the distance of men. Contestants for short runs were
divided into heats of about four men each by drawing lots,
then the winners of the heats ran to determine the final
victor. Races in armor, but without weapons, were introduced in the sixth century, and, after the Persian wars, they
became very popular.

The pentathlon consisted of competition in five events—
running, jumping, throwing the javelin and the discus, and
wrestling—to determine the best all-round gymnast. Jumping, and throwing the javelin and the discus, were practiced
very much in the palestra and gymnasium and were popular
sports throughout Greece, but at Olympia and in other
national games they were only a part of the pentathlon.
The broad jump and the hop-step-and-jump were the only
forms of jumping contested and the latter only rarely. All
competitors jumped from the same takeoff into soft, loose
ground; the distance was measured with a rod. The jumpers
generally used weights of stone or metal called halteres;
several of them have been found.

Throwing the javelin was one of the most popular and
practical sports in Greece. The art was necessary in war

and in the hunt, and every boy learned it in the palestra. Javelins eight to ten feet long and of varying weights with dull points were used for competition. Thongs were wrapped near the middle, leaving a loop for the fingers. This method of throwing trebled the distance that the javelin might be hurled and imparted a rotary motion to it.

In the original weight-throwing contests, stones and rough pieces of metal were used, but later the object took on the form of the modern discus. The many disci that have been found differ in weight and size, not only because some were for boys but also because different regulations were in force at different times. The discus was hurled without using the modern method of completely turning the body. Music from the flute frequently accompanied both discus and javelin throwing as well as jumping.

Wrestling, one of the most popular sports, was considered the most effective exercise for all-round development. It occurred as a separate event and as a part of the pentathlon. Of the two forms of wrestling, the "upright" and the "ground," the former was more common. The aim was to throw the opponent to the ground without falling with him; it took three falls to make a victory. There were no binding rules on holds, but those that caused torture or permanent injury were not looked upon as fair or sportsmanlike. The Greeks preferred speed, skill, and science to brute strength or foul play. When there were several competitors the modern method of matching by lot and elimination was used. In the palestra and gymnasium "ground" wrestling was frequent; the aim was to throw the opponent to the ground and then continue the struggle until he admitted he was beaten.

In boxing events the men were matched as in wrestling. In the place of the modern gloves, the Greeks securely wrapped the fingers, knuckles, wrists, and forearms with thongs of rawhide to protect the hands rather than soften the blow. The blows and parries were very similar to those of today. No ring was provided except insofar as the spectators formed one, there were no rounds; the fight went on until one was knocked out or until they rested by mutual consent. Boxers were not ranked or matched according to weights.

In the seventh century B.C. a combination of boxing and wrestling called the pankration was added to the events at Olympia. It was a free fight with hands unbound and all the tricks of both sports permitted: hitting, kicking, twisting of limbs, and strangling. Biting and gouging alone were forbidden. The fight continued until one contestant admitted he was defeated. Toward the period of the decline of Greek athletics, the pankration for boys was introduced.

Horse racing, both with chariots and with jockeys, found place in the Olympian games in the seventh century B.C., and, although they were very exciting, they did not harmonize with the aim and purpose of gymnastics and national games and were not permitted to overshadow the importance or detract from the honor of winning in the more athletic events. Contests for heralds and trumpeters were also held at Olympia. Originally all contests were finished in one day, but as the number of events and contestants increased five days were found necessary.

Rewards. The victor in any event at Olympia received both a crown of wild olive branches which had been cut from a sacred grove and a palm branch as a token of victory. He was honored in the celebrations and banqueting at Olympia, and his journey home was a triumphal procession. Frequently a city whose son had been victorious made a breach in the walls, so that he might not have to enter by the common path. His fame spread throughout Greece; sculptors carved his figure in stone, and poets wrote odes commemorating his achievements. The Greeks could name the victors of the various events for several years previous; it was common practice to recall an event to another by saying it was so many years after so and so won the pankration or the diaulos.

Training of Contestants. In the earliest times scientific training for athletics was not known, and the Spartans, because of their severe military training, won most of the prizes; but when contestants from other parts of Greece began practicing under scientific trainers, the Spartans, who continued to hold to military rather than athletic training, fell behind. The Athenian boy learned all the events and the proper forms of executing them in the palestra. If he excelled there, he continued his training in the gymnasia under skilled and scientific tutors, many of whom had been victors in the games. Exercises, such as punching the bag, shadow boxing, and dancing, were considered good training methods for the boxers; digging in the ground with a pick and jumping was recommended for wrestlers; using the halteres as dumbbells was encouraged for both boxers and wrestlers; the runners practiced in deep sand. Some thought was given to dieting.

Other Pan-Hellenic Festivals. The Pythian games were given in honor of Apollo near his shrine at Delphi, in the third year after every Olympian meet. In addition to the usual athletic sports and chariot races, competitions in the flute and lyre and in musical composition were held. The highest reward was a crown of bay leaves plucked from a sacred valley.

The Nemean games were held in Argolis in honor of Zeus in the early part of every second summer. The events were almost the same as those at Olympia. A crown of fresh parsley was the reward.

The Isthmian games, in honor of Poseidon, were given on the Isthmus of Corinth in the spring of every second year; wreaths of dry parsley leaves were given the winners. These four Pan-Hellenic gatherings never coincided but frequently came very close together.

Decline of the Games. During the second century B.C. a marked decline in Greek physical education is noticeable. The conquering Romans did not enjoy or have much respect for strictly athletic or gymnastic contests, and the Greeks were unable to maintain a national enthusiasm for them. The old gymnastics which aimed at complete development, exemplified in the pentathlon winners, gave way to athletics which implied prize-winning professionals who trained for one event only. The more exciting and brutal events such as chariot races, boxing, and the pankration became the most popular. The boxers fastened lead and iron pieces to the thongs which were wrapped about their fists, and science gave way to brute strength. The best people of Greece did not enter the games. Corruption and bribery were common.

Fig. 3. The Pankration. One attempts to gouge the other's eye and receives a beating from the trainer. (From a kylix, British Museum.)

The officials at Olympia held out determinedly against this destructive influence, but they could not remain entirely free from it.

In effect, professionalism destroyed the original concepts of physical education in Athens. Athletics which were carried to the extreme encouraged specialization in one sport, hero-worship, winning at all costs, large audiences, and the like. Trainers, often ex-athletes, trained their protégés to such an extent that amateurs experienced little or no success in competing against them. On the other hand, professionals often bought their victories and did not have to trust to superior physical strength and skill in order to win. These evils became so common that offenders were fined and punished, but nothing seemed to stem the tide.

Dance and Ball Games. The Athenians esteemed the dance almost wholly for its esthetic values and religious expression. In earliest times the gods were worshiped by large groups of dancers, including men of noble rank. The dances were very simple, but from them evolved the more complicated Dionysaic or Bacchic, which required a trained chorus. Nearly every dramatic production demanded the presence of a chorus of singers and dancers who, in the absence of scenery, gave the setting the proper atmosphere. The Pyrrhic was also danced in Athens by the Ephebi. Frequently professional dancers, girls and men, entertained the guests at the symposium or drinking bout.

The games that served as a means of physical education and recreation were all played with balls. The Greeks played a game very much like hockey. Another game, called episkuros, in which a large ball was kicked about, accounts for the statement that the Greeks played football.

THEORIES OF PROMINENT MEN

Any activity as popular as gymnastics would be sure to draw from the greatest minds opinions concerning its aims, values and theories. Xenophon reports Socrates as saying, "No citizen has a right to be an amateur in the matter of physical training; it is a part of his profession as a citizen to keep hmself in good condition, ready to serve his state at a moment's notice. Finally what a disgrace it is for a man to grow old without ever seeing the beauty and strength of which his body is capable . . . And in all the uses of the body it is of great importance to be in as high a state of physical efficiency as possible. Why even in the process of thinking, in which the use of the body seems to be reduced to a minimum, it is a matter of common knowledge that grave mistakes may often be traced to bad health" (*Memorabila* III–12).

Plato is said to have been nicknamed by his wrestling teacher because of his very broad shoulders. He, in all his writings, advocates physical training for its educational and military values but deplores every tendency toward professionalism and competitions for the purpose of amusing an audience. In his *Protagoras,* speaking of children, he wrote, "Then they send them to the master of Gymnastic, in order that the bodies may better minister to the virtuous mind, and that they may not be compelled through bodily weakness to play the coward in war or on any other occasion." In Book III of his famous *Republic* are found the following ideas: "Gymnastic as well as music should receive careful attention in childhood and continue through life. . . . Now my belief is not that the good body improves the soul but that the good soul improves the body. . . . Gymnastics will incline him to have as little as possible to do with medicine. . . . I believe that the teachers of both (music and gymnastics) have in view chiefly the improvement of the soul."

Plutarch, the biographer and historian, in his *Morals* says, "In the next place the exercise of the body must not be neglected; but children must be sent to schools of gymnastics. This will conduce partly to a more handsome carriage and partly to the improvement of their strength. For the foundation of a vigorous old age is a good constitution of the body in childhood."

Euripides, although not entirely opposed to gymnastics, rebukes the nation for worshiping the athletes because of their victories. "Of all the countless evils through Hellas, there is none worse than the race of Athletes. . . . Whoever helped his fatherland by winning a crown for wrestling or for speed of foot, or hurling the discus or striking a good blow on the jaw? Will they fight the foe with disci in their hands or driving their fists through the foemen's shields?" (Fragment of the play, *Autolycus.*)

Aristotle thought that "the education of the body must precede that of the intellect, it clearly follows that we must surrender our children in the first instance to gymnastic and the art of the trainer. . . . Up to the age of puberty gymnastic exercises of a comparatively light kind should be applied, with a prohibition of hard diet and compulsory exercises, so that there may be no impediment to the growth."

Hippocrates and Galen wrote on the values of physical training and advised their patients to take exercises in the gymnasia as a means of recovering from ills and weaknesses. Galen said, "He is the best physician who is the best teacher of gymnastics." Medical gymnastics and massage were known to both Greeks and Romans. Hippocrates asserted that "friction (may) be so violent that the body is made hard; so light that it is relaxed; so long-continued that it is decreased; so moderate that it is rounded."

THE GREEK IDEAL

The Greek military, education, and religious system promoted and strove for the physical perfection of its people. This ideal influenced every form of art and achievement. The finest odes from Pindar and Bacchylides are inspired by the victors of the games. A part of Pindar's *Seventh Olympian Ode* in honor of Diagoras of Rhodes, who won the boxing match at Olympia in 404 B.C., translated into prose, runs as follows:

Of garlands from these games hath Diagoras twice won him crowns, and four times he had good luck at famous Isthmus, and twice following at Nemea and twice at rocky Athens and at Argos the bronze shield knoweth him and the deeds of Arcadia, and of Thebes and the yearly games Boeotian and Pellene and Aigina where six times he won; and the pillar of stone at Megara hath the same tale to tell.

The gods alone rivaled athletes as subjects for the Greek sculptors. Naked contestants offered the carver of stone an opportunity to study nearly perfect human forms in action; the result was that their chisels produced that unexcelled if not unequaled statuary of all time. A great part of the knowledge concerning Greek athletics stems from the vase painter, who so universally used the scenes of the palestra and gymnasium and of the games as a means of decoration. In coin designs the athletes frequently displaced the statesmen and the gods. True Greek gymnastics, exemplified especially in Athens, discouraged professionalism, brutality, and excitement, and encouraged complete development of the individual, fair play, and nation-wide physical education for esthetic as well as utilitarian reasons. High ideals and noble objectives characterized the golden age of Greek gymnastics.

PHYSICAL EDUCATION
AMONG THE ROMANS

Near the end of the Homeric Age of Greek history a small settlement of sturdy shepherds and shrewd traders gathered near the famous seven hills on the banks of the Tiber. They were industrious, frugal, and earnest; they were practical in their view of life, stern in dealing with their fellowmen, reverent to their gods, and patriotic to their state. This small political unit of Latium extended its reign to eventually unite the entire Italian peninsula. The Roman Republic slowly gave the people more rights in return for military service. Emphasis on war and conquest led to placing great stress on physical vigor and relatively less concern for intellectualism.

EARLY PERIOD

The Roman father had undisputed control over his children and his wife. Disrespect might be punished severely and disobedience with slavery or death, but such measures were seldom necessary. The Roman matron was charged with rearing the children; she was honored and respected and given more freedom than were Greek women, excepting the Spartans. These people seem to have come to the idea very early that some day their city would rule the world.

The first duty of the family was to serve the nation and to that end rear robust children with true Roman ideals. Since there were no schools, the homes were expected to give both moral and physical training, and no homes ever discharged their duties more faithfully or more successfully. The parents in their daily and hourly contact with their children instilled in them pride of race, obedience, honesty, courage, industry, loyalty to the state, and reverence for the gods and the ancestors.

The Roman child, like the modern one, had his cart, tops, hoops, stilts, balls, and pets. The people were warlike and ambitious, and physical training was regarded as necessary to every Roman. The father, who was usually a soldier, was charged with the duty of training his son. The aim of physical training was to produce strength, agility, endurance, hardiness, and skill in the use of sword, spear, shield, and javelin, and in horsemanship and swimming. The Greek idea of gymnastics for grace, beauty, carriage, symmetry, or complete development of man could not have been understood by these early Romans. Virgil says (*Aeneid* IX–603), "We carry our children to the icy streams and harden them in the bitter icy waters; as boys they spend wakeful nights over the chase, and tire out the whirlwind, but in manhood, unwearied by toil and trained to poverty, they subdue the soil with their mattocks, or shake towns in war." In their play, boys competed with each other in swimming, wrestling, boxing, running, and jumping, although there was no palestra as in Athens. Ball games of many varieties were played by the early Romans. Throwing, catching, and juggling various sized balls was common practice, while a game similar to handball was popular. Many other ball games were also played, some being very vigorous and rough. Dancing was restricted to the royal families, religious ceremonies, funeral processions, and other public events.

The *Twelve Tables*, written in 450 B.C., summed up the social, political, and religious customs and ideals of Rome and made them the laws of the land. From that time, both in the home and in the schools, the tables became the basis for literary and moral instruction; all children memorized them.

Between the fourteenth and seventeenth year the boy laid aside the toga praetexta and other insignia of childhood. With ceremony and rejoicing he dressed in the toga virilis, and his name was inscribed as a citizen of Rome. He was then subject to service in the army.

The Campus Martius, a field dedicated to the god of war, Mars, lay outside the Servian walls. It was, first of all, a military parade ground and a training camp for soldiers. Male citizens, between the ages of seventeen and forty-seven, might be drafted into the army when needed and discharged when the war was over. Military training was very severe, and the discipline was strict. There were exercises in running, jumping, wrestling, riding, swimming (both naked and in armor), and sham battles. Wooden horses were used to train the recruit in leaping on and off the horse. They practiced long marches with heavy equipment, including intrenching tools, shield, helmet, sword, spear, breastplate, stakes for palisade, and food for seventeen days.

The Campus Martius served also as a resort for young men not in service. Here on any afternoon they competed with each other in the ordinary athletics, swimming, and games. Since boxing, running, jumping, and wrestling were not ends in themselves with the Romans, they never attained the skill and technique of the Greeks.

PERIOD OF EXPANSION

Rome owed her success in war to the moral and physical training of her youth. By 265 B.C. almost all Italy had submitted to Roman power, and by the end of the next century, Carthage, Spain, the Mediterranean islands, a part of Gaul, Greece, and Asia Minor lay prostrate before the conquering armies. By 31 B.C., which marks the end of the Republic, the whole of the Mediterranean world was governed by

Rome and for Rome. These conquests had an important and marked influence on Roman civilization. Contact with older and more advanced nations gave the conquerors greater breadth of mind and opened the way for alteration if not destruction of old Roman ideals. Wealth displaced poverty; luxurious habits took the place of simple living; thousands of slaves, sent back by the armies, degraded free labor; cheap grain from Sicily and Africa compelled the Italian peasant to give up his farm and move to the capital, where he and others of his kind formed the idle and dangerous mob. The prolonged campaigns tended to develop a professional standing army rather than a citizen army.

Recognition of the Value of Schools. As Rome evolved into a world power and came in contact with nations of superior intellectual attainments, the need arose for schools to produce statesmen and orators; so the homes surrendered the duty of training the youth to these institutions and to the slave pedagogue. Elementary schools taught reading, writing, and calculation; grammar schools taught the literature of Rome and Greece as well as the Greek language; and schools of rhetoric gave instruction in oratory, composition, law, and other higher subjects. Although the organization, the methods, and even the teachers and pedagogues were Greek, the Romans failed to accept the Greek idea that gymnastics and music were essential to a complete system of education. The Roman was too practical to see any value in music; and as for gymnastics, its real value was thought to be military. An ability to swim, however, was considered essential to every Roman. Complete ignorance was often expressed by the adage, "He has neither learned to read nor to swim."

Effect of Moral Decline. Toward the end of the Empire, the rich lived not only wantonly, but luxuriously. On the other hand, the contented small landowner of previous days faced both economic and political deprivations. The directions that both classes began to take marked the first steps toward undermining the patriotic and self-sacrificing attitudes of earlier days. This trend, in turn, caused many undesirable factors to arise, such as political corruption, a judiciary open to bribery, loss of civil freedom, emperors of a severe, despotic nature, and the like. An accompanying decline of the birth rate, increased divorce, and a loss of religious influence weakened the Roman Empire even when it was the great world power.

Rise of Games of Circus and Amphitheater. The growth of luxury, demands for intellectual training, and establishment of the professional army tended to destroy the slight favor which the Roman masses had shown for physical training. At the same time national sports arose, such as the games of the circus and of the amphitheater, which contributed nothing to the physical development of the nation. Conversely, these activities proved of great danger to the life and limb of the participants and of debasing influence on the audience.

The Circus Maximus was about 2,000 feet long and 600 feet wide and accommodated approximately 200,000 spectators. In the arena was a low wall called the spina around which charioteers raced. There were, as a rule, four horses to each chariot and eight chariots to the heat. Entrants lined up about 400 feet from the end of the spina in an arc so that all were equidistant from the end. At a given signal all dashed for the end of the spina to secure the inside position. The race was not fast, but very dangerous and exciting. The sharp turns at the ends of the spina afforded the collisions and overturned chariots which the audience came to witness. These hazards required caution, daring, and skill of the drivers. The races varied from two to four miles. There were no penalties for fouls; driving against another chariot, tripping the horses, and all kinds of trickery were encouraged. There were few races without casualties or deaths. The audience wagered large stakes on the success of their favorite driver or teams.

Gladiatorial exhibitions proved even more debasing and destructive of true sportsmanship. Here slaves and ruffians, trained for the purpose, fought their opponents, either man or beast, until death decided the issue. The emperors searched constantly for new methods of fighting, strange combats, and new varieties of wild animals, for the populace soon tired of the ordinary struggle between two soldiers. Men by the tens and hundreds were pitted against each other; authentic accounts state that the arena was often flooded and naval battles were staged, in which hundreds lost their lives. Training schools for gladiators have been found at Capua and Pompeii, consisting of a square field enclosed by buildings which contained trainer's quarters, kitchen, mess hall, property room, sleeping room, and guard house. The field was used for the exercises and combats.

The gladiator and the race driver (auriga) were idols of the populace and, in the decadent period of Rome, were honored by all classes. If they were slaves, they finally gained their freedom; if free, they received substantial rewards in money. Diocles, a Spaniard, entered 4,257 races, was victorious in 1,462 and won the equivalent of $1,800,000 in twenty-four years.

Importance of the Thermæ. In early times, Romans were content with the sponge bath, usually cold, or a plunge in the Tiber for hygienic and disciplinary purposes. With the increase of wealth and luxury, the government built the most magnificent public baths ever erected. At one time there were about 700 government baths. Some, much larger and finer than others and usually called thermæ, had arrangements for both recreation and social intercourse. The Therma of Diocletian accommodated about 1,600 bathers at one time and that of Caracalla about 3,200. These institutions are similar to the late Greek gymnasia except that more space was given to bathing and less to gymnastic facilities and they were more luxurious. Bathing privileges were usually free to all, but at times an admittance fee of less than one cent was charged. One of the best preserved thermæ is in the city of Pompeii.

There were separate apartments provided for men and women. Near the entrance was the apodyterium or undressing room; pegs were in the wall on which to hang clothing, or slaves were present to care for it. A palestra with a field open to the sky was incorporated in the therma. Here exercises and competitions of a light nature were engaged in to heighten the enjoyment of the bath and the evening meal. A spheristerium was provided where balls of various sizes and weights were tossed about for recreation and amusement. At least one therma has remains of what appears to be a bowling alley. The unctorium was the room where the body might be oiled before the exercises and anointed after the bath. In the frigidarium was the cold bath with pool and basins. The tepidarium was a very warm room, sometimes without any water, where perspiration might be induced and where one might accustom himself to the heat before entering the still warmer caldarium. The caldarium was usually the hottest room in most of the baths, but some had the sudatorium in which the water was almost to the boiling point. After the hot bath the bather returned to the tepidarium and cooled slowly, then used the strigil and towels to remove the perspiration. From there he went to the unctorium for ointment and perfumes. He might then dress and stroll about the corridors or gardens with friends, or he might seek the company of a poet, musician, philosopher, or a politician.

Roman Influence on Gymnastics. It has been stated before that the conquest of Greece by the Romans had a bad influence on the Pan-Hellenic games. Unable to value gymnastics as a means of attaining beauty, symmetry of body, grace, complete development and harmony of body and soul, the conquerors hastened the decay of the games, which had already begun under the later Greeks. Professionalism was encouraged, the more brutal and exciting sports came to be the most popular, money was given as prizes, and corruption and bribery followed. The games ceased to have any connection with general education; the moral values to be derived from friendly competitions disappeared.

The first exhibition of Greek athletics occurred in Rome in 186 B.C., but they did not prove popular. In the first century A.D., Nero built a gymnasium and instituted the Neronia games in which athletics had a part. Domitian, a few decades after that, built a magnificent stadium in the Campus Martius for athletics. The Olympiads were abolished in A.D. 394 by the Roman Emperor Theodosius, and physical training was no longer compulsory. All writings about these institutions are in the Greek language, and the athletes and trainers were Greek. Romans were the spectators, many of whom attended the games merely from curiosity to see the foreigners engage in their exhibitions.

Dance and Ball Games. In ancient times the sons of the proudest families of Rome practiced religious and military dances in public. But in the time of the Republic it became a disgrace for a man to dance on any occasion. In the times of the Empire some emperors introduced the Pyrrhic dance, usually executed by Greeks or children, for the amusement of the Roman populace. At the sumptous Roman banquets the guests were entertained by professional and slave dancers, usually girls. In the theatres the pantomimic dancing which interpreted the love stories of the gods were enjoyed by all.

The Romans, like the Greeks, played a game resembling hockey as well as harpastum, which was similar to soccer. Another game of throwing two balls at one time to an opponent who was supposed to catch both of them was popular. Many private homes and the thermæ were provided with handball courts; the game was played according to rules which were similar to modern rules.

Part II

Physical Education from the Teutonic Invasions to Modern Society

4

PHYSICAL EDUCATION
IN THE DARK AGES

Every phase of Roman society experienced a decay during the fourth and fifth centuries A.D. until the fall of the Roman Empire in the West in A.D. 476.

One of the many causes of the fall of Rome was depopulation. The numerous divorces, the few marriages, the low birth rate, and loss of manpower through incessant civil wars and gladiatorial games, as well as through suicide and homicide, tended to produce race suicide. A no less important cause was economic ruin. The decreasing number from whom taxes might be collected, the extravagance of the rich, the habit of giving grain to the populace, which not only wasted the public funds but also encouraged pauperism, the slave system which exterminated free labor—all contributed to the ruin of Rome's financial and industrial stability.

Finally, the eventual and almost complete moral and physical decay of the Romans was a contributing factor in the ultimate overthrow of Rome as an empire. The last decades of Roman history offer unequaled scenes of private and public extravagance and debauchery. From the emperor's court to the rabble, sensual excess seemed to be the aim of existence. The cry of the mob was for "bread and games," both of which were freely given. The period is memorable for its political corruption and dishonesty, and embezzlement of public funds. As one writer of the times said, "Virtue is the sentence of death." In early times the Romans had believed that virtue was the greatest and most valued thing in life. In the later era the moral and physical condition of the Romans changed. The long war tended to exterminate the vigorous, hardy, self-reliant young men who formed the early armies; those who were spared frequently fell victim to luxurious living and effeminate manners. As the Empire approached its final collapse, the young men, who should have borne arms in defense of the country, were enervated by luxury, wrecked physically by excesses, and frequently self-mutilated so that they might escape the rigorous discipline and the dangers of war.

SIGNIFICANCE OF THE TEUTONIC INVASIONS

Into this decaying Empire there migrated whole nations of Teutonic barbarians from Northern Europe. Through several centuries the Romans had met them in occasional wars and always managed to retain the Rhine and the Danube as the northern frontier, but they had never succeeded in conquering all Germany. In A.D. 376 the Visigoths began their successful invasion, and historians usually agree that A.D. 476 marks the end of the Roman Empire in the West. During that century the Visigoths occupied Spain, the Vandals seized Northern Africa, the Franks and Burgundians captured and settled in Gaul, the Angles and Saxons took Britain and the Ostrogoths occupied Italy itself.

The immediate result of the introduction of millions of victorious barbarians into a weakened though highly civilized nation was to produce the "Dark Ages." Literature and learning ceased to advance and, indeed, were only preserved in Europe by those who controlled organized monasteries. Bridges, roads, harbors, and even public buildings were neglected. Centralized government was destroyed; all great achievements of the ancients were endangered. Civilization has never before—nor has it since—experienced such a lapse.

Subsequent history demonstrated that the barbarian invasion of the Roman Empire was a fortunate thing for the world. What then was their contribution to the world's progress? Simply their own bodies. Mentally they were barbarians, but capable of assimilating a part of the conquered Roman civilization and ultimately progressing far beyond that civilization. Physically they were a young, vigorous, and stalwart race; the large families of sturdy children reveal their virility. Their simple but active life produced a race of giants in comparison to the Romans. The barbarian family, held together by almost unbreakable marriage bonds, lived in a rude log hut with thatched roof. Skins of animals and crudely woven cloth served as garments and provided the only protection against the disagreeable mists and cold winds of the forest. Herding cattle and sheep and primitive farming constituted the principal occupations. Hospitable to strangers but cruel to his enemies, loyal to his comrades, reckless in battle, he was a true barbarian unbridled and free.

This rugged people by their mode of living provided a rigorous training of the young. Boys learned early how to hunt, and the use of weapons became a part of their daily instructions. In addition, hawking, foot racing, wrestling, throwing spears and knives, ball games, and other physical activities were practiced. The endurance, strength, and skill required of their physical education fit readily into the vigorous life which these people led.

The world needed a young stock of humanity to replace that of the Romans. Although it took centuries for the Teuton to rise to the cultural level of the Roman and Greek, the newly reconstructed society rested on firm foundations; namely, that of strong, virile physiques, the broad shoulders and strong constitutions of the Teutonic invaders. The greatest civilized nations of the world today are partly or entirely their descendants.

INFLUENCE OF EARLY CHRISTIAN IDEALS

In the midst of the dissolute and immoral society of the declining years of pagan Rome was molded the theology and organization of the new religion of Christianity. Converts to the faith refrained not only from worshiping the gods of Rome but also from heaping adoration upon the emperor; they did not attend the games of the circus and the amphitheater or enjoy the luxuries of the bath; morally, they would not fight in the army. On the other hand, they must, if need be, die for their leader Jesus Christ. Because the new sect set itself off from Roman society, its members were misunderstood and despised by many and soon marked for persecution.

The revolting social evils and the persecutions, combined with a firm belief in the immediate return of Christ, gave rise to the doctrine that worldly and material things were not of God. The great emphasis which Christianity placed on the reward of eternal happiness in the hereafter minimized the importance of pleasure or social position in this worldly existence. The joy with which the martyrs died revealed that fact. If life for its own sake is not worth living but merely a time to prepare for the next world, all human culture is folly and one's life should be spent in prayer, penance, and meditation. The pagan Greeks and Romans promoted art, architecture, literature, and philosophy and sought the development and perfection of both mental and physical powers, but a Christian might endanger his soul in such worthless and foolish pastimes.

What is the status of physical education in a society with these doctrines and ideals? God deals with souls, not bodies. The degenerate Romans cater to their bodies; they wash them and ornament them; their every thought is of the sensual pleasure they derive from them. But bodies are mortal; the soul is immortal. The early Christian was concerned about his soul, not his body. The Greek theory that

body and soul harmonize almost into unity was challenged
by the Christian theory that the body was of Satan and the
soul of God and therefore antagonistic.

Theodosius, one of the early Christian emperors, abolished
the Olympian games in A.D. 394 because they were pagan
in their influence. As Christianity triumphed, chariot races
and other debasing sports of the Romans came to an end.

When the East, especially Syria and Egypt, accepted
Christianity, the idea that all worldly pursuits which gave
pleasure were evil fastened itself to the religion and became
the basis of asceticism. Asceticism was the highest ideal of
medieval Christianity. This ideal originally referred to the
discipline and training which an athlete pursues in preparation for a contest. But in religious and modern usage it re-
fers to a subjugation of the flesh with its passions and worldly
desires so that the soul may rise unhampered to great spiritual heights. Nearly all Oriental religions have an ascetic
phase, and the holiest adherents of the faith are the ascetics.

When it was found difficult to subdue the flesh, it was
regarded as insubordinate and to be tortured. It follows,
then, that asceticism and physical education in their treatment of the physical man are diametrically opposed. Even
dancing, which temporarily was retained as a part of religious ceremonies, later was forbidden because of its worldliness and impiousness. The earliest Christian ascetics were
the hermits of Egypt and the Near East, of whom St.
Anthony was one of the most famous. In caves and in the
desert, these holy men sought refuge from the evils of the
world and spent their lives praying, fasting, and meditating
on the hereafter. The more fanatical beat themselves until
exhausted, burdened themselves with heavy weights or
chains, lay constantly on beds of thorns, or sought out other
extraordinary forms of torment. For example, St. Simon
lived on a tall pillar for twenty years. Hair shirts, which
constantly pricked the flesh, were worn by monks in more
recent times. In those days uncleanliness was next to godli-
ness, and the ascetics were frequently infested with vermin

and often diseased, all of which added to their discomfort. Such treatment of the body, accompanied by incessant brooding and meditation, must surely have deranged minds and opened the way for hallucinations and visions similar to those which many ascetics are reported to have had.

INFLUENCE OF MONASTERIES

In about A.D. 529, St. Benedict organized monasteries in Europe where men who wished to lead a holy life might retire from the world with others who were similarly inclined. Monastic life was regarded as the ideal Christian life in the Middle Ages. The conduct of monks was regulated by detailed rules and enforced by strict discipline. Seven hours each day were devoted to manual labor and two hours to reading and study; time was specified for prayer, meals, and sleep. Manual labor was regarded as a means of subduing the flesh to escape the evils of idleness and thus gave rise to the maxim, "To labor is to pray." A new monastery was frequently situated in a swamp or on mountainous ground so that even greater labor would be required to construct it.

With the overthrow of classical civilization by the barbarians, the monastery, the church, and a few libraries became the sole depositories of learning. Monks rendered great service to subsequent centuries by preserving some classical learning, keeping records of the events of the time, and copying the works of many authors which might otherwise have been lost to modern times. Until the time of the universities, monastery schools and those of the cathedrals, which were usually staffed by monks, were almost the only institutions of learning in the Middle Ages. In these schools, reading, writing, and a meager knowledge of calculation were taught, all of which had a religious aim. In no school of the Middle Ages could physical education have found a place; education, in its aim, method, and content, was dominated by asceticism.

RISE OF MEDIEVAL UNIVERSITIES

In the twelfth century there arose, in some cases from the cathedral schools, a large number of universities. Among the most famous were the universities of Paris, Bologna, and Salerno. These institutions were quite free from civil and ecclesiastical control. Students numbered in the thousands and were of all ages. Many of them begged for a living; others did any work they could find. Many wandered from one university to another. The subjects—grammar, rhetoric, logic, astronomy, mathematics, law, medicine, and theology —were taught by the professors' lectures and debates by the students. All subjects were taught in accordance with, and supplementary to, the theological doctrines of the time.

No place was given for athletic sports or physical education; consequently, much of the students' leisure time was taken up in boisterous pranks, drinking, gambling, carousals, and riots in the town which finally ended in serious fights between "town and gown." These fights became so frequent that the method and place of trial of students came to be specified in the charter of the university. One of the arguments frequently given for the promotion of modern college and high school athletics is that such activities tend to prevent such things as these that happened in the medieval university.

PHYSICAL EDUCATION
IN THE AGE OF CHIVALRY

With the invasions of the Teutonic barbarians, centralized government in Europe became impossible. Feudalism arose in its place and provided a social, economic, military, and political system for society. The feudal system grew out of the lawlessness and barbarism of the time. The weak sought the protection of the strong and provided additional strength for the already powerful. The great landed noble became the lord, and those who sought his protection, the vassals. In spite of the teachings of chivalry and the prohibitions of the Church, the mailed fist generally ruled Europe. The lord who had a great following of vassals, sworn to serve him as trained knights, defied the king and usurped royal prerogatives in his immediate locality with impunity. The great mass of landless people sank to the position of serfdom, and, in order that they might have land to till, they pledged to surrender to the lord a part of the product of their labor and to pay certain other dues and penalties. Their lot was to toil, that of the clergy to pray, and that of the nobility to fight, govern, and engage in sports. A feudal army consisted of a lord or several lords, their vassals and their vassals' vassals, and so on but did not include the serfs. Private warfare was so prevalent that the nobles built fortified dwellings, castles with moats, massive walls, and battlements.

The Middle Ages offered only two fields of endeavor to the young nobleman—the church and chivalry. The former required a literary and religious education pursued in the quiet atmosphere of a monastery or cathedral; the latter demanded a physical and military education and training in social conduct, pursued in the active, gay, and pleasurable life of the castles of the high nobles. Needless to say, the great majority chose the training for knighthood. Specific training for war accompanied this program. However, hunting the wild boar or stag, hawking, swimming, wrestling, rope climbing, and horsemanship were engaged in and proved pleasurable as well as good preparation for future combat.

TRAINING FOR KNIGHTHOOD

At the age of seven the noble's son left his father's home to take up residence and begin training as a page in the castle of his father's lord. Here, in company with other boys, he played ball, marbles, seesaw, chess, and, in the later period, tennis. He imitated the active life about him and learned by observation many rudiments of chivalry. The purposive conscious training was in the hands of a lady who took upon herself the responsibilities of training a page. In return for her attention the page devoted himself to her and served her at all times and in all capacities. Under her direction the page learned to sing and to compose songs, to play the harp and dance, to dress properly, to be polite and respectful, to speak correctly in social gatherings, to be tactful, to conduct himself properly at the various important ceremonies and occasions. He was given religious instruction, taught to say prayers, and to revere the Church and its officials.

The page learned his lessons in actual service about the castle. It was his duty to wait on table—to carry in the food and dishes, bring water and towels for the guests, carve the meat, and pour the wine. He was always the errand boy and frequently the messenger of important news. Although the food and bed of the page was rarely different from that of the remainder of the household, it seems that in some localities there prevailed a Spartan attitude toward the page; no doubt, in the main the lot of the varlet was no easy one.

Toward the close of seven years as page, he helped the court in their sports of falconry by scaring up the birds to be chased and carrying extra falcons. He learned to ride, for it might be necessary to send him with messages to the neighboring castles. With the other pages he practiced swimming, running, jumping, fencing, boxing, and climbing around the walls of the castle.

At about fourteen the boy reached the status of squire. He remained attached to his mistress and continued to serve at the table, but more and more emphasis was placed on training for the most important activity of knighthood—fighting. He attached himself to a knight who required him to polish and repair the armor and weapons, care for the horses, and do other general service. In time of war he accompanied his lord, prepared him for battle, and watched him through the fight. If the knight's horse was killed, the squire brought another; if the lance or sword broke, he replaced it; if the knight was captured, the squire attempted a rescue; if he was set upon by more than one opponent at once the squire would join in the fight; if prisoners were taken, the squire guarded them. These responsibilities demanded intensive training.

The squire's spare moments were spent in running long races on foot as a means of procuring endurance, in constructing ladders of crude material and practicing the scaling of walls with them, in scaling walls without ladders, and in swimming with and without armor. Practice in fencing and swordsmanship was engaged in. The most important preparation was for horsemanship and for mounted combat. Mounting and dismounting gracefully, both at a stand and at full gallop, were practiced. To manage the horse, to carry the shield, and to use the various weapons effectively at the same time required years of training. The lance was a long sturdy spear with a thick shaft and an iron point. When this weapon was fixed for action, it projected six or seven feet in front of the horse's head. It took strength of arm and accuracy of aim to ride at full speed and deliver the lance head against a moving opponent. The squires constructed various targets for tilting; the most common was some form of the quintain. It might be a cross with a sandbag on one arm. When the squires struck the target on the other arm the cross turned on a pivot and dealt the attacker a blow with the bag of sand unless he was quick enough to escape it. Other quintains struck back only when they were not hit squarely. Training for accuracy was also secured by thrusting at the ring. In this exercise an iron ring was suspended in the air, and the squires charged at full speed endeavoring to place the lance point through the ring and carry it free from its support. Along with training in the use of the lance came the exercises with the sword, mace, and battle-ax in sham combat both with an opponent and with a dummy. It was also understood that the squire should discipline himself to withstand heat, cold, fatigue, and loss of sleep.

If, at the age of twenty-one, the squire had mastered the arts of chivalry, the ceremonies to create him a knight were arranged. First, he cut off a lock of hair, took a bath of purification, and dressed in pure white. The night preceding the event he spent in prayer, meditation, and fasting before the altar of the chapel, with the new armor and weapons near. At dawn he made confession and took the sacrament. At the appointed hour the court assembled to witness the ceremonies. The squire knelt before the lord to receive the accolade which was bestowed with appropriate words charging him to be a true knight. Then the new knight was assisted into his armor and, last of all, the sword, blest by the priest, was buckled on; then came the exhibition in the courtyard, where he demonstrated that he was worthy to be so honored.

The knight practiced physical exercise neither to attain complete development and establish harmony between body and soul, nor for any other lofty Greek ideal. He had nothing in common with the national patriotism of the Roman; rather, he sought an ability that was to be highly utilitarian and individualistic. The law of the fist necessitated a vigorous training for self-protection and self-preservation. Society and religion approved of the brave and skillful fighting man; the leisure of the nobility made possible the long period of training. Sports served as another incentive to attain a high degree of skill in horsemanship and the use of the weapons.

During the feudal period, physical education was completely divorced from intellectual education. These two disciplines had neither aims nor methods in common. Intellectual education was for the scholar and clergyman, physical education, for the knight. Hygiene and sanitation were never practiced in the castle or hut; consequently, the death rate was extremely high, disease was always prevalent, and epidemics, which decimated a district, were frequent.

IMPORTANCE OF TOURNAMENTS AND JOUSTS

Medieval tournaments served both as training for war and amusement. The joust was an engagement of two knights, tilting with lances; it might be spontaneous, resulting from a chance meeting or a wager, or it might be held in the lists under the regulations of the sport. A tournament was a contest arranged by a king or high noble in which many knights participated to exhibit and be rewarded for chivalric skill and bravery and to provide sociability and amusement.

The place of combat, known as the lists, was an oval-shaped field with seats arranged on each side. The contestants were stationed at the ends. The gay court of ladies, noblemen, and clergy assembled in splendid medieval pomp and pageantry; knights wore a gift-token from their lady-love and fought for her favor as well as for their own honor and fame. Contending knights were prepared for the contest by their squires; lances were tested; and the man and horse were clad in armor. Heralds read the rules of the joust and tournament. No pointed weapons were used. The lance head was blunted; only the broad sword without point was permitted, and the mace and battle-ax might be barred.

If the event was a joust the contending knights placed themselves at opposite ends of the lists, set the lance firmly in position, and, at the blast of the trumpet, amid the cries of their admirers, they dashed forward at full speed, bent low in the saddle, aiming the hard spearhead at the helmet or breastplate of the opposing knight. If both failed to strike their mark, the horses were wheeled about, and another charge followed. If one rammed the other with sufficient force to unhorse him, the former was declared the winner. If during several charges, square hits were made with such force as to break the shafts but neither rider was unhorsed, the one who broke the greater number of shafts was judged the winner. Sometimes the rules prescribed that when one was unhorsed, the other must dismount and continue the combat on foot; since both were encased in armor and pointed weapons were not permitted, the fight continued for a long time without much result unless one had been wounded in the fall or became exhausted.

In a tournament proper, a group of knights galloped from each end of the lists to the middle; each quickly chose an opponent, then turned back to the position to await the signal for the charge. On signal, all dashed forward to attempt to defeat their opponents with one blow; the unhorsed were trampled under foot; those with broken lances drew their swords; those with lances charged again into the melee; furious and unregulated fighting took the field, resulting in many serious wounds and considerable loss of life. When a great tournament ended in more deaths than usual, the church endeavored to end the sport but always failed. Dancing, feasting, and awarding of prizes in the castle ended the day of tournament and joust.

EFFECTS OF METHODS OF WARFARE

In the sixteenth century, the tournament became little more than a grand pageant which served as a pretext to show fine horses and beautiful armor and hold a social gathering. The rules of the game were altered so that it became a safe pastime. The change came partly as a result of new methods of warfare. From the eleventh to the fifteenth century, the cavalry of knights was the best fighting force, but with the increase in the use of missile weapons and the invention of the musket, a serf, so equipped, proved to be a better soldier than a knight. For many reasons feudalism, the age of serfs, nobles, and castles, was past.

Common methods of warfare from the earliest times to the decline of the feudal period demanded, in addition to courage and self-reliance, training in bodily strength, endurance, and skill plus accuracy in thrusting, striking, parrying, and hurling. Conflicts were man to man and hand to hand; the stronger and more skilled won, and the weaker and less skilled met death. The aim of physical education was closely related to self-preservation.

With the invention of missiles and the machinery of war, hand-to-hand combat declined to minor importance; the enemy was now defeated at a distance, and victory depended on the numbers of men, the accuracy of shooting, and the amount of effective machinery of war in action. Death on the battlefield came as a matter of chance rather than as the result of physical weakness. Progress in warfare has led to an increasing divergence in the aims and methods of military training and those of physical training. One draws its objectives from the possibility of war and the other from peaceful society.

6

PHYSICAL EDUCATION
DURING THE RENAISSANCE

The name Renaissance applies to the transitional period in European history between the Middle Ages and modern times. During the fourteenth, fifteenth, and sixteenth centuries, feudalism gave way to monarchy, private warfare to comparative peace, provincialism to nationalism, barter to commerce, ignorance of geography to discovery and exploration, institutionalism to individualism, superstition to investigation, faith to reason, asceticism to esthetics, preparation for the hereafter to enjoyment of the present, otherworldliness to worldliness, and, finally, handwritten manuscripts to printed books. At the same time, a widespread interest in the civilization of Greece and Rome arose. All who were touched with the Renaissance spirit found satisfaction in the study of classic philosophy, literature, and art. This emphasis upon things human rather than divine is called Humanism. The Humanists endeavored to revive and imitate classical literature both as to content and style.

In any society that promotes individualism and recognizes the worth of this life, the care and development of the body assume a place of importance. When the Humanists discovered the civilization of Greece and Rome, they were, of course, struck with the important consideration given to the physical man in these societies; consequently, nearly all

Humanist educators wrote on the necessity of physical education.

The Renaissance gave to Europe a system of secondary education, and names for these institutions were taken from the Greeks, for example, the German gymnasium, the French lycee, and the English academy. However, these secondary schools resembled Greek gymnasia only in name.

In effect, the Middle Ages, characterized by rigidity and repressiveness of both body and mind, gave way to a more broad and liberal education. The values of physical exercise and hygiene were highlighted. The racket, bat, club (golf), and other equipment for sports became common. Archery, tennis, golf, fencing, swimming, skating, and a multiplicity of dances were part of the culture. Although later discouraged or banned, such sports as bull-baiting, bear-baiting, cockfighting, and hawking occurred in one or various countries throughout Europe and England. The invention of the printing press and the discussion of gymnastics, sports, and other games in some of the publications tended to encourage wider acceptance and participation in these physical activities.

HUMANIST EDUCATORS AND PHYSICAL EDUCATION

The earliest teachers with Humanist views taught in the schools of northern Italy during the fifteenth century.

Vittorino Da Feltre (1378–1446) was called from the University of Padua to the court of the Prince of Mantua to teach children of the nobility. Da Feltre's methods and subject matter were in great contrast to those of the monastic and cathedral schools. The institution lived up to its name, "The Pleasant House," and enrolled forty bright and happy children eager to learn and anxious to please their schoolmaster who, instead of ruling them with fear, lured them to their lessons with kindness and understanding. Da Feltre, first because he was a Humanist and secondly because he was instructing boys who would one day be expected to bear arms, had great regard for health and physical exercise. The children were guarded in their diet and discouraged in the use of artificial heat. Daily exercises regardless of weather conditions were compulsory. In addition to playing the games of childhood, the children learned riding, fencing, archery, and ball playing. Competitions were held, and proficiency was encouraged in wrestling, running, leaping, and swimming. Teachers frequently took the children on long hikes through the country, both for the physical and the educational benefits to be derived from them. Da Feltre's aim in physical education was to discipline the body so that health might ever be present, the rigors of war endured, and weapons handled with good results. However, Da Feltre understood that the hours spent in play and in games also served as rest and recreation and tended to promote the learning of other lessons. He was one of the first schoolmasters to discover that ability to learn is partially dependent on physical condition, and except for the Greeks, he was the first to devise special exercises for invalid children. Further, Vittorino emphasized the need not only for small classes but also for shaping the program around the capacities of each individual.

Pietro Vergerio (1349–1428), of Padua and Florence, wrote an educational treatise, *De ingenius moribus,* in which he discussed, first, education for character; second, liberal studies; third, bodliy exercises and training in the art of war; and, finally, recreation. A few quotations from his work follow: "But where an active frame is conjoined to a vigorous intellect a true education will aim at the efficient training of both—the Reason that it may wisely control, the Body that it may properly obey. So that if we be involved in arms we may be found ready to defend our right or to strike a blow for honor or power. . . . Now war involves physical endurance as well as military skill." He then says that the boy must "be gradually inured to privations and grave exertion, to enable him to bear strain and hardship when he reaches manhood." Further, the boy should be "exercised in activity and courage by feats of strength or dangers of the field; in endurance by bearing both heat and cold, hunger and thirst. For as luxury enervates mind and body alike, so exertion fortifies both. . . . In choice of bodily exercises those should be adopted which serve to maintain the body in good health and to strengthen the limbs; and thus it will be necessary to consider to some extent the case of each individual

Fig. 4. Climbing exercises as illustrated in *De Arte Gymnastica,* by Mercurialis, 1672.

boy. . . . In childhood much care must be taken lest the growth be hindered, or the nerves of the body be strained by severe exertion; but, as youth develops, this may be slowly increased. The order perhaps to be observed is this; in childhood, learning first; in youth, morals, with physical exercises, varying in degree, for all." Then followed advice on specific training for war. Finally, "But as we are not so constituted that we are able to bestow ourselves all day long upon our ordered tasks, I will now set forth the true place of recreation." Vergerio then denounces "debasing games or such as cannot develop bodily gifts or powers of will." He favors "the sharp exertion of ball-play, the best refreshment alike for jaded spirits and for bodily fatigue."

Pius II, a pope of very marked Humanist ideas, wrote to a young prince concerning education as follows:

> As regards a boy's physical training, we must bear in mind that we aim at implanting habits which will prove beneficial through life. So let him cultivate a certain hardness which rejects excess of sleep and idleness in all its forms. . . . A boy should be taught to hold his head erect, to look straight and fearlessly before him, and to bear himself with dignity whether walking, standing, or sitting. . . . For such physical training not only cultivates grace of attitude, but secures the health play of our bodily organs and establishes the constitution. . . . Games, too, should be encouraged for young children—the ball, the hoop—but these must not be rough and coarse but have in them an element of skill. Such relaxations should form an integral part of each day's occupations if learning is not to be an object of disgust. . . . In respect of eating and drinking the rule of moderation consists in rejecting everything which needlessly taxes the digestion and impairs mental activity. . . . What but disease and decay can result from appetite habitually over-indulged? Such concessions to the flesh stand condemned by all the great spirits of the past."

Three outstanding leaders of the sixteenth century were Sir Thomas Elyot, Roger Ascham, and Hieronymous Mercurialis. Sir Thomas Elyot (1490–1546) was an English Humanist who wrote *The Governor,* a treatise on education. After discussing intellectual and moral education he discourses on recreation. Elyot agreed with all Humanists that the mind and body need recreation and that long hours of study should be broken by play and exercise. He was also aware of the physical benefit to be derived from games and exercises, for example, tennis, fencing, dancing, archery, wrestling, running, riding, swimming, and dumbbells. On the other hand, he questioned the value of football for "gentlemen," and he did not prohibit all forms of dancing.

Elyot, however, saw little reason for idleness, and he continually stressed the importance of physical activities, especially those which led to better bodily development.

Roger Ascham (1515–68), an English Humanist and a professor at Cambridge University, wrote *The Schoolmaster.* He advocated a study of the Latin and Greek authors as a means of obtaining a liberal education and recognized the importance of physical education. Ascham urged that young men "engage in all courtly exercises and gentlemanly pastimes. . . . All pastimes joined with labor, used in open place and in daylight, containing either some fit exercise for war or some pleasant pastime for peace, be not only comely and decent but also very necessary for a courtly gentleman to use." Ascham also appreciated the value of exercises as a means of resting the mind that it may be sharper at a later time. "The best wits to learning must need have much recreation and ceasing from their books, or else they mar themselves, when base and dumpish wits can never be hurt by continual study."

Hieronymus Mercurialis (1503–1606), a famous Italian physician, wrote a treatise, *De arte gymnastica,* in which he called the attention of his contemporaries to gymnastics of the ancients. His work was historical and descriptive, and he recommended the revival of the practice of gymnastics for the sake of health and individual welfare.

REFORMERS AND PHYSICAL EDUCATION

When the Humanistic spirit crossed the Alps, the tendency to enjoy life became a desire to seek the meaning of life: education for self-realization became education for social uplift; the study of the classics for pleasure and culture gave way to their examination for the light they might throw on the meaning of the Scriptures; training for good manners and courage became training for piety and character; literary education was replaced by religious education, especially in those countries that experienced a Protestant reformation. In the lands of Luther, Calvin, Zwingli, Knox, and other reformers, emphasis was again placed on the salvation of the soul rather than on the joy of living and preparation for life, but they did not preach salvation through asceticism or even through the Church alone. The reformers taught that the Holy Bible was the only source of religious truth and that one's salvation depended on understanding of and faith in its teaching. To assure this, the Protestant sects were therefore logically compelled to organize schools for boys and girls where at least reading, writing, and religion could be taught. The Reformation may be regarded as the cradle of the elementary school system of Europe which gave the masses an opportunity to gain a basic education. After private tutorial instruction, wealthy youths attended Latin grammar schools, and many progressed onward to the universities. Thus, a dual school organization based on a caste system developed in Europe.

Luther was determined that schools should be established in every Lutheran parish. In his famous "Letter to the Mayors and Aldermen of the Cities of Germany" he outlined the course of study and the methods to be used in these schools. He believed in gymnastic exercises because they were good for both the body and the soul. He said, "It was well considered and arranged by the ancients that the people should practice gymnastics that they might not fall into reveling, unchastity, gluttony, intemperance, and gaming. Therefore, these two exercises and pastimes please me best, namely, music and gymnastics, of which the first drives away all care and melancholy from the heart, and the latter produces elasticity of the body and preserves its health. But the great reason for these pastimes is that the people may not fall into gluttony, licentiousness, and gambling as is the case, alas! in courts and in cities. Thus it goes when such honorable and manly exercises are neglected."

Johannes Bugenhagen and Philip Melanchthon, the great organizers of the Lutheran Reformation, became the founders of the Volksschule and the Gymnasium, respectively. They arranged no place in the course of study for physical education but encouraged games and athletic competitions when time permitted outside of school hours.

Following the models of Melanchthon, Sturm organized and named the first German Gymnasium in Strassburg. His school organization remained almost unchanged until modern times. When John Colet organized the Humanistic school of St. Paul in England he formed the model for the English and American grammar schools. All these institutions soon lost their original aim, and the main course of study came to be the languages of Greece and Rome, not the literature or civilization. Instead of giving a liberal education and a preparation for life work, the schools prepared students only for institutions of higher learning. It naturally followed that training of the body was neglected and was not considered of sufficient importance to receive attention in the schools.

7

PHYSICAL EDUCATION
AND REALISM

The name, "realist," is given to those educators of the later Renaissance period who revolted against the formal drill on Latin and Greek grammar which characterized the secondary schools of Europe after the true spirit of Humanism began to wane. They advocated, instead of the narrow study of Latin and Greek works, a study of the real things of life. The Humanist Realists agreed that art, architecture, medicine, law, mathematics, and agriculture could best be studied through the classic authors; but the classics must be read and studied for their content and not for their style. The Social Realists believed that the aim of education should be to prepare one for a life career. They held that there were many good things in the classics but that not all of the valuable knowledge was contained there; further, that knowledge was not the end of education, but rather that the training of the mind, judgment, and character should be regarded as the true aim. Stress was placed on providing a student opportunities to test and explore so that his judgments would assure him a better way of life. The Sense Realists were influenced by the new discoveries in science and emphasized the fact that nearly all knowledge worth having could best be obtained through the senses—from objects, not words

69

about objects, and from observation and experience. Therefore, sensory training was advocated by this group.

As long as the schools were narrow in their curriculum and emphasized the mastery of classic language and Ciceronian style, and as long as the institution was regarded as a means of preparation for the university or at most a scholarly vocation rather than a preparation for participation in society, little place was to be expected for physical education. But the Realists, who advocated training the individual to meet the conditions of society, could not fail to restore physical training to an important position.

HUMANIST REALISTS

François Rabelais, one of the greatest of French educational theorists of the sixteenth century, wrote a satire on contemporary education and published his own views in a famous book called *The Life of Gargantua.* The hero Gargantua was first subjected to the methods and subject matter of the usual Latin grammar school, and after several years of such training, he "did profit nothing; but, which is worse, grew thereby a fool, a sot, a dolt, and a blockhead." Then an ideal tutor, Ponocrates, was secured, and after Gargantua was given a pill to make him forget all that he had learned, his education began again. Needless to say he studied the content of the classic authors and due care was taken for his physical welfare. Gargantua practiced difficult feats of horsemanship, the wielding of arms, the lance and the battle-ax, throwing the spear, exercises in swordsmanship, and the pastime of hunting. "He played at the great ball and made it bound in the air with both fist and foot. He wrestled, ran, and jumped. . . . He did swim in deep waters on his face, on his back, sidewise, with all his body, with his feet only, and with one hand in the air." He practiced diving "into pits and gulfs. . . . He did cast the dart, throw the bar, put the stone, practice the javelin, the boar-spear, or partizan, and the halbert." In addition to this he shot at targets with the strongest bows and crossbows; climbed ropes and trees and scaled the walls. When weather did not permit these outdoors activities, manual labor was to be provided indoors.

John Milton, the great English poet of the seventeenth century, wrote a "Tractate of Education" in which he set forth the ideas of the Humanist Realists. His famous definition of education, "I call therefore a complete and generous education that which fits man to perform justly, skillfully, and magnanimously all the offices, both private and public, of peace and war," reveals his realism. Milton first found fault with the contemporary education and then set up his own imaginary Academy for "gentlemen's sons" between the ages of twelve and twenty-one. The boys "should divide their day's work into three parts as it lies orderly—their Studies, their Exercises, and their Diet." With regard to the exercises, "therefore about an hour and a half, ere they eat at noon, should be allowed them for exercise and due rest afterwards. . . . The exercise which I commend first is the exact use of their weapon, to guard and to strike safely with edge or point; this will keep them healthy, nimble, strong, and well in breath, is also the likeliest means to make them grow large and tall and to inspire them with a gallant and fearless courage. They must be also practiced in all the locks and grips of wrestling, wherein Englishmen were wont to excel, as need may often be in fight, to tug or grapple and to close." Then while they are "unsweating themselves" he recommends recreation "both with profit and delight" in either playing or listening to the "solemn and divine harmonies of music"; he also advocates such recreation after meals.

At the giving of an alarm, all are called out to military exercises, either on foot or on horse, and are daily trained in the "rudiments of soldiership in all the skill of embattling, marching, encamping, fortifying, besieging, and battering, with all the helps of ancient and modern stratagems, tactics, and warlike maxims."

Like many other educators, Rabelais and Milton had in mind the training of gentlemen's sons only. The former thought solely of the tutorial method; consequently, physical training must be for gentlemanly sports, pastimes, and duties. The days of chivalry were not long past. The gentleman was still recognized as the fighting man and the leader in war; he should have knightly bearing and be ready to preserve his honor in duels if necessary. Milton wrote his tractate in the midst of the civil war between the Royalists and the Parliamentarians; he was partisan to the latter group, and it is likely that the conditions of the time are responsible for the militaristic tinge of his ideas on physical education. Even wrestling is to be taught, because fighting sometimes demands close quarters. The Humanist Realists failed to value play and games as a means of recreation, pleasure, and social training but thought of them as training in skill, alertness, courage, and similar attainments. Every hour of the day should be given up to some exercise or study of utilitarian value and its use must be obvious. The poetic and esthetic nature of Milton is revealed in the advocacy of the music hour; he said that the divine harmonies "have a great power over the dispositions and manners, to smooth and make them gentle." But not even the poet was able to see beauty in the human figure and its motions as the Greeks had done.

SOCIAL REALISTS

Michel De Montaigne, the great French sixteenth-century essayist, wrote "The Education of Children." Space in this text will not permit an adequate exposition of the excellent educational theories of this writer. Suffice it to say that the modern nations have hardly reached the high level of his ideals, although many of his theories have materialized in recent times. According to Montaigne, boys should be taught to do and to be that which a man ought to do and to be. His education would include training for character, right habits, manners, morals, and he agrees with Cicero that the best of all arts is that of living well. In regard to physical education, he regrets that parents so frequently spoil their children because "it would grieve them to see their children come home from manly exercise, sweaty and dusty, to drink cold water when they are hot, to mount an unruly horse, or to take a foil in hand against a skillful fencer. . . . It is not enough to fortify his soul; you must also make his muscles strong. The mind will be oppressed if not assisted by the body. . . . Now to be inured to labor is to be able to bear pain. . . . Our very exercises and recreations, running, wrestling, dancing, hunting, riding, and fencing will be a part of his study. I would have his manners, behavior, and bearing cultivated at the same time with his mind. It is not the mind, it is not the body we are training; it is the man and we must not divide him into two parts. Plato says we should not fashion one without the other, but make them draw together like two horses harnessed to a coach. By this saying would it not indicate that he would rather give more care to the body, believing that the mind is benefited at the same time? . . . Accustom him to heat and cold, to wind and sun, and to dangers that he ought to despise. Wean him from all effeminacy in eating and drinking, clothes and lodging, that he may not be a gay fellow, a dude, but a hardy, sinewy, and vigorous young man. I have been of this opinion all my life and still hold to it." Montaigne commends Plato for providing recreation for the youths of his city and encouraging them in races, sports, leaping, songs and dances, and "a thousand exercises for both mind and body."

John Locke, the famous physician and educator of the seventeenth century, wrote the treatise, "Some Thoughts Concerning Education." In this work, Locke gives these aims of education: first, vigor of body; second, virtue in soul; third, knowledge or mental acquisitions. His first concern is for the body, and the opening paragraph of his book is, "A sound mind in a sound body, is a short but full description of a happy state in this world; he that has these two has little more to wish for." Then farther on, "How necessary health is to our business and happiness, and how requisite a strong constitution, able to endure hardships and fatigue, is to one that will make any figure in the world, is too obvious to need any proof. . . . The consideration I shall have here of health, shall not be what a physician ought to do but what the parents should do for the preservation and improvement of a healthy, or at least not sickly constitution in their children." About one third of the book is made up of health rules, each supported by some argument or explanation. Locke advises that children be not too warmly clad, either in winter or summer, wear thin shoes and wash their feet in cold water daily, learn to swim, be in open air as much as possible, and become accustomed to heat and cold, sun and rain, and refrain from the use of tight clothing. Locke cautions against permitting children who are very warm from hard play to sit or lie on the cold ground and to drink cold liquids. Then follows a long discourse on diet, and eating habits, the values and dangers of various foods, value of thorough mastication, and the conclusion that simple foods are the best.

From what has been said it is plain that Locke's road to health and physical welfare is through a hardening and disciplining process; he has much to say about hygiene but little about the value of play. The remainder of his book emphasizes the importance of moral training, but he fails to see that physical education could be made an important item in that training. Locke seems to be only lukewarm in his attitude toward the training in knightly sports. Horsemanship is of value insofar as it conduces to health and to giving one a firm and graceful seat on the horse. "As to fencing, it seems to me a good exercise to health but dangerous to the life," meaning that it tends to make duels more frequent. In speaking so against the arts of gallantry, he recognizes that he is not in harmony with the traditional view.

Montaigne and Locke had in mind the training of the higher class, largely through tutors. All Social Realists took into account the necessity of health and physical training and realized the tendency of all families of the upper class to pamper and spoil their children. The earlier educators, for example, Montaigne, believed in the knightly sports; the later ones, such as Locke, discouraged them. All believed in rigorous discipline of the body. They, like the Humanist Realists, failed to understand the esthetic and social values of exercise and sports; of course, as long as the child is to be isolated from others by the tutorial system, group competitions and games would be impossible. For the most part the Social Realists had very little immediate influence on the schools of the time; however, the Ritterakademieen of Germany and academies in France did provide education for the nobles' sons along the lines advocated. In England instruction was left to the tutors followed by a finishing education in a school of arms on the continent.

Fig. 5. Vaulting and fencing exercises in a school of arms of the seventeenth century.

SENSE REALISTS

The modern nations in the last few decades have materialized some of the theories and followed some of the practices of the Sense Realists. A few of their beliefs were: all people, both sexes, rich and poor, should receive an education; the true end of education is to develop the faculties of both mind and body; teaching is best done through the senses of seeing and hearing, in short, experiencing rather than reading; to learn the mother tongue is more important than to learn Latin; the teaching process should be adapted to the learner and have a natural procedure; and teachers should be trained for the work of teaching.

The Sense Realists' school was filled with specimens, maps, charts, diagrams, pictures, and attractive textbooks. Because of their many new and radical ideas and methods, the Sense Realists were sometimes called Innovators.

Richard Mulcaster (1530–1611), the famous English schoolmaster of the sixteenth century, was for twenty-six years the head of the Merchant-Taylors school of London. He wrote one of the finest educational treatises of the English language, *Positions wherein those circumstances be examined, which are necessary for the training of children either for skill in their booke, or for health in their bodie.* He is among the first to call attention of the educators from the thing to be learned to the learner, thus laying the foundation for the science of education. There are forty-five so-called positions, and more than half of them deal with physical and moral training through games and exercises. Some of the chapter headings are:

Of exercises and training of the body. How necessary a thing exercise is. What health is and how it is maintained. What a part exercise playeth in the maintenance of health. Of exercise in general and what it is. And that it is athletic for games, martial for field, and physical for health. Of the particular exercises. Why I do appoint so many and how to judge of them or devise the like. Of dancing. Of wrestling. Of walking. Of running. Of leaping. Of swimming. Of riding. Of hunting. Of shooting. Of the ball. Of the nature and quality of exercise. Of the bodies which are to be exercised. Of exercising places. Of exercising time. Of the manner of exercise. Why the training of the mind and exercising of the body should be assigned to the same teacher.

No writer on education in this period insisted on the importance of physical education more than Richard Mulcaster. He even recognized the importance of good school sites with available sunlight and adequate space for play and exercise.

John Comenius (1592–1671), the great Bohemian educational reformer and schoolmaster of the seventeenth century, is better known today than he was one or two hundred years ago, because only in recent times have his theories and methods been understood and generally accepted. His school attempted to carry out the entire realistic program, giving the pupil an encyclopedic knowledge in an entertaining and natural way. Comenius wrote several texts to be used in the schools; the most famous of his books was the *Great Didactic*, which dealt with both the methods and subject matter for instruction.

As for physical education, Comenius says that gymnastics and games, running, jumping, wrestling, ball playing, and ninepins are to be encouraged. The teacher is to take the pupils on long hikes both for recreation and study. Comenius apparently understood the value of play to children, and he visualized play as a natural and vital medium in which education of the young could be enhanced. He, like Locke and others, believed in physical discipline and simple food. He suggests that the day be divided into three parts, eight hours for sleep, eight for work, and eight for nourishment, recreation, and physical development.

Nearly all Sense Realists, except Mulcaster, believed in universal education, and he too would carry it further than many of his contemporaries. Therefore, to advocate knightly sports as a means of physical development or even recreation would be ridiculous, for the common people could not ape the nobles. Schools of the type of Comenius' could not hire fencing masters, dancing and riding masters, and did not care to do so. Youths who wanted that kind of training would not want to attend schools where the common and the poor might come. Mulcaster's program is not entirely free from knightly education, but Comenius' and Ratick's and later Realists' are entirely so.

The theory of the Sense Realist was that exercise is a means of obtaining and maintaining health, that properly directed play and exercise produces what is modernly called physical fitness; they agree with the Humanists also that exercise serves as a rest from study and ultimately furthers the learning process. Perhaps one of the most important contributions of the Sense Realists was in the methodology of teaching they advocated. Although the principles upon which they based these methods were not substantiated scientifically, many of them have proved sound according to modern psychological findings.

8

PHYSICAL EDUCATION
IN THE AGE OF ENLIGHTENMENT

The eighteenth century was a period of transition to modern political, social, religious, and educational ideals. This transition is perhaps more easily traced in France than in any other country. During the early decades of the century France was governed by an autocratic king surrounded by arrogant, proud, but worthless nobles; the masses were abjectly poor and oppressed; a corrupt but powerful religious system executed heretics and allied itself to the monarchical government. The schoolroom practices were unscientific and actually cruel to the children. The society about the court was artificial and hypocritical: etiquette governed conduct, and punctilious religious observances served to veneer the gross immorality. Before the century was over, the teachings of Voltaire, who attacked the Church and State, and Rousseau, who denounced the society and education of the time, had been heeded. The activities of these men and their followers, combined with other forces, caused the upheaval known as the French Revolution, which wrecked the entire social structure of Europe beyond repair and led to its rebuilding in the nineteenth century.

ROUSSEAU'S EDUCATIONAL THEORIES

The emotional Rousseau (1712–78) was affected by the social inequality of man and the inhumanity of the upper toward the lower classes. He revolted against the artificiality and hypocrisy of life. He preceded Thomas Jefferson in the idea that all men are created free and equal. He believed that civilization was the cause of all the unhappiness in the world; "Civilized man is born, lives, and dies in a state of slavery." He advocated a return to nature and natural things. The essence of his teaching is, "All is good as it comes from the hand of the Creator; all degenerates under the hands of man."

Rousseau's *Émile* has had greater influence than any other educational treatise ever written: parliaments condemned it, the Church burned it and ordered its author arrested, philosophers praised it, and educators overlooked its exaggerations and adopted its sound principles. Rousseau condemned the contemporary practices of treating children as adults—dressing them in long, tight clothing and powder, paint, and wigs and compelling them to act as adults. He denounced the school for trying to teach them as though they were grown people and for flogging them when they failed to learn. "Nature wills that they should be children before they are men." Rousseau gives the imaginary boy Émile that which he considers to be an ideal education.

First of all, the boy is isolated from the contaminating influence of civilization by residing in the country. From birth to five years of age, the only concern for Émile is his growth and physical welfare. Accordingly he is placed under simple and healthful conditions; nature working in and through the boy is to have its way, unhampered by man. He is to be taught absolutely nothing. The second part of the book deals with the education or natural growth of the boy from five to twelve. Still no teaching of any kind is to be done, for Émile's nature demands that he continue to exercise his arms and limbs without interference. But at this age he becomes curious and desires to know things, to smell the flowers, to handle the rocks, to study the heavens and he "naturally" learns. "In order to learn to think, we must then exercise our limbs, our senses, and our organs which are the instruments of our intelligence." Émile wears very short, loose, scanty clothing, eats simple foods, accustoms himself to heat and cold; he swims, jumps, leaps over walls, scales cliffs, and grows into a healthy sturdy boy as naturally as he learns about his environment. After the age of twelve, the natural demands for physical activity have somewhat abated, and Émile is about ready to learn his moral and industrial lessons.

No educational theorist had conceived of education of mind and body as being so nearly the same thing as had Rousseau. Others were inclined to split the education of an individual longitudinally into two or more divisions—physical education, intellectual education, and moral education. But Rousseau had the idea of the continual growth of an indivisable entity, from birth until death. This growth might be cut into sections horizontally as nature had decreed. Physical and intellectual education are so intimately bound together that Rousseau found difficulty in determining when an activity ceased to be of physical value and became intellectual.

The following are some quotations from Rousseau's *Émile* which reveal his views on physical education. "The body must needs be vigorous in order to obey the soul; a good servant ought to be robust. The weaker the body the more it commands; the stronger it is the better it obeys. . . . A debilitated body enfeebles the soul. . . . If you would cultivate the intelligence of your pupil, cultivate the power which it is to govern. Give his body continual exercise; make him robust and sound in order to make him wise and reasonable; let him work and move about and run and shout and be continually in motion. . . . It is a very deplorable error to imagine that the exercise of the body is injurious to the operations of the mind; as if these two activities were not to proceed in concert, and the second were not always to direct the first." Rousseau seems to believe that a sound body makes a sound mind. "To spring from one end of the hall to the other, to estimate the bound of a ball still in the air, and to send it back with a strong steady hand, such sports do not befit a man but they serve to train a youth."

Rousseau understood the comparative educational values of different sports. He had little use for doctors, except when death was imminent, for then they could do no harm. "The only useful part of medicine is hygiene; and hygiene is less a science than a virtue." He resembles Locke in his ideas concerning clothing, food, sleep, and the general hardening process. Rousseau commends the writings of Locke and Montaigne on physical education and reflects that the vigor of mind and body of the ancients may be attributed to gymnastic exercises. He recommends games and outdoor activity for girls so that natural growth may produce healthy robust mothers.

During the last quarter of the eighteenth century, many of the theories and doctrines of the early decades were materialized and put into practice. This was particularly true of physical education. The theorists—Humanists, Realists, and Naturalists—had said enough; it was now time for action and practical reform. Since Rousseau's ideas were outlawed in France until after the Revolution, they received more immediate acceptance in Germany.

BASEDOW'S NATURALISTIC SCHOOL

Johann Basedow (1723–90) had been a teacher in a Ritterakademie in Denmark, where he saw students trained in the knightly sports and came to have some ideas of his own on the importance of physical activity. He was planning an educational reform when *Émile* appeared; he then determined to organize a naturalistic school along the lines of Rousseau, incorporating his own ideas. With the aid of the Duke of Anhalt he opened the Philanthropinum in 1774 at Dessau. So far as modern Europe was concerned, this was the first school admitting all classes of people to give gymnastics a place on the daily program. Although many of Basedow's ideas have eventually proved sound, the parents of his day did not accept his new methods of educating children. Because of poor enrollment and other factors he resigned in 1778, but others continued his methods until the school closed in the early 1790's.

Johann Simon was the first teacher of physical education in the Philanthropinum. During one hour of the morning and two hours of the afternoon the entire school engaged in a great variety of games, gymnastic exercises, sports, recreation, and manual labor. Some practiced the knightly sports of dancing, riding, and fencing; others, running, jumping, wrestling, and throwing. Ditches were dug of varying widths to leap across, and high-jump standards were constructed. There were also exercises in balancing as the pupils walked across a ditch on a narrow beam. The children played games, for example, shuttlecock and tennis, under the supervision of the teacher; the hoops and the seesaw were assigned to the younger ones. Later on, Johann Du-Toit, who succeeded Simon, introduced exercises on the ladders, swimming, skating, and archery. Manual labor—turning, cabinet making, and gardening—were also engaged in. The Philanthropinum won the favorable comment of the greatest men of the time and became the model for many similar schools. Basedow, its founder, is to be regarded and honored as the first modern educator to place physical education in an important position in the school.

Basedow's ideas of physical education were similar to those of Rousseau: nature and natural growth demand that the child be given time for play and bodily exercise; normal physical growth is more important in early years than mental training, and there are intellectual and moral values to be derived from the playing of games. These ideas were put into practice by Simon and his successors at the Philanthropinum.

GUTSMUTHS' INFLUENCE ON PHYSICAL EDUCATION

The Schnepfenthal Educational Institute, organized by Christian Salzmann in 1785, was modeled on the Philanthropinum. Rousseau himself could not have found a more ideal location for a naturalistic school than the Schnepfenthal estate near Gotha. A small court among the trees was prepared for the daily lessons in gymnastics, and Christian André was chosen to direct the exercises. Nearly all exercises that Salzmann had seen at Dessau were reproduced at Schnepfenthal and, in addition, throwing at a target, racing up and down hill, and pole-vaulting were practiced. In bad weather there were indoor exercises for correct posture and good carriage, which might be taken as the origin of free exercises. Sunday afternoons were spent in games and gymnastic sports.

Johann Friedrich GutsMuths (1759–1839) succeeded André as teacher of physical education after one year and remained at this school for fifty years. Although GutsMuths was not the first physical education instructor he is regarded —because of his long service and valuable literary contributions—as the real founder of modern physical education and the "grandfather" of German gymnastics. Whenever weather permitted, activities were held outdoors in a field designated as a place for exercise. All exercises used by André were continued. Climbing ropes, masts, and rope ladders, swinging, balancing rods on the fingers, going through exercises while standing on one foot, and a great variety of "stunts" (used perhaps to retain an interest in exercise) were added. Swimming was taught and became one of the most valued exercises. GutsMuths kept an accurate record of the work done by the individual pupils in order to ascertain progress. The students at Schnepfenthal also received a course in manual training and gardening. Long hikes were taken with Salzmann and GutsMuths leading the way; frequently their excursions lasted as many as four days. The school sought to promote the health of pupils by providing light, airy rooms and wholesome but simple food.

GutsMuths' wide influence rests on his two best-known books, *Gymnastics for the Young* and *Games*. These are not only the first manuals published by a practical physical educator but also are of high quality. GutsMuths realized that the theory and practice of gymnastics should be based on a knowledge of physiology and medicine; that games and swimming have a place in a system of gymnastics; that some educational institutions are not aware of the value of gymnastics, and others are not deriving the maximum benefits from the physical exercises; that contemporary educators can learn much from the Greeks and Romans on the subject of complete education; that the nation should promote the physical well-being of its people. He was also aware that if buildings are not suitable for gymnastics, use may be made of the school yards and neighboring fields; that serviceable apparatus may be made by hand; that exercises in practice should be pleasant and enjoyable and have for their aim a strengthening and harmonizing of body and soul, the development of a complete person; that physical perfection produces self-reliance and courage, which every citizen should have; that nature demands that the growth and development of the body must come first, in childhood and boyhood; and that girls and women should engage in light gymnastics and games, but not in the heavy work of men. To look for the means of producing strong healthy girls and women in the doctor's medicine case is ridiculous. He agrees with Rousseau that to be refined and pleasing one need not be weak and sickly.

In addition to these views, GutsMuths classifies various exercises and describes them in detail and gives his ideas concerning the time for their practice. No one since the Greeks had handled the subject of physical education more intelligently either in practice or theory.

GutsMuths' influence was immediate and far reaching. Prominent families urged the tutors to instruct their children in gymnastics; the schools of many localities began to take an unprecedented interest in the work; swimming schools were organized; universities began to consider the value of gymnastics. Not only did this movement occur in the German states but also in Denmark and Sweden. GutsMuths' *Gymnastics for the Young* was printed in Philadelphia in 1802. Jahn, Spiess, and scores of other prominent men visited his school.

A son of a tanner, GutsMuths not only became a well-educated man but also a real educator. He taught, in addition to physical education, subjects such as geography, French, and technology. However, GutsMuths' first love became physical education and, because of his wide contact

Fig. 6. Jumping and climbing exercises as illustrated in GutsMuths' *Gymnastics for the Young.*

with other scholars and his long service, he truly influenced the development of physical education. Had a period of political unrest and war not interfered, GutsMuths might have secured a prominent place for school gymnastics in general education, long before Spiess accomplished this.

PHYSICIANS' AND PHILOSOPHERS' CONTRIBUTIONS

While educators were coming to realize that physical education ought to be incorporated in the process of general education and that the need for physical welfare is no less important than the need for intellectual attainment, many physicians and writers were helping to mold public opinion in the same direction.

The *Medicina Gymnastica*, written by Francis Fuller (1670–1706), was published in England in 1705. The book dealt with the relation of exercise to disease. When translated into German, this treatise had as much influence in that country as it did in England.

In Germany, Friedrich Hoffmann (1660–1742), Professor of Medicine at the University of Halle, published a series of articles between 1700 and 1720. Among them were "On Motion, the Best Medicine for the Body," "The Incomparable Advantages of Motion and of Bodily exercises, and How They are to be Employed for the Preservation of the Health." These articles influenced GutsMuths some years later.

Johann Peter Frank (1660–1742), in his famous work, *A System for a Complete Medical Police*, by which he meant national policy, condemned the contemporary education for girls because of its seclusion and lack of physical activity. He further objected to the styles which tend to hamper bodily movements. He thought that the youth of Germany did not equal in vigor the youth of ancient Greece, and, therefore, he recommended gymnastics along Greek lines. Frank did not want the exercises to be too strenuous or too dangerous, and he objected to producing "athleten" or rope jumpers or jugglers. He demanded that open air places for gymnastics be provided, first of all for the school children. For inclement weather, a building should be ready for occupancy. He considered physical education a national problem that should be solved by the state.

As the eighteenth century closed, Gerhard Vieth (1763–1836), an expert gymnast and teacher of mathematics at the Haupte Schule in Dessau, was writing his third volume of the *Enzyklopädie der Leibesübungen*. The first volume dealt with the history of physical education, and the second with his own views. He contended that physical exercises promoted health, strengthened muscles, increased suppleness of the body, improved the carriage and physical beauty, stimulated courage and alertness, and "checked a too rapid development and misuse of the sexual instinct." He lamented that so few schools and universities promoted gymnastics among the students, and that they seemed rather to care only for the intellectual attainments.

Simon Andre Tissot (1728–97), a French physician, wrote *An Essay on Diseases Incident to Literary and Sedentary Persons.* He asserted that the life of the scholar entails much mental but very little bodily activity; consequently, there is no deep breathing, and the lungs always contain foul air. Very little attention is paid to food or drink, and, further, the sedentary life tends to seclude one from active and joyful companions. He recommended several exercises which would bring into play all parts of the body. With regard to children, he felt forcing them into hard study without regard for their physical welfare and growth proved injurious both to their development and health. He believed that girls should receive some kind of gymnastics also.

Clement Joseph Tissot (1750–1826), another French physician, exerted considerable influence in the cause of gymnastics through his work, *Medical and Surgical Gymnastics.* He complained that the gymnastics of his time had degenerated into mere games and pastimes and that the Greek sports were almost never practiced. Tissot discussed the effect of activity on the body and classified the exercises according to the result produced from a medical point of view.

Immanuel Kant (1724–1804), a famous professor of metaphysics and logic at the University of Konigsberg, wrote at length on physical education in his *Pedagogy.* He emphasized the disciplinary value of physical education: a strong, sturdy body and a keen, alert, and fearless mind were to result from its practice. Running, jumping, lifting, carrying, throwing at a target, and wrestling were all good exercises in his belief. Many games were to be recommended, but they must have a definite aim. The purpose was to develop a body and mind that would be fit to lead in society. Many of Kant's ideas and statements showed that he was influenced by Rousseau and by the visits which he paid to the Philanthropinum.

PESTALOZZI'S CONTRIBUTION TO PHYSICAL EDUCATION

At the beginning of the nineteenth century the great Swiss educator, Heinrich Pestalozzi (1746–1827) laid the foundation for modern pedagogy. Although influenced by the negative doctrines of Rousseau, he reformed and improved them along positive lines; as he said, he tried to "psychologize" education. This necessitated a study of the child through actual contact and especially a study of the child mind; the resulting knowledge was used as the basis for educational procedures. Pestalozzi compared the child to an unfolding plant and held that the end of education was to assist in the natural, harmonious, and symmetrical development of the mental, moral, and physical powers of the child. The child's part in education was observation, sense perception, and self-activity; the teacher's part was intelligent and sympathetic direction. In effect Pestalozzi considered good education as a method which encouraged natural individual development through concrete experiences. Pestalozzi began his educational efforts among the orphans at Stanz; he then established a model school at Burgdorf and, finally, the institution at Yverdun, which attracted the attention of Europe and America. His school at Burgdorf was provided with separate teachers of singing, geography, history, language, arithmetic, gymnastics, gardening, and manual training.

Pestalozzi's aim and theories demanded that he promote games and physical exercises under the supervision of an instructor in all of his schools. In observing his own child in 1774, he noted that after playing in the open air for a time the boy could then sit and concentrate on his studies for an unusually long period. In addition to this recreational value, he believed that to give vent to the play and competitive instinct was a means of accomplishing the harmonious development of mind, heart, and body. The following ideas, also, are found in Pestalozzi's writings. The strength, skill, endurance, hardihood, and command of the body which are to be derived from physical exercise are desirable and warrant giving physical education an important place in general education. But physical education should not be separate in aims or methods from education in general, for the child is a unity. Nature uses the physical and mental faculties alternately for the development of each other. For example, instinct urges the child to motion, but the exercise may sharpen wits, produce skill and a desire for fair play. To be able to jump is not the only end in the practice of jumping; nor to swim, in the practice of swimming. The school should not neglect this vital principle.

In Pestalozzi's school, at Yverdun in 1807, one hour per day was given to prisoners'-base, ball, and other games, as well as to mountain climbing, skating, jumping, wrestling, and similar activities. Informal play and sport, however, were not sufficient for Pestalozzi; he sought to develop a system of bodily movements arranged according to their difficulty and according to their effect on the body; these were to be practiced under the direction of a teacher. In this work Pestalozzi anticipated the free exercises of Spiess; he had already preceded him in his advocacy of the close relationship that should exist between physical and mental education. Pestalozzi was not an imitator of GutsMuths or Basedow.

Pestalozzi's educational theories are explained in his *Leonard and Gertrude* and *How Gertrude Teaches Her Children*, but his specific views on physical education are found in his article "Concerning Physical Education" published in 1807 and now incorporated in Hirth's *Das Gesamte Turnwesen*.

Phillipp Emenuel von Fellenberg (1771–1844) appropriated the theories of Pestalozzi and developed the industrial phase of education. In his schools the students engaged in shop work, gardening, and various kinds of manual labor.

The history of the manual labor school movement which was so popular in the United States in the 1830's traces its origin to these institutions. Fellenberg did not intend that manual labor should be regarded as a substitute for gymnastics; in all his writings he made it clear that systematic physical exercise and games were indispensable as a means of securing a complete education.

FROEBEL'S THEORIES

Friedrich Froebel (1782–1852) ranks with Pestalozzi as a founder of modern pedagogy. His educational experiences at Keilhau and Burgdorf resulted in the theory that education is acquired most efficiently through activity, self-expression, and social participation. Young children, he found, gave vent to self-expression most readily in their play. The kindergarten grew out of these theories, and Froebel presented the first well-organized program of education through play. Froebel's ideas and methods have been elaborated and accepted by the educational world. During the last few decades, volumes of literature on the subject of the educational values of play have appeared, and the world has, in a measure, ratified the theories of Froebel by the adoption of the play movement.

9

PHYSICAL EDUCATION
IN GERMANY SINCE 1800

The physical education programs in Germany paralleled to a great extent the political patterns of the nation. The leaders in the nineteenth century were Friedrich Ludwig Jahn, who championed liberalism and was most effective in his promotion of the turnverein, Adolph Spiess, who during a more conservative period organized gymnastics for school use, and Hugo Rothstein, who introduced the Swedish Ling system of gymnastics and attempted to impose it on the German army and schools. In the early part of the twentieth century, a reaction against formalism and militarism in the school program motivated the beginnings of the outdoor movement and participation in sports. But these more liberal and informal physical education programs were submerged about 1933 when the National Socialists came to power and imposed a strict militaristic pattern of exercise. After World War II, the pendulum swung back toward a program of sports and activities—this time, however, without political affiliation.

THE TURNVEREIN

The turnverein (German gymnastic societies) originated in the period of turmoil through which Germany passed in the first decade of the nineteenth century, and they are to a great extent the result of the labors of the patriot Friedrich Ludwig Jahn (1778–1852).

Contributions of Jahn to the Program. Jahn, though a Prussian by birth, felt that all Germany was his fatherland, and throughout his life he wrote, spoke, and fought for the political unity of the independent German states. When the citizen army of Napoleon swept away the feeble resistance offered by the inefficient and unpatriotic professional troops of Prussia at the humiliating battle of Jena, 1806, Jahn learned that radical reforms were necessary before his fatherland could be freed from the French conqueror. He possessed no political or social influence, but was endowed with a rugged constitution, a fighting spirit, and a vision, and he began the tasks of arousing his countrymen to a realization of the disgrace of tolerating the foreign despot and preparing them to escape it when the time was ripe. His first important publication *German Nationality*, called attention to the excellence of German achievements and asserted that the Germans should unite in order to protect them and prevent them from being corrupted by foreign invaders.

In the spring of 1810, Jahn was teaching in Plamann's Boys School and also in the Grauen Kloster in Berlin. Wednesday and Saturday half-holidays were spent with younger pupils out of doors for games and exercises. Occasional expeditions into the surrounding country by teachers and pupils were customary before Jahn came to the Plamann school; he, however, became the most active promoter of these affairs. He met the boys regularly outside the city and went with them to a neighboring hilly and wooded stretch of ground called the Hasenheide. Here they competed in running, jumping, wrestling, and played the games popular at the time. Jahn's enthusiasm, his personality, and his stories increased the popularity of the trips. Crude apparatus was improvised; jumping standards and horizontal bars were constructed. Sometimes the company did not stop for the games but took a long hike through the country singing folksongs and enjoying the stories of Jahn. That winter the outdoor games and trips were discontinued, but Jahn gave some of the boys instruction in crossbow shooting and fencing.

In the spring of 1811, balance beams, vertical ropes, ladders, additional horizontal bars erected between trees and standards for high jumping and pole vaulting, a jumping ditch, and a running track were added to the open turnplatz (exercising ground). The games and exercises now took place four afternoons per week, and frequently as many as two hundred boys and young men were present. Schools other than those with which Jahn was connected were permitting the boys to attend. Jahn adopted a gymnastic costume of long trousers and short linen jacket, which caused no little jesting from the idle and unwelcome onlookers.

There was no program for the day; freedom of action and individual effort was the rule. A boy invented a feat and dared the others to do it. The boys determined the games to be played. Jahn thought that the great values to be derived from this activity were physical power and harmonious cooperation. With these rugged constitutions and just and patriotic minds the fatherland might be freed, then united and made worthy of democratic institutions. When the opportunity arose, Jahn let his charges know of his hopes for Germany's future. In the winter his most enthusiastic pupils continued the exercises indoors and studied the works of GutsMuths.

The year of 1812 was one of still greater success. A more spacious turnplatz was secured, and more apparatus was added, including vaulting bucks and crude parallel bars, which were originally used for exercises preparatory to vaulting. Jahn became more systematic and noted down the various exercises, named them, and described the methods of performance. The number of participants reached five hundred at times; on Sundays and specially appointed days adults were welcomed at the turnplatz. Jahn, unable to oversee and direct the entire group, appointed several leaders, called vorturner, who were to assist him.

The great War of Liberation for Prussia was declared March 17, 1813. Jahn was among the first to volunteer to help free his land from France. During his absence Eiselin managed the turnplatz which was now financed by the government. The battle of Leipzig ended French power in Prussia, and Waterloo ended Napoleon's career in Europe. Soon after his return from war, Jahn published his famous book, *Die Deutsche Turnkunst* (German Gymnastics). This book became the turners' guide throughout Germany.

Jahn began by encouraging schoolboys in the gymnastic exercises and athletic sports. However, his ideas were adopted by those who were past school age, and the turner clubs, which came into existence, were made up of youths and men. Volksturnen (peoples' gymnastics) came to be more widely practiced in Germany than anywhere else. Jahn never lost sight of the fact that the turnplatz and turnhalle (indoor gymnasium) should have an important place near a school or a group of schools and that it is the duty of every city to provide them. Here, on every national holiday, games should be played, gymnastic sports engaged in, and prizes awarded. Only very severe weather should prevent the exercises from taking place outdoors.

Jahn's faith and work in physical education originated from patriotic motives. He believed that the hope of German freedom lay in the development of strong, sturdy, and fearless youths and that the continuance of Germany's greatness rested on the vigorous minds of the next generation. A nation with such people, he thought, would not rest until they had secured unity and constitutional government. He was aware of the great power of games and sports to break down class distinctions and generate social democracy. Jahn differed from John Locke, the English philosopher, on the matter of discipline through physical education. Jahn held that exercise should be regarded as a means of growth and development of political powers rather than as a hardening process, and Locke in no wise arose to Jahn's ideas of the mental and moral training to be received from the turn-platz. Locke believed that the program of physical education should develop a strong constitution, sustain healthful living habits, offer recreational exepriences, and develop sport skills essential for a "society gentleman." Jahn held that the turners should eat only simple food and refrain from overindulgence and intemperance. Tobacco and sweet-meats were forbidden near the turnplatz. He was aware of individual differences and did not expect all participants to do all exercises equally well. Jahn's methods were not based on the science of the human body but rather on a faith in physical education as a means of national regeneration. The sciences of anatomy and physiology were not fully under-stood and could not be applied to physical education.

During practice, Jahn says, the teacher should always be an example to the class. He should forbid bad conduct at the exercising place, be sociable and courteous to all, always be on time, observe all the rules, be enthusiastic about the work, learn the students' characteristics, and become their friend and advisor. When the exercises were to take up an entire afternoon, the participants chose their own activity for the first part; then, after a rest, came the orderly exercises in which all of certain age participated.

Die Deutsche Turnkunst contains a wealth of material on how to choose a location, how to lay out a turnplatz, and what apparatus to make. It describes many exercises, dis-cusses the value and the methods of playing several games, and describes the general management of a turnverein. A large part of the German terminology of physical education originated with Jahn, for example, the word turnen (to prac-tice gymnastics) and its derivatives and combinations.

Many of Jahn's contemporaries, for example, GutsMuths, thought that his ideas of physical education were somewhat narrow in that they were saturated with the patriotic motive; others, that his system was too heavy and difficult for chil-dren and defective because it had little or no free exercise and made no provision for the physical education of women. Spiess, of course, objected to Jahn's work on these grounds.

Jahn's gymnastics met with a ready acceptance through-out Germany, and in nearly all of the large cities, young men formed turnvereins using the *Turnkunst* as a guide. Hans Massmann and others who had been associated with Jahn assisted in the organization of these societies. The student clubs (Burschenschaften) whose aims were to unite Germany and secure a free government for the people, promoted the spread of turnen, and in due course their members usually became turners.

Fall of the Turnvereins. Because turnvereins arose in times of political stress, they had for their aims certain political achievements as well as the promotion of physical education. To free the German states from the French was an aim welcomed by kings, nobility, and commons. How-ever, the idea of German unity was met by the kings with hostility and by the nobility with suspicion; to advocate constitutional freedom and government by the people was to tread on dangerous ground. But Jahn believed that all three were necessary to Germany's greatness, and turners in gen-eral were known to hold these ideas.

After Germany was freed and peace restored, the states-men of Europe inaugurated a policy of repression and re-action to counter the spread of liberal political doctrines. At a conference of ministers in the fall of 1818, Metternich, the minister of Austria, declared—and all agreed—that the Burschenschaften and the turner organizations were hotbeds of revolution. In March 1819, Karl Sand, a turner, assassinated Kotzebue, a famous writer in the employ of monarchy. Jahn, although innocent of any connection with the crime, was accused of a conspiracy and arrested in July, 1819. Imme-diately turnen was forbidden in Prussia.

Jahn was held in prison or under close guard during a long period of litigation and was not acquitted until 1825. Even then he was forbidden to live in Berlin or near a uni-versity or boy's school. He took up residence in Freyburg, and, although he was relieved of police restrictions and decorated with the iron cross by the new King Frederick

William IV in 1840, he took no active part in turnen and died in 1852.

Some of the German states followed the lead of Prussia and abolished turnen. Others did not, but the years of 1820 to 1840 are barren of progress in physical education, though much was written concerning the subject.

Revival of Turnverein. Frederick William IV, who came to the Prussian throne in 1840, soon removed the ban on turnvereins and issued the order of 1842 that gymnastics are "formally recognized as a necessary and indispensable part of male education and received into the circle of means for popular education." The tendency that immediately followed—to provide facilities for physical education in the schools—encouraged the turnverein to become more adapted to adult gymnastics and sociability as well as independent of school organizations. There was a rapid increase both in membership and number of societies. The various organizations found need of a national organization of societies (the Turnerschaft), conventions and gymnastic meets (turnfeste), and the newspaper (turnzeitung) as a means of maintaining comradeship and cooperation.

The years of 1848 and 1849 were again years of European revolutions in which the people sought more liberal government, and the turnvereins were suppressed because of their liberal political ideals. About 1860, signs of revival appeared, and turnen was encouraged by the government and flourished for many years. In 1870, the year German unity was practically achieved, the turner societies numbered 1,500; in 1880, 2,200; in 1890, 4,400; in 1900, 7,200; in 1910, 9,100; in 1920, 10,000. In 1915 the societies contained a membership of over 1,000,000, and in 1926 the numbers had reached more than 2,000,000. Adolf Hitler and the National Socialist Party, after seizing power in 1933, soon took control of all sports clubs and youth organizations as well as physical education in the schools. All such activities were placed under governmental control to further the movement toward a totalitarian state.

THE OUTDOOR MOVEMENT

The environmental conditions present in the congested German cities led to the growth of a new activity. The hosteling movement spread rapidly in the early part of the twentieth century. Wandering throughout the German countryside became so popular with those who sought occasional refuge from the cities that hostels sprang up so that people could always find a hostel at the end of a day's hike. By the early 1920's, over 3,000 hostels existed and accommodated approximately one-half million visitors annually.

During the same period, many of the German sports organizations devoted to various competitions began to include activities which took enthusiasts far beyond the confines of cities. Cycling and rowing increased rapidly to the extent that special maps, guides, expense reductions, overnight facilities, and the like were provided for those actively engaged. Skiing, climbing, and gliding attracted many followers interested in wandering throughout various sections of the nation to secure their recreative pleasures. Until 1932, no nation excelled the Germans in their persistent travels throughout the country to enjoy nature.

The solidification or the unification of the underlying concepts of physical education has occurred to a marked degree in the Germany of today. A Study Commission in 1913 was initiated by authorities in Germany who sought an answer to the success of American athletes—German-born or otherwise. After seeing the playground movement in Chicago and other cities, this commission recommended vast additional play areas in all German cities. The spirit of the recommendations was adopted, but no legal acceptance occurred. Furthermore, the practices of American colleges and universities in physical education service and professional curricula were adopted in German universities.

Now, after years of chaotic conditions, the German sports teacher still moves forward. However, newer concepts—the social aspects of physical education and the development of self-discipline and perfection through physical education—are the objectives of the present German program. The creative aspects of sports and art have challenged the imagination of German educators.

GYMNASTICS IN THE SCHOOLS

The development of public schools for the masses came in the nineteenth century. The German turnverein did not immediately alter the school practices or introduce gymnastics into the educational institutions. They tended to supplement the work of the school rather than to secure a place for physical education in it.

Contributions of Spiess to the Program. Germany is indebted to Adolph Spiess (1810–58) for the successful development and organization of school gymnastics. When a boy, Spiess attended a Pestalozzian school where he came in contact with GutsMuths' gymnastics. As a university student, he became proficient in gymnastic activities, especially fencing. He was acquainted with Jahn, GutsMuths, Eiselin, and other leaders of the time. After a few years of teaching in Hesse, he went to Switzerland and remained from 1833 to 1848. During these years he organized his system of school gymnastics in the cities of Burgdorf and Basel. When, in 1842, Prussia's interest in physical education began to revive, Spiess went to Berlin in order to get his ideas before the authorities but failed to make a favorable impression and returned to Switzerland. Incidentally, Massmann, a leading turner, was chosen to devise a plan of physical education for all the Prussian schools.

While in Switzerland, Spiess wrote *Die Lehre der Turnkunst* (System of Gymnastics) and began his manual, *Turnbuch für Schulen* (Manual of Gymnastics for Schools). In 1848 he accepted the task of introducing his system into the school of the Grand Duchy of Hesse and began work in Darmstadt. He took personal charge of the teaching of physical education in the gymnasium, the realschule, and a mädchenschule (girl's school). An outdoor and an indoor gymnasium were provided and equipped with vertical poles, bars, ladders, giant stride, and bucks. Classes for boys and girls were organized.

Spiess's aim and achievement was to secure the adoption of physical exercise as a vital part of the child's education and develop a system suitable to the schools. To that end he advocated the following ideas:

1. An exercising hall and a turnplatz should be established as a part of, or very near, every school.
2. One period per day should be set aside for gymnastic work.
3. Pupils should be given marks according to their proficiency in the work.
4. Gymnastic material should be graded according to its suitability for different ages and sexes.
5. A special system of gymnastics for girls should be arranged.

In short, gymnastics should be recognized and treated with the same degree of importance as any other school subject. His motive was similar to that of the Athenians: physical education was to produce bodily perfection, beauty, and grace, and weld body and soul into a perfectly harmonious entity capable of ideal social participation. He said: "The end of education is undivided, embracing the whole nature of the pupil, it is the school that divides the work and taking different courses aims in the same direction. . . . The intellect and physique constitute but one being." Spiess was also aware of the pedagogical value of physical exercise, its use as a rest and recreation and its moral and social lessons. The exercises and institutions of the turners were not considered satisfactory for the new theories of school gymnastics, especially for girls.

The material and classification of exercises used by the followers of Jahn did not seem satisfactory for children, and especially for girls of school age. Spiess's alterations and additions are explained in his books. In order to adapt gymnastics to the school methods, classes of pupils of approximately the same age were organized and directed by one teacher. Exercises suited to that age were engaged in for a specified period of time each day. In the interests of efficiency the gymnastic class accepted the usual school formalism. Since this program had to be carried out in inclement weather and in winter, an indoor gymnasium became necessary.

Spiess introduced the marching exercises into the German system and called attention to their value. Through their use the teacher was enabled to control a large group and to secure a desired position for the entire class without confusion and waste of time. For the pupil these exercises served as a training in discipline and erect carriage. Spiess also singled out free exercises for special elaboration and emphasis; he is frequently called the founder of that branch of physical education. His aim in this was to give to the entire class, in an orderly manner and in the short time available, a series of exercises designed to bring into play all those parts of the body whose activity was necessary to the ultimate complete development. Formalism was not practiced in Spiess's schools to the exclusion of games, sports, or dancing; the moral, recreational, and esthetic values of the latter were highly appreciated. He also called attention to the use of music; the rhythmical motions of marching and free exercise drills, indoors, offered an opportunity for the use of musical accompaniment.

Considerable stress was placed on gymnastic exhibitions; they were regarded as a means of holding the interest of the pupils as well as securing favorable public opinion. Spiess found that the excursions into the country, so enjoyed by turners, were also suitable for the school classes when time permitted.

Spiess was opposed to the Jahn system of teaching by vorturners (class leaders) and advocated the employment of a sufficient number of teachers who had training and experience equal to that of the teachers of other school subjects. To that end he established normal classes in Darmstadt in 1849.

Pestalozzi, GutsMuths, and Basedow antedated Spiess in the matter of fostering gymnastics in their schools, but he perfected the idea, stressed its importance, and attracted the attention of the authorities at an opportune time and is usually considered the founder of the system of German school gymnastics and of gymnastics for girls. His classes were visited by officials of nearly every state in Germany, and his methods were adopted so widely that his system became a part of the German system.

Fig. 7. The Basel Turnplatz

Program Since Spiess. To carry out the Order of 1842, which advocated gymnastics for the schools, Hans Massmann (1797–1874), a turner of the Jahn type, was chosen to plan a system for all Prussia. Much to the disappointment of Spiess and most of the school authorities, Massmann clung to the old idea of a municipal turnplatz separate from the school and the school management, and very little advance was made in physical education in the schools. Massmann retired in 1850.

This period of stagnation was followed by one of strife. Hugo Rothstein (1810–65), while director of the Royal Central Institute of Gymnastics (Königliche Zentral-Turnanstalt) in Berlin, attempted to introduce the Ling Swedish system to the exclusion of some vital principles in the German system. Opposition was too great, and he withdrew in unpopularity in 1863. After several changes of name and location, the Royal Central Institute became the present Landesturnanstalt at Spandau, where thorough courses in gymnastics are given to prospective teachers of physical education.

Following 1860, Germany continued as a leader in school gymnastics and attached more and more importance to that subject. In that year, all schools for boys, from the elementary institutions to the universities, received orders to secure teachers of gymnastics and give additional time and emphasis to physical education. Two years later a manual for instruction in gymnastics in the elementary schools was published and attendance at the exercises made compulsory. In spite of the frequent revision of the manual and of official encouragement, the school authorities neglected to carry out the program through the eighties and nineties. This resulted because of a tendency to crowd the curriculum and to engage an ever-increasing number of women teachers in the faculties.

By 1904, Germany awakened to the seriousness of this neglect and did much to combat it, partly through the playground movement and by insisting that women teachers prepare to teach the subjects of physical education. Following that date, the time allotted for physical activities increased to three hours per week and one play afternoon each week in nearly all schools. Some schools devoted ten-minute periods to deep breathing and correct posture exercises on alternate days. The boys' and girls' athletic clubs for the promotion of certain sports and games, supervised by teachers, supplemented the regular school work. The addition of gymnastics for girls in 1894 as a part of the curriculum in higher schools received continuing support, and a special manual of exercises for girls was published in 1913.

In addition to the Landesturnanstalt, the leading states of Germany established normal schools for teachers of physical education. Each state managed its educational system independently; therefore, each had its own individual history so far as dates, leaders, and events were concerned. However, their methods and objectives in physical education were very similar. This was partly a result of the efforts of the national organizations promoting physical education throughout Germany, for example, the Turnerschaft and the German Society of Teachers of Gymnastics. The latter organization, through its conventions and publications, tended to make uniform the best methods and aims in physical education.

EFFECT OF WORLD WAR I

The great mental and emotional strain and the food famine had a very detrimental effect on the physical welfare of German children. In addition to a rehabilitation movement which evolved to influence the total physical education program, more emphasis was placed on the games and athletic sports, and additional attention was given to health education. This rejuvenation related directly to the governmental support that physical education received from the Weimar Republic. Regulations required all schools to include physical education in the curriculum, and it received equal status with other school subjects. Athletic meets, graded performance, presidential certificates, increased facilities of all kinds, and other factors brought physical education in Germany to a new high level. Those phases of physical education which flourished before World War I were retained as excellent means for restoring the mental and physical health of an exhausted nation. The spirit of play manifested itself in the organization of athletic and recreation clubs for all ages, in playgrounds, summer camps, new courses on play in normal schools, greater emphasis on dancing, rhythmic gymnastics, and in sport publications of books and magazines. The employment of school doctors and nurses, vacation camps, nutrition classes, school clinics, open air schools, and sex education evolved as advancements in the health education movement.

PHYSICAL EDUCATION DURING NATIONAL SOCIALISM

In 1933 when National Socialism came to power, Adolf Hitler appointed a military officer as National Sports Commissioner. Amateur sports organizations and youth groups were either dissolved or reorganized. The Commissioner specified 16 unions to control all the sports that were to survive. In addition, these unions controlled the "Sports Physicians," teachers, and youth groups. A national representative association was developed which included one member from each of the 16 unions. In turn, corresponding groups were established on district and local levels. In addition to these major steps, approximately 165 unions were dissolved by Hitler, and the leisure time of the workers and employees was planned in accordance with Nazi purposes. As sports were adequately handled by the amateur clubs, competition with their efforts was avoided.

Physical education became a required subject in schools, and passing physical fitness tests became part of the requirements for graduation. Even entrance into secondary schools depended upon the ability of a student to pass physical as well as intellectual tests. Special schooling awaited those rated high in both leadership and physical capacities. The usual physical education requirements were two or three hours weekly for elementary school children and four or five hours for secondary pupils. Universities stressed physical education and prospective teachers met such classes daily.

At the end of the school day (1:00 P.M.), club activities for Hitler Youth were specified. At this time, hikes and drills continued to complete the physical fitness program while Nazi indoctrination and party work received a fair share of attention. To increase the physical vigor of out-of-school 14- and 15-year-olds, a compulsory program in a

farm setting was required. The total program finally culminated in a half-year of service through labor followed by
induction into army life.

EFFECT OF WORLD WAR II

Many schools, colleges, and training institutes let physical
education die after 1945. This appeared as only a period of
adjustment. The sports teachers aspect of Berlin University
(dissolved by National Socialism) was replaced by a similar
undertaking in 1947 called the Cologne Sportshochschule.
This is a three-year course for men and women, which may
be taken either separately or in conjunction with university
studies at Cologne or Bonn. Primary teachers may also take
a one-year post-certificate course.

The sports clubs began to reappear by 1946, but without
political affiliation. Old and young alike met in the German
Light-Athletic championship in 1946 in Frankfurt. The following year this same national event occurred in Cologne.
The occupying authorities disallowed any central organization for sports, but nothing seemed to dim the desire of
Germans to participate in sports.

Most schools in Germany have physical education classes
which meet from 45–60 minutes twice each week. German
physical education includes the native turnen, English games,
Scandinavian corrective gymnastics, creative dancing, and
other activities. In the spring and summer, outdoor sports
receive major emphasis, and during the winter gymnastics
and other indoor activities are stressed.

Sports clubs and turnverein abound everywhere. All such
organizations sponsor very active youth sections. Full-time
instruction is usually provided. In most instances, schools
do not have their own playing fields but depend upon the
facilities controlled either by the clubs or the municipalities.

As previously mentioned, the movement back toward
sports and other physical activities during all seasons of the
year quickly gained momentum following World War II.
This trend has continued to flourish and the German child

of today compares favorably from a physical standpoint with English children or other European children. In other words, few, if any, effects of the shortages resulting from World War II are visible.

The culmination of all this effort toward physical activities seems most apparent during week ends, vacations, and holidays when favorable weather prevails. Hiking, boating, hostelling, gliding, winter sports, aquatics, and other outdoor activities attract thousands of families and other groups to the parks and other natural areas. The love of the out of doors and the desire for enjoyable physical activity seem to be a part of the German culture.

PHYSICAL EDUCATION
IN SCANDINAVIA SINCE 1800

Denmark and Sweden have contributed much to the development of physical education. Throughout the years the interests of Scandinavian people have led to a continuous effort to improve the gymnastic system and develop fitness for all.

PHYSICAL EDUCATION IN DENMARK

The progressive nation of Denmark has occupied an important position in the over-all development of physical education. Danish interest and achievements in gymnastics began in the stormy Napoleonic period when Denmark suffered humiliation at the hands of the great powers. The evident need for strong national defenders, combined with the Danish love for sports and athletic competition, made Denmark a fertile soil for the growth of the institutions of physical education. So throughout the nineteenth cenutry, Danish physical education emphasized programs which led to developing good soldiers and reverence for Denmark. The outstanding leader in the history of physical education in Denmark is Franz Nachtegall (1777–1847).

Contributions of Nachtegall. Nachtegall, when a university student, was a gymnast of the first rank. This proficiency and the reading of GutsMuths' works started him on the career of physical educator. He secured the position of teacher of gymnastics in a club of university students and later in a naturalistic school similar to that of Basedow. Nachtegall's career showed that he possessed boundless energy, tact, flexibility, and, above all, he was a good teacher with the ability to organize. In 1799, he directed his own private open air gymnasium in Copenhagen which proved to be very popular and the first of its kind. In 1804, Denmark turned its attention to the need for a larger and a better trained army and navy. The authorities recognized that the practice of gymnastics should be an essential part of that training and founded the Military Gymnastic Institute, the first gymnastic normal school of modern times. Nachtegall was made the first director. On his recommendation the government decided to extend the benefits of gymnastics to the schools and to encourage the participation of adults outside the military branches; to that end, civilians were permitted to attend the school.

In 1809 schools of the secondary grade were requested to give instruction in physical exercise. Five years later, in 1814, elementary schools were ordered to provide instructors and to secure grounds and equipment suitable for the practice of gymnastics. This is the first school ordinance establishing physical education as a part of general education in any European nation.

To prepare a large number of teachers for the work, courses in gymnastics were established in the various teachers' colleges in addition to the instruction given in the gymnastic institute. Nachtegall was chosen to fill the office of Director of Gymnastics for all Denmark. During the third and fourth decades of the century, progress was slow but worthy of notice. The Military Gymnastic Institute secured permission to establish practice classes for student teachers among the school children. A manual of gymnastics, published at national expense and distributed to the teachers of physical education in the various schools, became the guide. Gymnastics for girls was accepted and classes for women teachers of physical education were established in the Military Institute. Some localities far exceeded others in the practice of gymnastics; success or failure depended upon the attitude of the educators in a given community.

Revival of the Sixties. On the death of Nachtegall new and less able leaders took charge, and at times school gymnastics was threatened with extinction. The disastrous war of 1864 with Austria and Prussia aroused a renewed interest in gymnastics, especially as a means of augmenting national defense. The Danish Rifle Clubs, modeled after those in England, date from this period. At first all activities took place out of doors, but around 1871 the first of many buildings for exercise began to appear. Soon after they were organized these clubs took on the features of gymnastic societies. Members participated in, and encouraged others to engage in, gymnastics and games, and they held track meets and offered their buildings to classes of school children when no others were available.

Folk high schools, a Danish innovation, also evolved after 1864. These institutions, privately operated, were open to young men and women between the ages of 18 and 25. The majority who attended came from farms or rural communities. Many subjects have been or are taught (these schools still exist), but examinations are nonexistent. Gymnastics always have held an important place in the curriculum, and it was through the young adults attending these institutions that renewed interest in gymnastics took place in the nineteenth century.

Through the entire early period, GutMuths' system, as altered by Nachtegall, and the Jahn-Eiselin system of the German turners prevailed in Denmark. During the eighties, the Ling system of Sweden, which was introduced in a folk or people's high school, began its invasion. The resulting controversies concerning the values of the Ling system increased the popularity of gymnastics in general and tended to revive school gymnastics, which had been neglected. A committee, appointed for the purpose, arranged a system thought to be suitable for Denmark and published a manual of exercises. This new *Handbook of Gymnastics* contained many innovations from Sweden but retained much of the material already current in Denmark.

Since 1900 the most noticeable movements have been the demilitarization of educational gymnastics, extension of teacher training facilities, national financial aids in the promotion of physical education, recognition of the value of sports and games, and the contributions of Niels Bukh (see p. 114).

Demilitarization of School Gymnastics. For nearly a century the leaders in gymnastics were military men, from the highest directors and inspectors to the class teachers. This condition was, of course, a survival of the originally dominant military aim of physical education. The disadvantages were that the aims, methods, and theories were not suitable to the school conditions and that the exercises did not become a part of the school but remained supplementary to it.

In 1904 school gymnastics was divorced from military gymnastics in every way. The University of Copenhagen in 1909 offered gymnastics as a subject and provided a laboratory. To provide civilian teachers, the normal colleges and universities established both complete and brief courses in physical education and an independent Central Institute of Gymnastics was opened in Copenhagen. By this means the opportunities for securing preparation as a teacher of physical education have been increased and made inexpensive. Consequently great numbers of well-educated teachers have gone from these institutions into the schools of Denmark and other countries.

An act passed in 1937 requires public elementary and secondary school education, which is compulsory between the ages of 7–14, to include physical education as a part of the curriculum. The official allocation of school time in Denmark to physical education follows: children between 6 and 11, 11 and 14, and 14 and 18 have a minimum of two, three, and four activity periods respectively each week. An annual mark for physical education is given each student, and it receives equal status with marks given for other subjects.

To meet the handicap which many localities experienced in not having sufficient funds to equip a gymnasium and employ an instructor, the national government makes significant grants and loans. A government order in 1946 required all country schools to erect a gymnasium and install various pieces of apparatus and equipment. In conjunction with these requirements for physical education, the School Medical Service Act of 1946 insures free or substantially free school meals, dental care, nursing, and various types of medical supervision.

The Play Movement. The comparatively recent worldwide recognition of the value of play and playgrounds is noted in Denmark in 1896. Earlier, however, many private schools had emphasized group games and outdoor sports, and the Copenhagen Playground Association had been established. Under the leadership of this organization, the national government appropriated funds to be used by a committee for the purpose of promoting group games among school children by furnishing playground equipment, giving consultant services, and helping prepare teachers. Hundreds of schools accepted the plan and were aided and financed by this committee. Teachers' courses have been altered to give time to the theory and management of games popular in Denmark and suitable for physical education, such as Danish ball, cricket, football, and hockey.

Early in the 1900's many Danish children and youth recreation groups sprang up, such as The Boys' Voluntary League, Boy Scouts, Girl Guide Corps, and Y.M.C.A. programs. Hostelling became very popular in the 1930's with thousands of members joining and the necessary hostels being established. With at least twelve holidays for all working citizens, many clubs, schools, trade unions, municipal governments, and private interests cater to the leisure interests of the Danish people.

Primitive Gymnastics of Bukh. In 1921 Niels Bukh (1880–   ), the Director of Gymnastics in the People's School at Ollerup, Denmark, developed a new interpretation of the Ling gymnastics. Bukh recognized the many defects of the untrained body, the stiff round back, the forward projecting neck, the sets of overdeveloped muscles and underdeveloped muscles, and the like. His aim was to produce the perfect normal physique. To that end all bad postural habits, occupational deformities, and other defects must be eliminated first. Strength, suppleness, and coordination of the entire body must be obtained. The exercises for this purpose are called "Primitif Gymnastike." They differ from the ordinary exercises in that there are no "held" positions and no cessation of movement. In practice the work resembles a long memorized drill of big muscle exercises executed rapidly and with rhythm. His system does away with much of the old apparatus and relies mainly on wall bars, mattresses, and vaulting boxes. Marching (often while singing) accompanies the usual physical education sessions.

The ideas and methods of Primitive Gymnastics have influenced not only Denmark but Europe and America as well. Bukh and other Danish gymnasts have toured the United States and left their mark. However, the pattern of the American system of teacher education has been adopted by the Danes to a marked degree, even to the courses of instruction. Similar to the American system is the previously mentioned official allocation of school time in Denmark to physical education.

PHYSICAL EDUCATION IN SWEDEN

The history of physical education in Sweden runs parallel to that in Denmark. Although each exerted an influence upon the other, Sweden was more outstanding in her development of new methods and new objectives in addition to her international influence. Like Denmark, Sweden began with the military motive for national participation in gymnastics, and when the immediate danger of foreign attacks slackened, she continued physical education as a means of increasing national welfare and prosperity.

Contributions of Ling. The Swedish emphasis on the curative and corrective value of gymnastics, commonly known as medical gymnastics, has given the Swedish system adherents throughout the world. This movement resulted largely from the work of Per Henrik Ling (1776–1839), the founder of the Swedish system. As a university student, Ling showed great aptitude for foreign languages and literature. After attending the Swedish universities he went to Copenhagen, and remained from 1799 to 1804. While there he studied the old Norse literature, Danish and German languages, and took a course in fencing. He also visited Nachtegall's private gymnasium and very probably read GutsMuths' *Gymnastics for the Young*, which was popular in Denmark at that time. Apparently these events induced Ling to take up the work of physical education. His fencing exercises seemed to improve an arm affliction, and he came to believe in the curative possibilities of gymnastics.

In 1804 Ling accepted the position of fencing master at the University of Lund, in Sweden. He required his students to supplement their fencing with riding, vaulting, and other gymnastic exercises. At the same time, he studied anatomy and physiology, because he believed that a thorough knowledge of the human body and nature's laws was a minimum for an intelligent understanding of physical education. As Ling became more and more acquainted with the science of the human body he came to believe that the medical value of gymnastics had been too little emphasized and that gymnastics for the weak were as important as gymnastics for the strong; that exercise must be prescribed for the individual rather than for a group; that a system of gymnastics must be based on an accurate knowledge of the effect of the various exercises on the human organism; that teachers and instructors must know the purpose and effect of every exercise; and that the aim must be physical harmony and perfection, "The one-ness of the human organism; the harmony between the mind and the body."

During these formative years of Ling's work, Sweden was defeated by the French and Russians, and, deserted by England, she lost the states of Pomerania and Finland. Like Jahn in Germany and Nachtegall in Denmark, Ling saw that the only hope for national honor lay in a brave and sturdy citizenry, and he set out to accomplish that through physical education. These political disasters also called from his pen patriotic verses and articles which rank high in Swedish literature.

When Ling became fencing master in the Royal Military School, he proposed that a national institute of physical education be established where teachers might be prepared for the ultimate purpose of the physical upbuilding of the Swedish people. The idea met the approval of the authorities, and the Royal Central Institute of Gymnastics was opened in Stockholm in 1814. Its most important immediate work was along the line of military gymnastics looking toward national defense. Ling and other instructors taught the soldiers in the Institute and in the neighboring barracks. Ling's system of bayonet fighting and his supplementary exercises and *Handbook of Gymnastics* were used in the courses. The Institute became the center of this phase of military preparedness.

Ling laid the foundation both in the theory and practice of the Swedish system; his successors have added to and elaborated but never radically altered his original ideas. His *Gymnastikens allmänna Grunder* remains the cornerstone of the structure. In 1913, the centennial of Ling's proposal to establish the Central Institute, Sweden held a national celebration, including addresses, parades, gymnastic meets, and the decoration of Ling's grave.

On the death of Ling in 1839, Lars Gabriel Branting became the director of the Central Institute. The period of wars having passed, the military motive for gymnastics became less important, and Branting expanded the field of medical gymnastics. He pointed out that the greatest benefit of many exercises did not accrue to the muscular system but rather to the nervous and circulatory systems and to the viscera.

Medical gymnastic theories caused much controversy among medical men, but, in spite of the opposition, they were accepted in Sweden and had great influence in the leading countries of the world.

Physical Education in the Schools. The spread of gymnastics in Swedish schools came more slowly than in Danish. The earliest legislation on the subject was a law in 1820 requiring a course in physical education for the secondary schools for boys. The gradual adoption of a physical education program in all public schools did not result from compulsory legislation but rather from a genuine belief that physical exercise is an indispensable part of general education.

During the 1860's the Royal Central Institute of Gymnastics was reorganized, and three separate departments resulted, the pedagogical, the military, and the medical. Hjalmar Ling (1820–86), the son of Per Ling, became the head of the pedagogical department. The adaptation of Swedish theories to the school room is largely his contribution. This adaptation necessitated the construction of suitable apparatus, the arrangement of group exercises, grading, and progress of the work, and a classification of movements for young boys and girls. Through the work of H. Ling the rational "days order" of the Swedish system was evolved.

A healthy and gradual growth characterizes the history of physical education in Swedish schools during the last half century. Schools controlled by the Board of Education and the Supervisory Board of Trade Schools require compulsory physical education. The requirements apply to all state-supported elementary and high schools.

For school children between seven and nine years of age, either one forty-five minute period or two shorter periods are required each week. The other elementary classes may have up to three required hours a week. The secondary school classes devote from three to four hours each week to physical education. The physical education program in Sweden deals, in the main, with gymnastics, games and sports, and winter activities such as skiing.

To supplement this phase of physical education, Swedish schools set aside outdoor days to further insure that the young people lead a vigorous outdoor life. These outdoor days amount to a half day being set aside so that outdoor activities in games and sports balance the other school subjects. Schools schedule these days at their own convenience, and some schools combine two half days into one full day of outdoor activity. The number of required outdoor days varies from a required ten to twelve per year in secondary schools to as many as sixteen to twenty-four in some elementary schools.

In the practice of physical education, the exercises of the Swedish system, supplemented by games and sports, form the foundation of the activities. The Ling system always has been regarded in Sweden as superior to all other systems for its contribution to correctives. Also, its efficiency, orderliness, and adaptability to school methods are regarded highly. Stall bars and other wall apparatus prove functional in schools which have no gymnasia and where the classrooms or hallways must be used for physical education. Most high schools have well-equipped gymnasia, but many trade schools and elementary schools lack the necessary facilities for a well-rounded program.

The physical welfare of university students in Sweden receives as much attention as in any other country with the possible exception of the United States. The universities differ greatly in the facilities offered for gymnastics and sports. Some have abundant and well-equipped facilities, while others provide practically none. However, private gymnasia and gymnastic societies are readily available for those students desiring activity in gymnastics or sports.

A physical fitness program has developed in Sweden in which people voluntarily participate in gymnastics. The women began participation in this program in about 1942, and since that time thousands have begun to participate. As many as 5,000 women have participated in a Lingiad. Teachers are trained by the Gymnastic Association to circulate among working people and give them a few minutes of calisthenics.

The spirit of recreation play and sports competition has invaded Sweden as well as most other countries. Games have become a part of the physical and moral education program, and they have gained in importance in a program once dominated by gymnastics. Provision for outdoor games and sports is made at nearly every school at the present time. During the short summer the Swedes flock to the lakes and seashore for swimming, sun bathing, boating, and other aquatic activities. Skiing of all kinds, skating, curling, ice hockey, and many other similar activities predominate during the winter. Further, singing and dancing with participants dressed in colorful costumes are enjoyed throughout Sweden.

The Swedish system has done much to enrich the field of physical education both in theory and practice. Physical education has reached a high educational plane because of the insistence of authorities that prospective physical education teachers make a thorough study of the human organism through anatomy, physiology, and kinesiology. Exercises are then arranged with respect to that knowledge. Especially important are these basic sciences to the application of physical education in the corrective phase of the program. In all modern countries the field of corrective physical education has increased in importance in the past half century.

Preparation of Physical Education Teachers. Since its origin in 1814, the Royal Central Institute of Gymnastics has held a prominent position as a normal school. Three- and four-year courses are given and include both the theory and practice of physical education in the curriculum. Courses

in physical education are given in all institutions which prepare elementary school teachers. Public schools provide the
practice classes in which prospective teachers apply their
skills and knowledges while learning. In the twentieth century the teacher education program is reflected in a new
emphasis which the physical education teachers have made
on caring for the needs of all age groups. By encouraging
a broader program with additional stress on sports and
games, the program gives less of the total effort to military
aims.

11

PHYSICAL EDUCATION
IN GREAT BRITAIN, AUSTRALIA,
NEW ZEALAND, AND CANADA

Throughout the various parts of the British Empire, the sports and games of England have become a part of the culture in the new lands. The English people, therefore, have had a profound influence on physical education and leisure activity among the countries of the world.

GREAT BRITAIN

While continental countries created systems of gymnastics and developed the science of physical education, the British people continued their participation in outdoor sports. Britain's isolated position and her powerful navy shielded her from dangerous foreign invasions and, consequently, made unnecessary the strict discipline and training to which the nations of the Continent subjected themselves for national defense. The conditions which prompted Jahn to advocate the physical development of his people never existed in England. Britain's free institutions, personal liberty, and individualism tended to give free rein to the play and sporting instincts of her people. Her large manufacturing and trading population found leisure time and inclination to imitate the nobles in their outdoor sports. The temperate climate was always inviting to outdoor activity. English nature had a bent for competitive sport, but, on the other hand, it rejected formal drill except for purposes of military training.

History of British Sports. All people, savage or civilized, engage in some kind of sport, and it goes without saying that English sport is as old as the English people. As early as the year 1200, writers were expressing opinions on the value of games in general and comparing the benefits to be derived from the different sports. A proclamation of Henry VII (c. 1500) read, "It ever hath bene of old antiquite used in this realme for all lustye gentlemen to pass the delectable season of summer after divers manner and sundry fashions of disport," and established a series of athletic contests, the victors of which were to be rewarded. This national enthusiasm for play led to the invention of many games and to the adoption and alteration of several that were introduced from other lands.

In feudal England, the joust, tournament, and other knightly sports predominated. With the decline of feudalism and the rise to importance of the bowmen, archery became the most practiced sport and the one most encouraged by the royal authorities, both for nobles and commons. It was valued as a preparation for war—not as a means of physical education. Archery continued to have the royal favor and protection until the invention and common use of the musket lessened the importance of the bow as a weapon.

Golf probably originated in Holland, but when the same was introduced to the Scotch and English, it received such a welcome and added development that it is more commonly identified with Britain than with its native land. During the fifteenth century, laws forbidding the playing of golf were passed because it threatened to destroy the popularity of archery. This opposition did not long exist, for in the next century the nobles and the king himself accepted the game.

Then golfing clubs were formed by the wealthy people of England, but it was not until the nineteenth century that this game was played by great numbers of commons. Since 1880 it has had a remarkable increase in popularity in England as well as in Europe and America.

Hockey was played by the Greeks and Romans and has been a sport of the nations of Europe since that time. The modern name seems to have come from the hooked sticks with which it is played. In Scotland the game was called shinty and in Ireland, hurley. Its recent popularity dates from 1875, when the English Hockey Association was established. Hockey clubs were then organized throughout the British Isles. Games between the teams representing England, Ireland, Scotland, and Wales were frequent. Since 1900 matches between England, France, and other Continental countries have been common.

Cricket originated in England about the thirteenth century and evolved in the direction of the modern game during the fourteenth century. In spite of the hostile legislation and the scorn of the nobility, the game became popular. In the sixteenth century the higher classes took up the sport, and, slowly but gradually, it took the position of the national game.

Bowling originated in the Netherlands and Germany but was soon carried over the world by the Dutch traders. The English and the Scotch "naturalized" the alien pastime but never accepted it with the popularity that golf received.

Pitching quoits became the pastime of the lower classes near the Scotch and English border in the fifteenth century. Neither laws against it nor Ascham's statement that "quoits be too vile for scholars" was sufficient to prevent its encroachments on archery. Rustics found that horseshoes were a good substitute for the regulation quoits.

Tennis seems to have had its origin in France and was played by kings and nobles of both France and England as early as 1300. It was forbidden to the peasant in both countries, but with the winning of political freedom it was taken up by the commons. Only in the last century, however, has tennis gained its great popularity.

Games resembling football were played by the Greeks and Romans and were probably introduced by Roman legions into northern Europe and Britain. In the twelfth century the young men of London were in the habit of going to the country green to play football. Henry VIII and Elizabeth outlawed the sport, and Sir Thomas Elyot spoke against it in 1537. He said, "Foot Ball wherein is nothynge but beastlye furie and exstreme violence, whereof proceedeth hurte; and consequently malice and rancour do remain with them that be wounded; where of it is to be putt in perpetuall silence." Another writer expressed his opinion: "For as concerning football playing I protest unto you that it may rather be called a friendlie kinde of fyghte than a play or recreation —a bloody and murthering practice than a fellowly sport or pastime." In Ireland, on the other hand, a law of the sixteenth century forbade all sports except archery and football. Because of its crude "rough and tumble" features, it became a game of the commons. Shrove Tuesday was regarded as a special day for playing.

During the eighteenth and nineteenth centuries some larger schools of England accepted the game as suitable for boys and devised their own local rules for playing. Rugby purchased its first athletic field in 1749 and played football there. It seems to have been a kicking game rather than one of carrying the ball. An honorary tablet at Rugby explains how the game came to be changed. "This stone commemorates the exploit of Wm. Webb Ellis who with a fine disregard for the rules of football as played in his time, first took the ball in his arms and ran with it, thus originating the distinctive feature of the Rugby game A.D. 1823." The Rugby school rules predominated and laid the foundation for the modern football game.

Hammer throwing competition is of Celtic origin and very early became popular in Scotland and Ireland. A common sledge hammer was used, and the trials were made for distance only. This was one of the few sports favored by the governing authorities. Changes in the rules of the game and the style of the hammer have altered the fundamentals of the competition very little.

Pole vaulting originated from the method of jumping canals and drain ditches in England; every homestead kept a pole for that purpose. It soon became a form of sport and was engaged in at the fairs and holiday gatherings. Pole vaulting found its way into Germany and was advocated by Jahn and GutsMuths as a valuable exercise.

Skittles, wrestling, boxing, fencing, pitching the bar, prisoners'-base, slinging, skating, rowing, and many more activities kept the nation physically fit. A greater number of people, men, women, and children, engage in these sports than ever before. Wherever the British go their games go with them, whether it be Australia, India, or America. Britain's position in this field has made her a center from which ideas and inspirations have been drawn in the international playground and recreation movements. Germany, the Scandinavian countries, and America have felt her influence.

The encouragement and development of many sports in England show, with few exceptions, that the English people did much more in the way of refining and popularizing these activities than in inventing new ones. Perhaps traditional British reverence for freedom and individuality proved a welcome environment for sports and a less likely context for gymnastics and other activities designed for military purposes. This observation does not deny the use and acceptance of gymnastics in schools, clubs, and the military, but it does point to the most valuable contribution England has made to physical education. Of added significance is the fact that in many of its colonies, such as Canada and Australia, the English successfully introduced both the sports and the sports attitude.

Gymnastics in Great Britain. Britain did not remain free from the theories and achievements of physical education in the Continental countries. First of all, an urgent need was felt in the army for a system of physical training that would combine the benefits derived from formal drill with those derived from competitive sports. In 1822 the government obtained the services of the Swiss army officer and director of gymnastics, Phokion Clias. He was given charge of all physical training in military and naval schools and also was employed to teach in the Charter House Public School. His theories and methods were largely those of GutsMuths and other Germans. Because of an accident he left England in 1825.

Gymnastics for the army and navy was continued, but no very important leaders appeared until the coming of the Swedes, Ehrenhoff and, later, Carl Georgii, about 1850. Both were graduates of the Royal Central Institute, and both opened private institutions in London. These leaders claimed so much for their system that the British people were brought face to face with the question of whether their sports were sufficient or whether the Continental systems had anything better to offer.

Contributions of Maclaren. Archibald Maclaren (1820–84), a Scot by birth, was on the Continent at that time giving considerable study to the whole question of physical education. On returning to England in 1858 he established a private gymnasium in Oxford. A few years later the government decided to reorganize and regenerate the system of military gymnastics, and Maclaren was placed in charge of the work. His ideas were incorporated in a manual *A Military System of Gymnastic Exercises* which was to be used as a text. There was sent to his gymnasium a group of officers who were to be instructed in the theory and practice of gymnastics; they were then to return to the military center at Aldershot, where a normal school for other officers was to be established. The entire plan was carried out, and Maclaren's system came to be used in the military and naval schools to supplement the games and sports as a means of increasing the physical fiitness of the soldiers and sailors.

Maclaren was not satisfied with that; he believed that educational gymnastics was the direct and more important means of improving the physical standard of the British. His book *A System of Physical Education,* printed in 1867 and again in 1885, and again, by his son, in 1895, reveals the following theories:

1. Physical training should accompany the growing period of life.
2. Physical training and mental training should go hand in hand, and each should be of benefit to the other.
3. The much-practiced games in England will not produce a well-balanced organism, but on the other hand, they will tend to develop a onesidedness.
4. Only trained instructors should be employed.
5. Health rather than strength and skill should be the aim.
6. "Mind and body should be viewed as two well-fitting halves of a perfect whole, designed in true accord mutually to sustain and support each other and each worthy of our unwearied care and unstinted attention."
7. School games, sports, and pastimes are recreational while systematized exercise is educational.
8. Exercises should be regulated by individual fitness.
9. Systematic exercise is not only good for children and soldiers, but for the men of the shops and factories.
10. Exercises must be progressive and organized in a rational manner.
11. Gymnastics must not interfere with the playtime in the school, but rather it should become a part of the regular educational program.
12. Gymnastics "mean a gradual progressive system of physical exercise, so conceived, so arranged, and so administered, that it will naturally and uniformly call forth and cultivate the latent powers and capacities of the body, even as the mental faculties are developed and strengthened by mental culture and exercise."

Maclaren found fault with the Swedish system because he thought it was too much limited by the medical and corrective aims, and he objected to the German system because of its music and rhythm and its efforts to attain precision in group exercises. However, he invented very little that was new, either in theory or practice, but rather culled from all systems those theories and practices that suited him. Maclaren was a pioneer in the study of anthropometry and kept records of measurements and weights of his pupils for the purpose of studying the results of exercise.

Period of Investigation. The system introduced by Maclaren did not prove a great success. Nearly all teachers of the Maclaren gymnastics were from the army, and school exercises looked very much like military drill. Various investigations resulted in many but feeble efforts to revise physicial exercise in the interest of recreation and health.

Meanwhile, Danish and Swedish teachers brought to England the Swedish system of physical education. This system proved exceedingly popular especially with women and girls. In 1903 the Education Department of Scotland recommended to the school officials a new course which was based on the Swedish system. A year later the English Board of Education published a *Syllabus of Physical Exercise,* which was also founded on the Swedish system. This syllabus was revised in 1909 and again in 1919. During this period many educational laws favoring the spread of school gymnastics were passed, and several training schools for teachers of physical education were established.

Throughout the ensuing years, formal exercises have continued to be stressed. The reasons for this perpetuation of such a program seem to be threefold:

1. The general conception of physical education by both lay and professional people continues to be limited.
2. The stress on physical fitness during war periods has encouraged the continuance of the program.
3. Adequate facilities and space for a games and sports program are generally lacking in the English schools. This condition exists in spite of the fact that plans for the extension of hundreds of sites have been approved.

The Changing Concept. In England there appears to be an awakening among educational leaders which is bringing about a recognition of the connection between the school physicial education program and the leisure program for those who have left school. Leaders now place a greater emphasis upon the recreation element. Athletics, games, swimming, canoeing, hiking, and dancing receive some emphasis in schools. In addition, the emergency schools (clusters of huts) built during World War II in rural areas are used by local school authorities. Children sent to these camps for a short period each year receive opportunities in many outdoor activities; however, regular academic work still continues during this outing. The relationship between many of these activities and those which people in England voluntarily select after leaving school may bring about general public understanding of the desired over-all program. Fortunately, the idea of a highly specialized coach employed to coach the few best players has not been readily accepted.

Health Movement. England and Scotland have promoted the health and hygiene movement. As early as the close of the last century, medical inspection of the school plants and health inspections of the pupils were considered indispensable. The concept that exercise, food, and general hygiene are all elements of good health has been readily accepted. Not only does physical education extend from infanthood to boys and girls of 15 and 16, but each child is provided three or more health examinations during his school life. In addition, milk and hot meals are available as additional nourishment for those in need. Needy children often may be aided by schools to secure proper footwear and clothing. The Central Council for Health Education, formed in 1927, the Education Act (1944), and the National Health Service Act (1948) have combined to ease the burden of maintaining the health of children as well as the total family. The Departments of Education seek to promote a close cooperation between physical education, including recreation activities, and the general health program, which is bolstered with doctors and nurses.

Preparation of Physical Education Teachers. England has attempted to improve the quality of the physical education program by improving the teacher education curriculum and developing more competencies among all teachers. To improve the physical education competencies of these teachers, students in the two-year training colleges receive instruction in a course in physical training and hygiene. On the other hand, for the specialists, advanced courses of 400 hours are now offered and extend over a two-year period. Over a dozen training colleges now offer opportunities of this nature. A three-year course in physical education exclusively for women is now offered by several special colleges for women. On the whole, universities in England fail to recognize teacher preparation in physical education. An exception to this stand is Birmingham University, which gives significant emphasis to physical education in a general arts degree. Contrary to the elementary schools, the secondary schools tend to hire specialists in physical education or at least those classroom teachers that have undergone special preparation in physical education.

The aristocratic secondary boarding schools operate without governmental control of physical education, and their practices relating to the employment of qualified teachers of that subject vary from the public schools. These independent schools usually designate either a teacher (master) who formally participated in sports or a professional to organize and direct the program. School and national spirit appear as important aims of these instructors. In the universities, physical education is not required, so organizational help only is provided for those who voluntarily participate. Obviously, in the above type of boarding schools and universities, students who wish to participate find themselves in a position where they must use their own initiative to instigate and organize physical education activities.

AUSTRALIA

Australia, far removed from the mother country, is an island continent comprised of six states. The Dutch, who landed in Australia during the first decade of the seventeenth century, receive credit for being the earliest Europeans to do so. The Chinese, however, as early as the 1200's had a knowledge of this continent. In 1770, Captain James Cook landed at various places along the east coast and took formal possession for Britain by hoisting the Union Jack.

Australia is not a heavily populated continent, having only between seven and eight million people. The climate ranges from temperate cool to subequatorial. Alien immigration has been according to the "white Australia" policy, and the admission of southern Europeans and Orientals has been, in the past, seriously limited.

Each of the six states has developed and controlled education independent of the Commonwealth. An examination of Australia's public school system shows definite influences of both English and United States systems of education. However, the Australians do not establish school boards but put the control in the State Offices. Depending upon the state, education is compulsory up to the fourteenth or sixteenth year. Church schools and private schools, much like those in England, supplement the public school effort.

Culmination of the educational plan occurs in the universities in each state capital, the agricultural colleges in each state, the National University in Canberra, the teacher education colleges in each state, or in the technical colleges recently established. Extension courses, a form of adult education, and mobile libraries comprise other education efforts being made.

The Australians have emphasized the fitness aspects of physical education. Systematic physical activity programs have long been advocated as a means for producing a strong virile citizenry capable of protecting the nation from outside forces. Thus, the physical education programs in schools have stressed fitness and health purposes as major concerns.

Even though fitness has received considerable emphasis in schools, sports activities have not been overlooked. Teaching sports is well organized, and leisure time skills are stressed in schools. Schools develop their own sports and athletic clubs and associations. These organizations have developed in secondary schools in such sports as cricket, swimming, basketball, track, and rowing. The love for sport has carried on into the winter, and mountain areas near the cities play host to thousands who regularly visit them on week ends and holidays.

The Australians probably love sports more than any other national group. However true this may be, the vast number of spectators and the variety of sports played by the population show the distinct bent these people have toward physical activity. Their recent world-recognized feats in swimming, tennis, track, and other sports indicate that this relatively sparsely populated continent takes physical education rather seriously. Other sports such as golf, bowling on the green, boxing, field hockey, wrestling, and cycling have a long history in Australia and continue to interest both young and old alike.

The development of physical education in Australia originally stressed physical fitness, especially in the school programs. The fitness of Australian soldiers shows how vigorously this concept has been accepted. However, it must be realized that a broad program has developed in schools, as well as nationwide, and the sports activities have become an integral part of the total physical education program.

NEW ZEALAND

New Zealand is comprised of a group of islands which lie east of Tasmania and slightly over 1200 miles east of Sydney, Australia. The two main divisions of this British Dominion are the North and South Islands separated by Cook Strait. This channel varies from 16 to about 90 miles.

Polynesian canoe-men apparently came to the islands as early as the 1300's. But it was not until 1769 that Cook, the British navigator, visited the islands. New Zealand receives bountiful rainfall in most sections which encourages an abundance of evergreen vegetation. Fjords, rivers, waterfalls, fertile valleys, lakes, and mountains combine to make this Dominion as beautiful as any country in the world.

New Zealand has remained very close to England throughout the years. Many British customs prevail, and the people, from a social standpoint, remain quite conservative. On the other hand, social welfare legislation including social security, old age pensions, and a short work week (40 hours) have, to a great extent, been nurtured in New Zealand.

Education in this Dominion is controlled by a Department of Education on the national level. The local departments confine their major efforts to problems relating to educational areas and facilities. Secondary schools have more local autonomy than do elementary schools. Whereas local secondary schools employ their own teachers, elementary schools depend upon the National Education Department to do the hiring. The National Department rates teachers biennially, advertises teaching positions, and attempts to fill the vacancies.

A National Superintendent acts as a dominion-wide administrator for physical education in both secondary and primary schools as well as universities. In physical education and in other subject areas, the influence of the British point of view is blended with the progressive educational philosophy of modern education in the United States.

The Maoris, natives of New Zealand, fought a ten-year losing war (1861–71) with the settlers. These natives showed bravery and tenacity but very little skill in warfare. Their most visible contribution to physical education is in the area of rhythmical dances and related activities, which have been adopted by the school program.

In addition to the dancing program, physical education in the New Zealand schools includes many of the popular sports common to the English public schools. Among these rugby, cricket, and field hockey receive considerable emphasis. In fact, a criticism of the program is in terms of the great amount of attention given to the highly skilled player and the small degree of concern for the less skilled.

Because of its geographical location, aquatic activities such as yachting, swimming, and boating of all kinds exist as popular recreation activities. On the other hand, many of the popular leisure activities of England have been wholeheartedly adopted. Such pursuits include horse racing, bowling on the green, tennis, and golf. Men and women alike participate, but interest in women's sports is not high.

CANADA

Canada is an autonomous political unit with Great Britain the nominal head. It is composed of ten provinces in which approximately 14,000,000 people live. The Canadian Parliament has the general powers of legislation and government, and the provinces legislate on factors relating to civil rights, education, and local affairs in general. Canada stretches from the Atlantic to the Pacific Ocean, is bounded on the north by the Arctic Ocean from the border of Alaska eastward, and its southern border is the United States.

Canada is about 20 per cent larger than the United States, but the most desirable areas to live in lie relatively close to the United States border. Canada, originally noted for its fishing, furs, and lumber, now has a large pulp industry, hydroelectric power, and it has become a vast grain and agricultural center. In recent years, mining for aluminum, nickel, copper, gold, silver and other minerals has expanded. Petroleum resources are beginning to be exploited in Canada as well as uranium deposits.

The cultural problems have proved enormous in Canada. Native Indians not destroyed to the degree they were in the United States, a tightly knit French-speaking minority, and a large English-speaking population all combine to make patterns of living of Canadians complex. Since World War I Canada has increased in prestige considerably, and in the years following World War II her place in international affairs has developed rapidly.

The Dominion's responsibilities for education have been mainly limited to financing schools in federal areas, granting subsidies to those pursuing agricultural and vocational pursuits, sponsoring war emergency preparation programs, and stimulating health and physical fitness programs. The National Physical Fitness Act gave strong support to recreation. Provinces without adequate physical education and recreation programs were, through financial grants, encouraged to make agreements with the federal government. Some results included leadership education, cooperating with other interested governmental agencies, financial aid to localities, information services to communities, and the like.

Control from the federal government is avoided in all Canadian provinces and in all grades of Canadian schools. The purposes of physical education throughout Canada include development of organic vigor, health, leisure attitudes and skills, social habits and attitudes, and neuromuscular skills. These goals closely resemble those sought through physical education in the United States. To accomplish these purposes, the Canadian schools offer a sports and games program which balances the calisthenics and gymnastic program which predominated formerly.

Physical educators are prepared in a number of institutions of higher learning in Canada. McGill University in 1945 began offering a four-year course leading to the Bachelor of Science Degree in Physical Education. This culminated a series of adventures in the field which included participation by such prominent men as A. S. Lamb, R. Tait McKenzie, and James Naismith. The Universities of Toronto, Western Ontario, Alberta, and British Columbia represent some of those also offering the baccalaureate in physical education.

The Canadians are a sports loving people. The opportunities for fishing and hunting are as good as any in the world. The weather encourages extensive participation in winter sports. And such athletic games as ice hockey, rugby, soccer, and lacrosse have been popular for many years. Basketball is growing in popularity, and such professional games as Canadian football, ice hockey, and baseball have drawn considerable support from the people.

12

PHYSICAL EDUCATION
IN OTHER EUROPEAN COUNTRIES

In modern times, all European countries have programs in physical education.[1] There appears to be, for the most part, a great similarity among these programs. The following short descriptions of these selected programs give a general over-all picture of the status of physical education in many European countries.

FRANCE

The effort to develop nationalism in France following the French Revolution included, among other factors, education of the child by the state. Napoleon gave strength to this movement, and he developed from the previous decentralized program a centralized educational system. From that time forward, much emphasis has been given to developing a strong nationalistic feeling in all youth who go through the curriculum.

The physical education program in France was developed, in the main, by borrowing from other countries those physical activities and concepts which seemed to fit best. Foreign teachers were also employed to carry out such

[1] The lack of reliable information forthcoming from some European countries since World War II makes it impossible in those instances to give an accurate account of developments in education and physical education.

theories and practices. Such leaders were selected usually because of their success in their own countries regardless of the peculiar needs of the French people. In the 1800's France followed the pattern of other European countries and developed numerous sports and gymnastic societies and clubs. To gain financial support from the government, these clubs often included training in preparation for military service. To accommodate the interests of the people in these clubs, many play fields, stadiums, swimming pools, and other facilities were constructed.

In spite of the foreign influence, a Frenchman, Baron Pierre de Coubertin (1863–1937), brought his dream of modern Olympic games into fruition. These games, with the accompanying spirit of amateur participation, have done much to mold the present and almost world-wide ideal of physical education. The modern Olympic games became a reality in Athens in 1894. These games still flourish, but often the spirit or ideal of De Coubertin is abused as various countries try to gain world-wide recognition through the prowess of their athletes. In reality De Coubertin visualized the revival of the games as one means through which he could focus on the necessity for improved health and increased physical vigor.

A dominant military flavor controlled the viewpoint on physical education following World War I. However, a gradual shifting of authority from the Ministry of War to the Ministry of Public Instruction began to appear before the 1930's. This trend included establishing a Physical Education Bureau, and eventually physical education received direction through a youth and sports section of that bureau.

France has experimented with a number of different physical education systems through the years. These programs have run the gamut from the Ling gymnastics, to the George Demeny system which aimed to improve posture and a vigorous body, to Hébert's system which stressed running, climbing, balancing, and other natural movements.

Today the French physical education program includes many activities generally accepted in the United States.

Corrective physical education receives considerable emphasis with much attention being given to the development of large muscles through body building types of exercises. Games, dances, athletic skills practice, swimming, and track and field are included in the program. However, unlike the United States, the compulsory curriculum does not stress sports education and competitive events. Viewing the evolution of physical education in France over a period of years, the impact of the Olympic games and the many activities included, plus the concern for using leisure in a worthwhile manner, is revealed in the direction the program has taken.

RUSSIA

The development of a new social order in Russia, a country covering about 16–17 per cent of the earth's surface, has consumed the efforts of its people in the past few years. To help foster this change, education has been used extensively to indoctrinate all youth with the principles of communism. Much time is spent in schools to teach children the communistic viewpoint toward collectivism, work, cooperative groups, patriotism, and the like. In reality, the effort teaches the individual subordination of the self for the socialistic cause.

Tsarist Russia did not regard education as the important means for indoctrinating people as do the Communists. Similarly, physical education, which is now widespread throughout Russia, received little recognition before the development of the present socialistic state. Physical education, like education in general in Russia, should be studied as one way in which they strive to reach political and economic goals. Education for a free mind, or sports for leisure enjoyment, are ideals which Soviet patriotism does not embody.

Basically, the Soviet Union strives for mass participation in its physical education program as a means for attaining universal physical fitness. All citizens, not only those attending school, are encouraged to regularly take part in physical exercise and to follow approved health habits. Through these practices, the Soviet citizens are supposed to become more efficient and productive workers. On the other hand, this regimen is designed to intensify the patriotism of Soviet youth. Not to be overlooked is the emphasis placed on training for military life through the exercise program and the hygienic practices.

The Soviet Union has developed a very extensive and complex educational system. At the present time, compulsory education includes as many as seven years for children in urban areas. The present compulsory requirements are temporary, and the goal is for at least ten years of required education for all. Evening schools, correspondence courses, industrial trade schools, and technical high schools supplement the present basic educational plan.

Physical culture has become an integral part of the school curriculum at all levels. Lessons are usually about forty-five minutes in duration and, depending upon the grade level, range from once or twice to three or four times weekly. This formalized instructional program is supplemented by many extra class groups in athletic activities, dancing, and other forms of leisure interests. These groups or "circles" are centered in the school and meet two to four times each week following the regular school day. Education, the armed service, and trade unions support these activities. Many trips and excursions are planned for these groups on Sundays, holidays and vacation periods.

In addition to the above, the Communist party organizes a series of youth organizations to insure complete indoctrination in the Soviet ideology. Through these organizations much additional training in athletic sports and hygienic practices becomes possible. Further, the All-Union Committee of Physical Culture and Sports directs sports schools for gifted athletes. The trade unions, the government, and education support these special schools.

The development by the Soviet Union of many recreation facilities such as camps, rest centers, travel stations, swimming pools, gymnasiums, ski areas, and the like makes it possible for adults as well as the youth to participate regularly. Adults become members of athletic clubs and by taking advantage of all facilities tend to continue participation in sports longer than people in many other countries.

Each summer Physical Culture Day highlights sports participation in a nation-wide celebration. This event not only permits the results of the fitness program to be exhibited, but also it provides an opportunity for the politicians to speak before the people and encourage greater attainments in physical activities in the future.

In considering the physical culture program as a whole in the Soviet Union, it is apparent, first, that gymnastics are stressed in the early school grades, then as a preparation for the military, and finally as a means both for keeping adults fit and for providing enjoyment during leisure. Athletics and sports of all kinds receive considerable attention also. Soccer seems to be the most popular sport, but basketball and volleyball both receive considerable emphasis. Swimming, boating, hiking, and bicycling are also very popular. Skiing, hockey, and skating comprise the major outdoor winter sports. In fact, in some areas, skiing becomes the only means of transportation for school children so they must learn this activity.

Testing for physical fitness receives considerable support with emphasis being given to sports and activities of a military nature. Examinations include health and hygiene factors, gymnastic exercises, track activities, swimming, riflery, skiing, and various military activities. The "Master of Sports" award is the end toward which all athletes strive. This award, granted by the All-Union Committee of Physical Culture and Sports, designates that individual athlete as outstanding.

The amount of emphasis placed on physical fitness and prowess is perhaps best appreciated by the way in which the Soviet Union trains its Olympic games competitors. Nothing is left undone to produce winners, and their skilled representation in a vast number of sports is significant. Irrespective of the motives behind their Olympic games effort, their successes indicate clearly that the development of physical strength and skill has become an important factor in the Soviet culture.

ITALY

Many changes have been wrought in Italy since the time of the Roman Empire, and among these has been the attitude toward physical education. The gladiatorial combats of course no longer exist, but a program of physical education seems to be well established.

The nationalistic feeling built up in Italy before World War I became more solidified as Italy engaged vigorously after that war in the politics of Europe. The Fascist party, which came into power in the early post-World War I period, began immediately to devise means for organizing the youth for eventual political purposes. A Department of Physical Education was established to conduct both in- and out-of-school activities as one means for inculcating the Fascist spirit in the youth. Physical activity for fitness and club activities dominated this program.

State manuals for both boys and girls outlined the program conducted in elementary and secondary schools. In the elementary school the classroom teacher handled the four required thirty-minute physical education periods each week, while a specialist in physical education conducted the required four-hour weekly program. Physical education teachers also taught in the out-of-school program directed by Department of Physical Education. Athletics and track and field activities supplemented the calisthenics and gymnastic program.

The out-of-school program received government grants in addition to membership fees and local support. Youth organizations, two for boys and two for girls, were established. The age range for both sexes was eight to thirteen and fourteen to eighteen years of age. The political influence was carried to the extent that participants in these youth organizations even wore black shirts like those of the Fascist party. Sports, camping, gymnastics, winter sports, riflery, and work projects characterized the program. Many facilities and areas were developed throughout Italy to accommodate this program.

World War II abruptly changed the organizational character of the physical education program in Italy. However, the experimental work, the research in education in general and physical education, combined with the interest in physical activity, prevailed, and today Italian physical education has many fine features. Excellent work is being accomplished with the physically handicapped, gymnastics are directed toward meeting individual interests and needs, camping is stressed, and a fondness for sports is being instilled in the youth. Italians have continued to hold a prominent place in international sports, and they have produced many outstanding athletes. Among other activities, Italy has produced exceptional athletes in both fencing and soccer.

BALKAN STATES

Albania, Bulgaria, Rumania and Yugoslavia have experienced many conflicts either among themselves or with neighboring countries. This continual brush with war has placed emphasis on the need for physical fitness among the peoples of these countries. To attain a state of physical readiness for military service, various systems of gymnastics have been employed.

Albania has had a long history of being occupied and controlled by countries such as Serbia, Greece, and Italy. During World War II, its plight became even worse when the puppet government declared war against the Allies, but Albanian guerrilla forces fought viciously against the Axis powers. Physical education in this small country has stressed developmental exercises which prove advantageous from a military standpoint. Naturally, the instillation of patriotism and a spirit of nationalism through physical activity has prevailed.

Bulgaria was once a dominant power which extended its rule over the whole Balkan peninsula except for Greece but eventually collapsed and came under the control of first

Serbia and then the Ottoman Empire. Turkish rule was severe, and over a period of centuries the struggle of Bulgarians to free themselves created a strong nationalistic feeling. In 1915, Bulgaria joined forces with Germany in World War I. The restoration of peace resulted in Bulgaria losing much territory, but the climate of World War II gave Bulgaria the opportunity to restore its territory. After accomplishing this, Bulgaria once again joined Germany in its world conflict.

These associations with Germany, especially in World War I, resulted in Bulgaria's adopting the physical education methods and exercises of Germany. In the period between the wars, physical education progressed in Bulgaria. By the early 1930's compulsory physical education for all girls and boys below 21 years of age became a reality.

A half-hour a day is set aside for physical education in elementary schools. Special teachers of physical education are employed in many of the large schools. In secondary school a daily game period is set aside, and gymnastics are required two hours weekly. Hiking and trips into the country supplement these programs. Also, university students meet a two-hour-a-week physical education requirement by belonging to student groups which sponsor sports.

Those not in school or college also partake of systematic exercise. Organizations provide physical activity opportunities for the members. Industries are required to either provide the necessary facilities for employee physical education or pay the fees necessary for employees to join physical education organizations. Military and civic advantages go to those youth who pass an examination at the culmination of five years of physical education.

Rumania, too, has been plagued for centuries with military conflicts and occupation and rule from without. Although in 1916 Rumania entered World War I on the side of the Allies, it was forced by its geographical location to become a neutral partner of the Axis.

Although the Rumanians have been exposed considerably to German gymnastics, that system never took a firm hold.

The Swedish system, with variations, has proved more acceptable to Rumania. The emphasis on development of physical fitness for military advantages has strongly colored the physical education program. Gymnastic activities seem to be the core of the program, but considerable attention is given to sports and various outdoor activities. The Rumanian folk dances, performed by both men and women in colorful dress, depict the customs of these peoples as they have developed over many centuries.

Yugoslavia as a state came into existence after World War I. Six small republics, two independent states and four states belonging to the Austro-Hungarian monarchy were combined to form Yugoslavia.

This country is noted for its native folk dances. Kolo, its national dance, is performed vigorously by both men and women. In fact many dances are performed in Yugoslavia, as well as in other Balkan countries, by men without women. The German and Danish programs of gymnastics apparently influenced physical education more than the Swedish type. Tumbling, apparatus work, games, and sports all receive considerable emphasis. The necessity for maintaining a large and rather powerful military force under the regime of Tito has influenced the direction in which physical education has developed in recent years.

Reliable information about physical education programs in these countries is often as difficult to obtain as is trustworthy data on political and economic affairs. However, the physical activities sponsored by schools have not been of great significance. The major developments and the climate of the physical education movement is reflected in the organizations' programs and other community events and celebrations.

CZECHOSLOVAKIA

Like the Balkan countries, Czechoslovakia has experienced long periods of domination from without. The Czechs joined with the Allies in World War I and seemed to be in a favored position following that war. Hitler's rise in Germany led to eventual control of Czechoslovakia and the never to be forgotten slaughter at Lidice. A temporary Czech government was established in England during World War II, and Czech units fought with the Allies. In recent years the government has been dominated by the Communists.

The struggle to free themselves from the tyranny of the Hapsburg Empire during the 1800's caused the Czechs to develop a program of physical education that aimed to give the people physical and spiritual strength to gain their independence. The Sokol organization came into fruition early in the 1860's, and within a span of less than ten years a boys' branch and a girls' and women's division were added. This was a patriotic gymnastic movement that focused directly on strengthening nationalism. A festival, the Sokol Slet, is held at times to demonstrate movement, timing, precision, and form in large group activities. More than 95,000 school children and 270,000 men and women have participated in a Sokol Slet.

Physical education has become an integral phase of the educational system. Compulsory education exists for children to the age of fifteen, and a section on sport is included in the Ministry of Education. In all schools, primary, secondary, college preparatory, and universities, two hours per week of physical education are required. The typical program consists of calisthenic-type exercises, a variety of sports, track and field, aquatic activities, winter sports and folk dancing. Hiking and camping supplement the program.

The colleges at Bratislava, Brno, and Olomouc plus Charles University at Prague offer specialized physical education programs for preparing teachers. All elementary teachers average an hour of physical education each day during their two years of study. Special physical education teachers for college preparatory schools receive intensive training in physical education, both practical and theoretical, during their four years of preparation. The great number of independent organizations, including the Sokol, also conduct training schools for their leaders.

FINLAND

Finland was completely under the control of Russia for over 100 years, but in 1920 the U.S.S.R. recognized Finnish independence. During World War II, after very stiff resistance, Finland once again capitulated to the Russians. Finland once again became independent after World War II but only after severe territorial, financial, and economic difficulties.

Finland's contribution to the physical education movement has proved significant. In building up the spirit of nationalism, the German and Swedish systems of gymnastics were introduced very early. This in part has led to their striving for perfection of execution of the exercises. Even though this emphasis exists, the Finns tend to seek fun and enjoyment in their physical education. In the same manner the dances of the Finnish people stress perfection, but a recreative atmosphere seems to persist throughout.

Physical education has been introduced into the schools of Finland. Since the 1920's the Finns have expanded the exercises, marching, and gymnastics programs for pupils to include games and sports, track and field, and winter activities. The program for girls stresses rhythmic calisthenics, other rhythmic activities, and games. Athletic competitions for girls receive little backing, and even the Finnish Women's Gymnastic Organization recommends no competitions or championships in highly competitive athletics.

The enthusiasm of the Finns for physical activity of all types is marked. The feats of some Finnish athletes have been outstanding in international competition and in the Olympic games, especially in track and field activities. People from many countries have studied the methods that Finnish athletes use for conditioning themselves. The Finnish people love festivals, which include many exhibitions of sports, gymnastics, dancing, and other physical activities.

The part that the Finnish women have played in furthering physical education deserves special mention. A modern program of gymnastics for women has been developed by Miss Elli Björksten, Helsinki University. A vital interest in individual needs led her to develop a system which varied markedly from the Swedish system. As in physical education throughout Finland, this system stresses, as far as possible, informality and joyful participation. Another woman, Miss Anni Collan, has spent considerable time in preserving the old native folk dances by introducing them in the school program and generally encouraging their preservation by stimulating people to engage in these dances.

Many voluntary organizations promote physical education in Finland. These agencies have done much to advance athletics throughout the country. For the boys their program has stressed competition and perfection in sports activities. The girls' programs offered by these voluntary programs has remained mainly noncompetitive.

NETHERLANDS

The people of the Netherlands support a complex school system that is on the elementary level predominantly private. However, both public and private schools are supported by the state. The influence of the churches (Catholic and Calvinistic) has been considerable, and marked support exists for the viewpoint that play and recreation are wasteful.

The formal school curriculum has left little room for physical education. Until 1940 physical education was not compulsory. However, since that time advances have been made in introducing physical activity and health into the school day. In addition teachers now receive opportunities in their preparation to study gymnastics, which, incidentally, are similar in nature to those of the Germans. The influence of natural gymnastics of the Austrians is prevalent.

The Dutch, in spite of the restricted school program and an unenthusiastic church attitude, seek pleasure through sports and games. Skating, hockey, boating, dancing, basketball, volleyball, and korfball (similar to basketball) represent a few of the more popular leisure sports. The accomplishments of the Dutch in international speed skating, and of the women in swimming and track in the Olympic games, have been outstanding. Further, the Dutch girls in their wooden shoes and colorful costumes as they participate in folk dances are a symbol of the Netherlands throughout the world.

BELGIUM

The Belgians are divided into two language groups. Flemish, a Dutch dialect, is spoken in the north. In the south, French is the official language, but considerable German is spoken. Almost the entire population is of the Roman Catholic faith, and thus the church plays a very important part in shaping the educational pattern. During most of the nineteenth century Belgium was free of foreign domination, but her neutrality was ignored by Germany in both World Wars. The country was not only dominated temporarily from without, but widespread destruction took place.

Belgium's school system adheres to certain state standards. All schools, private included, receive state aid when minimum requirements are satisfied. Swedish gymnastics dominate the physical education program, but the German gymnastic influence is strong in the northern part of the country. Games and sports as a part of the physical education program in schools have been gaining acceptance since World War I. Soccer, track and field, basketball, and volleyball represent a few of the more popular sports.

Physical education in Belgium has been viewed with regard to the contributions it makes to health. In fact, the Belgians seem very interested in personal and community health as evidenced by industrial health programs, welfare benefits, labor legislation, and the close cooperative work with the Red Cross and various voluntary health organizations. Research in medicine and physiology are often related either directly or indirectly to physical education. Remedial exercises make important contributions to the over-all physical education program.

SPAIN

Spain, whose civilization dates back to the Stone Age and whose role in international affairs has declined from a very significant to an insignificant influence, has done very little to develop organized physical education programs. Although Spain requires eight years of compulsory education, the regulation is often overlooked, and organized physical education receives little or no attention. Even though Spain through her military force was an international power at one time and now operates as a dictatorship, physical education for nationalistic and military purposes has never seemed to permeate the regular lives of its people.

Bull fighting is the national sport of the Spanish people, yet few participate. Jai alai, a sport played in a large court (side, front, and back walls) and resembling handball except for a basket-type throwing implement attached to one forearm, originated in Spain. Spectators watch and bet on the results of this game. The people of Spain are also noted for their lively, colorful dancing which highlights many of their holiday and festive occasions. Fencing has remained popular in Spain, and considerable boxing takes place.

SWITZERLAND

The people of Switzerland have remained neutral during two world wars, yet all able-bodied men remain in the reserve army until they reach the age of 60. German dialects are spoken by most Swiss, but French, Italian, and Romansh (a Rhaeto-Romanic dialect) are official national languages. Not only do the languages differ, but the country is split from a religious standpoint with Protestantism prevailing over Catholicism in the ratio of about five to four.

Switzerland, which was the home of the League of Nations, is a confederation of twenty-five federal states or nineteen cantons and six half cantons. All these cantons have considerable autonomy, and consequently their educational systems differ. However, education is compulsory, and all children attend until they are at least 15 years of age.

Swiss education reflects the philosophy of the great educator Pestalozzi. Thus, physical education and play receive considerable emphasis. For the most part, special teachers usually conduct gymnastics three mornings each week and sports in the afternoon. Rhythmic group calisthenics tend to increase interest and add vigor to the exercises of the participants. Because of the differences of nationalities in Switzerland, other forms of gymnastics are prevalent such as the Jahn gymnastics with apparatus and the Dalcroze movements accompanied by music.

A vast number of sports clubs exist in Switzerland. Many of the clubs include such activities as mountain climbing and hiking, soccer, basketball, rugby, rifle and pistol shooting, and skiing. Winter sports and hiking are particularly adapted to the geography and climate of Switzerland, and much attention is given to promoting tourist trade. Summer tourists are provided additional inducements in the form of well-developed beaches, swimming pools, parks, and other facilities in or near the larger cities.

13

PHYSICAL EDUCATION
IN JAPAN, CHINA, INDIA, AND
SOUTH AFRICA

Most Eastern countries, until about 1900, functioned at a rather slow pace, some operating as the European countries did during the Middle Ages and others as colonies of Western countries. The strong nationalistic feeling prevalent in Japan for a long time has been developing in many other Eastern countries in the twentieth century. Accompanying this phenomenon has been the introduction of gymnastics, games, and sports through such media as armies and occupation forces, visiting sports teams, the Young Men's Christian Association, missionaries, and tourists. Interest has developed in physical activities to the extent that the Far Eastern games have been organized, and many of these nations now participate in the Olympic games.

JAPAN

Japan, an overpopulated nation, is made up of four major islands and numerous smaller islands. Although contact with the West was made as early as 1542 and some trading took place, a repressive feudal government arose in the seventeenth century and continued for about 250 years to

1867. This date marked the Meiji restoration, which led to trading once again with the West. Also, many Japanese went abroad to study and returned to Japan with knowledge about foreign developments in military science, political institutions, and industrial developments. Japan also developed a strong army and navy.

With this surge to become a world power and with the continued trend toward a strong nationalistic feeling, physical education became an important factor. Military drills and gymnastics (later the Swedish type) have given way to a sports and games program. Following World War II, in which physical activity for military preparedness dominated, new education laws completely reorganized the school program including physical education. Six years of elementary school are followed by two three-year periods for junior and senior high schools. Physical education is required throughout this entire educational experience. In addition compulsory physical education exists as a part of the university general education plan.

Physical education in Japan at present resembles that advocated in the United States. An attempt is made to integrate physical education with other subjects. Individual interests, needs, and capacities receive attention as boys and girls participate each day in physical education. Sports, games, dancing, and forms of outdoor education comprise the major activities. Emphases are placed on improving health, personality, motor skills, and social acumen through wise selection of activities and proper methods of teaching.

Japan has always been noted for its wrestling and judo. The Japanese are very strong participants in the Far Eastern games, and they also enter the Olympic games. Swimmers from Japan have gained world-wide recognition, and their accomplishments in international competition have been outstanding. The development of after-school athletic programs and the activities of many clubs and organizations indicate that Japan will continue to produce outstanding athletes. Japan has adopted baseball as a major national sport and in the process has developed thousands of amateur teams and some professional teams.

CHINA

China has never been a closely knit country with a strong and influential central government. Great Britain, France, Germany, and Russia all had concessions for trading with China until the Open Door policy, advocated by the United States, gave all countries equal access to China's trade. This foreign influence has always been resented by the Chinese. At present China is controlled by the Communist party, and a militaristic atmosphere prevails throughout the country.

Physical education in China made little progress until the twentieth century. Missionaries and the Young Men's Christian Association introduced gymnastics and some games. American educators later encouraged the introduction of a sports program, and in 1929, a compulsory physical education law was passed. Physical education then became more organized, and standard programs were developed by the Ministry of Education for all levels of education, including college. Standardization becomes less rigid in the higher grades, and the informalized program of sports and games receives most attention. In fact the recommended college physical education activities resemble those advocated for a well-rounded American college program.

The Chinese have not developed professional sports, but a great amount of local amateur competition takes place. This practice grew in China despite the fact that there was no required physical education until relatively recent years. The Chinese National Amateur Athletic Federation conducts National Athletic Meets, and in many cities local competitions are held once or twice each year. In recent years women's events have been added to these meets in which general enthusiasm prevails.

This participation by girls and women has been increasing rapidly since the democratic approach to education included girls. They were quick to take advantage of this opportunity, and as a result physical education also became a requirement in schools for girls. Popular activities for girls include swimming, volleyball, basketball, tennis, and softball. Many institutions have trained women physical education teachers throughout the past twenty-five years.

INDIA

India, long under the domination of England, has been a self-governing nation since 1947. The traditional caste system of India was legally abolished by the new constitution, but regardless of this important advance the country is involved with internal conflict. In addition the outmoded farming methods, lack of flood control, poor housing, dense population, many different languages, and other factors thwart attempts to move forward with social and economic reforms.

Education is hindered by all the above conditions, but the many languages, the lack of adequate educational facilities, and the sparsity of qualified people to teach loom as major deterrents. The central government gives some financial assistance to education and provides over-all leadership. Plans for educating the people of India include a compulsory free elementary education for all children which already is taking shape. Also planned are limited secondary school and college programs plus a literacy program for all adults.

Although leadership comes from the central government, each province and the city councils therein assume responsibility for education. Thus the ascetic philosophy and the taboos and traditional practices may have definite effects on the development of the educational program at the local or state level. Some of the progressive states require physical education through all educational levels including college.

A few schools—some of which are located in Calcutta, Bombay, Madras, Amraoti, and East Punjab—offer teacher preparation programs in physical education. The affiliation of such schools with the universities is progressing slowly, and completion of this movement should result eventually in a better educated physical education teacher. Short-term courses for classroom teachers also help them in becoming better prepared to conduct the physical activities for children. Already India's educational leaders view physical education as a way of helping to attain the total educational development of the individual. Health, personality development, neuro-muscular skills, and social adjustments are some desired outcomes of the physical education program.

India seems determined to nurture the present physical education program and expand it considerably in the years ahead. Many voluntary and public groups are stimulating progress. The National Association of Physical Education and Recreation was formed in 1946 at the initial National Physical Education Conference. Advisory Committees on Physical Education exist in many states as well as on the central government level of India. A National Sports Club is in the process of planning and making available modern physical education facilities and areas. The Indian Olympic Association not only has many affiliates of sports groups with national governing bodies but also helps further sports which have no national governing bodies. Interscholastic and college athletic associations abound throughout the country, and sport and gymnastic tournaments are conducted by many private associations.

The emphasis on physical education in India has spilled over into community life. Communities throughout the nation have exercise centers, and some cities are setting aside recreation areas as centers for leisure pursuits. The establishment of leisure programs is being encouraged because individuals, local government, and some central government departments view recreation as the means through which people will be diverted from drinking alcoholic beverages.

Today, the program of physical education for India varies markedly from school to school, but regarded as a whole it is quite comprehensive. Some school camping, classical Indian dances, folk and modern dance, gymnastics, a variety of dual and individual games, team games, and swimming comprise major activity categories included in the school program. As India advances its social and economic programs and as the philosophy which supports subordinating the body to the spirit becomes less popular, physical education should attain a real place in the educational program.

SOUTH AFRICA

South Africa is bordered by the Atlantic Ocean on one side and the Indian Ocean on the other. A large country, almost a half million square miles, it is mostly plateau (2,000 to 5,000 feet high) although some mountainous areas exist in the east and some lowlands along the long coastline. South Africa is dry and warm, and irrigation is often necessary to supplement the rainfall. The Dutch were the first white settlers at Capetown, but the British took over in 1841. Finally, in 1910, following the South African War, the British established the Union of South Africa, a federation of four provinces: Natal, Orange Free State, Cape of Good Hope, and Transvaal. Mainly a farming and cattle country, South Africa also mines many products, such as diamonds, gold, copper, asbestos, and chromium.

South Africa has established an educational system organized on a basis of 12 grades, either 8–4 or 7–5. Education is compulsory from the ages of seven to fifteen or sixteen, depending upon the province. The various races and languages result in a complicated social structure which is reflected somewhat in the school systems. The European group is provided with fine teachers and superior school facilities. However, the colored and Asiatic groups receive less benefits, and the natives have been seriously neglected from an educational standpoint. This condition is of great consequence because approximately 10,000,000 natives, 2,500,000 whites, about 1,000,000 colored (i.e., part-white), 300,000 Indians, and a small group of Chinese make up the population of South Africa. This obviously leaves the vast majority of inhabitants without adequate educational opportunities.

The Union Department of Education is the central government authority, and it guides the physical education programs of universities, special and technical schools and colleges, and various governmental departments of the Union. The provinces control elementary, secondary, and teacher education institutions. Compulsory physical education exists on all education levels.

Dr. Ernst Jokl has contributed much to the advancement of physical education in South Africa. In 1938 he produced a film which portrayed the type of physical activities for use in physical education. The film was shown to various groups and it was generally well received. Two years later Jokl also developed a *Syllabus of Physical Exercises* for South African Schools. Printed in both Afrikaans and English, it describes by word, sketches, and diagrams the activities ranging from simple children's games to complex activities. Jokl held the position of Director of the Physical Education Department at Wetwatersrand Technical College, Johannesburg, the largest institution of higher learning in the country.

The goals of physical education in South Africa include organic fitness, desirable health habits, neuromuscular skills, continued recreational interests, and desirable social habits and attitudes. To accomplish these ends, gymnastics are stressed, especially in physical education classes, but activities such as rugby association football, cricket, hockey, golf, tennis, and rhythms represent some of the other activities that are used extensively.

Special preparation of teachers for physical education is offered in four universities. Specialization is accomplished during a four-year study period. However, at all teacher training colleges in the four provinces, those who have completed their regular education may take advantage of a one-year physical education program which qualifies them to supervise physical education in the elementary schools.

14

PHYSICAL EDUCATION
IN SOUTH AMERICA AND MEXICO

The countries of Latin America have had many internal difficulties, and one of the consequences has been the failure to build strong educational programs. In recent years, these countries south of the United States give evidence of working toward educational goals which will provide educational opportunities for all. European influence has always been strong in these countries, and it is reflected in the physical education programs that have been developed.

ARGENTINA

Argentina, the second largest country in South America, is more than one-third the size of the United States. Approximately 17,000,000 people live in this country. Argentina has some of the finest cattle herds in the world, but it also produces wheat, corn, mutton, wool, wine, and lumber. Argentina has most every kind of climate and a varied topography that includes mountainous territory, a huge fertile plain, and tropical forests and swamps.

British, French, Germans, Italians, Swiss, and East Europeans have settled in Argentina and developed it considerably. Argentina is not only one of the world's granaries, but also considerable manufacturing has been initiated. The lack of power, resources, and power tools has tended to retard industrial developments.

The native Indian population, which caused the Spanish settlers to abandon Buenos Aires in 1841, five years after it was founded by the Conquistador, Pedro de Mendoza, has almost disappeared. In effect, the population is European, favoring French culture. Even though Argentina produces vast amounts of farm products and beef, almost seven out of ten people live in cities.

Education in Argentina is the responsibility of the national government, through the Department of Education, and the provincial governments. The provinces support elementary education often aided by federal funds, but secondary education is left to the federal government. Most provinces require children to attend school from ages six to fourteen. However, this requirement is not strictly enforced, especially for girls. The secondary schools, called national colleges, generally have a five-year curriculum. Normal schools have a four-year primary teacher education course or a seven-year secondary (national college) curriculum. Beyond this level a national university system exists.

The teaching in Argentina differs from that in the United States in many respects. The federal government appoints teachers to the schools it provides; local school councils have little or no authority with regard to federal schools; teachers in universities and secondary schools support themselves by holding an additional job; schools, especially those federally administered, have identical textbooks and other materials; and teachers on the elementary level are not required to have as much education as those on other levels.

Physical education on all levels is under the jurisdiction of the Ministry of Education and supervision is carried out to insure compliance with regulations. Physical education is required from elementary school to the university. Classroom teachers instruct physical education on the elementary level, but special physical education teachers are employed above that level. Buenos Aires is the home of the National

Institute of Physical Education, which has a three-year curriculum for preparing men and women teachers.

European influence has undoubtedly resulted in the emphasis given to gymnastics, and there is a trend toward Bukh exercises and away from Swedish gymnastics. Rhythms and folk dancing also play an important part in the physical education program. Sports and athletics are very popular in Argentina; in fact, with few exceptions, most games popular in America are played enthusiastically. In addition to the required physical education program, extra class activities are organized for the children and youth.

Physical education in Argentina is viewed as the way to keep individuals fit. Further, the social values and the aspect of leisure education are stressed as very worthwhile outcomes. The leisure goal seems to be realistic because, in general, the people avidly pursue sports activities. Many clubs with a variety of facilities for games, sports, and other activities serve the interests of people throughout Argentina.

Riding and handling horses has long been a favorite pastime in Argentina. Polo is a popular sport. Another game, el pato, is played with horses, but riders roughly contend for a six-handled ball which they attempt to throw through the opponent's basket. The gauchos, nomadic herdsmen of an earlier era, receive credit for inventing this game and passing it on to the present sportsmen.

BOLIVIA

Bolivia, like Paraguay, is an inland country in South America with a population of less than 4,000,000 people. It is part mountainous and part tropical. The mountains hold Bolivia's wealth—its minerals. Tin, silver, copper, zinc, lead, and gold are a few of the minerals mined. The tropical area in the east is unsettled, and its potential value has never been adequately appraised.

More than half the Bolivian population is pure Indian. In the east many tribes have not been influenced by white culture whatsoever. In the west Spanish culture and Catholicism prevail, but the Indians maintain their customs and language. Around 35 per cent of the population are mestizos, called cholos, and the remainder are white. The cholos and whites control business and politics, and the native Indians do the labor.

The Ministry of Education, Fine Arts, and Indian Affairs supervises Bolivian education. One of six bureaus is organized to direct and supervise physical education throughout Bolivia as well as many special institutions. Free, public elementary and secondary education exists, and all children between the ages of seven and fourteen must attend. A six-year elementary curriculum is complemented by a six-year secondary school which is divided into two parts. Another peculiarity of the educational system is that private secondary schools equal the number of public institutions.

Physical education is compulsory in both elementary and secondary schools. Two to three hours of activity are required each week. At the university level no physical education requirement exists. The curriculum in schools includes formal gymnastics, many sports such as volleyball, basketball, and rugby, and rhythmics and folk dancing. Education is conducted quite formally in Bolivia, and this holds true in the health education classes.

Boys before reaching eighteen years of age take training in preparation for two years of compulsory military service. Physical education is stressed during this training period.

BRAZIL

Brazil is the largest land mass by far in South America, and approximately 50,000,000 people reside there. Because of its size, Brazil has variety in its climate and topography. The people, too, come from diverse origins, and the new Brazilian "race" is an amalgamation of Indian, Negro, and European strains. Although Portuguese is the official language, German and Italian prevail in certain southern areas, while Indian languages are used in the north.

The huge Amazon River basin occupies much of the north and north central portions of Brazil. Here, the steaming jungles, although providing rubber, hardwood, and other products, remain virtually unexploited. The northeast is a farming and cattle region, while the east and southeast form the populous section of Brazil. Much industry is springing up in parts of Brazil as evidenced by the rapid growth of both the state and city of São Paulo. Brazil has the natural resources to eventually develop industry to the utmost. For instance, the iron reserves are considered as fine as any in the world.

By law, primary education is compulsory in Brazil, and the states are supposed to spend at least 20 per cent of their total incomes and the national government 10 per cent or more for education. Of course opportunities for education vary according to the economic wealth of a state. The federal government directly supervises secondary schools and institutions of higher learning, while the states, for the most part, maintain primary and normal school education. About three types of normal schools exist: (1) those offering four years beyond elementary school, (2) those having two or three year post junior high school curriculums, and (3) those maintaining a five-year course emphasizing cultural and professional education.

A Ministry of Health, developed in 1930, has a physical education office. The Ministries of the Navy and War direct their own physical education programs. State offices are generally maintained for supervising physical education. Physical education is required on all education levels, and it occurs usually twice a week for periods of 30 to 45 minutes.

Physical education has been focused on gymnastics and body-building activities, but recently some emphasis has been given to activities designed to develop desirable social characteristics. Gymnastics, however, do form the basis of primary and secondary physical education at present. Encouragement of sports as a part of the required program is taking place and reflected in the programs of the more progressive schools. Some institutions already have begun to compete in sports among themselves.

At the present time in Brazil it is necessary for a group interested in a sport to secure the approval of the federal government and then form a single sport federation such as the Brazilian Basketball Confederation. A National Council of Sports was created as a department of the Ministry of Education to supervise sports governing bodies on the national level. The young men and women of Brazil have shown great interest in sport. Because the climate in most of the settled areas of Brazil is warm, swimming is a very popular sport and recreation activity. Soccer, as both a professional and amateur sport, is the most popular team game. Over 200,000 fans may be accommodated in a single stadium in Rio de Janeiro. Horse racing, other equestrian sports, and hunting are very popular leisure activities.

CHILE

Chile is a long narrow country with hot deserts in the north and mountains running into the sea in the south, accompanied by wet wooded areas along the coastline. The central part of Chile, a long central valley, accommodates the main population concentration. The people of Chile are approximately 60 per cent Spanish mestizos, 30 per cent white, and 5 per cent pure Indian.

Chile has a compulsory education system for children between the ages of seven and fifteen. The program of physical education is required on both primary and secondary levels but not at the University of Chile. Classes run about 45 minutes two or three times each week.

Joaquim Cabezas Garcia became director of the Institute of Physical and Manual Education in 1906. This agency later became a university school and now is known as the Institute of Physical and Technical Education. Garcia received his preparation in Sweden. Coupled with this was the influence of a German team of instructors who came to Chile in 1885. The formal gymnastic program consequently has always predominated, and sports assume an inferior place in the required physical education curriculum. However, the interscholastic programs in both primary and secondary schools are well organized in basketball, soccer, football, track and field, and other sports.

The emphasis on physical fitness and health stressed in schools also carries over into adult life. Many people in Chile belong to associations that have a formal tie to the National Sports Council. The Council, composed in part of government officials, concerns itself with the development of sports for adults. Other governmental bodies also are involved in the over-all sports program, and there is an apparent tendency to emphasize personal and national physical fitness.

COLOMBIA

Colombia, with both Atlantic and Pacific coastlines, is a land of contrasts—disease-infested jungles to majestic Andean peaks. Colombia is a big producer of platinum and gold and is second only to Brazil in the production of coffee. Milling cotton textiles, food processing, manufacturing clothing and chemicals, distilling liquor, and processing the country's chief exports represent a few of the industrial activities that have made great strides in the past twenty-five years.

The Ministry of Education supervises public education in Colombia. Before 1930 the Catholic church controlled the schools, but now the local boards of education, the state, and the ministry combine to finance the program. However, the Ministry of Education, for the most part, sets standards and minimum requirements on the secondary level and requires private agencies to follow them. The national government has established only a few secondary schools. On the other hand, primary education is publicly financed by state and local governments in the main. The organizational pattern is usually a 4–6 plan. Free, compulsory education between the ages of seven and fourteen is the unenforced requirement.

Elementary school terminates the education of many students. Physical education is given three times a week in elementary, secondary, and normal schools. Classroom teachers assume the responsibility for conducting these activities on the elementary level, and specialists continue from that point on. Gymnastics and folk dances are given an important place in the physical education program. However, sports are becoming popular, and secondary schools organize intramural sports programs in addition to the regular class periods. Health, loyalty to the democratic way of life, preserving the cultural heritage, and fitness appear as major foci of the physical education program.

ECUADOR

The small country of Ecuador has not even made an accurate survey of the wilderness of plains and jungle east of the Andes. The central area is a plateau on which most inhabitants live, and farming is the main occupation. The coastal area produces most of Ecuador's chief exports, cacao, cyanide precipitates, gold, petroleum and other products. The main bulk of the population is either Indian or part Indian, about 15 per cent of the population is Negro, and the few white people are landowners and control politics.

Education is compulsory between the ages of six and fourteen. Elementary schools in urban and rural areas are of six- and four-years duration respectively. High schools are designed so that a two-year specialized course is offered beyond a four-year general cultural curriculum. The Ministry of Education supervises almost all educational agencies.

Physical education is compulsory daily for one-half hour in elementary school and two or three hours on the secondary level. Gymnastics (rhythmic gymnastics for girls), dances, and various sports including boxing comprise the program on both educational levels. Track and field, basketball, football, tennis, and volleyball are some of the sports receiving most emphasis. Intramural and interscholastic competition have not developed appreciably.

PARAGUAY

Paraguay, a small inland republic, is a subtropical land with a small population exceeding 1,000,000 people. The land west of the Paraguay River is largely unproductive, but some authorities believe it may contain petroleum. The area east of the Paraguay River produces cotton, tobacco, sugar cane, rice, beans, corn, and other farm products. Rum, molasses, and alcohol are manufactured, and the orange groves supply about three quarters of the world's petitgrain supply, which goes into flavorings and perfumes. The native Guarani Indians had a high standard of culture before the white men arrived, and they have freely mixed with the Spanish people. Although Spanish is the official language, Guarani is spoken throughout Paraguay.

The Chaco War with Boliva (1932–35) left Paraguay exhausted though victorious. Thereafter, improvements begun in health, education, and roads have been thwarted by rapid successions of government (except between 1940–48) and many internal conflicts.

Free elementary education is compulsory for six years, but the regulation is not strictly enforced. A Minister of Public Instruction supervises education, and, through joint operation with the National Council in Education, plans the curriculum and enforces policies. Private schools make up the secondary education program, and they continue for five years. A sixth year of specialization is available for those who intend to pursue university preparation at the National University in the capital city, Asuncion.

Bodily development appears to be the focus of the physical education program. Sports and games have been introduced into the program, and the leisure use of such activities receives emphasis. An academic tradition prevails, and physical education has not gained the important place in education in Paraguay that it has in some other South American countries.

PERU

Peru has a great variety of topography and climate as it stretches from the mountain area of the Andes down to the rain forests of the West Amazon basin. The eastern area has a rich potential, but the difficulty of transportation has thwarted its exploitation. As in the time of the Inca Empire as well as during the Spanish conquest, mining still remains an important industry with gold, silver, copper, lead, zinc, and bismuth being produced. The potential for producing abundant agricultural produce is great, and the forests in Peru are extensive.

The number of natives in Peru has not been accurately determined, but it is undoubtedly true that at least half the 8,000,000 population is pure Indian. The larger part of the remainder is mestizo, with a few Orientals (mostly Japanese), some Negroes, and a larger group of European whites (Spanish, German, and Italian). The Indians generally live in the east and in the mountainous areas, while the whites have established themselves in the cities and along the coastal area.

The Ministry of Public Education supervises education and is divided into six departments for administrative purposes. The Department of Physical Education and Hygiene is one of these departments and supervises the compulsory physical education program required in elementary, secondary, vocational, and normal schools. Lima, the capital of Peru, is the home of the National Institute of Physical Education where students follow a comprehensive three-year curriculum. Entering students are required to meet certain health and physical standards.

Gymnastics in Peru are stressed as preparatory exercises for activities in sports. In general, the needs and interests of the participants receive consideration, as does the section of the country because of the diverse climates. Testing of students is frequent, and emphasis is placed upon health and body development.

Sports are organized in cities for the leisure or upper classes. Golf, polo, tennis, and swimming are some of the sports designed for, and considerably limited to, this special group. In addition, horse racing and bull fighting are popular, but all classes seem to find one way or another to enjoy these sports.

URUGUAY

Uruguay separates Brazil and Argentina, so its topography varies from the humid Argentine pampas to the South Brazilian uplands. For the most part, rain is sufficient and falls evenly throughout the year. Thus, this country with a temperate climate produces many agricultural products on a small amount of land. Raising sheep and cattle are basic to Uruguay's economy.

Uruguay is a prosperous country with exceptional communication and transportation facilities. Its people are progressive and have introduced much social legislation. Child labor laws, the eight-hour work day, accident insurance, and pensions for the aged have all been effected. The 2,225,000 people are made up of about 10 per cent mestizos, practically no pure Indians or Negroes, and the rest of white European extraction, mostly Spanish and Italian.

Four directorates under the Ministry of Public Instruction and Social Welfare are organized so that each is responsible for the control of one of the following levels of education; (1) elementary and normal school, (2) industrial, (3) secondary, and (4) higher. Six-year elementary schools predominate, but some rural schools only extend for three or four years. Secondary school curriculums are divided into two phases, a four-year general course and two-year special curriculums designed to prepare students for the universities they select. Various other types of educational institutions exist including the National University at Montevideo, the capital. Citizens and foreigners may attend all public education without cost.

The National Commission for Physical Education maintains public playgrounds, and it is to these, because of a lack of school space, that elementary school children are often taken three times weekly for physical activity. Although gymnastics receive attention, objectives relating to leisure education and social habits and attitudes become more important each year. As a result, sports like soccer, baseball, tennis, basketball, and aquatics have been introduced. Uruguay has become a vacation and recreation resort attracting many people from outside the country, and so it seems natural that the leisure aspects of physical education should be encouraged.

VENEZUELA

Venezuela is bounded by the Caribbean Sea on the north which gives it a long coastline. It has steep cliffs, waterfalls, and generally inaccessible territory in the south. The Orinoco basin is a rich cattle country, the coastal highlands in the northwest area is the main center of population, and the coast and jungle areas are extremely wet and very hot.

In northeast Venezuela astoundingly rich oil fields exist. New discoveries near Caripito make Venezuela one of the very top oil producing countries in the world. A few oil refineries have been developed, but most of it is processed outside the country. Cattle and agriculture are the leading industries, but manufacturing has developed rapidly in the last few years.

The great majority of Venezuelans are a mixture of white and Indian blood. Some mulattoes, Zambos (Indian and Negro), and Indians also inhabit the country. The powerful landowning class, although small, is Spanish for the most part.

The Ministry of Education controls and supervises the elementary and secondary schools. Only four years are available at that educational level. Secondary schools have a four-year curriculum plus a one-year course for specializing. Public education is free in Venezuela. A National Teachers College, in addition to normal schools, prepares teachers.

The National Ministry of Education has an Office of Physical Education which supervises and organizes physical education in the schools, constructs areas and facilities, prepares teachers of physical education, and promotes and organizes public sports activities with those of private groups. The program of physical education has been traditionally oriented toward preparation for the military. Gymnastic activities have predominated in the past. Recent trends indicate a swing toward considerable emphasis on sports on all levels. Basketball, soccer, volleyball, track and field, and other sports, are becoming very popular. Physical education curriculums also now include the voluntary intramural program of activities.

MEXICO

Mexico, a country of approximately 23,000,000 people, stretches south from Texas, New Mexico, Arizona, and California to the borders of Honduras and Guatemala. Three territories and twenty-eight states combine to form the administrative units of Mexico. Aridity and mountainous terrain are the curse of Mexico as they make agriculture in many parts of the country impossible. Due to an inadequate water supply, irrigating the interior is most difficult. The central plateau is the area most populated, and it offers opportunities for agriculture. The primitive means of agriculture, still used extensively in Mexico, slow agricultural developments considerably. Oil production near the city of Tampico is considerable. Homecrafts, such as pottery making and basket weaving, abound in Mexico. Industries found in the central plateau area, especially in the cities of Mexico and Monterrey, include textiles and clothing, tobacco, construction materials, paper, iron, and the brewing of alcoholic beverages.

Since Cortes undertook the conquest of Mexico in 1519 and eventually divided the country among Spaniards, there has been much stress. Even though the Catholic Church spread Christianity, there are three separate groups which never coalesced easily—the whites, the mestizos, and Indians. The revolution which lasted most of the nineteenth century gives real evidence of the unrest which has existed in the past in Mexico. Since the early 1930's, advances have been fairly steady in Mexico, and today definite progress can be noted such as: (1) better transportation, (2) political stability, (3) making the Indians an organic part of the state and increasing their literacy, (4) increased irrigation, and (5) increased industry which is leading toward self-sufficiency and an export surplus of some products.

The Constitution of 1917, which specified agrarian and labor reforms, also made educational and religious provisions which caused trouble with the church. This document ruled out religious elementary schools and placed the responsibility in the hands of the Ministry of Education. Although each state controls its own government, the national government maintains some very direct controls over religion, public health, land, education, and other societal factors.

Physical education is required for two hours weekly in upper elementary grades, normal schools, and secondary schools. The goals of physical education deal with better physical well-being, health, leisure, education, courage and confidence, and fitness for the military. To accomplish such ends, gymnastics for boys, dancing and rhythmical gymnastics for girls, games for both sexes, and individual and team sports make up the required curriculum.

Elementary classroom teachers conduct physical education classes in many elementary schools. Specialists in physical education direct the classes in some urban elementary schools. The secondary schools in the city and many rural areas also have special physical education teachers. The Normal School for Physical Education, situated in Mexico City, prepares a carefully selected student body which undergoes comprehensive and specialized curriculum.

Health education and hygienic living have been stressed since 1922. The original Public Health Department established then has undergone certain changes and is known as the Ministry of Public Health and Welfare. This agency and the Ministry of Education work together. School health services have been established in Mexico City, dental clinics exist in some of the large cities, and medical examinations are given to teachers and pupils in other places.

Mexicans traditionally enjoy festive occasions, and folk music and colorful dances play a vital part in such activities. Dances may be either religious or light, but always colorful costumes, masks, and head ornaments add richness to the occasions. Sports have become very popular in Mexico. In addition to the games of the Mayas and Aztecs which remain, the Mexicans have long sponsored such sports as hockey, jai alai, soccer, horse racing, other equestrian sports, and bull fighting. In recent years, baseball (even professional), basketball, football, softball, and swimming are a few of the many sports which have gained additional popularity.

Part III

Physical Education in the United States of America

15

PHYSICAL EDUCATION
IN THE COLONIAL PERIOD

In the first half of the eighteenth century there were but a few small colonies scattered along the Atlantic seaboard of America. By the opening of the Revolutionary War settlements had spread inland toward the mountains and a few even beyond into the Ohio Valley. By then the population of the thirteen colonies was reported to be around three million with Boston a metropolis of thirty thousand. The colonists were of divergent national origins. For the most part they were earnest, God-fearing people. A deep desire for freedom was the common cornerstone of their zeal which eventually led them on unfalteringly through hardships and tribulations to the formation of a new form of government which, 350 years after the arrival in America of the first of them, is the envy of the entire world. All, in spite of their varied religious and national backgrounds, were bound together by their common worries—the unfriendly native Indians, the constant dread of French conquest, and the unjust demands of the British crown.

Throughout Colonial days the population was almost 95 per cent rural. Settlements were far apart, and as travel was by foot, horse, or boat it was difficult for people to get together. The days were filled with the struggle for existence —the conquest of the soil and of the forests, protection from the Indians, building and repairing homes, obtaining food, and preparing meals. Also, the men had to make their own tools and much of their own furniture while the women had to prepare the cloth and make the clothing and home furnishings. The children had to help in whatever way they could. Everyone was busy most of the waking hours. However, since work at arts and crafts was a necessity everyone had some form of creative work to do, and therein lay much contentment for all.

EDUCATION IN GENERAL

From the very start the colonists sought a common education for all children. One of the earliest acts of the new nation was to pass an ordinance granting land to the various states for educational purposes. Locke's *Thoughts on Education* exerted great influence on the colonists, and his theory of formal discipline held sway. By the close of the eighteenth century the education theories of Rousseau, Basedow, and Pestalozzi were filtering through to America, and they were changing the thinking of the people as to the aims, curriculum, and methods of education. However, in most of the land the church had a firm hold on the school curriculum and claimed the aim of education to be solely piety and preparation for a life of hard work, with play looked upon as sin. Many national leaders, especially George Washington, Thomas Jefferson, and Benjamin Franklin took a deep interest in the schools. Jefferson, in particular, used his great influence for the establishment of free universal schools.

Lower Schools. The elementary education of boys and girls was cared for through private tutors, district schools, and public schools for paupers. Secondary education was provided for by so-called "grammar schools." In 1647 the colonies of Massachusetts Bay and Connecticut enacted laws stating that a town with fifty families should establish an elementary school and a town with one hundred families should maintain, also, a Latin grammar school. Girls rarely attended any of these schools. The teachers hired to "keep" school were quite unprepared for their task. Books were few, the school hours were long, and discipline was severe. In the elementary schools reading, writing, ciphering, and spelling comprised the curriculum. The Bible was the main textbook, and all children were taught the catechism.

Although these secondary schools were generally called "free" schools they were not free. As yet the colonists had not envisioned the idea of taxation for the support of schools, so the schools were maintained by tuition and by subsidy from the local government. In New England these schools were looked upon mostly as instruments to prepare young men for the ministry or the practice of law or medicine. Therefore, they offered courses in Latin and Greek, logic, elocution, and rhetoric, and some also offered Hebrew. For the most part only the sons of the professional classes attended. But there was, even at that early day, a "voice crying in the wilderness"—the voice of Benjamin Franklin (see p. 183). As early as 1743 in his *Proposals Relating to the Education of the Youth of Pennsylvania* he recommended that academies be organized whose aim would be to prepare young people for life in the world of their day. He called for schools with a "healthful situation" with garden, orchard, meadow, and fields and with provision for students to engage in games, running, leaping, wrestling, and swimming. Franklin founded the first academy in Philadelphia in 1749. Samuel Moody (see p. 184) followed in 1763 with the first boarding school.

In Colonial days the Latin grammar school dominated education, but after the Revolutionary War and as a result of Franklin's interest the new kind of school—the academy—became an influential part of American education. The academy was geared not to preparation for college but to preparation for life in general. Although the first academy was established in the mid-eighteenth century the idea did not "take hold" widely until the Revolutionary War was ended. Now these schools, frequently founded by philanthropists, spread rapidly and soon became the most popular type of secondary school.

In Colonial days boys and girls went to Quaker schools together wherever these schools existed, but for the most part girls did not attend school until after the Revolutionary War. However, in New England and in the Middle Colonies many young girls went to so-called "Dame Schools" where they were taught reading and writing but no arithmetic. Some authorities permitted the girls to use the boys' schools from five to seven in the morning before the boys came, and frequently girls of sixteen would be starting elementary school work while boys their own age would be attending secondary schools. Moreover, in a few localities where there was a sufficient number of girls desiring to attend secondary school, special private schools called "female seminaries" were organized. But, by the close of the Revolutionary War girls were quite generally permitted to attend all elementary schools. Also, private and day schools for girls were being established in large numbers so that many, by then, were receiving secondary education.

Higher Schools. Harvard, established by the Pilgrim Fathers in 1636, was the first college in America. Following this came William and Mary in 1693, Yale in 1701, Princeton and Brown in 1760, and Dartmouth in 1770. The University of Pennsylvania, founded by Franklin as an academy in 1749, and set up according to his educational theories, was the first state university in America.

PHYSICAL ACTIVITIES

Since the responsibilities of meeting the needs of everyday life were so time-consuming in Colonial days and the post-Revolutionary War period, there was little free time for recreation. But the spontaneous urge for people to get together for companionship brought forth forms of recreational activities which, although born of their daily needs, resulted in much merrymaking for the great mass of the

people. Also, some did manage to find time occasionally
to engage in dance and sports.

Leisure Activities. From the needs of the people to combine recreation with useful labor there arose quilting parties,
corn-huskings, house- and barn-raisings. Even though the
stern hand of the church was strongly felt in the land, the
pious, who considered anything not connected with work or
worship as a waste of time, could conscientiously join in
this fun. The less pious and the young people engaged in
the dances and the sports which some of the colonists had
brought from the mother countries with them. Also, the
need to market their products brought forth fairs, and
amusements grew up around these such as wrestling matches
and chasing greased pigs.

A leisure class developed around the large plantations
of the South where there were slaves to do the work. Fox-
hunting and extravagant balls filled the leisure hours. In
Philadelphia, as early as 1627, British soldiers quartered
there brought to that community a form of old English
pageantry, and other groups kept alive the traditional Maypole dances of England. Practically all the colonies except
the strongly church-controlled ones of Massachusetts, New
Hampshire, and Connecticut soon developed some forms of
festivals, fairs, and pageants.

Children of Colonial days played marbles, "fives," leap-
frog, hop scotch, blindman's buff, and hop-skip-and-jump.
They did a lot of kite-flying and fishing, and in the spring
they danced around the Maypole. The children of the New
England colonies, where the obdurate Puritans ruled both
church and state, found it difficult to engage in these activities as much as they would like. The recreation movement
of the twentieth century was far away, even in dreams, in
those days. The grown-ups, too, had their difficulties with
stern authorities. On Christmas Day, 1621, when the Governor of Massachusetts ordered the men of Plymouth out to
their daily work, the newcomers who had recently arrived
on the "Fortune" excused themselves saying it was against

their conscience to work on Christmas Day. So, as Massachusetts archives tell the story:

> . . . he led away ye rest and left them: but when they came home
> at noone from their worke he found them in ye streete at play, openly:
> some pitching ye barr & some at stoole-ball and shuch like sports. So
> he went to them and took away their implements and tould them it
> was against his conscience that they should play & others work. If
> they made ye keeping of it a mater of devotion let them kepe their
> houses, but ther should be no gameing or revelling in ye streets.
> Since which time nothing hath been attempted that way, at least
> openly.

Church rules or no church rules, the young people of Boston played football and squibs and in the winter threw snow
balls so actively that "His Majesties Justices" passed a law
in 1701 "for preventing danger by Footballs, Squibs, and
Snowballs." Toward the latter part of the period the boys
and young men of all the English settlements played football, cricket, fives, rounders, and many other games. The
village commons, or "greens" as some called them, served as
the first municipal playgrounds in America. The Dutch
brought to New Amsterdam their great love of skating and
ninepins. They used the Old-World Dutch skates and sleds,
and, in their merrymaking, both old and young were a great
contrast to the dour New Englanders.

In Virginia nearly all the British sports flourished. Muster
day, when all men were to report for military instruction,
was an occasion for athletic competitions and games; foot
races, jumping, boxing, wrestling, cockfights, and horse-
racing were the main attractions at these gatherings and at
the fairs and picnics. The winners received prizes and considerable notoriety. Such meets were crude but enjoyable
and were engaged in without training. Fox hunting was the
universal sport of the Virginia gentlemen.

Shortly after the Revolutionary War, the Methodist
church, fearing the trends of the day, issued the following
statement on play for the students attending the schools
under their management.

... we prohibit play in the strongest terms. ... The students shall rise at five o'clock ... summer and winter. ... Their recreation shall be gardening, walking, riding, and bathing without doors, and the carpenter's, joiner's and cabinet-maker's business within doors. ... The students shall be indulged with nothing which the world calls play. Let this rule be observed with the strictest nicety; for those who play when they are young, will play when they are old.

Dance. The early settlers brought various forms of dance to the New World with them. The British gentry brought their stately and dignified dances while the lower classes brought the jigs and reels and boisterous squares. The French brought their cotillions, waltzes, and quadrilles. After the Revolutionary War the few girls' schools then in existence were advertising dancing as one subject that would be taught to "the young ladies."

Sports. Before the war, school hours were so long that there was little opportunity for the boys to engage in sports. But after the war, the new academies, which replaced the old grammar schools, permitted some time for sports and athletic competition. As for the colleges, the games of the students are as old as the colleges themselves, but from the very start they met with opposition from the authorities, who were quick to rule against them as harmful. As related in Princeton College archives, the boys at that school were playing some sort of ball game in 1761 as is evidenced by the outcry of the trustees of that year as follows:

The Trustees, having on their own view been sensible of the Damage done to the President's House by the Students playing at Ball against it, do hereby strictly forbid all and any of the Sd Students, the Officers and all other Persons belonging to the College, playing at Ball against Sd President's House, under the penalty of Five Shillings, for every offense, to be levied on each Person who shall offend in the Premises.

At all events, the Princeton trustees were not forbidding the playing, merely moving it to some other setting. Providing a playing field for the boys was as yet out of the picture.

Nine-Pins. In 1714 the British Coffee House maintained a bowling green in Boston which was open to "all gentlemen, merchants and others that have a mind to recreate themselves." In New Amsterdam a green was laid out in 1732 at the foot of Broadway for the use of the public, the land being leased from the city. Bowling Green of today's New York City marks the site of these activities. Originally nine pins were used, but, because of excessive betting, the game was outlawed, and later, to evade the law, a tenth pin was added.

Rounders. Played with a bat and ball, rounders was a very popular game in all the Colonies and flourished throughout the years until the game of baseball replaced it.

Shinny. The boys at Princeton College played a game "in the back common of the college" with balls and sticks which caused so much annoyance to the faculty that in 1787, as reported in the college archives, they voiced their objections declaring:

The game is in itself low and unbecoming gentlemen Students and in as much as it is an exercising attended with great danger to the health by sudden and alternate heats and colds and as it tends to accidents, almost unavoidable in that play, to disfiguring and maiming those who are engaged in it . . . the faculty think it incumbent on them to prohibit both the Students and Grammar Scholars from using the play aforesaid.

The diaries of the students of later years testify that the faculty prohibition was of no avail and that shinny was for many years the main college game.

Swimming. The first swimming pool in America was built on the banks of the Schuylkill River at the foot of Race Street in Philadelphia in 1791. It was not a floating pool as were many later ones of that day but stationary with the bottom of the pool resting on the bottom of the river. It was called a "plunging bath." Privately owned, it had connected with it two showers and a bowling green.

STATUS OF PHYSICAL EDUCATION

Although Franklin strongly urged recognition by the schools of the physical activity needs of children, physical education not only had no acknowledged place in education in Colonial days but the educational spirit was even hostile to the idea of physical education as well as to play. Military drill was the only physical activity accepted as part of the school program. In New England, in particular, the boys from ages ten to sixteen were given military drill six days a year. But with the coming of the academies after the war, there arose an emphasis on the physical welfare of the students and the desirability, if not the necessity, of physical exercise as a part of the school program.

Jefferson, also, in his writings on education expressed his belief in the necessity of physical exercise as a part of general education. The influence of these great leaders was gradually felt, and educators began to re-evaluate their educational objectives.

PROFESSIONAL LITERATURE

Since no profession of physical education existed as yet in the early days of United States history there was, of course, no professional literature as such. However, there was developing a literature on physical activities which is of historic interest. The earliest known book to be brought forth by the colonists was a book on football published in 1702. Following closely thereafter there appeared several books of American origins, chief among which was Hugh Gaines' *A Little Pretty Book* of 1760 which contains woodcuts of games and gives the first mention in the United States of cricket and baseball.

LEADERS IN PHYSICAL EDUCATION

Benjamin Franklin (1706-90). America's first recorded promoter of physical education was Benjamin Franklin. His was the first voice raised in the Colonies in behalf of physical education. Not only did he as an educator interest himself and others in the kind of school and curriculum needed for the youth of the land but he also went far beyond that to offer detailed instructions and advice on setting up a physical-activity school program. He even gave instructions on the techniques of teaching some of the activities, notably swimming.

As a young boy Franklin became deeply interested in the skills of swimming. He experimented with a kite to draw himself across the water as he floated on his back and with cork paddles for his hands and feet to propel himself more effectively through the water. He investigated the problem of muscle-cramping and the physiological effects of sudden plunging into cold water. He became such an expert swimmer that when a young man he gave an exhibition of swimming in London and later gained an international reputation as an authority on the subject.

Samuel Moody (**1727–?95**). Before the Revolutionary War, Samuel Moody, first headmaster of the famous Dummer Grammar School of Byfield, Massachusetts (the first private boarding school in America, which opened in 1763) became the chief exponent of physical activities as an important part of education. After Franklin he was the foremost person of this period to promote this part of the program. He, himself, taught the activities to the pupils and participated in them with the boys. Among his pupils were two signers of the Constitution, twenty members of the Continental Congress, and two Chief Justices of the Massachusetts Supreme Court.

16

PHYSICAL ACTIVITIES OF THE
EARLY NINETEENTH CENTURY

By 1830 the population of the United States had increased from the three million of Revolutionary War days to ten million, and throughout the 1830's, '40's and '50's immigrants from many lands continued to pour into America at every port. To Europe, America had become "the promised land" —the home of the free. In Germany, Metternich's Carlsbad Decrees of 1819 stifled political action and instituted strict censorship of the press and supervision of universities. Through the thirty years in which these decrees were in force, German students and professors by the hundreds fled to America bringing with them their deep interest in education and freedom. Many of them, also, brought their enthusiasm for physical education, materially enriching the educational system of that period.

At the same time the Irish were being ruthlessly suppressed by the English, and from 1816 on Irish immigrants poured into America in astounding numbers. The trickle of 6,000 for the year 1816 mounted to 18,000 in 1818; to 65,000 in 1832; to 92,000 in the year 1842. From 1820 to 1920 over four and a quarter million Irish immigrants came to the United States. Highly individualistic—an open critic of the established order, a "squatter," most active, hard, and pugnacious, a bold and resolute spirit—this Irishman became the typical frontiersman of the early days of our nation.

These two groups—the Germans and the Irish—played an important part in shaping the nation's destiny and, as counter-balancing forces, in shaping the educational philosophy which materially influenced the path which physical education would follow.

EDUCATION IN GENERAL

With the opening of the nineteenth century, elementary schools rapidly increased in number, and the academies gained in popularity over the Latin grammar schools of Colonial days. Coeducation was becoming a recognized form of education, but "free" public high schools open to all children were unknown in the early part of this era, and college education for women was but a dream of a few advanced thinkers.

Treatises and books on education by European leaders were becoming readily available in the United States. Particularly did Froebel, the German founder of kindergartens and champion of education of women, begin now to have marked influence on American educational philosophy. It was also in this period, thanks to the German immigrants, that there emerged the widespread idea that exercise and games are necessary for the proper growth of children and that the schools are responsible for the physical as well as the intellectual education of youth.

The number of schools financed by public taxation grew rapidly between 1800 and 1850, but the private schools continued to carry the great burden of the responsibility for the education of the youth of the land.

Lower Schools. In 1837 Horace Mann (1796–1859), a famous educational reformer, remodeled the Massachusetts system of public school instruction, centralized the supervision of local district schools, severed religious domination wherever it still existed, and introduced new methods based on the best to be found in Europe. His methods and theories were soon adopted in all common schools.

Heretofore secondary schools had not been considered necessary for the great mass of the people but now the idea was growing, and education was expanding in all directions. Also, by the end of this era the public schools had started to make deep inroads upon the enrollment of girls in private schools.

Higher Schools. Immediately following the Revolutionary War the emphasis of education was shifted from the colleges to the lower schools. Now, in the new century, a trend for "higher education" began. The state universities and the church colleges expanded materially while the first woman's colleges (Mt. Holyoke and Elmira Female Seminaries), the first private coeducational college (Oberlin), the first normal school (at Lexington, Massachusetts), and the first graduate course (at Yale University) put in their appearance. Most of the colleges established in this period were founded by religious groups and in their beginnings were of the manual labor type of school. About 1790 the combining of industrial training with intellectual education was first advocated. The plan seemed well suited to the growing spirit of democracy in education because the students, without financial means, could defray a part of their educational expenses with the products of their labor. However, it was not until the theories of Pestalozzi and Fellenberg, the two noted Swiss educators of the day, came to America that these ideas were put into practice. In 1831 the advocates of the movement for manual labor met in New York City and organized the Society for Promoting Manual Labor in Literary Institutions.

Colleges founded on this idea sprang up throughout the Middle West from 1833 on. In Indiana, the Presbyterians organized Wabash Manual Labor College in 1833 and Hanover in 1834; the Baptists founded the Indiana Baptist Manual Labor School in 1835; the Methodists, Asbury University in 1837; and the Friends, Earlham College in 1842. All these institutions long ago dispensed with the manual labor phase of their work and now exist as Wabash, Hanover, Franklin, Depauw, and Earlham Colleges. Mt. Holyoke, the earlist female seminary (although at first of secondary school level), was also established in the thirties on the idea of manual labor called, for girls, "domestic duties."

PHYSICAL ACTIVITIES

Leisure Activities. The quilting bees, corn-huskings, and square dancing of earlier days were still popular. Organized competitive sports had not yet come to the American scene, but there were informal games and contests to claim many participants.

As the people conquered the wilderness and settled down to establish homes and form communities, there grew up a division of labor made possible through group-living which produced some semblance of leisure time. None but those pushing ever westward had still the hard life of the early colonists. Now there developed new forms of physical activities to claim the attention of the people.

With the coming of the steamboat and railroads, recreation took on a new form. The New York Herald in 1838 advertised round-trip boat excursions to Coney and Staten Islands and Hudson River trips with dancing and band concerts included.

By the late 1840's many Germans had come to Ohio, bringing their Old-World ways of celebrating special occasions which set the pattern for the Fourth of July celebrations throughout the Middle West with their parades, singing, bunting and flags, picnics, patriotic speeches, and reading of the Declaration of Independence. Games and contests filled the day and lasted far into the night. Freedom was indeed something very personal to these people who had so recently fled their native land to find it here in America. They threw themselves wholeheartedly into these celebrations. With Czech immigrants, they also, initiated festivals and sharpshooting contests, the first one held at Washington, Missouri, in 1840 when they crowned the first United States King of the Sharpshooters.

Dance. To some school authorities, lessons in dancing seemed sufficient for the physical education program for girls. Mrs. Emma Willard (1787–1870), a famous woman educator of the day, set the thinking in that direction when, in a speech of 1819, she said: "Exercise is needful to the health and recreation to the cheerfulness and contentment of youth. . . . Dancing is exactly to this purpose. . . ."

Just what form of dancing was used in these school programs other than the ballroom forms of the day is not made clear; but since the dance advocates suggested the use of dancing as a substitute for calisthenics the forms used for class work, no doubt, had some calisthenic type and content, probably the forerunner of the "fancy steps" of a later day.

Gymnastics, Calisthenics, and Exercises. All three terms, gymnastics, calisthenics, and exercises, were used in this era to designate activities other than play or dancing. When the newly arrived German immigrants used the term gymnastics, they meant the German form so that the older settlers became accustomed to use the other two terms to designate exercises other than those of the German system.

German System. The great influx of German political refugees, who came to the United States in the early part of the nineteenth century bringing their love of gymnastics with them, gave this system a running head start in America. Among these refugees were three of Jahn's own close friends, who were excellent teachers and devoted followers of his theories: Charles Follen, Charles Beck, and Frances Lieber (see pp. 208–09). These three men interpreted to America the turner movement with its great fervor for freedom and its great hatred of oppression of every kind. In fact the coming of these men to America in 1824 and 1827 marked the real beginnings of a physical education program in the schools.

When a new high school opened in New York City in 1825 it was announced that included in the new school program would be gymnastic exercises. In that same year the four leading men's colleges—Yale, Harvard, Amherst, and Dartmouth—offered instruction in gymnastics under the leadership of these recently arrived German refugees. This initial effort of the 1820's to introduce German gymnastics in America was not a sustained effort, and by the 1830's this enthusiasm had died down, and the practice of gymnastics in the literary schools of the nation ceased. But the conviction that something should be done in the schools for bodily development endured in the minds of leading doctors and educators so that there remained some fertile ground ready for a revival in the 1850's and 1860's.

Catherine Beecher's Calisthenics. The program of useful exercise through domestic duties which was set up at Mt. Holyoke Female Seminary was copied in many schools, but it held no appeal to many educators as a real physical education program for girls. Nor did the German gymnastics get a favorable response from women educators who felt that they were too strenuous for most girls. So Catherine Beecher (see p. 209), a fighter in her day for the education of girls, devised a system of calisthenics of her own. Adapting the word "calisthenics" from the Greek *kalos* meaning "beautiful" and *sthenos* meaning "strength" she devised a system of physical education built around twenty-six lessons in physiology and two courses in calisthenics, one for schoolroom use and one for exercises in halls.

The exercises, made up of simple movements to be accompanied by music, acquired much popularity throughout the country and were accepted by many schools as a substitute for dancing. She preferred that they be practiced in a hall arranged for the purpose, but, where that was not convenient, the ordinary schoolroom would suffice. The aims were to produce grace of motion, good carriage, and sound health. This marked the first attempt of an American to devise an exercise program for Americans.

Strength Seekers. Dr. George Barker Winship (1834–76), a graduate of Harvard, became famous throughout the United States as the advocate of heavy gymnastics. His ideas appealed to all young men who sought to have bulging

muscles and great strength. From 1859 to the early seventies he toured the United States and Canada, lecturing on
gymnastics and giving weight-lifting exhibitions. The Winship Gymnasium in Boston became the most famous school
for strength seekers in the country. Winship's exhibitions
tended to confirm the popular idea that the gymnasium was
a place for strong men, prize fighters and wrestlers, and
that great strength was the aim of gymnastic training and
was synonymous with health and well-being. It has taken
physical education almost a century to live down this concept that developed from these strength seekers.

Dio Lewis' System. Dr. Dio Lewis (see p. 210), a well-
known temperance and health lecturer, attacked vigorously
the popular idea that great strength was the mark of well-
being and that gymnasia were primarily for gymnasts. In
his writings he strove to prove that light wooden dumbbells
were better suited to the real practice of gymnastics than
those of iron. He took pains to destroy the common belief
that free, unsupervised play of children was sufficient to
develop sound and properly formed bodies. He held that a
gymnastic teacher was as essential to the proper development of the body as the ordinary school teacher was to the
development of the mind. Those who advocated military
training for the schools, of whom there were many, found
the promoter of the New Gymnastics against them. He
believed that military training not only failed to develop the
upper half of the body but was conducive to rigidity and
to strained positions. Also, he maintained that athletic
sports, as a means of physical education, fell far short of
organized gymnastics because of their overexertion of certain parts of the body and neglect of other parts.

So he devised a system of exercises for America's schools
according to his own ideas. He advocated the use of music
or a drum to mark the rhythm of the exercises, which should
be fast enough to increase the rate of heart beat and respira-
tion. He also originated the idea of tossing beanbags as an
exercise. He preferred the beanbags to balls because they

were more easily grasped with one hand. The gymnastic crown, weighing from three to one hundred pounds, was one of his contrivances. It was worn to secure erect spine and good carriage. Many of his exercises were with wands, dumbbells, clubs, and hand-rings. He claimed to have invented 500 exercises and advocated their use in place of military drill, skating, riding, and dancing.

Fig. 8. Gymnastic costumes recommended by Dio Lewis in 1862.

Dio Lewis was a good salesman and engendered much enthusiasm for his system of gymnastics. He was widely acclaimed all over the country. Many magazine articles were written about his system and about him. The celebrated writer, Thomas Wentworth Higginson, took note of him saying in the *Atlantic Monthly* in 1861:

Gymnastic exercises are as yet but sparingly introduced into our seminaries, private or professional, though a great change is already beginning. Until lately all our educational plans have assumed man to be merely a sedentary being; we have employed teachers of music and drawing to go from school to school to teach those elegant arts, but have had none to teach the art of health. . . . It is something to have got beyond the period when active sports were actually prohibited. It would be unpardonable in this connection not to speak a good word for the favorite hobby of the day—Dr. Lewis and his system of gymnastics; or more properly of calisthenics. . . . Dr. Winship had done all that was needed in apostleship of severe exercises, and there was wanting some man with a milder hobby, perfectly safe for a lady to drive. . . . It will especially render service to female pupils so far as they practice it; for the accustomed gymnastic exercises seem never yet to have been rendered attractive to them on any large scale and with any permanency.

Sports. The earliest settlers of Colonial days participated in many sports; these were played without organization and without universally recognized rules. But in the nineteenth century, rules were developing for certain sports, and organizations to formulate them were being established. Examples of these sports follow.

Baseball. Although Cooperstown, New York, claims that baseball originated there in 1839, a game known as baseball was played in the United States before 1760 for it was mentioned in *The Little Pretty Book,* published in that year. The old English game of rounders came to America with the earliest colonists, and it is quite generally agreed today that throughout the years the game gradually evolved into today's game of baseball, which in its present form is essentially American.

The first printed rules in the United States under the name of baseball appeared in *The Book of Sports* of 1834, which copied the rules from an English book on rounders. These facts would seem to challenge the Cooperstown claim. However, there is a possibility that someone there may have established the diamond-shaped field, thus partially legitimatizing that town's claim to baseball fame, aside from the fact that it now possesses the Baseball Museum and Hall of Fame, which was established there on the basis of the earlier and now challenged claim.

Although Abner Doubleday (1819–93) is named as the originator of the game in Cooperstown in 1839, the claim scarcely holds up in light of the facts about his life. In 1839 he was a student at West Point, and his home was not located in Cooperstown. During the Civil War he was one of the commanding generals at the Battle of Gettysburg, and he devoted much of his later life to writing and lecturing on military topics. Never did he, in his writings or lectures, show an interest in the game of baseball or make any claims for himself as originator of any part of the game.

In the game as played in this era base-running was done clockwise. The Knickerbocker Baseball Club of New York City, organized a few years earlier, drew up new rules for the game in 1845, and these became the foundation of the modern game.

Football. Though the early colonists played a kicking game which they called football (an adaptation of "futballe," a game played in England as early as the eleventh century), it was not until the first half of the nineteenth century, when American collegians blended soccer with rugby and added other methods of play, that the game began to resemble present-day football. Students at Yale University played football as early as 1807 on the public green of New Haven. Both Harvard and Yale Universities used the game to haze freshmen. By 1827 Harvard, and by 1840 Yale and Princeton, were promoting interclass matches.

Swimming. In the early 1800's Philadelphia boasted of floating baths such as were popular at the time in France and England. They were located in the Delaware and Schuylkill Rivers and according to Watson, ". . . lay upon the water like low houses with white and yellow sides and green Venetian shutters with boatmen at hand to convey bathers to the establishment." The walls of these houses had openings through which the river water ran to make the pools. Some were elaborate having galleries and several bath chambers.

In 1827 Lieber opened the first swimming school in America in connection with the Boston Gymnasium. John Quincy Adams attended this school and became an excellent swimmer and diver.

In 1821 there was in existence an organization known as "The Humane Society" whose purpose was the restoring of life in persons apparently drowned. Aquatic activities even spread to the colleges as evidenced by the fact that in 1848 Girard College opened in Philadelphia with four indoor swimming pools, one each in the basement of the four dormitories, and one outdoor pool—all of which were planned by Lieber and were in use for over fifty years. This marked the first school in America to have a swimming pool.

Sports Clubs. The first of the sports clubs, to be established in the United States was the Savannah, Georgia, Golf Club of 1795. The second, known as the United Bowmen of Philadelphia, was in existence in 1830. The first baseball club, the Knickerbocker Club of New York City, was organized in 1845 and played in the first match game in 1846.

During the fifties baseball clubs increased rapidly, and by 1858 there were twenty-five teams playing in and about New York City. That year the National Association of Baseball Players was founded. Through the National Association the players agreed on the rules of the game and specified that the ball was to weigh six and one-half ounces and was to be ten and one-half inches in circumference. The bat might be any length but must not be more than two and one-half inches in diameter. The pitcher, who pitched, rather than threw, the ball, might stand anywhere on a line twelve feet long placed forty-five feet from the home plate. Only amateurs who had been members of the club for thirty days were permitted to play in the regular games. During the Civil War the clubs charged admission to see the games, and the players received a share of the money; this was the beginning of professional baseball history.

Intercollegiate Athletics. During the late 1850's a few colleges began to play baseball as a definitely organized sport. There soon arose the desire to pit their prowess against other colleges. The first game of any sport played between colleges was a baseball match at Pittsfield, Massachusetts, in

July, 1859, when Amherst played Williams winning by a score of 66 to 32. There has been preserved at Amherst College a copy of an "Extra" of the *Amherst Express* of July 1st and 2nd, 1859, which proclaims: "Baseball and Chess! Muscle and Mind!" After a report of the many preliminaries undertaken to arrange the contests the paper goes on to report the events. The Amherst players had a 90-mile journey to Pittsfield which they made the day before. The Williams teams arrived at the rendezous the following morning having only "20 miles to overcome." The two baseball teams put up at different hotels, and the chess players were entertained by the Pittsfield Chess Club. The Williams baseball boys were dressed "in the uniform of club . . . Amherst decidely in undress." Each team furnished its own ball, Amherst's weighing two and one-quarter ounces and measuring six and one-quarter inches around, while Williams' weighed two ounces and was seven inches around. The teams from both colleges were chosen by ballot from the student bodies. It was rumored that the Amherst "thrower" was the town blacksmith, hired for the occasion. So the first gun was fired that day at Pittsfield in "intercollegiate athletics." And in that very first engagement rumor of unfair advantage lifted its ugly head.

17

ORGANIZED PHYSICAL EDUCATION
IN THE EARLY NINETEENTH CENTURY

At last the idea of physical education in the schools was spreading but not without setbacks provoked by three distinct groups: the overly ardent advocates of manual labor, those still strongly influenced by the Puritan's idea that play in any form is sin, and the many scholars who felt that, although play might not be a sin, it was most certainly a waste of time.

The many German educators who came to America fleeing political persecution brought an enthusiasm for German gymnastics which, in its ebb and flow of popularity for more then a hundred years, greatly influenced physical education in the United States. Heretofore the English love of sports had set the pattern of physical activity, but from now on there developed the two interests—gymnastics and sports. By the close of the Civil War, gymnastics had such a strong hold that the term "physical education" (which was in use as early as 1859 according to reports of the New York State Department of Education) had come to mean to most people merely gymnastics, and there arose the custom of speaking of physical education *and* sports as if they were two different things.

STATUS OF PHYSICAL EDUCATION

Lower Schools. The Round Hill School at Northampton, Massachusetts, founded in 1823, was the first secondary school in the United States to make physical education (gymnastics) a part of the regular course of instruction. However, the Latin School of Salem, Massachusetts, was encouraging play for its educational, as well as recreational, value as early as 1821, and it may have had some simple gymnastic and play apparatus. Four years after the founding of the Round Hill School, gymnastics was added to the course of instruction with Charles Beck (see p. 209) as the teacher—the first officially recognized teacher of physical education in America. He set up an outdoor gymnasium with apparatus such as was used in a German gymnasium and the entire school was divided into classes, each meeting for an hour three times a week for gymnastic instruction. Beck was succeeded by Charles Follen (see p. 208), another German refugee.

Following this lead about fifteen other secondary schools organized gymnastic classes for their students. When the Chauncy Hall School was organized in Boston in 1828, provision was made for exercises and games. The head master was especially interested in the promotion of the physical welfare of the students. He provided some crude apparatus for physical exercises and at recess periods took the boys to the Boston Common to play games.

Many educational leaders of the day advocated that education for health, by means of regular exercise and instruction in hygiene and physiology, was necessary for complete education. None of the academy faculties, however, had a well-defined idea of the real scope and significance of the science of physical education. The popular concept was that the place for games and physical exercise was after school hours, and that special teachers were not necessary. The work of the superintendent of schools to secure a place for physical exercise on the daily program of the schools of Boston constitutes one of the earliest efforts made by school administrators. In his school report of 1852 he said: "In addition to the exercise allowed at the time of recess each half day, all the younger children need provision for some gentle exercise as often as once in every half hour, such as riding, walking, marching accompanied with such motions of the arms as would tend to give fullness and erectness to the chest." The next year a rule that every "scholar" should have daily some kind of physical or gymnastic exercise was passed but scarcely enforced.

In the annual report of 1858, the superintendent of the Boston schools again spoke out for physical education saying: "While the intelligence is in training, the conscience and the body must not be neglected. Liberal playgrounds ought to be provided for every school at whatever cost, and they should be used."

In the 1850's educators were also awakening in the Middle West and on the West Coast. Many school yards of St. Louis were equipped with play apparatus which was used at recess periods, and some schools were practising "manual exercises," while in Cincinnati there were a few parallel bars, horizontal bars, horizontal ladders, and circular swings in four school yards. In 1857 the superintendent of the Cincinnati schools proposed that all teachers employed in the schools should be instructed in a system of gymnastics adapted to the several grades of the schools from the first through the sixth. A year later a department of physical education was established with a special teacher in charge of the work.

A daily program of calisthenics and free play was inaugurated in 1854 in the Rincon School of San Francisco, and two years later a public exhibition of the work of the pupils consisted of exercises on horizontal bars and rings, and with wands, dumbbells, and Indian clubs.

Several other cities made efforts to organize a system of physical training for the public schools in the fifties, but none were able to entirely overcome either the obstacles of lack of funds, facilities, and trained leaders, or the general skepticism regarding the value of the work. The time was ripe, however, for the enthusiasm and confidence of Dio Lewis.

The Dio Lewis system of calisthenics was first established in a private school in West Newton, Mass., in 1860. The superintendent of the Boston public schools then secured instruction for his teachers, and the system was generally introduced into the Boston schools. The teachers were to give not more than one-half nor less than one-quarter of an hour to the exercises once during every school session. In 1862 there were seventy teachers who had had training and were giving the work to Boston school pupils.

Girls' Schools. In this era many people deplored the health condition of young girls and urged that physical education be made a part of their school programs. The editor of the *Boston Courier,* after attending a school festival in 1858, wrote that "not one girl in ten had the air or look of good health." Catherine Beecher in her two schools in Hartford and Cincinnati used the system of calisthenics which she had developed for girls in an effort to combat this state of affairs, and many schools adopted her system. In her *Reminiscences* there is preserved a speech which she gave in Cincinnati, in 1837, in which she said, in part:

When physical education takes its proper place in our schools, young girls will be trained in the classrooms to move head, hands and arms gracefully; to sit, stand and walk properly and to pursue calisthenic exercises for physical development as regular school duty as much as their studies; and these exercises set to music, will be sought as the most agreeable of school duties.

Some private schools for girls of this era gave their students a physical education program that was indeed rich for that day including skating, archery, riding sidesaddle, dancing, swimming, croquet, walking, and calisthenics. A few schools, notably Mt. Holyoke Female Seminary in Massachusetts, offered physical education as early as 1837 but substituted domestic duties for a large part of the program. Rockford Female Seminary in Illinois offered its students a physical education program as early as 1849.

Colleges. On the whole, college authorities evidenced little interest in the physical well-being of their students. They provided no gymnasiums and no facilities for sports. What little interest there was came from a small handful of individuals devoted to an educational ideal. A superintendent of the United States Military Academy resigned from the service in 1818 and began an agitation for the reform of the higher educational institutions of the nation, maintaining that one of the great defects of the educational system was the neglect of physical education in all the principal seminaries.

In 1826 Harvard gave permission to Charles Follen, who was then an instructor of German in the college, to organize gymnastics for the students although the activity was not recognized as a part of the educational program. On a piece of ground called the Delta, the students, directed by Follen, constructed some crude apparatus consisting of bars, ladders, wooden horses, and suspended ropes, and laid out places for running and jumping. It was a German "turnplatz" transplanted to America. The authorities also appropriated one of the vacant halls for indoor work. The student body showed great enthusiasm, and Follen had large numbers on the Delta and on the hikes and cross-country runs.

Soon thereafter other colleges, Yale, Amherst, Williams, Brown, and Bowdoin, set up outdoor gymnasiums. In many cases the faculty and students worked together to clear the ground and construct apparatus. Instructors were employed, and classes were held from two to five times per week. In addition to the outdoor gymnasium a room was usually provided for indoor work. The apparatus consisted of parallel and horizontal bars, ladders, ropes, mats, and wooden horses. Running and hiking were encouraged. In some institutions fencing and boxing were taught.

Physical Education Through Manual Labor. Throughout the 1830's and 1840's the colleges of the manual labor movement clung to their theory that manual labor was the best form of exercise and would conserve the time that participation in gymnastics would waste. These manual duties, therefore, were a substitute for physical education in all of these schools in their early years. Hence there was little progress in the development of physical education in colleges in general until in the 1850's when a nation-wide interest in the subject manifested itself and became felt in institutions of higher learning. The University of Virginia took the lead in this aroused interest and, in 1852, employed an instructor who created much interest in gymnastics among the students. In fact the university even built a gymnasium. However, as in other schools, this physical education work was not given recognition as a real part of the educational program.

Amherst College Department. The President of Amherst College, in his 1855 report to the trustees, said: "No one thing has demanded more of my anxious attention than the health of the students. The waning of the physical energies in the midway of the college course is almost the rule rather than the exception among us, and cases of complete breaking down are painfully numerous."

In 1859 the construction of a gymnasium was begun at the total cost of $15,000, and the trustees voted to establish a department of physical education, the first college department in the United States. They set forth the following requirements for the person to be selected as its head: he must be "thoroughly educated, a doctor of medicine and he must know something of gymnastics and sports and adhere to the principles that (1) the object of the gymnastics was not to learn to perform difficult feats but to keep the body in health, (2) the exercises used should be suited to all who engage in them and (3) students should be guarded against overwork in exercising." This person was to be given a seat on the faculty and the title of Professor of Hygiene and Physical Education.

Dr. Edward Hitchcock (see p. 264), recently graduated from Harvard Medical School, was selected for the post—becoming the first officially recognized College Director of Physical Education in the United States. At the same time, he achieved the rank of Professor—the only physical educator to hold that title in any college in the United States for many years to follow. He took over his duties at Amherst in August, 1861, remaining in that post for fifty years until his death in 1911 at the age of eighty-three.

This department was not only the first of the modern type to be organized at a college, but for twenty years it stood alone, unequalled in efficiency and professional excellence— years ahead of its day. At first Hitchcock built his program around heavy gymnastics, but soon coming to the conclusion that light gymnastics, when executed rapidly, were more beneficial he revised the program. He stressed hygienic living and regular strenuous exercise of a pleasant, recreative type.

From the first year at Amherst, Hitchcock compiled statistics of measurements of the students and thus became the first physical educator in America to apply the science of anthropometry to physical education. Measurements were made soon after the student came to the college and again at the close of each school year. The records were kept so that the student might know how he compared with others and how he changed from year to year.

First College Gymnasiums. In 1820 Harvard University constructed the first college gymnasium. Although privately owned, it was maintained for the use of Harvard students. It was well equipped with German apparatus of the day. Other gymnasiums followed: Williams College in 1851—a gymnasium with baths, owned and controlled by the students; University of Virginia in 1852—a building destroyed during the Civil War; Miami University (Ohio) in 1857—a building renting for $60 a year. Harvard University, in 1859, constructed a building that cost $8,000 including the cost of equipment. This new Harvard gymnasium, an octagonal building of brick, was a gift of the class of 1822. It had two bowling alleys and dressing rooms but no baths and was opened in 1860 to all students for a two-dollar fee per term. In that same year, 1859, Princeton University built a little shack painted red which it acquired after an uprising of students in a demand for a gymnasium; and Yale University at a cost of $11,000 built a gymnasium which had a bath and bowling alleys in the basement.

In 1860 Amherst College built a two-story stone gymnasium, in 1861 Oberlin College built a men's gymnasium, and in 1864 the students at Williams College raised $5,000 and erected a stone gymnasium which, like the one built in 1851, was completely owned and controlled by them.

Teacher Training. Although normal schools had by now come into the educational picture, none as yet offered special courses for the preparation of teachers of physical education. However, in 1859 the New York State Normal School asked for recognition of physical education in the schools and for the preparation of teachers to handle the subject. As early as 1827, Follen at Harvard University took things into his own hands and trained students as monitors to teach under his supervision.

At the Pittsburgh convention of the turners in 1856, it was proposed that a normal school be established as a means of filling the demands for trained instructors, and in the early part of 1861 the school was opened at Rochester, N.Y. This was the first attempt to establish a normal school of gymnastics in the United States. However, the school was no more than started when the Civil War effort claimed both pupils and teachers, and the school closed, to be revived later.

Founded to train teachers of physical education, the Dio Lewis Normal Institute of Physical Education opened in the summer of 1861 in Boston with such a distinguished faculty that it augured well for a bond with education in general. The president of Harvard University was the school's first president, and he had a board of directors of distinguished gentlemen and an imposing faculty of four medical doctors: one as professor of anatomy, one as professor of physiology, one as professor of hygiene, and Dio Lewis, himself, as professor of gymnastics. The school opened with fourteen pupils. It offered two full courses of ten weeks each and included two periods of gymnastic drills daily, covering a series of 200 exercises to be learned in a ten-week period. In the second year, elocution and a course in Swedish Movement Cure were added to the curriculum. By 1868 the school had conducted nine sessions and issued diplomas to 421 persons who went out to teach mainly in the large cities of New England, although some went to other sections of the United States. His graduates were greatly sought by schools and colleges. By 1869, Dio Lewis had turned his attention to other interests and, after a highly successful eight-year period, the school closed its doors.

Nonschool Programs. The German turner groups, the YMCA, and the public gymnasiums that were established in this era furnished opportunities for large numbers to pursue physical activities outside the schools.

Turnverein Movement. After its popularity of the 1820's and its subsequent dying out in the 1830's, the German system of gymnastics again rose to a position of importance in the United States. In 1848 revolutionary movements again swept over Europe. In Germany, in particular, the government used a policy of reaction and suppression against those demanding a liberal form of government. As a result of this suppression, thousands of Germans migrated to the United States settling mainly in the north. They represented a high level of intellect and broad cultural interests. Deeply interested in both physical and mental development for a "chainless mind in a fetterless body" they soon, wherever sufficient numbers had collected, organized the Old-Country German gymnastic society—the turnverein.

The first such group was organized in Cincinnati, in 1848. At this time the Germans in Cincinnati still wore German peasant costumes of black velvet with red vests and big silver buttons. In that same year the second society was formed in New York City. The turnverein held its first national turnfest (outdoor gymnastic meet) in Philadelphia in 1851. Its aims were to promote physical education, intellectual enlightenment, and sociability among the members. The turnverein building was always provided with a gymnasium where classes in the German system of exercises were conducted for men, women, and children. The teachers in the early period were men who had had experience in Germany. The Know-Nothing Party, which was against all foreigners, took every opportunity to oppose the turners and even to jeer and ridicule them. But when the call came for volunteers for the Union Army the turners joined in such numbers that many societies ceased to exist, and their newly founded normal school closed.

Young Men's Christian Association. In 1851 the first YMCA in the United States was organized in Boston, ten years after George Williams (1821–1905), a London clerk, had started the movement. Within ten years there were over two hundred associations in the country, and very soon all had established boys' departments. As early as 1856, at the Third International YMCA Convention at Montreal, the question was raised about serving the health and physical development of the members.

Public Gymnasiums. Shortly after the two immigrants, Beck and Follen, arrived from Germany and began their teaching of gymnastics at the Round Hill School and Harvard University in the 1820's, prominent citizens of Boston began agitation for a public gymnasium. Dr. John C. Warren (1778–1856), Professor of Anatomy and Physiology at Harvard University, was a leader in the movement. The Board of Aldermen granted a request for a piece of ground for the purpose of establishing a school for gymnastic instruction and exercise. Money was raised by public subscription to guarantee a salary for a teacher and to provide apparatus. By September, 1826, the first public gymnasium, located in Washington Gardens, was ready, and Follen had been secured as the teacher. The gymnasium proved very popular and enrolled students until 1832. But even the expert gymnast could not keep the Boston Gymnasium alive. The novelty soon wore off, the participants became the target for the humorist and caricaturist, and the gymnasium closed its doors.

When the movement was revived some thirty years later Thomas Wentworth Higginson commented as follows in the *Atlantic Monthly* in 1861.

It is one good evidence of the increasing interest in these exercises that the American gymnasia built during the past year or two have far surpassed all their predecessors in size and completeness, and have probably no superiors in the world. The Seventh Regiment Gymnasium in New York, just opened by Mr. Abner S. Brady, is 180 by 52 feet in its main hall and 35 feet in height, with nearly 1,000 pupils. The beautiful hall of the Metropolitan Gymnasium in Chicago, measures 108 by 80 feet and is 20 feet high at the sides, with a dome in the center 40 feet high and the same in diameter. Next to these probably rank the new gymnasium at Cincinnati, the Tremont Gymnasium at Boston, and the Bunker Hill Gymnasium at Charlestown, all recently opened. Of college institutions the most complete are probably those at Cambridge and New Haven. The arrangements for instruction are rather more systematic at Harvard.

With the growth of gymnasiums in the schools, colleges, and YMCA's, the public gymnasium eventually died out.

Professional Organizations. Teachers' associations had by now come into existence, and, at their meetings, physical education became a topic for discussion. In August, 1830, a convention of "Teachers and Other Friends of Education" met in Boston and organized the American Institute of Instruction. At this convention, Warren lectured on *The Importance of Physical Education,* speaking on the effects of poor ventilation, unsanitary school buildings, and improper seating, and on the relation of physical exercises to the problems of general education.

Physical Education Literature. Several books and one periodical on physical activities came off the presses in the United States in this period. Most books published in this era were on sports, but there were three books on gymnastics besides the 1831 book of Warren, *The Importance of Physical Education,* which might be called the first publication in the field of philosophy of physical education. From *Youthful Sports* of 1801 to *Medical Parlor Gymnastics* of 1859 a great variety of activities is covered. Foremost among these books are: William Turner's *Art of Swimming* published in 1821, which included Benjamin Franklin's "Advice to Swimmers"; Charles Beck's translation of Jahn's *Treatise on Gymnastics* published in 1828; Catherine Beecher's *Course in*

Calisthenics for Young Ladies in Schools and Families published in 1831, containing sixty-two illustrations and a discussion of teaching methods and course material—the first American book on curriculum and methods; followed in 1858 by her *Physiology and Calisthenics;* and Dio Lewis' book *New Gymnastics for Men, Women and Children* published in 1862, which had wide circulation and ran through twenty-five editions.

The first American periodical in the physical education field was established by Dio Lewis and named *Gymnastic Monthly and Journal of Physical Culture.* It was published in Boston, beginning in December, 1861, but it did not survive long.

LEADERS OF PHYSICAL EDUCATION

For the first time in the United States there now arose leaders who fully devoted some period of their lives to the cause of physical education—three men born in Europe and one man and one woman of American origins. They are discussed chronologically.

The first three—German immigrants of superior education —were, in spite of their training in philosophy, law, the classics, theology, political economy, and history, deeply interested in physical education. In laying the foundations of physical education in the United States, they brought to the groundwork a scholarly approach.

Charles Follen (1796-1840). Born in Romrad, Germany, Charles Follen, a pupil and friend of Jahn, fled the country when Jahn was arrested in 1819 for his political activities. He went first to Switzerland with another of Jahn's disciples, Charles Beck. None too safe there, the two soon went to France where the Marquis de Lafayette, then a deputy in the French Chamber of Representatives, urged them to go to America. Armed with letters of introduction to Lafayette's friends, they arrived in Philadelphia in 1824. Follen, who held the degree, Doctor of Civil Laws, from the University of Geissen, soon found employment at Harvard University to teach German. Later he added the teaching of gymnastics to his schedule and soon took on the added responsibility of teaching at the first public gymnasium in Boston. Later he gave up the teaching of gymnastics and devoted his time completely to the teaching of German, ethics, and history at Harvard.

Charles Beck (1798-1866). Charles Beck was born in Heidelberg, Germany, and procured the degree, Doctor of Theology, from the University of Tubingen. He fled to America with Follen, and almost immediately upon his arrival the head master of the famous Round Hill School in Boston procured him to teach gymnastics, baseball, hockey, football, and Latin. This marked the first time that German gymnastics was taught in the United States. Beck left the school in 1830 to assist in the establishment of Phillipstown Academy in New York. Two years later he became Professor of Latin at Harvard University. His last years were spent as a Unitarian minister and a leader in the fight for the abolition of slavery.

Francis Lieber (1800-72). Born in Berlin, Germany, Francis Lieber was educated at the University of Jena where he procured the degree, Doctor of Philosophy. Also a friend of Jahn, he found life increasingly difficult in Germany and escaped to America in 1827. At that time Follen gave up his teaching at the Boston Gymnasium, and Lieber was offered the position. He opened the first swimming school in the United States at the Boston Gymnasium. In the 1840's he was invited to make plans for the new Girard College which was opened in Philadelphia in 1848. Following this he took up the teaching of political economy and history and became known as America's "first academic political philosopher." His *Political Ethics,* published in 1838, and *Civil Liberty and Government,* published in 1853, marked him as one of America's scholars.

Catherine Esther Beecher (1800-78). Catherine Beecher was born in East Hampton, Long Island. She was the daughter of the well-known preacher, Lyman Beecher, and sister of Harriet Beecher Stowe, author of *Uncle Tom's Cabin,* and Henry Ward Beecher, the famous preacher and reformer. Reared in a home of unusual educational advantages, she was tutored at home by her father and did not attend her first school until she was ten years old. Twelve years later after the family had moved to Hartford, Connecticut, she opened her own private school for girls, the Hartford Female Seminary. It achieved such fame that shortly she had over one hundred pupils. Sensing that they needed an exercise program, she investigated the German gymnastics that had come into prominence in the Boston area but rejected them as too strenuous for the average frail girl of that day. Becoming interested in physiology, she combined this interest with her attempts to devise a system of exercises advisable for girls. In 1831, she produced her first book, *A Course of Calisthenics for Young Ladies*—the first manual of physical education in America—and in 1858 her second book, *Physiology and Calisthenics.* A sustained effort of twenty-seven years was required to perfect the system of exercises which she developed to produce good posture and grace.

When her family moved to Cincinnati she opened the Western Female Seminary there and soon thereafter launched upon a career of lecturing in an attempt to sell education, in general, and physical education, in particular, throughout the East and Middle West. In 1864, she joined the staff of Dio Lewis' new school for girls in Massachusetts, but the two soon disagreed on fundamental philosophy concerning their two systems of calisthenics, and Miss Beecher resumed her educational promotion work. She organized women's educational societies in the East to raise money to send women teachers to the Mississippi Valley as missionary teachers to start schools there. She may justifiably be claimed as the originator of the first American system of gymnastics and as the first woman physical education leader in America.

Dio Lewis (1823-86). Dio Lewis was born in Cayuga County near Auburn, New York. Quitting school at the age of twelve, he began his teaching career three years later.

When nineteen he embarked upon medical studies through a combination of a few courses at Harvard University and study in a physician's office. At twenty-eight he received an honorary degree of Doctor of Medicine and shortly thereafter embarked upon a five-year lecture career on temperance and health topics which took him all over the country.

In his travels he encountered the German system of gymnastics, but, in spite of its great popularity, he felt that it was not what the United States needed. So he devised a system of calisthenics of his own, and in 1860 he went to Boston and organized evening classes to present his system to the public. Achieving immediate acclaim, he organized his Normal Institute of Physical Education. Thus began the first teacher-training for women in this field.

In 1864 he established a school for girls at Lexington, Massachusetts, and brought Miss Beecher to its staff. Within three years the school had three hundred pupils from various parts of the country, mostly girls of delicate constitution sent there for their health. One year later, tiring of this venture, Dio Lewis renewed his lecturing, and the school closed. He now organized The Woman's Crusade, which later developed into the Woman's Christian Temperance Union, and he added Europe to his lecture itinerary.

He popularized physical education and sold the need for it to many educators who, through his influence, put it into the school programs. A man of exceedingly good looks and with much personal charm, he was a sensation wherever he went.

18

PHYSICAL ACTIVITIES OF THE
LATTER NINETEENTH CENTURY

The United States was fast becoming the "melting pot" of the nations. It was producing a new person—the American—a blending of peoples of all nations. By 1870 the population of the United States was 38 million; by 1880, 50 million; and by 1900, 76 million. From the end of the Civil War until the close of the nineteenth century over 13 million immigrants had been admitted into the country. However, by 1885 only 20 per cent of the population was foreign born. By 1880, the rural population was 71 per cent of the entire population, but, by 1890, it had dropped to 64 per cent.

Although the churches still banned card-playing, dancing, and theater attendance as evil, the old rules for strict Sabbath observance were fast disappearing. Nationalism had become the great emotion of the world, and the United States, because of her particularly strong belief in the equality of men and in the dignity of the individual, came to feel that all children must receive an education to be worthy of the new nationalism.

EDUCATION IN GENERAL

This was a period of great educational awakening in the United States. Schools were now being established rapidly in all parts of the country. The Civil War brought to the people a realization of the need to wipe out illiteracy and to give an ever-widening segment of the population an education—girls as well as boys. In fact compulsory education was born now, not from a desire to force anyone to do anything but as an expression of the firm belief that every child has a right to an education. But a great handicap to this movement was the lack of teachers and the inadequacy of those who were teaching. Most of the teachers had no more than a high school education if, indeed, even that. Up to 1850 there were but eleven public high schools in the United States, but they were increasing gradually, and by 1885 approximately 160,000 pupils were enrolled in these public high schools.

Coeducation, too, was spreading. By 1900, 98 per cent of all public schools and 56.7 per cent of all private schools in the United States were coeducational. Moreover, by the close of the century practically all the forty-five states then in the union had established higher schools of some form—university, normal school, or agricultural college. Also, church-dominated colleges had opened in practically all states, and eleven of today's leading women's colleges were established between 1865 and 1891 with a twelfth (Elmira College) already functioning as a college before the Civil War period.

ACTIVITIES OF PHYSICAL EDUCATION

In their informal leisure the people still enjoyed quilting bees, corn-huskings, square dancing, hunting, and fishing. By the 1890's bicycling, athletic contests, and prize fighting had become popular. The great German immigration to the Middle West brought to that region the love of Sunday picnics and outings, much gay music and dancing—all frowned upon so vigorously by the dominating Puritan stock throughout the Colonial period and early years of our national life. Now things began to change in America with this in-pouring of blithe spirits who did not fear the Puritan's God. Near the end of the century electric trolley cars came to the cities, and they transported the willing throngs to the amusement places that were springing up in the outlying districts.

Gymnastics became the core of the physical activity program across the land in nonschool organizations as well as in the schools. The sports and games pursued by school children and college students under their own organization and management still received but scant attention from the schools except in a few situations. However certain groups of adults now began to promote athletics and games, foreshadowing today's rich sports heritage. Here and there dancing claimed some attention—it, too, presaging an interesting future.

Dance and Rhythms. The free exercises of Catherine Beecher were performed to music, and in some schools they developed into a sort of dance form which later replaced calisthenics, but they had no permanency as did the dance forms discussed below.

Ballroom Dance. It would have been unthinkable in the nineteenth century to teach any form of ballroom dancing in a public institution. It was taught only in private dancing schools. The minuet of Colonial days had about died out as a social dance by the time of the Civil War, but the Virginia reel kept its popularity. In the early part of this era the most popular dances were the schottische, polka, gallop, lancers, quadrille, mazurka, varsovienne, Newport, and gavotte. The waltz was not popular until later and then was danced only in the East for quite some time. In the 1890's when the famous band leader, John Philip Sousa, toured the country, his band music became so popular that its two-step rhythm popularized the new dance step, driving all other forms into the background.

Esthetic Dance. America's first popular dance teacher to align himself with the schools to offer dance as part of the physical education program was Melvin Ballou Gilbert (1847–1910) of Boston who, in the early nineties, developed for school use the so-called "esthetic dancing." He based his work on a modified ballet form and first taught it at the Harvard Summer School of Physical Education in 1894 and a few years later at Vassar College and the Boston Normal School of Gymnastics. This form of dancing became very popular throughout the country, particularly with girls.

Folk Dance. The early immigrants brought their various native dances to America, but they did not display them publicly probably because, in their eagerness to become Americanized as rapidly as possible, they did not care to give others a chance to accuse them of trying to keep their homeland customs alive in the New World. Not until teachers of physical education, themselves, went to Europe and collected the dances did they become known and used in the schools. When Anne Barr (1867–1945) of the University of Nebraska studied in Sweden in 1898–1899 she collected Swedish folk dances. Upon her return to the United States she had several of them published in sheet-music form. This was, as far as records now indicate, the first publication in the United States of folk dances of other lands. Miss Barr taught them at the University of Nebraska the following year and introduced Swedish folk dances at the Chautauqua School of Gymnastics in the summer of 1899.

Square Dance. As the frontiers moved ever westward the pioneers carried to their new homes a form of dance brought originally from England known as country dancing which, by now, had developed several American forms of its own— the Kentucky and Tennessee mountain form; the formal one of New England; and that of the plains and the cowboys. However, square dancing did not carry over into school physical education programs in the nineteenth century. Its popularity existed in pioneer communities as the recreational dance form of the people, and it was handed down from parents to children. Thus it persisted enthusiastically in the Middle West, South, and Far West throughout the century.

Gymnastics. In the nineteenth century there were practically no public school "exercise rooms" in the United States. Class work had to be carried on in the regular schoolroom with large groups served in a small space by teachers who were totally unprepared to teach physical activities. A class form that must be learned by rote had to be committed to a program of formal gymnastics in order to exist at all. This form served its day and, in many places, served well in this formative period of the physical education profession. It gave children as well as many adults excellent physical fitness training, albeit a narrow program. The horse and buggy, the pony express, and the kerosene lamps of that day were inadequate, too, but while the pioneer period was passing on to the period of automobiles, railroads, electricity, and supervised play, gymnastics, as well as the other things, served their purpose well.

German System. The German system of gymnastics, which had been introduced to Americans about a half century ahead of the Swedish system, had gained a real stronghold by the close of the Civil War. With another wave of German immigrants coming right after the war, German gymnastics took a still firmer hold and throughout the rest of the nineteenth century was very popular.

Many people, though, refused to accept German gymnastics. Americans of other national strains were repelled by the intense German nationalism of the promoters of this system. Dr. Edward Mussey Hartwell (see p. 270), of Johns Hopkins University, felt it necessary to point out to these critics in his remarks at a conference in 1889 that "the fondness of the German people for gymnastics is as marked a national trait as is the liking of the British for athletic sports." Much misunderstanding has always existed about the German system which might have been avoided had the German immigrants differentiated between German gymnastics and the over-all German physical education program. To them, the word "gymnastics" embraced the over-all program, but to non-German Americans the word meant merely calisthenics and apparatus work. Americans in general do not interpret the word to embrace sports, games, and rhythms as well as free-standing exercises and apparatus work. Hence the consternation of the German Americans when the system was so bitterly attacked because it was accused of being so narrow. The true German system of gymnastics consisted of five types of activities, all evolved from Frederick Ludwig Jahn's work, namely: (1) tactics and marching; (2) free exercises with short and long wands, dumbbells, rings, and clubs; (3) "dance steps" for girls; (4) apparatus work using balance board, buck, horizontal bars, long and side horse, ladders, parallel bars, poles, ropes, round swing, suspension rings, and vaulting box; and (5) games and play—a graded set as developed by GutsMuths in 1793.

Since both the German and Swedish systems held the serious attention of both the school and nonschool groups for a rather long period, a somewhat detailed description of what they actually offered as exercise is of historical significance. In the May, 1894, *Mind and Body*, is a chart outlining the German system of gymnastics then in use in the United States. The main features of the program consisted of the following:

1. General exercises of strength, acquired through:
   a) wrestling, weights, and putting the shot.
   b) straining a large number of muscles to the utmost, combined with the act of exertion thus increasing "the strength and dimension of the muscle."
2. Localized exercises of strength acquired through:
   a) calisthenics with weights—the movements frequently repeated combined with long holding.
   b) work on horizontal bars, parallel bars, rings, or pole vaulting.
   c) straining a small number of muscles to the utmost.
3. Exercises of skill done through "compound and flourishing calisthenics," balancing exercises, work on horse, buck, horizontal and parallel bars, far and high jump.
4. Exercises for quickness acquired through:
   a) walking, marching, running, rope-jumping, dancing, hopping, climbing ladders or hills, swimming, rowing with moveable seat, bicycling, skating, sawing wood, mountain climbing.

    b) "rhythmically repeated movements distributed over a great number of muscles with intention of moving forward quickly . . . or as rapidly as possible straining the activities of the heart and lungs to the utmost and causing temporary exhaustion of these organs."

5. Exercises of endurance acquired through:
    a) exercises listed in numbers 3 and 4 above.
    b) moderating the speed to preserve "equilibrium of different organic activities" so that the "motion may be continued for hours."

6. Exercises of attention acquired through tactics and "rhythmical motions as in May dancing, etc., where a single member is but a part of the whole."

7. Exercises of alertness acquired through:
    a) wrestling, fencing, intricate running, and ball games.
    b) mastering of the unforeseen and need of suddenly necessary motions on the impulse of the moment.

Swedish System. The system of gymnastics of Per Henrik Ling soon challenged the German system in America. Great rivalry developed between the advocates of the two forms. In fact the famous Conference of 1889 concerned itself primarily with discussions of the relative merits of the two systems. At that meeting Dr. Edward Hitchcock, Director of Physical Education of Amherst College, threw the weight of his influence behind the announcement of the Boston Public Schools that they were going to try out the Ling System. But Dr. Luther H. Gulick (see p. 323) of the YMCA school in Springfield, Mass., opposed the use of either system saying that both demanded "too much attention to detail and too much patience for what it was worth." However, he approved of the Swedish System for school children who had to exercise in the school room but not for adults nor for free hours out of school.

The Germans held that the Swedish method was too formal, uninteresting, failed to obtain recreational values, and was very weak in social and moral training. The Swedish supporters claimed that the German system lacked scientific foundation, that too much music and rhythm accompanied the exercises and thereby prevented the maximum physical benefit from being derived, that too much emphasis was given to the recreational and not enough to the educational results, and that the system was unable to cope with problems of individual and specific weaknesses.

In light of all the arguments it is interesting to note that several women physical educators went to Sweden to study, but records reveal no names of leaders among the women who sought foreign study or even local instruction so that they might bring the German system of gymnastics to the girls and women of America. Senda Berenson (1868–1954), head of physical education at Smith College, was the first woman from the United States to study at the Central Gymnastic Institute in Stockholm.

Swedish gymnastics of that period was characterized by (1) the Day's Order, (2) progression of exercises day by day and week by week from easy to difficult, from light to strenuous work, (3) use of word of command for all movements, (4) stress upon correct holding of positions, and (5) corrective or remedial effects. In fact out of the Swedish system grew the corrective gymnastics that have assumed so important a place in the school physical education program of the twentieth century. The apparatus work of Swedish gymnastics was quite different from that of the German system. In the Swedish form the following apparatus was used: high and low boom, swinging ladders, swinging and travelling rings, climbing ropes, bar stalls, rope ladders, and vaulting box. In the free-exercise part of the program no hand apparatus of any kind was used, nor was there any musical accompaniment.

The advocates of this system of gymnastics claimed that the functioning of the heart and lungs was the fundamental function of the body, and that Swedish educational gymnastics served to develop these organs. They were not concerned with the development of muscle strength or speed. As Dr. Claës J. Enebuske (1855–?), who held medical degrees from both Harvard University and the University of

Paris and the Ph.D. from the University of Lund, Sweden, said to his pupils at the Boston Normal School of Gymnastics: "Get the heart and lungs right and the muscles will meet every reasonable demand." The Day's Order consisted of the following schedule of exercises.

1. Order movements
2. Leg movements
3. Strain bendings
4. Heave exercises
5. Balance exercises
6. Back exercises
7. Abdominal exercises
8. Lateral trunk exercises
9. Jumping exercises
10. Slow leg exercises
11. Respiratory exercises

Each lesson contained an exercise for each of the eleven items listed above and in that order. From lesson to lesson the exercises became more strenuous and difficult either by increase in the number of repetitions or by advancing to exercises requiring ever greater skill of execution. Enebuske's book, widely used throughout the United States in this era, gives three series of twenty-five lessons each, all progressively arranged from lesson one through lesson seventy-five. To show the progression in the Day's Order, Lessons 1 and 75 are outlined below using the short-cut writing system used for Day's Orders at that time.

	Lesson 1	*Lesson 75*
1. Order	Fund. std and rest	Order movements
2. Leg	Std., ft. placing sideways	Stret. ½ horiz. std., knee bending
3. Strain bend	Std., back bend hd	Stret. bow std., alt. leg raise and heel raise
4. Heave	Wing std. position	Std. 2 arm ext. and alt. arm ext. in various directions
5. Balance	Wing stride std., 2 heel raising	Stret, ½ toe std., arm sinking sideways downward slowly

	Lesson 1	*Lesson 75*
6. Back	Cross std., 2 arm rotation	½ stret fall-out std., chg of arms and ft. with adv. in zigzag and about facing.
7. Abdomen	Std., back bending of tnk (gently)	Stret. horiz. ½ toe lean std., arm parting
8. Lateral Trunk	Std., side bending	Stret fallout twist std., side bending and strd prone falling, alt arm and leg raising
9. Jumping	Mark time	(a) Wing toe knee bend std., spring jump in place with alt. stret of knee. (b) Std., free jp in place with facing 360 degrees.
10. Slow leg	Wing std., 2 knee bend	Stret walk toe std., 2 deep knee bend
11. Respiratory	Std., 2 arm raising with deep breathing	Cross twist outward fall-out std., arm flg sideways with chg of ft in series, alternate with std. circumduction of arms with deep breath

Delsarte System. During the early nineties the Delsarte System of Physical Culture received much fame, and great numbers were converted to its theories. This system took its name from its founder François Delsarte (1811–71), a French vocal and dramatic teacher. Finding that ideal poses and gestures could best be taught through physical exercises, he devised a system for use in his work. Although he had no thought of devising a system of gymnastics, many elocution and dramatics teachers accepted his methods and, adding their own ideas, evolved a system of exercises which they claimed would produce poise, grace, and health. These claims gave the Delsarte system a universal appeal entirely aside from its connection with the vocal and dramatic arts, and elocution teachers were in demand to teach this system in many schools, where it was accepted as a physical education program. This system was characterized by a series of relaxing, "energizing," and deep-breathing exercises augmented by poses to denote various emotions. Without sound principles back of it, this system proved but a fad, and it soon died out although it enjoyed much acclaim in its day.

Sports and Games. The post-Civil War period brought new sports to the national scene and changes to others—all of which are discussed in the material that follows.

Baseball. The game of baseball was popular in many army camps during the Civil War, particularly among the northern soldiers, and after the war it fast became a popular national game. By 1876 all young America was playing the game. In 1866 the ball was made smaller, the pitchers began to throw curves, and the distance and force of the batting and throwing increased to such an extent that padded gloves became necessary. The overwhelming popularity of baseball hurt cricket, which had heretofore been popular particularly in those parts of the country with large settlements of English descendants. Now cricket became almost an unknown game in the United States.

The first conference of the National Association of Baseball Players was held in 1867. At that time Illinois had fifty-six baseball clubs and Iowa, forty-two. Soon after that, intersectional contests were organized. In 1869 the Red Stockings of Cincinnati turned "pro" and toured the East winning all games. The Chicago White Stockings, Philadelphia Athletics, and Washington Nationals were formed, and in 1871 ten such clubs played championship series. So much gambling, drinking, and corruption came to be attached to the games that professional baseball was no more than started when it became threatened with extinction. Out of efforts to lift the game to a respectable position came the National League of Professional Baseball Clubs in 1876. Other leagues soon followed, such as the American Association in 1882 and the American League in 1900.

Basketball. Basketball is exclusively American in its origin. Invented in 1891 by Dr. James A. Naismith (1861–1939), then a young teacher at the YMCA Training School in Springfield, Massachusetts, it claimed immediate popularity both as an indoor and outdoor game and as a sport for men and women. In the first try-out game, played at the YMCA school in 1892, using peach baskets for goals, Naismith and Amos Alonzo Stagg (1862–   ), another young teacher, who later became a famous football coach, were captains of the two teams, and Dr. George L. Meylan (1873–   ), a visiting YMCA director, who later became Medical Director of Columbia University and a foremost leader of the camping movement, played on one of the teams.

Naismith, trained for the ministry and honored with a Doctor of Divinity degree, lived to see his game used by gamblers for their own ends. Not only did this grieve him but he was ill at ease in the world of intense training and coaching that grew up around the game, maintaining always that basketball was a game to be played, not coached.

Bicycling. The bicycle was invented in 1816 in Germany after an earlier unsuccessful attempt in France in 1769. The velocipede was developed in 1862. In 1872 came the high front-wheeler leading to the smaller wheels with chains and gears which was devised by an Englishman, and the craze for bicycling was on. "The Bicycle built for two" led to "triplets, quads, quints" and even to wheels with eight and ten saddles. Cycle racing soon became the sport sensation of the world, and the top racers were *the* athletic heroes of the day.

Women in their long, voluminous skirts of the early 1890's took to the sport, but the skirts had to be shortened. They receded to ankle length causing consternation in many communities, but that was nothing compared to the uproar that arose in every village all over the country where the bolder of the young women, abetted by liberal parents, adopted the dress reform sparked in an earlier day by Amelia Bloomer (1819–94), a prominent writer, lecturer, and champion of women's rights and dress reform. The cities less stormily accepted the shortened skirts and the "bloomers" along with the bicycle-riding for girls and women.

Everyone of all ages took to wheels. On week days the streets were full of people going to work on bikes and on the week-ends full of bicycle club members who were on their own outings or following "bike" races somewhere nearby. By 1900 bicycling was the fashion of the day among all classes of people—it was, indeed, the biggest sports craze of the past hundred years. So many people took to wheels that bicycle speeders became a menace in the large cities, and police were mounted on bikes to catch these speeders who were endangering the lives of the other citizens at 20 miles per hour. Then, with the coming of the electric car the fad ended almost overnight—ending almost as suddenly as it arose. Bicycling then fell into its twentieth-century niche as a means of recreation for children and youth and as a means of transportation for school children and, in the earlier years of 1900, also for the working man. But while this fad lasted, in the 1890's and the first decade of the 1900's, bicycling brought splendid physical developmental exercise to the great masses of the population.

Bowling. It was not until the 1860's that bowling, popular from Colonial days on, became a well-regulated sport. Beginning then, bowling clubs were organized in great numbers, and in 1875 the National Bowling League was founded. In 1895 a national reorganization was accomplished which resulted in the formation of the American Bowling Congress which revised the rules and standardized the equipment.

Football. Since 1873 football has been the most popular sport connected with college life and the most opposed and condemned; it has caused more college conferences and agreements than all other games combined. The earliest games of football were so rough and so devoid of rules that the "class rush" was substituted for it as a safer activity. As the game grew it was more like "association" football (soccer) than the present style of game. There follows a brief review of the growth of football.

In 1869 Princeton and Rutgers played the first intercollegiate football game in America. The game was played at New Brunswick on November 6 with twenty-five players on each team. At this game yelling was introduced by the Princeton players, using an imitation of the Confederate rebel yell—a bloodcurdling cry of Civil War days. In this first match the Princeton players used the yell to frighten their opponents, but it took so much breath from the players that in the second game they asked their fellow students on the sidelines to give the yell for them. Thus started the United States custom of sideline yelling at games. Following this game, Columbia, Yale, Cornell, Pennsylvania, and Harvard were soon playing against each other. When Columbia and Yale Universities played a match in 1872 they used twenty men to a team. In 1875 representatives of a group of colleges met in New York City and drew up rules which all adopted. The following year Harvard students organized a football team using a form of soccer rules and challenged the students of several colleges in the United States. When none accepted, they challenged the students of McGill University of Montreal, Canada, who accepted the challenge, and the game was played in May, 1875. McGill was playing rugby rules, kicking, catching, and running with the ball, which were unfamiliar to the Harvard players. The Harvard men asked them to explain their rules, and the two teams agreed to play the first half of the game by McGill's rugby rules and the second half by Harvard's soccer rules. One year later (1876) Harvard and Yale played their first match with Yale the victor. The Harvard men asked the Yale students to play by some of McGill's rugby rules to which they consented. In that same year several colleges, not satisfied with the rules adopted in 1873, met in Springfield, Massachusetts, to revise and standardize the game. Upon the insistence of the Yale and Harvard delegates that some rugby rules be incorporated, the group acquiesced, and the following year (1877) they revised the rules again setting fifteen as the official number of players to a team.

Football was abolished at Harvard following a report by the president in 1885, stating that his investigating committee was "convinced that the game of football as at present played by college teams is demoralizing to player and spectators and extremely dangerous."

In 1890 playing between Yale and Harvard was revived, and that year Harvard won its first victory over Yale. This was a stupendous event with 20,000 at the game and a special train to bring in the "fans." The first professional football match was played at Latrobe, Pennsylvania, in 1895.

Swimming. From Frances Lieber's swimming school of 1825 grew the popularity of the "floating baths." It was in 1866, however, before Boston established its first baths and 1870 before New York City built their first of twenty-seven baths, five of which were in use up to 1904. Some of Boston's eleven floating pools and New York City's twenty-seven were for men and boys only, some for women and girls only, and some for both sexes but at different periods for each. Some had both deep and shallow pools for adults and children. Gradually, because of the changing sanitary conditions of the rivers, these pools changed to "fill and draw" type. Some converted to the use of city water and emptied into the rivers. Many of this type were in use as late as 1939.

Harvard University put in the second college pool in 1880, a wooden affair. The year 1885 brought the first YMCA pool (in Brooklyn) and the first municipal pool (in Philadelphia). These pools had no showers, no water sterilization, and no hot water. They were open only in the summer and with no instruction offered. About 1896 word came from Germany that the spread of diseases could be traced to swimming pools. In the nineties Milwaukee, Utica, San Francisco, Chicago, Newark, Brookline, and Boston put in municipal pools. Of these cities, San Francisco was the first to offer instruction and Milwaukee was the first to have its pool open all the year and to have warm water and showers. After

1896 showers became a common requirement for all pools. The size of these first pools ranged from 11½ to 150 feet in width and from 2C to 300 feet in length.

Tennis. Tennis came to America in 1874 and found a welcome among those who had seen the game in Europe and among the English descendants. Within a year the girls at Mt. Holyoke Female Seminary were playing the game. The Staten Island Cricket and Baseball Club was the first organization to give the sport any attention. At first the game was ridiculed as being fit only for frail girls and women. Nevertheless, a tournament was held in Philadelphia in 1880, and the next year the United States Lawn Tennis Association was organized.

Track and Field Sports. Scotch immigrants brought the "Caledonian games" to Boston in 1853, and from there they spread throughout the country until by the seventies they had become very popular. These games were the forerunners of today's track and field sports.

Other Sports. Badminton was first played in this country in 1878, softball was invented at the Farragut Club in Chicago in 1887, handball was first played in this country in 1888 with the first tournament put on by the Amateur Athletic Union in 1897; and volleyball was invented in 1896 by William Morgan, a YMCA physical director of Holyoke, Massachusetts. The first public golf courses were built in Boston, Indianapolis, and New York City around 1895, and the United States Golf Association was organized in 1894.

Women's Sports. As early as the eighties, Wellesley College had its crews and competitive rowing on the campus lake. In the nineties, women's colleges were engaging in a variety of sports.

In 1894, Miss Berenson, head of physical education at Smith College, modified the rules of basketball for girls, and her modified form spread rapidly throughout the country. Within the year the game had reached the Pacific Coast where it was primarily a girl's game until 1910 when boys, also, finally became interested in it.

Sports Clubs and Associations. To many educators and laymen as well, the poor physical condition of the soldiers drafted for the Civil War called for greatly increased sports in schools and national life. This gave impetus to the rise of sports and gave arguments in favor of physical education in the schools and colleges. Leagues of amateur and professional athletes, athletic clubs, Young Men's Christian Associations, and similar organizations contributed to the wave of enthusiasm and promoted athletic games and contests. This upsurge brought the first permanent amateur sports clubs and intercollegiate associations.

Amateur Sports Associations. By 1879 participation in sports had grown to such proportions that a need for standardization, control, and nation-wide promotion was felt, and the National Association of Amateur Athletes of America was organized. Its aims were to check the evils of professionalism, keep athletics on a respectable level, promote legitimate sports, define rules, and conduct competitions in an orderly and fair manner. From this organization developed the Amateur Athletic Union, which held its first meeting in 1888 in Detroit. With about 125 member clubs, it was completely reorganized in 1891, becoming a union of amateur athletic associations, rather than an organization of individual clubs.

Following the AAU's lead these organizations appeared: National Archery Association in 1879, with its first tournament in Chicago; Ski Club of Red Wing, Minnesota, in 1886; St. Andrews Golf Club of Yonkers, New York, in 1888 with a six-hole course; and the Amateur Fencing League of America in 1891.

Intercollegiate Sports Associations. The earliest intercollegiate associations were as follows: Intercollegiate Association of Amateur Athletes of America, organized to promote track and field sports, in 1875; Intercollegiate Football Association, organized by Pennsylvania, Harvard, and Columbia Universities in 1876; Intercollegiate Athletic Conference organized in New York City in 1883 as the first attempt at faculty control of college sports; the American Football Rules Committee, organized in 1893 to replace the old Intercollegiate Football Association of 1876; and in 1895, the Western Conference (now the Big Ten), organized when the presidents of the Universities of Chicago, Illinois, Michigan, Minnesota, Northwestern, Purdue and Wisconsin met and created the Intercollegiate Conference of Faculty Representatives.

Interscholastic Sports Associations. There was no control of high school sports until 1896 when a group of teachers in Wisconsin set up a committee to control their contests. Schools in the states of Michigan, Illinois, and Indiana soon followed suit. These efforts marked all that was done in this direction in the nineteenth century. Teachers, principals, and even janitors played on high school teams before organizations arose to control these sports.

Intercollegiate Athletics. Student interest in intercollegiate contests, which were first held in the 1820's, came to a head in the 1850's, and after the Civil War grew until in the 1880's they began to assume an important place in college life. As interest in gymnastics brought about the erection of gymnasiums so the interest in sports now brought about the building of athletic fields and stadiums. The first organized efforts at restrictions in college sports took place in this era. In 1882 a three-man faculty committee was set up at Harvard after faculty complaints that students were missing too much school work because of their games. Dr. Dudley A. Sargent, Director of Physical Education, was a member of the committee, and the following year he called a conference of other colleges for December, 1883, in New York City to consider faculty control of athletics. Nine colleges were represented at the meeting with three college presidents present.

In 1884 a committee representing twenty-two of the leading institutions attempted to secure the agreement of the college authorities to the following propositions: that athletic and gymnastic instructors shall be appointed by the faculty and not by the students; that college teams must be confined to games with college teams; that a standing committee of college representatives shall pass on the rules and regulations for conducting the contests; that no student may play on a team more than four years; and that games shall be held on college grounds only. These principles were not generally accepted.

With but little improvement in the contests, the President of Harvard University, following his earlier denunciations of 1885, again protested in 1894 and made proposals that stirred up great dissent among the students. The March issue of *Mind and Body* lists the three main proposals: no freshman to play in intercollegiate contests; no one to play in more than one contest a year; and intercollegiate contests to be held only once every two years. Following this, serious quarrels took place. Harvard University severed athletic relations with Yale University in 1894 and again in 1897, and with Princeton in 1897, and the U.S. Military and Naval Academies broke athletic relations with each other in 1893 and again in 1899.

But football was not the only sport used in intercollegiate contests in this era. As early as 1874 the first track and field intercollegiate meet was held at Saratoga, and the first intercollegiate swimming contest was held between Pennsylvania, Columbia, and Yale Universities in 1897.

Women's Sports Clubs and Demonstrations. As early as the eighties some women's sports clubs were in existence in the colleges. By 1890 several women's colleges had bicycling, boating, tennis, and walking clubs and were conducting their first tennis tournaments. By 1892 basketball clubs had put in their appearance. Bryn Mawr united its various sports clubs into one organization in 1891 thus giving birth to the first Woman's Athletic Association. In 1895 Mt. Holyoke was presented the gift of an ice-skating rink, and the students organized an ice-hockey club. *Mind and Body* of November, 1895, reports the first women's field day to be held in any college in the United States—at Vassar—roundly condemning this innovation.

In the last decade of the nineteenth century, gymnastics demonstrations and gymnastic-drill contests were very popular with women in all colleges.

19

ORGANIZED PHYSICAL EDUCATION IN THE LATTER NINETEENTH CENTURY

The discovery of gold in California in 1848 brought a sudden rush of people to the Pacific Coast. The Oregon and Santa Fe trails were developed, and the Conestoga wagon became the symbol of advancing America. At last the great territory west of the Mississippi River was being opened up to settlement. Besides the miners and professional Indian fighters and scouts who piloted the wagon trains across the wilderness, cowboys, too, became important in the national life, bringing to it not only their "broncho-busting" but also their own interpretation of the dances of the Tennessee and Kentucky mountain folk.

With the opening of the first transcontinental railroad in 1869, the settling of the west took on new speed. The church, failing to keep pace with the westward moving settlers, began to lose its hold, and play and dance were no longer looked upon as sin except in those communities settled by the Puritan stock itself pushing westward. Back in the East where pioneer days were now long since past, industrialization had set in, and great portions of the population, no longer engaged in farming, had become engaged, instead, in factory work, thus changing materially the physical development and recreational needs of the people.

EVENTS AFFECTING PHYSICAL EDUCATION

Civil War. The aftermath of the Civil War was as bad, if not worse, than the war itself. Particularly were conditions deplorable in the conquered South. Public schools and colleges in both the North and South were impoverished. Almost all educational work had to start anew. The libraries wherever they existed tried valiantly to fill the educational gap until schools could be re-established and teachers found to man them.

Military Drill in the Schools. In 1862 Congress passed the Morrill Act creating the land-grant colleges of which the Universities of Cornell, Purdue, and Illinois were the earliest. In order to secure the land as an endowment the schools had to agree to teach military tactics as a part of the regular course and to require it of all male students. Following this lead scores of other colleges and universities adopted military training, too, using it as a substitute for, rather than a supplement to, physical education. Moreover, during the Civil War the military leaders of the Union took note of the excellent training and discipline of the Southern troops and ascribed it to the numerous military academies of the South. This resulted in an irresistible movement to introduce military training in the schools of the North, as soon as the war was at an end. Also, reports of the poor physical condition of over a million men recruits from sixteen to forty-five years of age who were examined during the Civil War resulted in a renewed drive for military training in the schools sparked by leading military men and statesmen—a combination of influences that gave physical education a setback still felt in some schools at mid-twentieth century.

State Legislation. In 1866 California passed the first state physical education law. It required that physical exercise be given to pupils "as may be conducive to health and vigor of body as well as mind." From then on things rested until the State Teachers Associations, the American Association for the Advancement of Physical Education, and the turnvereins of Ohio and Pennsylvania threw their organizations back of efforts in several states to procure such laws. Ohio's efforts were the first to meet with success in this renewed effort. It got its law through in 1892, followed in 1899 by North Dakota.

STATUS OF PHYSICAL EDUCATION

Physical education, as well as education in general, was neglected during the Civil War, and the advocates of physical education had to wage battle anew on every front. It was an uphill battle against the military leaders who were working to introduce military training into the schools which, of course, tended to take the place of physical education. In the 1870's the argument of the day among educators was that of military drill versus gymnastics. Dr. Dudley A. Sargent (see p. 267), then head of physical education at Yale University, led the battle for gymnastics against the principals of the Boston schools, who held out for military drill. When Bowdoin College gave its students the privilege of voting between gymnastics and military drill for a requirement they stood almost unanimously for gymnastics.

The calisthenics of Catherine Beecher and Dio Lewis, popular just before the war, soon began to lose their hold. But the German system of gymnastics was still receiving increased attention in many parts of the country, and by the close of the century the Delsarte and Swedish systems had put in their appearance. Throughout the nineteenth century sports and athletics still had no place in the official school or college programs. They were recognized only as the students' own after-school projects.

The 1880's and 1890's brought a period of great expansion for physical education not only in the schools but also in nonschool organizations. Many gymnasiums were built, and the schools began to demand teachers who were professionally trained.

Although the formal physical education programs borrowed from the Europeans played a major role in schools during the second half of the nineteenth century, a new attitude toward physical education began to gain momentum. The desires of people for recreation, the popularity of organized field sports, college athletics, and a changing educational philosophy gave concern to the staunch proponents of the traditional formal program.

The office of the U.S. Commissioner of Education reported in 1891 on the status of physical training in the schools of 272 leading cities of the United States. The figures showed that 83 cities had a special director of physical education for the entire school system, 81 others required the schoolroom teacher to teach exercises, and 108 permitted teachers to offer exercises if they so wished: 10 per cent of the schools had established exercise programs before 1887, and of those offering physical education, 41 per cent used the German system of gymnastics; 29 per cent the Swedish system; 12 per cent the Delsarte system; and 18 per cent a combination of these. At this time there were reported to be 31 gymnasiums in the schools of eleven cities of the 272 investigated.

Elementary and Secondary School Programs. Gradually a physical education program was being accepted as a "must" and introduced into the large city schools. In 1867 the Board of Controllers of Philadelphia made provision in the budget for two or three well-trained physical-exercise teachers with the class work to begin in all primary and grammar grades the following year. The teachers were required "to devote ten minutes during the course of each school session to such physical exercises as the size of the room and other circumstances might permit." Two years later they established a second department of physical education with its own special teachers—this one in a girls' high school—the first department of physical education for girls in a public school in America.

Schools soon divided into two camps—those using the German system of gymnastics and those using the Swedish system—if, perchance, they offered a physical exercise program at all. Of course, a few schools departed from the pattern, but the great majority adopted one of these two systems. The development from the 1870's on is discussed under these two headings.

The great amount of physical activity which children undertook on their own during recess periods was, except in schools with unusual teachers who assumed responsibility "beyond the call of duty," completely unsupervised and beyond the scope of physical education. The recess periods were great fun with much physical activity wherever a few natural born leaders and a lot of lively children got together. But the timid and less venturesome were neglected, and the sort of citizenship training that came out of this play was dependent solely upon the naturally good leaders or the "bullies," as chance dictated, who would "rule the roost."

Adoption of the German System. The following cities established physical education in their schools using the German system: Milwaukee in 1876, Chicago and Kansas City in 1885, Davenport in 1887, Cleveland and St. Louis in 1888, Denver in 1889, and Dayton in 1892. Many other cities joined the movement in the late 1890's procuring their teachers from the Normal College of the American Gymnastic Union (NCAGU), which was the revived school started by the turners in Rochester, N. Y., just preceding the Civil War.

The story of the founding of the department in the Kansas City schools depicts the part played by the turners in the establishment of the system in the schools of America. Carl Betz (1854–98), a graduate of the four-month training course of the NCAGU, then located in Milwaukee, was appointed instructor in the Socialer Turnverein in Kansas City, Missouri, in 1885. That same year he accepted an invitation to demonstrate a class of girls in wand and club drills before the teachers' institute. His work was well received, and all agreed that something of that kind should be a part of the schoolwork. Betz offered to direct the exercises for a few months without pay in order to demonstrate their practicability. The school board accepted his offer, and before the end of the year (1885) he was employed as director of physical education of all the schools of Kansas City, which position he held until his death in 1898.

Adoption of the Swedish System. Dr. Hartwig Nissen (1856–1924) introduced the Swedish system of gymnastics to America when he came to Washington in 1883 as Vice-Consul for Norway and Sweden. Immediately upon his arrival in Washington he began to acquaint the physicians with the value of medical gymnastics and massage and opened the famous Swedish Health Institute. Among his "patients" were prominent men such as Benjamin Harrison and Ulysses S. Grant. Next he introduced Swedish gymnastics into the Franklin School and, in 1887, among students at Johns Hopkins University. When Baron Nils Posse (1862–95), the son of a prominent family of the Swedish nobility and a graduate of the Royal Central Institute of Gymnastics of Stockholm, arrived in America from Sweden in 1885 he first visited Nissen and then went to Boston in the hopes of establishing himself there in the practice of medical gymnastics.

Mrs. Mary Hemenway (1820–94), the widow of Boston's prosperous shipping merchant, was deeply interested in the advancement of education. Her son had given the magnificent Hemenway gymnasium to Harvard in 1879, and she was prepared to give financial aid to projects in behalf of the public schools. Seeing in Swedish gymnastics possibilities for bettering the health of school children, she offered to finance the teacher training of over a hundred teachers per year provided the school board would give Swedish gymnastics a place in the school program for all pupils on an experimental basis. They consented to the project, and Mrs. Hemenway provided the services of Posse to train the teachers. By 1890 over four hundred teachers were prepared to give instruction in the Swedish system. The superintendent thereupon ordered "that the Ling or Swedish system of educational gymnastics be introduced into all the public schools of this city." Dr. Edward Mussey Hartwell (see p. 270), formerly of Johns Hopkins University, was elected to the position of Director of Physical Training and began his duties in 1891. This was the first time the title of Director was granted by a public school system for the head of the physical education work. Following Boston's lead, many schools now adopted the Swedish system for their physical education programs.

Shortly Nissen was persuaded to come to Boston as Hartwell's assistant. Thus Swedish gymnastics gained a firm hold in the schools, particularly in the Boston area.

Adoption of Other Systems. In spite of all the flurry of excitement over the relative merits of German and Swedish gymnastics, some schools installed physical education programs built around exercises devised by their own teachers or composed of their own revamping of the calisthenics of Catherine Beecher and Dio Lewis or perhaps even using the Delsarte exercises which had become popular in the 1890's. And still other schools, particularly those in small towns, occasionally had teachers who had heard of exercise programs in the city schools and, wanting to give their pupils something but knowing nothing of any of these systems, contrived some drills that produced activity if not founded on anything of a scientific nature.

One "independent" of the period was Brooklyn, which set up its own school program in 1895 with Jessie H. Bancroft (see p. 333) responsible for organizing the work, which was carried on at first in a church. Miss Bancroft had received some training as a pupil of Sargent and at the Harvard Summer School of Physical Education, but she was, in a large measure, self-taught. She devised her own set of exercises and built up a program for all the schools of Brooklyn. Shortly she was given the official title of Director of Physical Education of Public Schools—the first woman in the United States to hold such a title.

Program in Girls' Schools. In the 1860's the female seminaries, all of which were of secondary school level except

Elmira, were adding physical education in some form to the curriculum. Miss Beecher renewed her campaign in behalf of physical education in these schools.

In the era preceding the Civil War the emphasis of the school physical activity program was on the cure of physical defects which were supposed to be brought on by too much study, whereas in this era it had become apparent that girls could stand the stress of attending school and needed, in physical education, not so much cure as prevention of ills.

Facilities, Requirements, and Staffs. Schools were slow in supplying gymnasiums. By the end of the century there was in Chicago but one elementary school that had a gymnasium although 205 principals were requesting them. However, seven of the fifteen high schools had gymnasiums; and the others used hallways for classes and had wands, dumbbells, and Indian clubs in racks on the walls. This was, no doubt, typical of the situation throughout the country.

By the end of the century many schools were requiring at least five minutes of exercise of each pupil daily or twenty minutes, two or three times a week, or a half-hour, two times a week. The most averaged fifty minutes per week. This was, indeed, quite the accepted requirement in those schools that had a program at all.

In Chicago, typical of conditions in large cities, there was only one special physical education teacher assigned to an elementary school, but there were seven other specialized teachers to supervise the physical education work given by the regular classroom teacher in the other elementary schools. These handled 30,000 pupils in thirty-four schools. Each school was visited three or four times a year by a supervisor, and those schools where the hallways were outfitted with the exercise equipment were visited as often as every four or six weeks. In the seven high schools with gymnasiums each had a special teacher of "physical culture."

Physical Education For College Men. With the close of the Civil War, physical education began to develop in earn-

est in many colleges. Dr. Edward Hitchcock, at Amherst
College, was setting the example for all other schools. By
now the students there were having intramural athletics,
but Hitchcock was firm in his denounciation of "hot and
violent contests with professional gamesters," and he gave
but lukewarm acquiescence to games with other colleges.
Early in his work there he had instituted corrective work
for those needing it.

In the early 1870's, Sargent established a physical education program at Bowdoin College as he, himself, pursued
work for the bachelor's degree. He gave all the boys free
exercises varying the program the Freshman year with dumbbells, the Sophomore year with Indian clubs, the Junior year
with chest weights, and the Senior year with wands and
pulley weights—training in all of which he had "picked
up on his own." All gymnasium classes were dismissed in
the spring for military drill so Sargent went to Yale University each spring from 1872 on, and established a program
for that college while he pursued his medical studies. In
1875 the Yale authorities gave the students their choice for
requirement between Greek and gymnastics, and all but two
selected the latter. William Howard Taft, then a student
at Yale, destined later to become President of the United
States, was one who elected gymnastics, and he became one
of the class leaders.

Program At Harvard University. The Hemenway Gymnasium, costing $110,000, was ready for occupancy in 1879
replacing the old gymnasium of 1859. At that time Sargent
was appointed to take charge of the physical education work
with the title of Assistant Professor of Physical Training and
Director of the Hemenway Gymnasium. He relates in his
Autobiography that many faculty members considered the
new gymnasium as a vast waste of money and resented having a college graduate placed in charge of physical education
—work which they considered unworthy of a college-trained
man. Sargent was charged with the task of equipping the
new building, determining the policy of the department,

and arranging the work. Believing that the difference in the physical make-up and physical needs of the students was too great to allow uniformity of exercise he began building a program around the individual needs of the students. He took bodily measurements of all students and also gave them strength tests which he devised. Then he prescribed exercises for each, using the many different pieces of apparatus which he invented to meet specific physical developmental needs. For many years he worked on his mechanical contrivances which came to be called "Sargent machines." They included foot, ankle, wrist, leg, and back machines, rowing and lifting machines, chest expanders, chest weights, quarter circles, and short and long inclined planes. He also used some German and some Swedish apparatus, and, at the same time, he developed a more detailed system of measurements than was being used at Amherst College. His studies along that line added greatly to anthropometric knowledge.

Program in Other Colleges. It was a full half-century before other schools caught up with Hitchcock at Amherst and Sargent at Harvard. Of the private coeducational colleges Oberlin was the first to establish a department of physical education (1885). Of the state universities the University of Wisconsin offered the first classes in physical education (1870), although this date does not mark the establishment of a department. The following list shows dates for the actual establishment of departments in state universities:

1888–California	1891–Nebraska	1894–Michigan
1890–Wisconsin	1893–Utah	1896–Minnesota
1890–Texas	1893–Illinois	1897–Ohio State
1891–Indiana	1894–Kansas	1899–Iowa
	1894–Washington	

Facilities. Many gymnasiums were erected after the Civil War, starting with the Dartmouth building of 1867 which cost $24,000. Following that Princeton replaced its earlier red shack with a $38,000 "gym," the finest of its day. Bowdoin's gymnasium had no heat, and the men dressed for class even in zero weather, changing to cotton shirts and tights and cloth slippers. Jersies and woolen sweaters were unheard of as yet.

In 1870 the University of Wisconsin built a $4,000 gymnasium (the first state university to build one). The Yale gymnasium of 1875 had eight long bathtubs lined with zinc, which the students used only on payment of a special fee.

Fig. 9. Harvard University: Hemenway Gymnasium (1885) (Leonard and Affleck, *A Guide to the History of Physical Education*, Courtesy of Lea & Febiger)

Then 1879 brought the wonder gymnasium of the age—Harvard's $110,000 Hemenway gymnasium—followed in 1878 by the University of California's modest $12,000 Harmon Gymnasium. During the sixties and seventies many colleges that could not afford gymnasiums fitted up vacant rooms as drill halls.

Staffs. Yale University listed in the catalog an instructor in physical training for the school year 1860–61 and again in 1867 through 1872. In 1867 Harvard University named as its first teacher of gymnastics a pro-boxing teacher—a mulatto. Although listed as "Instructor and Curator of

Gymnasium," his name was not included in the list of regular faculty members. Amherst College gave Hitchcock the faculty status of Professor from the date of his first appointment. Later Harvard University conferred upon Sargent the rank of Assistant Professor. But in most colleges the earliest appointees to be placed in charge of the gymnasium were ex-prize fighters, weight-lifters, and janitors. At this time there were no schools in the United States preparing teachers of physical education.

Salaries. As to salaries, Sargent was paid $5 per week when he first went to Bowdoin College in 1869. Two years later the salary was raised to $500 per year. In 1872 he was paid $50 a week at Yale University on special assignment. In 1875 he asked Bowdoin for $1200 per year from which he would pay the janitor and his assistants, purchase the apparatus needed, and pay all other expenses except heat, light, and building repairs. The college refused this salary request, and he resigned.

Physical Education For College Women. As a rule physical education fared better in this era in the women's colleges than in coeducational schools. From their very founding the women's colleges offered physical activity classes to their students while in most coeducational schools such classes came most belatedly long after the establishment of the schools.

First Departments of Physical Education. Vassar was the first college in the United States to offer physical activity classwork for women as a part of the school program. This was in 1868. Mt. Holyoke and Rockford Colleges had been offering work since 1837 and 1849 respectively, but neither achieved collegiate rating before the 1880's. Oberlin was the first college to organize a department of physical education for women (1885); Goucher was the first of the women's colleges to organize a department (1889); Oberlin was the first to name a woman as the head of physical education for women and to give her recognition as such in the college catalog.

Program. The core of the college program for women was calisthenics or gymnastics with some sports hanging on as fringe activities without official college sanction. Mt. Holyoke College added to its requirement in calisthenics a daily walk of one mile in good weather and a three-quarter-hour walk in bad weather. The Dio Lewis system of gymnastics was the favored form for college women in the 1860's; in the early 1880's most women's colleges changed to the Sargent system; in 1888 Goucher College took up the Swedish system, and all the other women's colleges except Vassar swung over to this system, also; in 1890 Elmira and Rockford Colleges adopted the Delsarte system; but not one of the women's colleges accepted the German system.

The programs for women in coeducational colleges followed somewhat the pattern set by the women's colleges but the men's programs and men teachers on the same campus introduced forms of activities and a type of emphasis on methods and philosophy that differed somewhat from that originating in the women's colleges. The story of the beginnings of a department of physical education for women in a coeducational school during this era will illustrate the point. In the late 1880's, at the University of Nebraska, a group of women students urged the Military Department to give them military drill, and this it consented to do provided the girls would be content to drill indoors. In 1891, Wilbur P. Bowen (1864–1928), a mathematics teacher at Michigan State Normal School, was brought to the University to set up the Department of Physical Education for Men. The women pleaded so persistently for classwork, too, that Bowen and the new Commandant of the ROTC—Lt. John J. Pershing, recently graduated from West Point, who had, also, come to the university faculty in the fall of 1891—decided to do something about it. Pershing offered to teach the girls fencing and marching and Bowen to teach them dumbbell exercises and Indian-club swinging.

At the insistence of Pershing, who felt strongly that "ladies" should not be doing military drill at all and that in their physical activities they should be taught by a woman rather than a man, the Chancellor finally capitulated and the next school year (1892–93) he employed a local woman, Anne Barr, who had learned some Indian-club swinging at the local YMCA, to take over classwork for the women students on an hour-pay basis. Becoming interested in her teaching, Miss Barr went to the Chautauqua School of Physical Education the following summer and there began actual professional training for the position which she held for several years—first as Directress of the Women's Gymnasium and later as Director of Physical Education for Women at the University of Nebraska. Very soon physical education became a requirement of all young women for the first two years with four hours a week of activity and one of hygiene. Thus did women's physical education work get started in one state university. The story is, no doubt, typical of those of many other colleges.

Facilities. In the women's colleges, physical education classwork got under way in this period by using the out of doors, corridors, assembly halls, and store rooms. One school used a privately owned gymnasium in the local community—Radcliffe at Sargent's gymnasium. Vassar was the only college that started its physical education work with a special building constructed for the work. In 1860 it built a "Hall for Calisthenics" with footprints painted on the floor to indicate where students should stand during their exercise periods. Mt. Holyoke had a gymnasium by 1865 that cost $1900; Smith College, by 1875; Bryn Mawr, by 1885; Goucher, by 1888; and Mills College, by the end of the century.

The coeducational colleges lagged far behind the women's colleges in procuring facilities for women students. As a rule the women were permitted to use the men's facilities on occasion, and in many schools some large room in the women's dormitory was set aside for a women's gymnasium.

Goucher College constructed the first swimming pool for women in 1888, although it did not list swimming as an activity for students until 1904; Vassar built the second pool in 1889; Smith installed a "swimming bath" in 1892 which could be used by two to five students at a time and was used for over thirty years; Bryn Mawr built its pool in 1894, and by the end of the century Radcliffe College had built one. There were no pools for women or men in any coeducational college or coeducational university of this era.

Costumes. In 1865 the special costume which the Vassar College girls wore for gymnastics work was of gray flannel with the blouse high-necked and long-sleeved and the skirt anklelength with bloomers underneath. Elmira College girls in 1872 wore a costume of black alpaca, lined throughout, with a "Garabaldi" waist and a skirt reaching to within ten inches of the floor with Turkish drawers underneath with elastic leg-binding and falling to the length of the skirt, with skirt and blouse trimmed in scarlet "Gilbert opera flannel."

By the 1880's shorter costumes appeared with dark divided skirt reaching only to the knee at the leg binding and with deep folds of the material curving down well below the knee and caught up by the binding underneath. Amelia Bloomer, the champion of dress reform for women, unwittingly supplied the name for the newfangled gymnastic costume.

Staffs. Physical education in these early years was taught by teachers of other subjects who read a book or two on exercise and, from this, undertook to teach calisthenics or some dance-type activity called "fancy steps." As early as 1862 the Mt. Holyoke College catalog listed a teacher of calisthenics. The Smith College prospectus of 1874 announced that "regular gymnastic exercises in the gymnasium will be prescribed under the direction of an educated lady physician."

In the 1860's and 1870's women's departments were able to procure pupils of Dio Lewis who offered the first teacher-training in physical education to women in America. Later the Sargent School of Physical Education, the Harvard Summer School of Physical Education, and the Boston Normal School of Gymnastics opened, and from then on practically all women teachers of physical education in colleges with the exception of those who "just picked it up" came from these three schools. At some state universities instructors in elocution and oratory taught the first "physical culture" classes to be offered to women. Oberlin, the first coeducational college to appoint a woman to teach physical education, selected Dr. Delphine Hanna (see p. 272), a graduate of the Sargent School, for the position in 1885. Two years later she was given the title, Director of Physical Education. Following that Goucher College appointed a physical education teacher from the Central Gymnastic Institute of Stockholm. Mt. Holyoke had two women teachers with the Ph.D. degree teaching gymnastics along with their special subjects, most obviously women not trained in this field. However, when these women teachers of academic subjects no longer taught gymnastics "on the side" and women trained in the field did come upon the scene, it was several decades before a Ph.D. degree again graced the women's physical education ranks. No woman physical education teacher in any women's college received recognition in academic rank of any sort in the nineteenth century. The coeducational colleges were more advanced in this respect.

Research. This period was one of great interest in anthropometric testing, which started in the United States with Hitchcock's work at Amherst College in 1861. From the very start, he used data from eight items in his research work: age, weight, height, chest girth, arm girth, forearm girth, lung capacity, and pull-up. For forty years he published, annually, anthropometric tables of Amherst men, which fill two large volumes of material. In 1873 Sargent, then a young medical student at Yale, started work on strength tests and later as a teacher at Harvard University started work on his own tests to try out ideas of methods of physical development. From 1880 to 1886 he collected data of Harvard men for his anthropometric charts. Following this lead charts were made from the measurements of Yale men and YMCA men from 25 to 35 years of age while research into the anthropometric measurements of women was carried on principally at Wellesley and Oberlin Colleges and the University of Nebraska.

In 1890 the first athletic achievement test was born— the Pentathlon test of the Athletic League of the YMCA's of America devised by Dr. Luther H. Gulick. This is the earliest record of the use of elements of sports and games as test forms. It was the forerunner of many such tests which, at the turn of the century, so markedly motivated the promotion of physical education in the schools. As developed further in the early 1900's by Gulick for the Public School Athletic League of New York City, these tests consisted of throwing for accuracy and speed, running for speed, and jumping for distance.

Teacher Training. In an address on *Female Suffrage* given in 1870 in the Music Hall of Boston, Catherine Beecher made a public appeal for trained teachers of physical education for girls in which she said:

> The department of the physical training of all the institutions should be committed to a woman of good practical common sense, of refined culture and manners and one expressly educated for this department. By the aid of both parents and teachers, she would study the constitution and habits of every pupil, and administer a method of training to develop healthfully every organ and function, and to remedy every defect in habits, person, voice, movements, and manners.

At that time, however, there were only two schools in the United States offering teacher training work in physical education, both offering at first only a two months course. (Some claim that the Dio Lewis school offered a ten months course from its very beginnings.) By the time other schools had been established in the 1880's the curriculum was fairly well established as a seven months course. Gradually it grew to a ten months course and by the 1890's all schools offered at least two years of training. Although normal schools for the training of teachers of physical education had opened in Stockholm in 1814, in Dresden in 1850, and in Berlin in 1851, this era marked the real beginnings of professional training in physical education in America.

From the early 1860's to the close of the nineteenth century thirty-four normal schools of physical education were established. None, however, was of collegiate rank. In the school year of 1897–98, 192 graduates of these schools were teaching in the public schools across the land, some teaching the German, some the Swedish, some the military, and some the Delsarte system. The more notable of these schools in the order of their founding were: 1861, Dio Lewis Normal Institute of Physical Education in Boston, which did not carry over into this era; 1861, The Normal School of the American Gymnastic Union in Rochester, New York; 1881, the Sargent School of Physical Education in Cambridge; 1886, the Brooklyn Normal School of Physical Education; 1887, the Harvard Summer School of Physical Education, and the YMCA International Training School in Springfield; 1888, the Chautauqua Summer School of Physical Education; 1889, the Boston Normal School of Gymnastics; 1890, the Posse School of Physical Education in Boston, and the Chicago YMCA Training School; and 1898, the New York Normal School of Physical Education, later known as The Savage School.

Normal College of the American Gymnastic Union. The Civil War disrupted the teacher training work started by the German turners in the school which they established in Rochester, New York, in 1861. With the conclusion of the war the school was re-established in New York City. In 1869 it was moved to Chicago with George Brosius (see p. 276), one of the foremost leaders of the turner movement, as one of the teachers. Forced to close because of the great fire in Chicago, the school moved again to New York City in 1872, and then in 1875 it moved to Milwaukee where it remained throughout the rest of the nineteenth century except for a two-year interval (1889–91) when it was located temporarily in Indianapolis.

During these years the course had been lengthened to require ten months of study, and it included the history and literature of physical education, anthropology, anatomy, physiology, hygiene, first aid, principles of education, the German and English language and literature, fencing, swimming, observation, and practice teaching. Graduates of this school taught in public schools throughout the country although most located in the Middle West.

Sargent School of Physical Education. Dr. Sargent, having become head of physical education at Harvard University, was so importuned by young women of the town of Cambridge and of Radcliffe College who desired some training in the art of teaching exercises, and by heads of schools who desired teachers trained to teach his type of exercises rather than the German system, that he took over an old carriage house, converted it into a gymnasium, and set up such a course in 1881. He offered the courses at first gratis with the stipulation that the students would actually go out to teach. At that time most people felt that if they knew a dumbbell drill, a few exercises with Indian clubs and a list of chest-weight exercises they were really professionally trained in physical education. By 1891 he had thirty pupils, and the course had developed into a thirty-two week session for a $100.00 fee. Then he extended the course to a two-year course, the attendance doubled, and the school took on the title, Sargent School of Physical Education.

Brooklyn Normal School of Physical Education. The Brooklyn Normal School of Physical Education was founded in 1886 by Dr. William G. Anderson (see p. 274), then Physical Director at Adelphi Academy in Brooklyn. When Anderson became Associate Director of the Yale University Gymnasium in 1892, the normal school was moved to New Haven and renamed the Anderson Normal School of Gymnastics.

Harvard Summer School of Physical Education. Dr. Sargent obtained permission from Harvard University in 1887 to offer a summer course in teacher training, open to

women as well as men. In his *Autobiography,* he relates
that, although Harvard was not too happy about opening
classes to women and the granting of teacher's certificates,
the authorities finally gave permission providing he would
assume all financial responsibility for the project. So intense
was the local feeling against Harvard's being a party to such
a venture that Radcliffe College discouraged its students
from attending the course and the *Boston Medical and Surgeon's Journal* opposed it and denounced Harvard for allow-
ing such a course. In spite of the initial storm of criticism
the summer school prospered and carried on for thirty-one
years under Sargent's expert direction. The very first session was so successful financially because of the unexpect-
edly large enrollment of fifty pupils that, beginning with the
second session, Harvard officials took it over, relieved Sargent of the burden of collecting the fees and paying the bills,
and named him Director of the Summer School of Physical
Education, with salary.

YMCA International Training School. The YMCA International Training School was founded in 1885. Two years
later it set up a two-year teacher-training course in physical
education with Dr. Gulick at its head. In 1888, Robert J.
Roberts (see p. 276), who had just completed twelve years of
highly successful work as the director of the gymnasium of
the Boston YMCA, joined the teaching staff. In 1895 Dr.
James Huff McCurdy (see p. 335), Director of Physical Education, New York City YMCA, succeeded Gulick in the
directorship of the physical education training department
and extended the course to three years.

In 1886 the YMCA opened the Western YMCA Secre-
tarial Institute in Chicago and four years later added a
summer course for the training of teachers of physical education under the auspices of the Springfield School. That
same year the Institute was incorporated as the YMCA
Training School of Chicago offering a two-year course.

Chautauqua Summer School of Physical Education. The
Chautauqua Summer School of Physical Education was the

second school to be founded by Anderson. He established it in 1888. In the 1890's and early 1900's the school enjoyed much popularity among teachers seeking refresher courses in a summer-resort setting as well as among teachers seeking help so that they might handle "gym" classes along with their other work.

Boston Normal School of Gymnastics. Mrs. Mary Hemenway, the Boston philanthropist, founded the Boston Normal School of Gymnastics in 1889. It should not be confused with the Boston Normal School, which is an older school established to train teachers in the field of general education. Mrs. Hemenway installed her secretary, Amy Morris Homans (see p. 265) as the Director of the school. In 1891 it graduated its first class of twelve from its two-year course. Two years later it graduated forty-three with thirty others receiving a one-year certificate. The starting salary of these graduates ranged from $1,000 to $1,800, considered excellent in those days.

From the beginning, the school maintained a distinguished faculty, numbering in its ranks in its earliest days the Professor of Philosophy of Harvard, the Dean of Harvard Medical School, and the Professor of Biology of Massachusetts Institute of Technology. Continuously until the school merged with Wellesley College in 1909 there were Harvard and Massachusetts Institute of Technology professors and heads of departments on the staff on a part-time basis, and, even after the transfer of the school to Wellesley College near Boston, many of these teachers were retained as special lecturers.

In its second year the school increased its staff and expanded its curriculum to include general anatomy, applied anatomy and physiology, histology, hygiene, and supervised teaching in the public schools of Boston. In the third year it added anthropometry, emergencies, general psychology, pedagogy, and voice training. To augment the activity program it added dance. In its fifth year it added to the curriculum physics, chemistry, comparative anatomy, embryology, and sanitation, all taught by Massachusetts Institute of Technology professors.

Colleges and Universities. Besides the private normal schools, one private coeducational college (Oberlin) in the 1880's and six state universities—Indiana in 1892, Washington in 1896, California and Nebraska in 1897, Illinois in 1898, and Wisconsin in 1899—started to offer courses to prepare students to teach physical activities along with their major subjects. But it was not until the fall of 1897 that the first opportunity came actually to specialize in the field in college. In that year both the universities of California and Nebraska offered a special professional-training curriculum now known as a major in physical education. Two years later (1899) Oberlin College combined its various isolated courses in teacher training and set up a 20-unit curriculum in specialization.

The University of Nebraska course carried a 28-hour requirement of specialization, and, in the spring of 1900, the first students taking the course were graduated—two young women—who thereby became the first women students in the United States to receive a college degree with specialization in physical education. In 1902 Oberlin College graduated their first women physical education majors.

Nonschool Organizations. Several forces were at work in the last half of the nineteenth century to bring physical education to all the people. In the era preceding this, the turners and the YMCA got their start. Now the Sokols and the YWCA's join the other groups in offering physical education to other citizens.

North American Gymnastic Union. The 150 turner societies with their 10,000 members of prewar days and their Normal School at Rochester, New York, had been disbanded while the men fought in the Union army. Now with the Civil War at an end the NAGU was revived, and by 1872 there were 187 societies functioning. Before the 1880's little was known about the work of the turnverein in America outside German-American circles. The membership of the

societies and the participation in the turnfests were confined to those of German origin. The German language
was used, to a great extent, in all the activities, and no effort
was made to interest other Americans in the educational,
social, or gymnastic work. Throughout their history the
turnverein met with vigorous hostility in some communities,
for the turners were abolitionists, free-soilers, and opponents
of prohibition. They fought all foes of progress, the moneyed
aristocracy, and the church.

During the 1880's their membership grew to 36,000 in 277
societies. They now began agitation for physical education
in the public schools and contributed moral and financial
support, material, publications, and leadership to that end.
In some communities they purchased apparatus and placed
it in the school yards. Some served as teachers free of
charge in order to convince reluctant school boards of the
value of their work. Their normal college demanded that
its graduates be able to give instruction in the English
language, that they might be prepared to enter the schools.

From 1881 on, the turner societies held turnfests every
four or five years with from 1,200 to 3,400 participants in the
competition. At the World's Fair in Chicago, 1893, they
gave daily exhibitions of their work and distributed thousands of pamphlets. In 1894 the organization began publication of a monthly periodical, *Mind and Body*.

Sokols. Bohemians, as well as Germans, came to the
United States in large numbers in this era, and the gymnastic enthusiasts among them organized Sokol clubs which
are similar to the German turnverein—democratic, patriotic
organizations for the practice of voluntary discipline aimed
at both moral and physical fitness. The first American
Sokol was established in St. Louis, Missouri, in 1865. Never
as numerous as the German immigrants, the Bohemians did
not become so widely known although the first of them came
to America with the earliest Dutch settlers, having fled to
Holland to escape religious persecution. The late-comers
of the nineteenth century settled mainly in the Middle West

and there enthusiastically pursued their physical activities —gymnastics, folk dancing, and sharpshooting.

Young Men's Christian Association. The wave of athletics and gymnastics which swept the country during the 1850's began to influence the Young Men's Christian Association. At their 1860 convention they favored the formation of gymnastics and athletics as a "safeguard against the allurement of objectionable places of resort." In 1866 the president of the New York City YMCA, proposed a four-fold program—physical, mental, social and spiritual—which was adopted. By 1869 the first buildings equipped with gymnasiums were erected in New York, San Francisco, and Washington, D.C. with Boston's building coming in 1872. In 1885 the Brooklyn Central Branch put in the first YMCA pool.

Until their school at Springfield, Massachusetts, began turning out teachers for the YMCA's, they had to resort to the use of circus performers and professional athletes as part-time teachers. In 1886, Gulick became National YMCA Physical Director, and in 1887 a department of teacher training in physical education was added to the Training School, and a summer course was inaugurated as a refresher for those already teaching. Also, an International Committee was established to supervise the physical education work in the YMCA's over the country with Gulick serving as head of this supervisory work.

The 1890's brought historic events to the YMCA. In 1890 Gulick devised the YMCA equilateral triangle known today the wide world over. In 1891 and 1896 the games of basketball and volleyball were developed in YMCA's as previously discussed, and in 1896 the Athletic League of the YMCA's of North America was founded.

By 1900, the YMCA had 294 physical directors and 22 assistant directors for 491 gymnasiums with nearly 80,000 men and 20,000 boys registered in their classes.

Young Women's Christian Association. The Young Women's Christian Association was established in the United

States in this era. In 1882 the first association, which was established in Boston, set aside a nearby park for calisthenic classes and installed chest weights in the hallway of the building with a girl member of the association leading in classwork in these activities. Two years later Boston erected a new building which was the first YWCA in the country to include a gymnasium as part of the facilities, and, in 1887, the first classes in calisthenics were offered using a combination of Dio Lewis and Delsarte work.

In 1886 a national association of YWCA's was organized at a conference at Lake Geneva in Wisconsin, and in 1891 the eleventh conference created the International Board of YWCA's to send general secretaries and physical education teachers to YWCA's all over the world.

The physical education program generally in the 1890's consisted of Indian-club swinging, dumbbell drills, wand drills, "esthetic marching," and basketball. As early as 1895 the latter had become a very popular activity in the YWCA.

Movements Related to Physical Education. Although the great mass of the population still worked long hours all six week days and had but little leisure themselves, a concern was growing in this era for the welfare of children in their out-of-school periods. Out of this concern developed two important movements which America has given to the world —the recreation and the camping movements.

Recreation Movement. As happened in so many movements in America which were for the enrichment of life, it was Boston, with its sand gardens, that started the ball rolling in the development of the playground and recreation movement. Brookline near Boston was the first town to vote public funds for a playground. This was in 1872. Chicago, in 1876, opened the first public park in America (the present Washington Park) and offered recreational facilities although without supervision. Boston in 1888 designated seven school yards as playgrounds and the following year added eleven more to these, all open to children of all ages. Also, in 1888, New York City opened its school buildings in the evenings for recreational use by the citizens, and, in 1889, Boston established several so-called "outdoor gymnasiums" for older boys and men to take care of leisure hours brought on by the shortened workday. A few years later sections were set aside in the parks for older girls and women.

Citizens of New York organized The Outdoor Recreation League and secured from the municipal government an appropriation of about $30,000 with which twenty school yards were operated as play centers. The city then began the purchase and equipping of tracts of land at a very great cost. Seward Park alone cost $2,500,000. Jacob A. Riis, the leader of the Anti-Slum Movement to get children off the city streets and Secretary of the Committee on Small Parks, did more than any other person to secure adequate space for play in New York City. He was identified with the playground movement throughout his life.

The playground system of Chicago began with a vacant-lot play center managed by Hull House in 1893. Six years later New York City opened several school yard playgrounds modelled after that of Hull House, and the establishment of this type of facility quickly spread to all other parts of the country. Ten cities set up playgrounds between 1890 and 1900. In nearly all the cities the work was begun by philanthropic and humanitarian organizations; in some cases the city gave financial support, and in some it gave no encouragement whatever. The playground movement was definitely identified with the anti-slum and the social service movement.

Camping Movement. Although the camping movement got an actual start when the head of the Gunnery School for Boys in Washington, Connecticut, took the boys on a camping expedition in 1861, it did not develop into a movement until after the Civil War. The first private camp was established in 1876, the first church camp in 1880, and the first YMCA camp in 1885. The YMCA camp, Camp Dudley, is the only one of the early camps still in existence; hence it is today the oldest camp in America.

The first private camp—a boy's camp on Burnt Island on Asquan Lake near Holderness, New Hampshire—was established for the specific purpose of meeting educational needs of young boys of well-to-do families who were wont to idle away their time at summer resorts with their parents. This first camp started with a program built largely around physical activities, thus setting the pattern conformed to by the camps that followed and establishing for the camping movement objectives closely akin to those of physical education itself.

Professional Literature. Literature in the field of physical education began to increase materially in this era. For the first time not only books but periodicals and reports of surveys became available from the presses of the United States and from local authors. No longer were workers in the field of physical education dependent almost solely on foreign publications.

Books. Over twenty books achieved prominence in this period. Foremost among them were: William Blaikie, *How to Get Strong and How to Stay So* (1879), which influenced several who later became prominent leaders to take up the study of physical education and which, highly popular in both Europe and the United States, ran in many editions up to 1902; DuBois-Reymond, *Physiology of Exercise* (1885), translation of Berlin edition published in *Popular Science Monthly;* Robert J. Roberts, *Classified Gymnasium Exercises* (1889); Nils Posse, *The Special Kinesiology of Educational Gymnastics* (1890); Claës J. Enebuske, *Progressive Gymnastic Day's Orders According to the Principles of the Ling System* (1890), which sold over 5,000 copies; *Basketball Rules,* first edition mimeographed (1894); Dr. Jay W. Sceaver, *Anthropometry and Physical Examinations* (1896); and Senda Berensen, *Basketball Rules for Girls,* first edition mimeographed (1899).

Periodicals. As in the period preceding the Civil War there were several periodicals that frequently contained articles on physical education activities, but none were in any sense periodicals of the profession. But in the 1880's there appeared the *Reports of the Proceedings* of the annual conventions of the American Association for the Advancement of Physical Education covering ten years from 1885 to 1895. Then in the 1890's came an awakening, and four professional magazines burst upon the professional scene: *Physical Education* (March, 1892–July, 1896), in four volumes with Gulick as editor (preceding this he started a YMCA magazine called *The Triangle* in June, 1891, which carried much of interest to physical education); *Posse Gymnastic Journal*, which started with the issue of December, 1892, and ran for ten years after Posse's death in 1895 still carrying articles supposedly written by him; *Mind and Body*, published by the North American Gymnastic Union, starting with the March, 1894, issue; and *The American Physical Education Review*, the official organ of the AAAPE starting in the fall of 1896 with Hartwell as "Chairman of the Magazine." It was issued quarterly from 1896 through 1907.

As to the first magazine, there is some confusion. Careful scrutiny of the four volumes of *Physical Education* gives no clue as to what organization, if any, backed this magazine. There is not even the mention of the editor's name, but Gulick's biographer states that he edited a magazine named *Physical Education*. It may have been the private venture of Gulick alone or of him and a group of his friends. The subscription price was $1.00 a year, and it was published by the Triangle Publishing Company of Springfield, Massachusetts. It listed an Advisory Committee made up of the profession's most distinguished leaders of that day. Hartwell was in charge of the Current Topics Department, and G. Stanley Hall, America's leading psychologist, was a frequent contributor.

Apparently the sponsorship of this magazine puzzled the people of that day for the editorial in the April, 1895, issue says:

Our Purpose. There are some of our readers who have received the impression that this magazine was, or desired to give the impression that it was the official organ of the physical education department of the International Committee of the YMCA. We wish to state clearly that *Physical Education* is not the official organ of any body whatsoever, neither the International Committee Association Training School at Springfield, Massachusetts, nor American Association for Advancement of Physical Education. It stands merely for a subject—Physical Training—in its relation to the development of all-round character for manhood and womanhood.

Why a magazine backed by so illustrious a group lasted but four years is a puzzle these sixty-odd years later. The story may have died with the passing of the last of this group, Anderson, in 1947. (Issues of some of these early magazines are available in microcard from the School of Physical Education, University of Oregon. They make interesting reading.)

20

ORGANIZATIONS AND LEADERS OF
THE LATTER NINETEENTH CENTURY

Although general educators had, before the Civil War, formed organizations to pool their interests and ideas and to promote educational standards and objectives, there was not a sufficient number of physical educators nor was there a profession of physical education sufficiently recognized to warrant such organizations in the physical education field until in the 1880's. By then a goodly body of leaders had developed, and professional organizations arose out of their coming together for mutual aid.

PROFESSIONAL ORGANIZATIONS

The American Association for the Advancement of Physical Education. The national group known today as the American Association for Health, Physical Education and Recreation was founded November 17, 1885, as the American Association for the Advancement of Physical Education. The organization meeting was called by Dr. W. G. Anderson, then a young teacher at Adelphi College in Brooklyn, who earlier approached various influential persons interested in the advancement of physical education and found them enthusiastic over the idea of a meeting. It was a gathering of distinguished persons such as the Reverend Henry Ward Beecher, William Blaikie, the New York City attorney who had written the popular book, *How to Get Strong,* and leading educators, physicians, and newspaper men of New York City and Brooklyn besides the best known physical education teachers of the day. At its organization meeting forty-nine members joined. At the second meeting (the first convention) in 1886, enough others joined to bring the membership to 114. At the ninth annual convention held at Yale University in 1894, professional members were listed from California, Canada, Illinois, Iowa, Louisiana, Missouri, Oregon, and Wisconsin, as well as from all the eastern states.

In 1895 at its tenth annual convention held at Teachers College, Columbia University, in New York City it voted to reorganize along the lines of the North American Turnerbund. At the same time it named Boston as the national headquarters and for the first time accepted representatives of a district as members of the national council (the Eastern District).

The destinies of the organization were in most capable hands. Five men served as president in the first fifteen years to the close of the nineteenth century—first, Dr. Edward Hitchcock, of Amherst College; then William Blaikie, the New York City attorney (the only president in the history of the organization who was not working in the field of physical education); and Drs. Dudley A. Sargent of Harvard University, Edward M. Hartwell of Johns Hopkins University and the Boston public schools, and Jay W. Seaver of Yale University. Dr. Anderson, the founder of the organization, served as the first Secretary-Treasurer. Photographs of all presidents from 1885 through 1932 except two are shown in the *Journal of Health and Physical Education* of January, 1932. Also, all from 1885 through 1957 are listed with their years of service in the Appendix of this book.

This infant organization was destined to become the largest department of the National Education Association. By the close of the nineteenth century it was well on its way.

In 1895 professional workers in New England were called together at Clark University, and at that meeting the Physical Education Society of New England was organized as a combined several-state section of AAAPE. At this organization meeting G. Stanley Hall of Clark University addressed the group, and Sargent gave an illustrated lecture. This marked the first effort to organize by districts. In that same year the leaders of Ohio organized the first State Association of AAAPE.

Society of College Gymnasium Directors. In October, 1897, Anderson and Hartwell called all men college directors of physical education who were not using the German or Swedish systems exclusively in their work to come together to talk over where America stood in regard to gymnastics. Twenty-three directors responded to the invitation and they founded the Society of College Gymnasium Directors, which through the years has wielded strong influence in physical education in the United States. This organization is known today as the College Physical Education Association. Its purpose was to "promote the physical welfare of the students in the institutions of higher learning, to make surveys and conduct research and to promote a professional spirit among its members." Hitchcock, who had served as the first President of AAAPE, now took over as the first President of this new organization. (An interesting photograph of this group assembled in convention at Yale, December, 1899, is shown in the February, 1944 issue of the *Journal of Health and Physical Education*.)

Physical Training Conference of 1889. In this period there occurred the first conference on physical education to be held outside the framework of an organized group. Known as "The Conference of 1889 on Physical Training" it was destined to be the forerunner of many equally notable conferences to follow in the twentieth century. (This first conference is fully reported, and the report, long out of print, is now available on microcard.) The conference, financed by Mrs. Mary Hemenway of Boston, was called by the Secretary of the Massachusetts State Board of Education, the Superintendent of Schools of Boston, the Presidents of Massachusetts Institute of Technology, Boston University, and Colby College, the members of the Boston School Commission, and an imposing array of leading citizens of Boston. The United States Commissioner of Education presided at the conference.

Among the thirty-four speakers at the four sessions were sixteen medical doctors, one General of the Army of the United States, one Earl from England, two Barons (one, Baron Pierre de Coubertin [1863–1937] of France, who was touring England and America to study the sports activities, from which observations he soon thereafter developed his idea of establishing the modern Olympics), one Doctor of Laws and one a Doctor of Philosophy. Of these thirty-four speakers, five were women. The discussions and demonstrations centered around the German and Swedish systems of gymnastics. Two thousand people attended the conference, which was considered to be the most notable educational event of the era. Its success was a great boon to the advancement of physical education.

LEADERS OF PHYSICAL EDUCATION

There were six professional "giants" of this era—four men and two women—whose work laid a firm foundation for the profession of physical education in the United States. All were born in the period 1828–60 and are listed chronologically.

Edward Hitchcock (1828–1911). Edward Hitchcock's father was a professor at Amherst College and later became its third president. Edward graduated from Amherst in 1850, and after two years of teaching chemistry and natural history at a seminary nearby, he went to Harvard University, acquiring his medical degree in 1853. He then resumed his teaching until 1860 when he went to London to study comparative anatomy under the famous Sir Richard Owen. The following year he was offered the position of Professor of Hygiene and Physical Education at Amherst which he held from the fall of 1861 until his death in 1911. In his long directorship of this, America's first department of physical education, he blazed so excellent a trail that his department set a fine example for all that were to follow. The story of that department has already been told.

He was a genius at organizing and at seeing in the physical-exercise program a means to an end which transcended any system of gymnastics or calisthenics. He had no training in any form of gymnastics so he used the Dio Lewis system in the early days of his directorship as something tangible to start with. He immediately embarked upon research into physical measurements, thus starting the first anthropometric studies in America, which he carried on throughout his entire professional career. He was the first President of both the American Association for the Advancement of Physical Education and the Society of College Gymnasium Directors. He took the lead in the research work of both associations and was a frequent speaker at their meetings. His genius lay in his insistence upon a sound scientific basis for all his work and upon accurate and truthful observation. In this he left the profession a valuable heritage. He is a Fellow in Memoriam of the American Academy of Physical Education.

Fig. 10. Edward Hitchcock. (Courtesy of *Journal of Health—Physical Education—Recreation.*)

Amy Morris Homans (1849–1933). Although not trained in the specialized field of physical education, Amy Morris Homans was one of the profession's great women leaders. Born in Vassalboro, Maine, she was educated by private tutors as were most young girls of that day who received serious schooling. At the age of nineteen she became preceptress of a girl's seminary in Maine, and two years later went to North Carolina to become principal of two schools, one a normal school. After ten years of teaching and administrative work she became secretary to Mrs. Hemenway of Boston. The two of them organized, and Miss Homans directed, the Boston Normal School of Household Arts which the State of Massachusetts took over two years later as the Department of Domestic Science of Framingham State Normal School—one of the first of such departments in the country. Two years later when Mrs. Hemenway founded the Boston Normal School of Gymnastics she installed her secretary as director of the school. Under Miss Homan's skillful direction and farseeing educational philosophy the school quickly achieved leadership in the training of women. Under her management the school took the lead in acquiring collegiate status when, in 1909, it became the Department of Hygiene and Physical Education of Wellesley College. From that step she forged ahead until the department finally acquired full postgraduate status—another first in the profession.

Upon her retirement in 1918 at the age of seventy she was given the title of Emeritus Professor, the first woman in the profession to achieve this distinction. In 1909 she received the first honorary master's degree and in 1930 the first honor-

Fig. 11. Amy Morris Homans. (Portrait by De-Camp—gift of Mary Hemenway Alumnae Association. Reproduced by courtesy of Wellesley College.)

ary doctor's degree to be conferred upon a woman in the field of physical education in the United States. She was the second woman to be elected to membership in the American Academy of Physical Education.

Until the time of her death at the age of eighty-five her counsel was continuously sought because of her rare wisdom. A woman of marked culture and refinement, she insisted upon a liberal arts education coupled with professional training. A gentlewoman in every sense of the word, she set a pattern for all women working in the profession that brooked no compromise with femininity. A woman of high courage, she was unflinching in her maintenance of high standards, and she set for her students a professional code that also brooked no compromise. A woman of dynamic personality, of unusual administrative ability, and of superior standards of thoroughness of work, she was inexorable in her insistence that students make the most of their educational advantages. All these qualities marked her as an unusual leader who demanded near perfection for her pupils yet claimed their deep respect, sincere admiration, and devoted homage.

Dudley A. Sargent (1849–1924). In his *Autobiography,* Dudley A. Sargent gives a most interesting account of his life work. He was born in Belfast, Maine. His father died when the boy was seven years old, and he was sent to Hing-

Fig. 12. Dudley A. Sargent. (Courtesy of *Journal of Health –Physical Education–Recreation.*)

ham, Massachusetts, to live with relatives. There he got a taste of physical education and liked it. By the time he was eleven years old he was supporting himself chopping wood, lumbering, and farming, up at 6 A.M. in the winter and at 4 A.M. in the summer. At the age of fifteen he was studying Cutter's *Anatomy, Physiology and Hygiene* which he considered the most enthralling of all his school textbooks. As he grew older he took on carpentering and plumbing work to support himself, and at the same time he kept up his own physical development with gymnastic exercises which he invented for himself.

Returning to Maine to live he saw a gymnastic exhibition at Bowdoin College which interested him so much that he and his chums formed a gymnastic club using his uncle's barn for their gymnasium. He became so proficient that he joined a circus doing an act of some of his self-taught stunts. At the age of twenty he was appointed Director of the Gymnasium at Bowdoin College, and, seeing that the boys who worked on farms and in mills and lumber yards had superior physiques, he set out to devise a program of exercises and apparatus that would give the other boys similar development. Using the muscular movements of everyday labor and sports activities he originated a system of gymnastics that was indeed "natural" gymnastics, foreshadowing that movement of the twentieth century. At the same time he registered in the college to study for his own degree and also launched himself on serious anthropometric research contributing materially to our knowledge in that field.

Later he founded the Department of Physical Education at Yale University while he pursued his medical studies there, acquiring both the A.M. and M.D. degrees in two and one-half years. In 1879 he was appointed Director of the Gymnasium and Assistant Professor of Physical Training at Harvard University, and there he developed a scientific program based on the individual needs of each student. This led to the invention of his own anthropometric measuring apparatus which by 1889 was in use in 350 institutions. Wishing his inventions to become educational tools free to all, he did not patent them, and when a manufacturer took out patents on them he caused Sargent serious trouble which led him to regret that he had not at least "policed" his own inventions.

He founded the Harvard Summer School of Physical Education and the Sargent School of Physical Education, both teacher-training projects, turning out hundreds of teachers through the years, most of whom were heads of departments in colleges, high schools, and private schools in the United

States and in Canada, England, France, China, and Japan.
He established a camp connected with the Sargent School
near Peterborough, New Hampshire, and there he died July
21, 1924. He has been elected a Fellow in Memoriam of the
American Academy of Physical Education.

He was a self-made man—a man of learning and culture—
a handsome man of imposing bearing—a man of great dignity and personal charm. He took an active part in the professional organizations and was one of the early presidents
of the AAAPE. He lectured not only in America but also in
Europe. He, more than any other person, guided intercollegiate athletics into proper controls and regulations.

Always a student of philosophy and the sciences, he based
his work on sound scientific foundations. Perhaps his philosophy of physical education can be presented best by his
own statements. Always willing to speak out publicly in
behalf of physical education, and an excellent speaker, he
advanced the profession materially through his speeches as
well as through his writings. As early as 1864 he stated the
aim of physical education as he envisioned it: the attainment
of harmony in development and a well-balanced organism.
At the famous Conference of 1889 he gave public voice to
his professional credo when he said:

> One-half the struggle for physical training has been won when [a
> student] can be induced to take a genuine interest in his bodily con-
> dition—to want to remedy his defects, and to pride himself on the
> purity of his skin, the firmness of his muscles, and the uprightness
> of his figure.
> . . . .
> It is more to the credit of a university to have one hundred men who
> can do a creditable performance in running, rowing, ball-playing, etc.,
> than to have one man who can break a record, or a team that can
> always win the championship.

At this same conference, when asked what he thought
were America's needs in a physical education program, he
replied, "the strength-giving qualities of the German system,
the active and energetic quality of English sports, the grace
and suppleness of French calisthenics, the poise and pre-

cision of Swedish free movements—all of these systematized and adapted to our peculiar needs."

Edward Mussey Hartwell (1850–1922). Edward M. Hartwell was born at Exeter, New Hampshire, the son of a brilliant lawyer and the grandson of a surgeon. He earned many degrees—the A.B. and A.M. from Amherst, the Ph.D. from Johns Hopkins, and the M.D. from Miami Medical College of Cincinnati. He also studied at the Royal Gymnastic Institute of Stockholm and in Vienna and Bonn. Later, Amherst College conferred upon him the honorary degree, Doctor of Laws—the first such degree to be conferred upon a physical educator in America. As a pupil of Hitchcock, he became deeply interested in research, and he advanced the profession materially through both historical and biological research.

For seven years he was Associate Professor of Physical Training and Director of the Gymnasium at Johns Hopkins University. In the spring of 1883 he travelled from Maine to Tennessee visiting gymnasiums in colleges and other institutions for a survey of physical education for the United States Bureau of Education, producing a manuscript, *Physical Education in American Colleges and Universities*, which has through the years remained a masterpiece of surveys and, with the passing of the years, has been a valuable document of historical information. Following this, in 1890, he made a third trip to Europe visiting playgrounds and school gymnasiums (in his various trips he investigated physical education work in Russia, Scandinavia, Germany and Great Britain), and the following year he became the first Director of Physical Education of the Public Schools of Boston which position he held until 1898, building a program which served as a model for all public schools for many years. Later he became Secretary of the Department of Municipal Statistics of Boston serving in that capacity until his retirement in 1919.

He served the American Association for the Advancement of Physical Education as its president for seven years and

Fig. 13. Edward Mussey Hartwell. (Leonard and Affleck, *A Guide to the History of Physical Education.* Courtesy of Lea & Febiger, Publishers.)

was a constant contributor of reports and papers, all scholarly and scientific. He gave dignity to the profession through his scholarly approach to all of his work. He is a Fellow in Memoriam in the American Academy of Physical Education.

Delphine Hanna (1854–1941). Born in Markeson, Wisconsin, Delphine Hanna graduated from Rockport State Normal School in 1874 and for ten years taught in the grade schools of Kansas and New York. Becoming concerned about the lack of physical stamina of most pupils and teachers, she enrolled in the Dio Lewis Summer School in 1884 in the hopes of learning how to remedy this condition. Disillusioned over the lack of scientific basis of Lewis' physical education theories, she transferred to the Sargent School, graduating in 1885. The following year she worked with Boston orthopedic physicians to study the treatment of spinal curvature, and in the evenings she studied the Delsarte system at the Currie School of Expression. Later she incorporated the best of this system into her posture training work.

In 1886 she went to Oberlin College as Instructor in Physical Culture with the promise of living expenses but no salary and $300 to spend on equipment. She started classes in calisthenics, correctives, and "fancy steps," but the President had to be persuaded that there would be no harm in the "fancy steps" before she could proceed with them. She also offered classes to men students, and inspired several to take up physical education work, some of whom later became distinguished leaders in the profession. She continued her studies at Harvard Summer School and in 1890 procured the medical degree from the University of Michigan and after that the A.B. degree from Cornell University and A.M. from Oberlin. Early in her career at Oberlin she began anthropometric research, devising charts for women which were widely used by other colleges, and teacher-training courses—the first such courses for women in the United States at college level.

In her thirty-five years at Oberlin she held the titles of Instructor in Physical Culture; Director of Physical Training, Women's Department; and Professor of Physical Education and Director of the Department—the latter from 1903 to 1920. She was the first woman in physical education to hold the title of Professor in an American college. She

Fig. 14. Delphine Hanna. (Courtesy of Oberlin College.)

retired in 1920 as Emeritus Professor and became the first woman in the field to receive a Carnegie pension. In 1925 she was honored by election into the University of Michigan Hall of Fame. In 1931 she was among the first group to receive the Honor Award of the American Physical Education Association.

Dr. Hanna was a trail-blazer for American women in the field of physical education. She was the first to set up work for women founded on sound scientific procedures, the first woman to do scientific research in the field, the first to set up teacher-training for women founded on educational methods. She worked in the national professional organization and was one of the first women to serve on the National Council.

William G. Anderson (**1860–1947**). Born in St. Joseph, Michigan, William G. Anderson attended lower schools in Quincy, Illinois, and Boston. He later earned the A.B., A.M., and M.S. degrees at Yale University, the M.D. from Western Reserve University, and the Doctor of Public Health degree from Harvard University. Later he was the recipient of an honorary master's degree and the honorary doctor's degree—Doctor of Laws.

At the age of twenty-five he founded and became President of the Brooklyn Normal School of Physical Education. The following year he founded and became Dean of the Chautauqua Summer School of Physical Education which position he held through 1904. In 1893, after eight years in Brooklyn, he became the Associate Director of the Yale University Gymnasium and ten years later advanced to the Directorship which he held until his retirement in 1932. He served Yale a total of thirty-nine years acquiring the academic rank of professor in 1905. Concurrently with his early work at Yale University and the Chautauqua Summer School of Physical Education he served as president of the Anderson Normal School of Physical Education until 1903 when he became the Director of Physical Education at Yale University.

He was the founder of the American Association for the Advancement of Physical Education and served as its first secretary from 1885 to 1888, taking on the position of treasurer from 1888 to 1892. He also was one of the founders of the College Gymnasium Director's Society and served as one of its early presidents. He was one of the earliest writers in the profession, producing five books and numerous articles in periodicals, mostly on medical research. He invented the ergograph and several other pieces of equipment for Yale's Department of Experimental Psychology.

The American Association for Health, Physical Education and Recreation has created the Anderson Award in his memory and conferred upon him the Gulick Award. Travelling widely in Europe, he studied research methods there

Fig. 15. William G. Anderson.

and became a Fellow of the London Society of Sciences and Arts. He was a member of the American Academy of Physical Education.

Other Leaders. No account of the leaders in physical education of this era would be complete without mention of several other men and women who helped materially in opening the trails in the professional wilderness. All of these were born before 1860 and are listed chronologically on the following page.

George Brosius (1839–1920). Known as "the Father Jahn of America," George Brosius was the one person above all others who got physical education started in the public schools of the Middle West. A teacher for fifty years, he was the greatest leader of the German system of this era. In his work at the Normal School of the American Gymnastic Union he trained large numbers of students.

Eliza M. Mosher (1846–1928). One of the leading women physicians of the United States of this era, Eliza M. Mosher in her work at Vassar College, in particular, made important contributions to physical education through her work in physical examinations for women which set the earliest standards in the field, her advocacy of appropriate gymnastic costumes for women which broke down earlier barriers, and her posture-training work which blazed new trails in the education of women.

Robert Jeffries Roberts (1849–1920). As head of the Boston YMCA Department of Physical Education, Robert J. Roberts developed a program for hygienic bodybuilding which came to be known throughout the country as the "Roberts Platform" and became the cornerstone of all YMCA physical programs. He was recognized as the foremost YMCA physical director of the day.

William Stecher (1858–1950). Outstanding physician as well as the founder of the modern departments of physical education in the public schools of both Indianapolis and Philadelphia, William Stecher was a foremost leader in the turner societies. From 1907 to 1935 he served as editor of the turner magazine, *Mind and Body.* He was a member of the American Academy of Physical Education.

21

PHYSICAL ACTIVITIES OF THE
EARLY TWENTIETH CENTURY

By the turn of the new century the United States was fast
becoming industrialized. Only 40 per cent of the population
was still rural, by 1927 only 29.9 per cent. Cities were becoming large beyond all dreams of the century just ended.
Now the nation was populated "from sea to shining sea."
Families were not as large as in the century just closed,
children were spending more time in school, and much
social life was taking place outside the home. Telephones,
electricity, automobiles, and motion pictures were rapidly
transforming the American way of life.

In spite of all efforts to keep out of World War I, the
United States was finally drawn into the conflict. When the
armistice was signed November 11, 1918, the war ended
with the United States emerging as one of the great powers
of the world. The third decade of the century came to a
close with the stock market crash of October, 1929, which
ushered in the great depression of the early 1930's. This
was the political and social setting within which physical
education was coming of age.

As the new century opened, the schools had come to be
recognized as the cornerstone of democracy; more money
was appropriated, better buildings and equipment were
provided, and more highly trained teachers were available.

The result was that the best theories of educational procedure could now become educational practices. Coeducation was universally accepted for all public elementary schools and in the high schools of the smaller towns and villages. Social studies had gained prominence, and educators led by John Dewey (1859–1952), recognized as America's greatest philosopher of the day, were reappraising their objectives in terms of social philosophy. In 1918 the National Educational Association proclaimed its Seven Cardinal Principles of Education listing among them health, citizenship, and worthy use of leisure—three concerns to which physical education could so well contribute.

By 1923 there were thirty million children in the schools —two million of these in the high schools and eleven million in rural schools.

ACTIVITIES OF THE PHYSICAL EDUCATION PROGRAM

Dance. The "dance exercises" of the 1860's and 1870's gave way to the "fancy steps" of the 1880's and the 1890's. They in turn gave way to esthetic dancing which in turn gave way to other forms of artistic expression such as modified ballet and natural dancing which after their day bowed off the scene to make way for the so-called "modern dance." Social dance, too, had its vagaries, and various forms have come and gone with the fickleness of the other forms of dance. The more important of these will be discussed in relation to their impact on physical education of this era.

Clog and Tap Dance. A form of dance that became popular in schools in this era was clog, or tap dance as the school-used version of it came to be known. Clogging was a popular stage form in the 1890's, and children, on their own, had picked it up and had been clogging in play activities since the close of the nineteenth century. In the 1910's physical education teachers introduced this activity into the schools.

Esthetic Dance. Melvin Ballau Gilbert carried on dance instruction at the Harvard Summer School of Physical Education and the Boston Normal School of Gymnastics and in several other schools until his sudden death in 1910. He trained many young physical education students who took this form of dancing to the schools with them. But by the close of World War I "Gilbert dancing" as it was frequently called had passed out of the educational picture.

Folk Dance. The teaching of folk dance has increased through the years until it has become intrenched in the physical education program while other forms of dance have come and gone. Folk dance was the one stable form of dance of this era—stable because it was rooted in the real culture of the people. Elizabeth Burchenal (see p. 333), Inspector of Girls' Athletics for the New York City public schools, began in the early 1900's her popular collection of folk dances of all nations. Over a period of many years she visited various European countries collecting these dances at first hand. From 1908 to the 1940's she furnished the profession a total of fifteen books covering the folk dances of all countries of Europe and America. Early in this period the Playground and Recreation Association of America organized a National Folk Dance Committee to promote folk dancing in the playgrounds of America, and in 1916 the American Folk Dance Society was organized. Miss Burchenal served as chairman of both of these groups.

Natural Dance. As esthetic dance was coming "full circle" of the period of its popularity a new form of dance was developing, called by some "natural dancing," by others "interpretive dancing," and by still others "interpretative dancing." It developed from the earlier work of Isadora Duncan (1878–1927), America's first woman dancer of note who achieved world-wide acclaim. She made her debut at Daly's Theater in New York City at the age of seventeen. Five years later she started a revival of the study of the ancient Greek dance. Although she developed a dance form from the choric dance of the classic Greek theater, she was not interested in reviving Greek dance as such, merely using the Greek form for the expression of emotion. She did, however, adopt the classic form of dress and the custom of dancing in bare feet. She tried to bring the dance back to the people and tried to get people to dance for their own pleasure of self-expression.

At Columbia University there developed a modification of Miss Duncan's work for use in the schools which by the late 1910's and the early 1920's had completely replaced the esthetic dance of Gilbert's day. This new form of dance was characterized by the costumes of flowing draperies and bare feet and by its divorce from all ballet forms of techniques substituting much running, skipping, and leaping.

Margaret N. H'Doubler (1889–   ) developed at the University of Wisconsin a form of dance based, no doubt in its beginings, on this natural dance form. But it was peculiarly her own concept. To her pupils and followers it was merely "the dance" although in her book, *A Manual of Dancing* (1925), she herself labeled it "interpretative dancing." She broke with former techniques and developed fundamentals of dancing as basic teaching forms. Her work won quick acclaim as her pupils presented it throughout the country. By 1926 she had organized the first major in the field of the dance to be offered by any college or university in the United States.

These forms of dance in turn gave way to a new form— modern dance—which had its origins in the close of this era, but since it did not blossom until in the 1930's it will be discussed in the chapter that follows.

Square Dance. The first two decades of this era saw almost a blackout of square dancing except in small and widely scattered areas where the pioneers tenaciously clung to these old dances. Even then square dance was used mostly in annual revivals at what were called "old settlers reunions" when the young people had an opportunity to learn the dances which their parents remembered from their youth. In many Midwest communities this was, even as late as the early 1900's, the only form of social dance known to the young people where there still remained religious

objections to the waltz and the two-step. But to the rest of
the country square dance and the lancers had become but
memories of the past until, in the early 1920's, Henry Ford,
the industrialist, financed a revival which has grown, decade
by decade, until, in the 1950's, it has taken much of the
country by storm.

Gymnastics. As the twentieth century opened, gymnastics was the backbone of the physical education program.
Sports were approved and desired but in most places were
only a sideline—not as a part of the actual program. A
Health-Through-Exercise Movement began after the slump
in interest in gymnastics that followed the Delsarte popularity of the past era. By the 1900's many business and
professional men had a growing awareness of a personal
need for exercise. Without sufficient trained leadership
available a host of advertising physical culturists arose to
meet this demand. Announcements in the popular magazines of the period from 1899 to 1917 illustrate the point.
Some of the advertisers made large sums of money in a
single year. At the same time women developed an interest
in what Dr. Luther H. Gulick so aptly spoke of in 1907 as
"society gymnastics." This was a reaction to the Delsarte
system and became very popular because of its renewed
promise of Catherine Beecher's dreams of teaching women
how to sit and stand correctly, how to ascend and descend
stairs, and how to perform daily activities effectively and
efficiently.

The YMCA, by 1907, had developed a gymnastic program distinctly its own to meet its interpretation of the
needs of American boys and men not reached by the schools.
Their program was built by Robert Jeffries Roberts around
light gymnastics followed by a run, bath, and rub-down.
They used very little heavy gymnastics in this program and
gradually worked in exercises aimed toward athletic skills.

Up to 1915, 95 per cent of the colleges and universities
included gymnastics in the physical education program,
and up to 1919, 100 out of 145 normal schools still used them.

After World War I the use of gymnastics in physical education programs suffered serious decline.

Attacks on Gymnastics. The controversy of the 1890's and the early 1900's as to which system of gymnastics, German or Swedish, was better for America had, by 1900, developed into a controversy as to whether either should be used. Gulick dealt gymnastics a setback when he compared the gymnastic-trained man with the athlete. The former he described as a man of overdeveloped muscles, great shoulders and chest, weak legs and heavy carriage; the latter as erect, graceful, and fleet with splendid endurance. These statements made a deep impression on people for Gulick was popular with both the professional and lay public. In 1910 Dr. Thomas D. Wood (see p. 326) of Columbia University advocated a program of exercises built around natural activities, sports, and games, which started a movement for what came to be called "natural gymnastics." But Dr. Dudley A. Sargent, then near the end of a long and distinguished career in physical education, uttered a word of caution when he said in an address at the 1920 National Physical Education Convention:

> To condemn a thing simply because it is old or to recommend it simply because it is new, is not the best way to advance our cause. Read into physical education everything you can of the slightest value but don't read out of it the most fundamental thing of all—that is all-round *muscular exercise.*

German System. The YMCA's and the turners were the most successful agents in promoting German gymnastics in the early 1900's, making their appeal chiefly to the people of German origins. Other Americans did not stay with them long, perhaps because practice to become skillful in their form of gymnastics requires patience, thoroughness, hard work, and continued effort, and the German temperament fits that requirement. Americans of English origin wanted games in place of gymnastics in the physical education program. However, German gymnastics had a popular appeal and were carried on in and out of school, wherever there was a large German population. Mills College was the first women's college to adopt German gymnastics (1902). Elmira College soon followed. But this system never achieved popularity among American college women as did the Swedish and Danish forms.

By 1909 the turners who were practicing German gymnastics numbered 40,000, but this marked its popularity peak, and from then on the numbers participating decreased constantly.

Swedish System. The Swedish system of gymnastics carried with it the theories of medical and corrective gymnastics. Therefore, during the first quarter of the twentieth century, this type of physical education increased considerably in importance, largely as a result of the tendency to have concern for individual needs. It was taught in practically all college women's departments until Danish gymnastics came in the 1920's to challenge its hold. It was also used largely in the public schools except in the strongholds of German stock. The chief exponent of Swedish gymnastics of this era was Dr. William Skarstrom (1869–1951) who, born in Stockholm, Sweden, come to America as a young man and after graduation from the Boston Normal School of Gymnastics procured the medical degree at Harvard University. He modified the system to meet America's needs as he saw them. He reached large groups of teachers in training through his work at Columbia University and Wellesley College.

Natural Gymnastics. A new term, "natural gymnastics," arose in the first two decades of the new century from an attempt to formulate a system of gymnastic exercises for class use built on the fundamental skills of occupational, athletic, and dance forms of movements. Wood originated and fostered the movement and later Dr. Jesse F. Williams (1886–), Clark W. Hetherington (see p. 330) then of New York University (who as a student had worked with Dr. Wood at Stanford University), and Rosalind E. Cassidy (1895–), of Mills College, popularized it through their writings and teaching. This form of gymnastics was a return to the theories of Locke and Rousseau of the seventeenth and eighteenth centuries, which stressed recognition of individual differences and sought to measure a child's progress in terms of his own growth. It was also a return to GutsMuths and Jahn whose programs of play, sports, and outings had apparently been forgotten by the overly ardent advocates of German gymnastic exercises and apparatus work. And, too, it was a return to Hitchcock and Sargent of the previous era who had advocated a program adapted to the needs of the individual.

Danish Fundamental Gymnastics. The Danish system came to the United States in the 1920's sponsored chiefly by Americans who had studied under Niels Bukh in his school in Ollerup, Denmark. This system retained some of the formalism of the Ling Swedish system, but it substituted rhythmic action for sustained positions and precision. Although it is a strenuous form of exercise it made a greater appeal in the United States to women than to men. It enjoyed great popularity in women's departments in colleges during the 1920's and 1930's.

Sports. It was 1910 before sports were generally accepted by school authorities as a legitimate part of the school program although some physical educators themselves recognized their value in the education program and had been quietly including them in their class-hour activities for some time previous to this date. Wherever they were given a recognized place in the departmental offerings for boys and men, the department was usually spoken of as a department of physical education *and* athletics. Even now this distinction holds in many schools although women never have accepted this dual terminology. Sports as a part of the school curriculum developed more readily in the colleges than in the lower schools.

New sports activities that came onto the scene in this era were outing clubs started at Dartmouth College in 1910, shuffleboard introduced in Florida in 1913, and speedball created in 1921 by Elmer D. Mitchell (1889–) of the University of Michigan.

Baseball. At the opening of the century, professional teams began to overshadow the amateurs and claimed sectional loyalties that kept the populace in a frenzy of excitement when the winners of the big league pennants were being decided. In 1927 Babe Ruth of the New York Yankees made sixty home runs and a name for himself that will long top the lists of America's all-time greats in sport.

The intense interest in baseball brought about modifications to catch and hold the interest of the great mass of unskilled players for their own participation. In 1907 playground ball was developed in the Chicago South Park Playgrounds. In 1923 rules for this game were standardized by the National Recreation Association, and, by 1930, the game had evolved into the present game of softball.

Golf. Interest in golf now became countrywide. Even small towns constructed golf courses, at first all privately owned. In the early 1900's, the United States became a formidable rival of Great Britain in international matches. An American women's golf team captured the English women's championship tournament in Scotland in 1905. In the early years, due to the cost of the links, the game was confined largely to the members of the wealthy and exclusive clubs. When national, state, and municipal authorities began to promote recreation and play, this movement resulted in securing the necessary land, laying out golf courses, and placing the game at the disposal of the general public.

By 1910 there were twenty-four public golf courses in the United States; by 1920, seventy; and by 1931, five hundred in addition to many private clubs. The United States Golf Association by then listed 1,124 club members.

Swimming. Syracuse, New York, in 1900, Kansas City, in 1901, and Pittsburg, in 1903, joined the ranks of cities with municipal swimming pools. However, up to 1904, only a few offered instruction in swimming. In 1903, Chicago added to its older pools the new McKinley Natatorium, the largest in America—50 by 300 feet.

The first bacteriological studies of swimming pools in the United States were made in 1909. These brought about the early organization of the American Association of Hygiene and Baths in 1912 which established standards for pools (1915). The first indoor pool located above basement level (sixth floor) was at the 23rd Street Branch of the New York City YMCA. It was in this pool that the first Red Cross life-saving tests were given in 1914.

Track and Field. Track and field activities came into renewed popularity after World War I. In the early 1920's difficulties developed between the National Collegiate Athletic Association and the Amateur Athletic Union over the selection of the United States track and field athletes for the Olympic games. This brought about the establishment of the National Amateur Athletic Federation which forced better representation of college organizations and of the Army and Navy.

The first national championships in track and field were held in 1921. After that many famous Relays such as the Drake, Kansas, Penn, and West Coast Relays were developed, and, from 1922 on, indoor meets have been popular.

Volleyball. The United States Volleyball Association was formed in 1928. The game was played almost exclusively before World War I in the YMCA's and YWCA's, but, after its introduction to the armed services in their recreation programs put on by the YMCA physical directors during World War I, it spread rapidly in both school and nonschool groups.

Olympic Games. At the first modern Olympiad held in 1896 in Athens the United States won the high jump, the pole vault and the hop-step-and-jump. In the new century the U.S.A. track and field teams romped off with most firsts, and many seconds and thirds besides, to give the United States an enviable record in the sports field. The United States was represented by athletic teams at all Olympic games of this era—at Paris in 1900, at St. Louis in 1904, at London in 1908, at Stockholm in 1912, at Antwerp in 1920, at Paris again in 1924, and at Amsterdam in 1928.

Outing Clubs. Although many outing clubs flourished temporarily in colleges in the 1880's and 1890's, none achieved permanency. The first to claim that honor was the Dartmouth Outing Club organized in 1910. In 1922 Smith College organized the first women's outing club to achieve permanency. From then on outing clubs became popular in many colleges. They sponsored all forms of outdoor activities in all seasons of the year, many maintaining clubhouses.

INTERSCHOLASTIC AND INTERCOLLEGIATE ATHLETICS

The story of interscholastic competition is largely the story of the State High School Athletic Associations which will be discussed later in this chapter. The story of intercollegiate athletics of this period is largely the story of football.

This era brought highly paid coaches, training tables, large expenditures of money for sports, and huge gate receipts undreamed of in the nineteenth century. The all-too-common attitude of the college authorities toward the student athletic sports was that they were a necessary evil, to be tolerated and at times restricted.

Quarrels such as had occurred in the 1890's over football now increased between leading schools. Many schools broke off athletic relationship. Theodore Roosevelt during his presidency of the United States (1901–09) remarked that "when money comes in at the gate, sport flies out the window," and called a White House Conference of football leaders and coaches in the hopes of bringing some order out of the chaos. But even that helped for but a short time. Soon quarrels were rampant again. In 1912 and again in 1916 Harvard and Princeton Universities severed athletic relations, and in 1928 Army and Navy had a break over football disputes. Many other schools were engaged in similar quarrels and breaks, but the news managed to be kept under cover.

In 1928 a sportsman journalist of the era voiced the disgust of a large segment of the citizenry over the decay of athletics when he wrote of "The Great Sports Myth"—the myth that football players are heroes of high moral qualities, "purified and made holy by their devotion to intercollegiate sports." He claimed that intercollegiate and international sports do not produce nobility of character and strengthen the bonds between nations and individuals but produce instead "broken ankles, bad feeling, cursing, and revelry in the sanctity of dressing rooms; coarse accusations and cheap humor in the publications of a great university."

The first night football games came in 1928, and in that same year one single contest at the Yale bowl drew a crowd of 80,000 with special trains running from several cities carrying the private cars of the affluent as well as long strings of coaches for the common herd.

By the close of this era, the National Collegiate Athletic Association had instigated reforms in football and brought it under faculty control, eliminated the hiring of seasonal coaches, promoted the growth of football conferences throughout the country, and established rules committees and national tournaments. By this time the Amateur Athletic Union, the YMCA, the National Federation of State High School Athletic Associations, and the Canadian Physical Education Association were all working with the rules committees.

INTRAMURAL SPORTS

The intramural form of athletics preceded the intercollegiate and interscholastic forms by many years. Indeed for almost the entire nineteenth century it was the only form of sports competition for boys and men except in a few rare cases. But when extramural competition put in its appearance as a widespread movement near the end of the nineteenth century, it grew to such proportions and to the neglect of all but varsity prospects that educators found it necessary to give special thought to the organization of intramurals for the mass of college men and school boys.

In Colleges. In 1913 both at the University of Michigan and the Ohio State University a physical education staff member was appointed specifically to organize and administer a sports program for the many quite apart from the program offered for the skilled few. According to the Athletic Research Society, by 1916, 114 colleges had such programs under way. In 1919, Mitchell became Director of Intramurals at the University of Michigan, the first college to give the title to the head of this work. In 1926 he published *Intramural Sports,* the first book on this subject, and in 1928 the University of Michigan opened its Intramural Sports Building, a building devoted entirely to these activities—the first such specialized building in the United States.

In Lower Schools. The movement to recognize intramural athletics in elementary schools gained momentum by 1905 after Gulick organized the Public School Athletic League of New York City. After starting with a spectator type of sports which immediately showed up bad attitudes, they changed the emphasis to the educational aspects of sports. However, in most schools, competition in the public schools, as well as in colleges, developed along with the desire to cater to spectators.

By 1925 the intramural idea had filtered from the colleges into the high schools, and this form of sports became popular, particularly in the large schools where the extramural program reached only a small group of students out of the total enrollment.

WOMEN'S ATHLETICS

At the opening of the new century women's sports in colleges and high schools began gradually to come under the control of the physical education departments although at Bryn Mawr College students held out as late as 1929 in turning over their own control and promotion of sports to the physical education staff. This era brought several new sports to women in the United States such as lacrosse, field hockey, volleyball, cricket, water polo, and soccer.

In Colleges. From a mild start in the 1890's in a few isolated places, intercollegiate competition for college women now increased in the 1900's. In the East a few colleges played intercollegiate basketball occasionally, from 1900 to the World War I period, but during the 1920's, intramural competition had almost completely superceded all such competition. In the Middle West the University of Nebraska started a program of varsity basketball in 1900 managed by a woman English teacher, playing high schools, YWCA's, and an occasional college team, but by 1906 this type of competition was replaced by an intramural program of interclass games. In the West, the University of California's Sports Past-time (*sic*) Association ran off intercollegiate matches with the University of Nevada, Stanford University, and Mills College from 1900 to 1903 when because of unfavorable publicity the school authorities put a stop to the games.

In the early 1920's about 22 per cent of the colleges sponsored some form of intercollegiate sports for women. In 1930, only 12 per cent were engaging in intercollegiate competition. So interest in this type of activity was on the wane by the close of this era with intramurals, sponsored jointly by women's athletic associations and the departments of physical education, gaining in popularity.

By 1925 play days had become popular, the first held at the University of Washington as an intramural affair. The University of Cincinnati was the first to sponsor an intercollegiate play day in which girls from various colleges were scattered among many teams—no one school putting any one team into play in any activity. In other words the players played with other schools rather than against them.

In Lower Schools. In the early years of the 1900's, girls in some high schools in all parts of the country competed in interschool activities, although the games were not organized or controlled by school authorities. Some played college teams; some, other high school teams, and some, boys' grade school teams. By 1910 girls' interscholastic basketball had become big excitement in many small towns of the Middle West and South, and this continued throughout the era.

Partly in imitation of the college women's athletic associations and partly to combat interscholastic games, girls' athletic associations sprang up, and, sparked by them, intramurals took the stage in most high schools. These GAA's found support and encouragement in the State Leagues which began to be established in the 1920's.

In Industry. It was in this era that there first arose exploitation of girls through athletics. Certain men's sports organizations, some industrial and business groups, unthinking Chambers of Commerce, a few ill-advised school men, and a number of men's athletic coaches—all supported by undiscerning parents of possible "star" performers—found the temptation too much to resist once they realized that skilled girl athletes made good publicity for their promoters. By the 1920's the Women's Athletic Section of the American Physical Education Association and the Women's Division of the National Amateur Athletic Federation and State Leagues were vigorously opposing these forces in behalf of what they called educational athletics for girls. The AAU took the lead in organizing girls in industry for competitive sports. In the 1920's national championship tournaments sprang up across the country—all man-inspired, man-managed, man-coached and man-financially-rewarded from the prowess of the worthwhile athletic "finds." This phase of sports for women was well on its way in the 1920's. It came to its flowering in the period to be discussed in the next chapter.

In Olympic Games. American women first took part in the Olympic games in 1928 at Amsterdam and then only over the vigorous protests of the Women's Division of NAAF, Women's Athletic Section of APEA, the National Association of Physical Education for College Women, the

YWCA physical director's group, and with the vigorous supporting protests of the foremost men leaders of physical education. The women athletes were recruited from industry—at that time a somewhat difficult environment for women protesters to storm. But these women athletes made no showing of particular interest to either the home or foreign sports world.

22

ORGANIZED PHYSICAL EDUCATION
OF THE EARLY TWENTIETH CENTURY

As physical education began to find a real place in the schools two groups maneuvered for control of the program: those who held that gymnastics should be the core of the program and those who were trying to break with this early concept to widen the educational objectives. The latter group tried to redirect the program of formal gymnastics, apparatus work, and therapeutic exercises—mainly based on the medical—toward a less formal program of sports and games which they considered a method of education. The new trend toward a sports and games program did not cast aside gymnastics. Formal exercises and apparatus activities still retained a place in many school and college programs and under the direction of a professionally trained teacher served a real educational purpose—body building.

The playground movement of 1900 helped to sell physical education to the public, and the play activities, athletics, and folk dance which were now added to the program helped immeasurably to popularize it.

EVENTS AFFECTING PHYSICAL EDUCATION

World War I. Thirty-three per cent of the men drafted for the United States armed services for World War I were rejected as unfit to serve. Out of the ensuing accusations and recriminations came an awakened conscience. People were now ready to give backing to a real program of physical education in the schools. This postwar impetus brought greatly expanded facilities and increased staffs. Swimming pools, football stadiums, spacious gymnasiums, and large athletic fields sprang up all over the country. A growing consciousness that physical education and athletics were for the many, not just for the few, brought a great upsurge for intramural sports and increased required work in physical education in the schools and colleges.

In their conduct of the war the government turned to physical educators to advise on many special projects. For example, Jessie Bancroft (see p. 333) was called to serve as Chairman of the Government Commission on Training Camp Activities and President of the War-Camp Service. Elizabeth Burchenal (see p. 333) was appointed a member of the U.S. Department of Labor's Commission of Wartime Community Services and a member of both the U.S. War and Navy Departments' Commission on Camp Activities. Dr. Joseph M. Raycroft (1867–1955), of the University of Chicago, was appointed Chairman of the Athletic Division of the War Department Committee on Training Camp Activities and was sent by the Secretary of War to Europe to study conditions affecting the morale of the American Expeditionary Forces. Edward C. Schneider (1874–1954), of Wesleyan University, was a member of the Medical Research Board of Aviation with the AEF, and Dr. Thomas A. Storey (1875–1943), New York State Director of Physical Education, was made Executive Secretary of the Government Inter-departmental Social Hygiene Board.

State Legislation. The movement for state laws requiring that physical education be taught in the schools, which started in the 1890's, lagged in the 1900's. Up to 1914 only three more states had acted: Pennsylvania in 1901, Michigan in 1911, and Idaho in 1913. But by 1930 thirty-nine states in all had passed physical education laws. With state legislation came state physical education directorships set up in the state departments of public instruction. New York in 1916 became the first state to create such a position with Dr. Storey, of the College of the City of New York, in the directorship. California was the second with Clark W. Hetherington serving as state director from 1918 to 1921. By 1930 twenty-two states had state directors of physical education. (See Appendix for list of early directors.) The rising tide of state legislation which increased physical education work in the schools showed up the shortage of teachers in this field, and private schools, normal schools, colleges, and universities stepped up their teacher training work.

Most of the early laws required the teaching of physical education in the larger schools and made it permissive in the smaller ones. Later the laws carried provisions for time allotment and required physical education credits for graduation. Whereas the first laws specified the teaching of calisthenics and/or gymnastics, the later laws specified instead sports and rhythms. However, the crowded conditions and lack of facilities of many elementary and high schools encouraged the use of calisthenics rather than games and sports.

STATUS OF PHYSICAL EDUCATION

Aims and Objectives. Educators, parents, and the public in general now began asking what were the aims and objectives of physical education. Although Hitchcock and Sargent in an earlier day had both voiced their own aims, the profession as an organized group had not faced up to the challenge. Now Hetherington, President of the Physical Education Department of the National Education Association, voiced for the profession the aims in this new century as: (1) organic education for vital vigor, (2) psycho-motor education for power and skill in neuro-muscular activities, (3) character education for moral, social, and spiritual powers, and (4) intellectual education acquired through free play or development of social thinking. These aims were a far cry from the single, narrow aim of the earlier eras, that of relieving the tedium of the school room.

Terminology. The term "physical culture," used widely from the 1860's on, continued in use in some quarters as late as the 1910's with its use at its height in 1895. The use of the term does not seem strange when it is realized that interest in the classics predominated in higher education in the nineteenth century, and the word "culture" was used generally by the classicists. In 1895, for instance, the University of California called its Arts and Science College the "College of General Culture." Many colleges offered courses entitled, "religious culture" and "social culture." Also, physical education came to many schools in those early days through the elocution departments, which called their course, "voice culture"; so it was natural for them to call the physical activity courses, "physical culture."

The word "training" crept in when military departments were assigned the responsibility of the physical activity courses, and it was natural to make the two terms, "military training" and "physical training," conform. When the social and psychological objectives came into the picture the word "education" naturally came to the front. At this same time educators began to replace physicians as physical directors, and the term "physical education" came into its own. It must not be forgotten that when Hitchcock in 1861 set up at Amherst College the first department in any school in the United States it was officially designated as the Department of Physical Education and that many of the physical education leaders used this term in the 1890's. By the 1920's physical education had become the accepted term.

Lower Schools. Whereas practically none but the large city schools had organized physical education by the end of the last century and only a smattering of small towns had added it after the turn of the century, the post-World War I period brought great and sudden growth in this branch of education. For example, Alabama, California, Ohio, and Virginia not only employed state supervisors of physical edu-

cation but county supervisors as well; the entire state of
Florida had but three full-time physical education teachers
in 1924, but by 1927 it had 73; Indiana had but few schools
in 1900 with special teachers of physical education, but by
1930 it had 802 in 477 schools; and Minnesota had only 108
full-time and 63 part-time teachers of physical education in
1924, but by 1930 it had 301 full-time and 698 part-time
teachers. These are typical examples of what was going on
throughout the country.

Facilities. Although gymnasiums of this new era far
outnumbered those of the 1890's, building did not keep
abreast with the growth of the programs. The medium-
sized towns made the best showing in facilities according
to the findings of the White House Conference of 1930,
which reported, for example, that Ohio had gymnasiums in
80 per cent of its public schools; New York, in 62 per cent;
the Dakotas, in 51 per cent; and New Hampshire, in 44 per
cent.

The National Education Association through its Committee on School House Planning set up standards for physical
education facilities in the schools calling for every junior
and senior high school to have a gymnasium which "must
be a Hall of Health with an abundance of fresh air and sunlight." The Committee on Reorganization of Secondary
Education went further and recommended for every school
two gymnasiums, one for boys and one for girls, and many
schools strove to meet these requirements. In 1908 Detroit
opened a swimming pool in its Central High School—the
first high school pool in the United States. As to playing
fields the Society of State Directors of Physical Education
called for a field of three to four acres for every 400 pupils,
and the NEA asked for fields of at least ten acres for all rural
high schools.

Requirements. Most state departments of education set
a minimum requirement in the schools, and many city and
town schools set their own minimum above that. In the
1920's many schools set a minimum of 415 minutes per week

of physical education classwork in the elementary schools and 300 per week in junior high schools.

The question of granting school credit for physical education classwork was fought out seriously in this era. A survey of 582 schools of New York State in 1924 revealed that 82 per cent of the principals and superintendents were in favor of granting credit. Of the 17 per cent opposed one said, "I am opposed to giving credit for digging potatoes, etc. in lieu of Latin"; another said, "Schools are for training the young to read and write"; and yet another said, "It would be as much out of the general scheme as giving credit for eating well-balanced dinners." So it was obvious that as late as 1924 many educators still held a narrow concept of both physical education and education. However, by 1930 credit was being granted in seventeen states. From a survey of 254 school systems it was shown that 70 per cent were granting credit by that date.

Staffs. In 1903 when Gulick became the first head of the physical education department of the New York City schools he inherited a staff of thirty-six teachers, the largest group in any school system in the United States at that time. Before that there had been four independent heads of physical education, one for Brooklyn, one for the Bronx, one for Manhattan, and one for Queens. Now all were united under one head. In 1909 Ethel Perrin (see p. 336) of the University of Michigan faculty was made the Supervisor for the Detroit public schools with three men and two women on the staff. This department soon became the model public school department of the period.

The elementary schools followed the general pattern of placing the responsibility for physical education on the classroom teacher, and the high schools tended to employ coaches for a particular sport such as football or basketball and then assign them the physical education work.

Physical Education for College Men. In the early 1900's much antagonism still existed within the college faculties toward physical education as a part of the educational program. Nonetheless those colleges that had not yet developed physical education departments before the end of the nineteenth century now began to carry on the programs heretofore carried on unofficially by the students themselves. For the first quarter or more of the century most colleges found it difficult to meet the high standards of a few of the institutions which pioneered the physical education movement in the nineteenth century.

By 1913 the University of Michigan and the Ohio State University had inaugurated departments of intramural sports, completely taking over the informal sports programs formerly managed by the students. A study of state universities of this era revealed that fifteen universities maintained separate departments of physical education for men and women with five of these completely separated in all respects and ten separated but coordinated under a Division of Physical Education.

Facilities. This was a period of gymnasium building and rebuilding: funds were made available, and many fine buildings were provided. William Ralph LaPorte (1889–1954) of the University of Southern California invented the self-service locker-basket system which added much to the efficiency of dressing rooms and facilitated classwork materially. The increased popularity of indoor intercollegiate athletic sports caused architects to increase the seating capacity of the structures. Gymnasiums with a gallery running-track became popular at the turn of the century, but interest in this feature had practically died out by 1930. Not only fine gymnasiums were built in this era but also great football stadiums.

Early in this era when football was becoming "big business" in the colleges and universities, Harvard University built the first of the large stadiums (1904). It seated 23,000, an unheard-of seating capacity before this date. Other colleges slowly fell into line, but most stadiums of this era were not built until the 1920's. By 1920 the total seating capacity of stadiums then in existence was 929,523; by 1930 the total had risen to 2,307,000. The stadium at the University of Michigan first seated 87,500 and was later enlarged to seat 97,000; the Ohio State University stadium seated 77,000, later increased to 85,000 capacity.

Requirements. The University of Pennsylvania was the first university to require all students to take courses in physical education for all four years. Beyond this, following the advice of their own Benjamin Franklin given 150 years earlier, the authorities also made the ability to swim a requirement for graduation. The land-grant colleges lagged in their physical education offerings because of their commitment to require military drill of all male students. By the close of the era in the other colleges and universities, physical education was quite generally required for both men and women for three hours per week for the first two years of college work.

Staff Rank. The University of Pennsylvania again set a record by giving R. Tait McKenzie (see p. 328) the rank of full professor when they brought him from McGill University in 1904 to become head of the physical education department. The University of Missouri followed this lead by offering the same rank to Hetherington when he joined the faculty in 1910 as head of the department. After that many colleges offered professorial rank to physical educators.

The College Physical Education Society reports that by 1927, 27 per cent of the college physical directors had the M.D. degree; 87 per cent, the Ph.D. or Ed.D. degree; 20 per cent, the master's degree as top degree; and 38 per cent, the bachelor's degree. Seven per cent had no college degree.

Physical Education for College Women. By the time of World War I practically all colleges and universities with women students had established departments of physical education for women. In the coeducational schools, some were placed under the men's departments, some were coordinated with them, and some were completely independent of them.

Many forceful women were at the helm at this time shaping the destinies of these college departments and setting the pattern of a United States philosophy for the physical education of women which materially affected programs in the lower schools and in nonschool groups as well as in the colleges.

Facilities. In most coeducational colleges and universities the women's physical education facilities were quite meager compared to those for the men. The women used the men's gymnasium floor and playing fields when the men did not wish to use them. But in a few colleges women were fortunate to have their own facilities. In 1900 Hearst Hall, a gymnasium for women, was built at the University of California (Berkeley). Women of the University of Texas had their own gymnasium in the basement of the Woman's Building early in this era, and the University of Washington had a small building for a women's gymnasium. The Mary Hemenway Gymnasium of Wellesley College of 1909 was then years ahead of the times in many of its details, such as central-controlled showers and costume-disinfection system. But all too frequently the women fell heir to the men's old gymnasiums when they acquired new ones, but at that it was better than none at all.

However, it was not until the 1920's that women students really came into their own in physical education facilities. The new Hearst Memorial Gymnasium at the University of California at Berkeley, built in 1927 in semi-monumental style of architecture, was particularly magnificent in its architectural design and in its scope of facilities.

Four well-designed and equipped gymnasiums were constructed for college women in the 1920's at the Universities of Oregon, Washington, and California (Berkeley), and at Smith College. Other notable buildings of that decade were those at North Carolina College for Women built in 1923, and at the Universities of Minnesota, Colorado, and Illinois.

For outdoor facilities Mills College built the first college outdoor swimming pool in 1924 to be followed shortly by the three outdoor pools for women at the University of California. Athletic fields for the exclusive use of women in coeducational institutions were first developed in this era. The women's colleges have always led all other schools in their playing space for women. In 1902 Wellesley College constructed a boathouse and bathhouse on the shores of its campus lake, and by 1929 boasted twenty-two tennis courts, several hockey fields, and a like proportion of other play areas. Smith College by 1930 led all other colleges in its outdoor facilities for women. This college maintained in one field twenty tennis courts, ten archery lanes, a running track, and in another field of twenty acres, four hockey fields, a soccer field, a baseball diamond, a golf-driving range, several badminton courts, and a bridle path. Smith College also had three outing cabins, a boathouse, a crewhouse, and riding stables.

Programs. Although women engaged in sports in colleges from the earliest days of their enrollment in these schools, they, like the men students, organized them on their own, quite apart from any officially recognized physical education classes. The latter consisted almost exclusively of calisthenics and gymnastics with a taste of rhythms. Wellesley College was the first of the women's colleges to accept activities other than gymnastics and rhythms as a part of the physical education required program. It was not until the 1910's that sports were accepted as a part of the all-year school programs by most colleges.

In the 1920's there was a marked increase of emphasis on corrective work (individual gymnastics) for those needing special developmental or protective measures in their exercise program. A few colleges offered this work in the 1910's, and a rare few, influenced by the Swedish Movement Cure of the late nineteenth century, offered this work in the first decade of the 1900's. The women's departments in all eras have been far in advance of the men's departments in this field of work in the United States.

Staffs. In the 1890's a department of physical education for women was considered sufficient in size if it had one teacher with possibly one or two student assistants. By 1900, however, several women's colleges had as many as two or three full-time teachers, and by 1929 most had two or more full-time teachers. Wellesley College boasted thirteen. Early in the century in many colleges and universities the instructors of elocution and oratory taught "physical culture" until sports and games become an important part of the program, and their training proved inadequate for the new trends. A few colleges employed women trained in Sweden and England but most used graduates of American schools of physical education. As to academic training, Oberlin College was the only one at the turn of the century which employed a woman teacher trained in physical education who also held a college degree. Gradually teachers with college degrees came on the scene, and by the end of this era practically all heads of women's departments in colleges held at least the bachelor's degree, and most of them had from one to two years of graduate work.

The several women heads of departments who held the medical doctor's degree in this new era were different from the M.D.'s of the earlier century who held these positions. This era's M.D.'s were trained in physical education as well as in medicine and so really were of the physical education profession.

In the earlier century the only title recognized for a woman physical education teacher except in one or two rare cases was that of Director or Directress of the Gymnasium. Even into the 1920's many colleges conferred upon their women physical education teachers no academic rank whatsoever. On the other hand, as early as 1885 and 1895 Oberlin College and the University of Nebraska accorded the rank of instructor to their women directors of physical education. Oberlin advanced their women's director to the rank of full professor by 1903—the first college to grant this rank to a woman physical educator—and the University of Nebraska upgraded their director of women's physical education in 1900 to adjunct professor, in 1912 to assistant professor, and in 1915 to associate professor until by 1924 it granted to the head of the department the rank of full professor. This was the first full professorship granted to a woman physical education teacher in a state university. Wellesley College, in the 1910's, became the first of the women's colleges to accord the head of the department of physical education the rank of professor.

Costumes. The most universally accepted costume of the first part of this era was the long, full bloomers of three to five yards of woolen suiting, a middy blouse and middy tie, or a blouse of the same material as the bloomers worn with a stiffly starched dickey with complicated underarm harness to hold it in place, long, black cotton hose, heavily ribbed, and leather, orthopedic-style gym oxfords. By the 1910's a decided change came about, and in the 1920's still another so that by 1930 the woolen costume had given way completely to cotton, and the full bloomers had practically vanished from the scene replaced by scant bloomers with elastic well above the knee or by shorts.

Research. The interest in research which was started by Hitchcock and Sargent in the preceding century grew with the years, and the new century brought new and wider interests in testing. Whereas anthropometrical measurements and strength tests held the main interest in the earlier days, physical achievement tests and tests of cardiac efficiency now took the stage of interest, motivating for improved programs.

From the first physical achievement tests for school children (devised by Gulick for the New York City Public School Athletic League in 1904 from his earlier Pentathlon tests of the 1890's devised for the YMCA) to those given in 1928 by the National Recreation Association to 44,117 boys and girls of 450 cities, there was a great advance in testing techniques and standard-setting. The American Physical Education Association produced its athletic badge tests with established standards of achievement in 1913, and its national committee, set up under Dr. James H. McCurdy in 1922 to work on motor ability tests, developed a physical intelligence quotient. The APEA Athletic Badge Test consisted of, for boys, (1) arm strength, (2) jumping for distance, (3) running for speed, (4) throwing a baseball for accuracy, and (5) throwing a baseball for distance; for girls, (1) balancing, (2) running for speed, (3) throwing a baseball for accuracy, (4) throwing a baseball for distance, and (5) efficiency in fundamentals of a game, either baseball, basketball, or volleyball.

In the college field Dr. George L. Meylan of Columbia University devised, in 1919, the first achievement tests for college men using elements of sports in running, jumping, climbing, vaulting, throwing, etc., and in the same year Agnes Wayman (1880–   ), of Barnard College, presented the first such tests for college women. In 1921, Sargent first presented his Physical Test of a Man, which achieved much prominence throughout the country. This test consisted of a vertical jump using the factors of height and weight with ability to overcome the force of gravity. The efficiency index for this test was arrived at by the formula of weight in pounds multiplied by height of vertical jump in inches divided by height in inches. In the 1920's Frederick Rand Rogers (1894–   ), of Boston University, started work on a physical fitness index (PFI), which is still in use in the 1950's. This index is the achieved strength index divided by the normal strength index for the individual's age and weight. Tables of norms for age and height were worked out for the formula.

By the opening of the new century it had become apparent to the medical men both within and outside the profession that children, for their protection, should be classified for exercise according to the functioning of their heart and blood vessels. In 1905 McCurdy started work on adolescent changes in heart and blood pressure, and Schneider developed his cardio-vascular efficiency tests, in 1917, which were used by the aviation services during World War I.

Teacher Training. This period saw the demise of most of the private noncollegiate training schools of physical education and the birth of teacher training in this field in colleges and universities and public normal schools as related below.

Private Schools. All schools preparing physical education teachers before 1900 were private schools without collegiate rank. By the turn of the century most of them began arranging affiliations with colleges. The Boston Normal School of Gymnastics was the first of these early private schools to affiliate with a college. In 1909, it became the Department of Hygiene of Wellesley College. In the fall of 1917 it was granted graduate status, fulfilling the thirty-five-year-old dream of Amy Morris Homans. A notable exception to the movement for affiliation was the Sargent School of Physical Education, which, in 1902, lengthened its course to three years and retained its private, noncollegiate status until 1941 when it finally affiliated with Boston University. Upon the death of Sargent in 1924, Carl L. Schrader (1872–) (then President of the American Physical Education Association, later to become the first state physical director of Massachusetts and still later President of Ithaca College) became head of the school.

In 1907 the Normal School of the North American Gymnastic Union moved to Indianapolis, Indiana, and was authorized by law to confer degrees. Under the leadership of Emil Rath (1873–1943), who served as Dean of the school from 1909 to 1934, the school widened its curriculum, but it did not affiliate with a college in this era. (In 1941 it affiliated with the University of Indiana.) Other private schools that did affiliate with colleges in this era were the following: The Anderson School of Physical Education, which, starting out as the Brooklyn School of Physical Education, moved to New Haven and in 1901 became the New Haven Normal School of Gymnastics; it later achieved collegiate rank as Arnold College and still later affiliated with the University of Bridgeport; the Boston School of Physical Education affiliated with Boston University; the Bouvé School of Physical Education, with Simmons College; the Central School of

Physical Education, with Russell Sage College; the Posse School of Physical Education, with Tufts College; and the Savage School of Physical Education, with New York University.

The State of Massachusetts gave the YMCA Training School of Springfield, Massachusetts, authority in 1905 to confer the degrees of bachelor of physical education (B.P.E.) and master of physical education (M.P.E.), and, in 1912, the name of the school was changed to the International YMCA College and still later to Springfield College. By 1916 it had lengthened its course to four years. Dr. McCurdy was head of the physical education work of the college for thirty-five years from 1895 to 1930. In 1913 the YMCA Training School in Chicago achieved collegiate rating and became George Williams College.

New private schools of physical education established in this era were: the Chicago Normal School of Physical Education (1905), the School of Physical Education of Battle Creek College (1909), the Columbia Normal School of Physical Education in Chicago (1915), the Newark School of Health and Physical Education (1917), the Marjorie Webster School of Expression and Physical Education in Washington (1920), and the Ithaca School of Physical Education (1925), later to become Ithaca College.

Colleges and Universities. Although a limited number of colleges and universities, such as Oberlin College and the Universities of Indiana, California (Berkeley), and Nebraska, had started teacher training work in physical education before the turn of the century, none had started their professional work early enough to graduate their first students before 1900.

As the teacher training work in this field developed in various universities it was sponsored in some by the liberal arts colleges, in some by the teachers colleges, and in some by the schools of education. The last two named had gradually absorbed practically all teacher training in physical education by the 1920's with the exception of Stanford University where a new development took place when, in the 1920's, it established a School of Health and Physical Education— the first in the United States. It was under the direction of Dr. Storey, who guided this precedent-breaking experiment until his retirement in 1940.

Many colleges and universities followed the lead of Oberlin College and the Universities of California and Nebraska of the past era and established major departments in physical education as follows: Illinois (1905), Washington (1906), Oregon (1907), Wisconsin (1911), Utah (1914), Missouri (1914), Iowa (1918), Indiana (1919), Minnesota (1919), Kansas (1920), Michigan (1921), Texas (1923), Ohio State (1924), and Wyoming (1925).

Public Normal Schools. One of the first public normal schools to offer specialization in physical education was the one at Ypsilanti, Michigan, whose course started in 1913 under the direction of Wilbur P. Bowen. Soon thereafter many normal schools, spurred on by state legislation that required teachers in ever-increasing numbers, established specialization in physical education.

Graduate Preparation. In 1901 Teachers College of Columbia University, inspired by Dr. Wood, became the first institution to offer the master's degree with specialization in physical education, and soon thereafter a few other schools followed their lead. However, Wellesley College was the first to set up a graduate curriculum in physical education which was open only to persons who had completed full undergraduate requirements for a major in physical education. By 1930, twenty-eight schools were offering graduate work in physical education, and two, New York University and Columbia University, were offering courses leading to the doctor's degree, both beginning in 1924.

Nonschool Organizations. Physical education developed rapidly in the 1900's in nonschool organizations with the YMCA's and YWCA's leading all other groups.

Young Men's Christian Association. The YMCA expanded its program of physical activities working with all types of community agencies to promote physical activities for young boys in particular, yet giving increased attention, also, to its offering for young adults and older men. The national organization now maintained two colleges, one in Springfield, Mass., and one in Chicago, Ill., both of which specialized in the preparation of teachers of physical education to man their so-called "physical departments."

In 1906 Dr. George J. Fisher (1871–   ), then a YMCA director at Brooklyn, was named head of the Physical Department of the International Committee, and in 1910 Dr. John Brown, Jr. (1880–   ), a former YMCA Director at Montreal and New York City and just out of medical school, joined the staff of the National Board. When Dr. Fisher became Deputy Scout Executive of the Boy Scouts of America in 1919, Dr. Brown succeeded to the directorship which he held until his retirement in 1941. Under the management of these two men the international physical education program expanded remarkably. Figures covering the period of 1900 to 1920 show the following increases: gymnasiums from 507 to 838; athletic fields from 143 to 205; physical directors from 294 to 633 (820 by 1930); and participants in the program from 80,433 to 488,478.

During World War I large numbers of YMCA physical directors worked with the allied troops both at home and overseas. The program which they offered to the servicemen was designed to occupy leisure hours through recreational sports participation aimed at developing morale and a sense of brotherhood with all other servicemen. They also worked with the convalescents in hospitals helping with muscle reeducation and recreational activities.

Young Women's Christian Association. In this new era the YWCA added swimming to its activity programs with the first classes opened at Montgomery, Alabama, and Buffalo, New York, in 1905. In 1911 they organized the first National Conference of YWCA Health Education Directors. The National Board uses the term "health education" in preference to "physical education." The Centennial Report of 1916 stated that there were 65,000 women attending YWCA gymnasium classes and 32,000 in the swimming classes.

Turners and Sokols. With the public schools assuming the responsibility for the physical training of children, the Turner and Sokol clubs now placed their emphasis on programs for adults. With the coming of World War I so much feeling arose against Germany that it became highly advisable for groups bound together by their common German background to dissolve and to identify themselves exclusively with other Americans as Americans. This materially affected these societies and they waned markedly.

Movements Related to Physical Education. Many important movements related to physical education in various aspects of their programs originated in this era, such as the Boy Scouts of America (1910), the Girl Scouts of America (1912), the Camp Fire Girls of America (1914), and the National Park Service (1911). The recreation and camping movements grew ever more important with the coming of the twentieth century.

Recreation Movement. The promotion of recreation had become an accepted part of American life in the large cities by 1900. Now those groups that had previously supported settlement yards and school playgrounds broadened their activities to include municipal, state, and national recreation areas. Sums of money which were enormous for those days were spent for these ventures.

In 1900 Chicago appropriated $10,000 for the equipment of playgrounds in densely populated districts. Congress began the annual appropriations for playground work for the District of Columbia in 1905. Chicago, in 1903, voted a $5,000,000 bond issue for small recreation parks, and ten were opened in 1905. By 1910 the city was operating 65 playgrounds and bathing beaches, and its South Park system was regarded as the finest in the world. Boston, New York, and Philadelphia also made provision for playgrounds and parks. In all, more than 150 cities reported playgrounds before 1910, and many other cities had them in the planning stage. Los Angeles appointed its first Board of Playground Commissioners in 1904.

The increased interest in recreation which followed World War I brought greatly expanded facilities: play fields, swimming pools, bathing beaches, golf courses, day camps, and winter sports facilities. By 1925, 748 cities had community recreation leaders, and 688 cities had 5,121 playgrounds with 17,177 leaders representing a yearly expenditure of $1,900,000.

Camping Movement. Organized camping is a movement which America has given to the world. By 1900 there were twenty-four or more camps established in the United States, and the movement grew rapidly from then on.

In the first sixty years (from 1860 to 1920) the movement was largely a recreational one. During the 1920's it began to take on its educational stage when camping became an extension of the school. Many schools now established their own camps. Omaha, Nebraska, established its school camp in the early 1920's—one of the first such camps.

Professional Literature. Now arose a great flurry of writing in the United States to make up for the dearth of local professional material of the nineteenth century. Many "firsts" came in this era—written for the profession by persons working in the profession—such as: Jessie Bancroft's *School Gymnastics and Light Apparatus* of 1900; Luther H. Gulick's *Physical Education* of 1907, the first book on philosophy and principles; Elizabeth Burchenal's *Folk Dance Tunes* of 1908; Jessie Bancroft's *Games for School, Home, and Playground* of 1909, one of the professional all-time best sellers; Clark W. Hetherington's *Normal Course in Play* of 1909; and R. Tait McKenzie's *Exercise in Education and Medicine* of 1909.

The second and third decades also brought forth several firsts such as Thomas D. Wood's *Health Education* of 1910, the book that started the modern natural gymnastics movement; Gulick's *The Healthful Art of Dancing* of 1911, which was used for over twenty years in the schools of America; the state of Michigan's *Physical Training for Public Schools* of 1912, the first state manual; Wilbur P. Bowen's *Manual of Physical Education for Ypsilanti Schools* of 1915, the first city manual; and his *Action of Muscles* of 1912, the first on kinesiology; Frederick E. Leonard's *Pioneers of Modern Physical Training* of 1919 and *History of Physical Education* of 1923; James H. McCurdy's *Physiology of Exercise* of 1924; and Elmer D. Mitchell's *Intramural Sports* of 1928.

The two periodicals started in the 1890's, *Mind and Body* (1894) and *The American Physical Education Review* (1896), continued through this era. The latter, which had been a quarterly from 1896 through 1907, became a monthly in 1908. Dr. William A. Stecher was editor of *Mind and Body* from 1904 until its demise in 1935. Gulick was editor of *The American Physical Education Review* from 1900 through 1902 and McCurdy from 1905 through 1929 when it became the *Journal of Health and Physical Education.*

Four new magazines were established in this era. *Physical Training* was started by the YMCA in 1901 with Gulick as its editor. In 1905 Fisher took over the editorship; in 1924 it changed its name to *The Journal of Physical Education,* and in 1926 Brown became its editor. The magazine *Playground* put in its appearance in 1907 as the official organ of the Playground and Recreation Association of America.

A periodical called *American Gymnasia and Athletic Record* was started in September, 1904. Published by the American Gymnasia Company of Boston, it claimed to be "The Only National Physical Training Publication Giving News of the Profession." The few issues available for perusal are full of interesting news of meetings, programs, and teachers—much that the other periodicals of that time did not carry. The periodical did not survive long, but while it lasted it maintained a book sales division and a teacher's exchange—both in the field of physical education.

In March, 1909, another magazine entered the field, *Hygiene and Physical Education.* This magazine had purchased the mailing list of the defunct *American Gymnasia.* It carried articles on health education and hygiene as well as physical education, and its first few issues gave promise of a brilliant future in the educational field, but it, too, soon vanished from the scene. It apparently took the backing of a national organization to keep a professional periodical on its feet in those days.

23

ORGANIZATIONS AND LEADERS
OF THE EARLY TWENTIETH CENTURY

The new century brought increased interest in the promotion and control of athletics as well as advancement in the profession of physical education so that many new organizations came into existence in the early 1900's. Also, the number of trained personnel in the field increased materially, and a new group of leaders arose to carry on the work started by the stalwart pioneers of earlier days.

PROFESSIONAL ORGANIZATIONS

Interests had become sufficiently specialized by the coming of the twentieth century to support several different types of professional organizations. The continuing history of those already in existence at the opening of the century will be discussed in the material that follows along with the history of new organizations, listed in the order of their founding.

American Physical Education Association. The American Association for the Advancement of Physical Education, founded in 1885, changed its name in 1903 to the American Physical Education Association. By 1903 it had built up a federation of local societies, some of them city groups, some state groups and one a regional group of several states. Now it undertook to organize its workers into sections of interests. By 1904 it had three sections—the Section on Normal Schools and Professional Training, the Section on Gymnastic Therapeutics, and the Section on Anthropometry—and three affiliated organizations—the Secondary School Directors' Society, the Public School Directors' Society, and the Society for Research—all of which later developed into sections. By the end of this era it had eleven sections and five affiliated organizations. Also, it united its many local groups into district societies with the Eastern, Middle West, and Southern districts coming into the mother organization in the order named. (The Presidents of this era are listed in the Appendix.)

Society of College Directors of Physical Education. The Society of College Gymnasium Directors, founded in 1897, changed its name in 1909 to the Society of College Directors of Physical Education. Throughout the 1910's and 1920's it held its annual meetings in connection with those of the National Collegiate Athletic Association and the American Health Association. During World War I the Society offered the services of sixty men in fifty colleges and universities to the United States government, all experienced medical examiners and practical physical educators. It also gave serious study to the problem of the relation between the departments of gymnastics and those of athletics, which in most colleges had developed as two separate departments.

Physical Directors Society of the YMCA. There were enough men working in physical education in the YMCA's by 1903 to found the YMCA Physical Directors Society at that time, joining forces to improve the standards and enlarge the field of service in physical education in the YMCA's of America.

Playground Association of America. During this era many organizations important to physical education came into existence. In 1904 the Big Brother Movement, Inc., was born in New York City to help underprivileged boys. From it came the idea of such an organization on the national level.

In 1906, sparked by Gulick, the PAA was formally organized in Washington with Gulick as its first president and Theodore Roosevelt, its Honorary President. It immediately started to work for the development of year-round programs and for municipal support. It sent out field workers to conduct campaigns in cities to get playgrounds organized, and it also set up programs for playgrounds and started a drive to find leaders to man them. In 1911 it changed its name to the Playground and Recreation Association of America (PRAA) with Joseph Lee (1862–1937), a philanthropist of Boston, known as "the father of the playground movement," taking over the presidency and continuing in that office until his death in 1937.

National Association of Physical Education for College Women. In 1909 Amy Morris Homans invited all directors of physical education in women's colleges in New England to meet at Wellesley College to discuss their mutual problems. In 1915, again meeting at Wellesley, the group enlarged to include all Eastern colleges, and they organized the Eastern College Women's Physical Directors Society. Two years later the college women physical directors of the Middle West met at the University of Chicago where they organized their district association. In 1921 the Western group organized at Mills College. Then in 1924 these three regional groups met together in Kansas City and affiliated as the National Association of Directors of Physical Education for College Women to work together for the common good. It immediately embarked upon investigations into physical examinations of women, excuses from required work, programs, and credits. In the early days of the organization none but directors of departments were accepted into membership, but before the close of this era membership was opened to all members of the staffs of physical education for women in colleges and the word "directors" dropped from the title.

American Academy of Physical Education. An early Academy of Physical Education was organized by Gulick in

1904. This was an informal group of physical educators who desired to get together for discussion free of formalities and red tape. They met annually for an entire week in early September at the summer camp of Dr. George L. Meylan on Sebago Lake in Maine. The group included the pre-eminent men leaders of that day. The meetings produced much fine thinking for the advancement of the profession, but with the interruption of World War I and the death of its guiding spirit, Gulick, in 1918, this organization broke up.

In 1926 a new group organized the present American Academy. Three of the five original members—Hetherington, McKenzie, and Storey—had been members of the earlier group. The other two originating members of the new organization were Dr. William Burdick (1871–1935), of the Baltimore Athletic League, and Jay B. Nash (1886–   ), of New York University. These five selected five others to join them, and these ten selected five more the following year. This process was continued until 1930 by which time the charter membership list was completed. This group then proceeded to draw up a constitution and to get the organization work under way. Of the earlier group Sargent, Gulick, and Leonard had passed away by 1926 and were elected Fellows in Memoriam. The others of the earlier group were elected into membership. Throughout this four-year organization period, Hetherington acted as Chairman of the group, and in 1930 McKenzie was elected its first President, serving in that capacity for many years. The purpose of the organization is discussed in the chapter that follows.

National Physical Education Service. After World War I, many conferences were held patterned after the famous Boston Conference of 1889. The most far-reaching in its effects on physical education was one held in 1918 when the United States Commissioner of Education called sixty leaders of physical education to Atlantic City for a conference. Out of this meeting grew the formation of a National Committee on Physical Education with Dr. Thomas D. Wood at its head. It immediately established the National Physical Education

Service to promote state and federal legislation on physical education programs and playgrounds in all schools under their jurisdiction. The Playground and Recreation Association accepted the sponsorship of this service, and $10,000 was contributed to finance it. James E. Rogers (1885–   ), who had been on the National Staff of PRA since 1911, was appointed head of the service, and from then on he travelled constantly all over the United States until his retirement in 1950, promoting state and federal programs of physical education. It is impossible to fully appraise the advancement which this work brought to the profession.

ATHLETIC ORGANIZATIONS

With the coming of the new century, athletics started to take such a prominent place in both school and national life that many organizations came into existence for their promotion and control. Some of these were already under way in the 1890's, and now new ones came into existence. The most important of these new ones (listed in the order of their founding) are discussed in the material that follows.

Public School Athletic League. In 1903 Gulick, then Head of Physical Education of the schools of Greater New York City, set up the Public School Athletic League. Although it was not a part of the school program it was sponsored by the Board of Education and also by the President of the College of the City of New York and by the Secretary of the Amateur Athletic Union. Wealthy citizens gave it financial support so that the school budget did not have to carry it. None but boys of good standing in their schools could enter the activities, and an effort was made to interest all boys, particularly those of only average ability. Early in its program the organization developed an Athletic Badge Test, and McKenzie, who had considerable skill as a sculptor, designed the first trophies.

In 1905, a Girls' Branch of the League was organized by Elizabeth Burchenal of Columbia University with the help of prominent women in New York City. Miss Burchenal became its first secretary and was the official instructor of folk dance and athletics. From the very start, the League refused to sponsor interschool contests. It started as did the boy's organization as a volunteer group outside the school program. However the Board of Education acknowledged it as the arbiter for all girls' athletics in the schools. In 1909, when Miss Burchenal was appointed Inspector of Girls' Athletics for the public schools of New York City, this organization became a branch of her department.

National Collegiate Athletic Association. Because of the great number of injuries and brutality that had developed in the game of football, serious criticism arose from many quarters at the opening of the new century. Many universities, including Stanford and Columbia, and several colleges abandoned the sport altogether. Doctors, educators, and ministers spoke and wrote against it. In 1905 a convention of delegates from twenty-eight leading colleges, called together by the Chancellor of New York University, formed the United States Intercollegiate Athletic Association. This body was empowered to make rules and regulations governing all major sports played by colleges. At the 1916 meeting the name was changed to the National Collegiate Athletic Association, football rules were revised so that play became more open, and penalties for violation of regulations were provided. Later the organization undertook to develop rules of other sports and to control the eligibility of the players.

Athletic Research Society. A group of people interested in the improvement of physical education, recreation, and athletics organized the Athletic Research Society and, in 1910, took up the first serious study of professionalism in athletics. Since then it has tackled other serious problems, making resolutions and recommendations to the proper authorities.

American Olympic Association. The American Olympic Committee was created in 1911 to take charge of the participation of American athletes in the Olympic games of 1912. In 1921 it developed into a permanent organization called the American Olympic Association with its membership made up of a federation of independent associations.

Athletic Conference of American College Women. Under the sponsorship of Blanche M. Trilling (1876–   ), Director of Physical Education for Women, this organization was born at the University of Wisconsin in 1917. Women student delegates from twenty-three colleges and universities met there for a conference to discuss the problems of athletics of college women. From its beginnings this organization has taken a stand against varsity intercollegiate athletics for women, promoting instead intramural programs for all. Throughout this period the organization held triennial conferences starting with the conference at the University of Indiana in 1921.

Women's Athletic Section of APEA. A Committee on Women's Athletics was set up in 1917 within the APEA to establish standards and formulate sports rules for athletics for girls and women. Miss Burchenal was appointed the first chairman of this national committee, and in 1927 it became the Women's Athletic Section of APEA.

Athletic League of North America. The Athletic League of North America was established in 1919 by the YMCA for the promotion of amateur athletics for boys and young men in out-of-school situations. By 1952 it had 7,500 athletes registered for its national sports competition.

National Federation of High School Athletic Associations. In the 1910's high schools in both Indiana and Illinois joined forces and created their two state associations. Shortly thereafter schools of other Midwest states followed their lead. Then, in 1920, representatives of the Illinois, Indiana, Iowa, Michigan, and Wisconsin associations met in Chicago and organized the National Federation of High School Athletic Associations. The meeting resulted from dissatisfaction over contests which were being sponsored for high school boys by various colleges and universities and by some sports clubs and promoters without attention to eligibility rules and high school regulations. The present name was adopted, in 1922, when eleven states had joined the association. By the close of this era twenty-eight states had joined to work for their common interests in control and direction of sports for high school boys.

National Amateur Athletic Federation. Shortly after World War I, great dissatisfaction developed among parents, educators, playground leaders, youth-group leaders, and laymen in general over the trend of athletics in the United States, which were under a leadership that seemed to have no guiding principles other than to produce winning teams at any cost. National leaders in several organizations concerned with athletics came together to discuss these problems. The Secretaries of the United States War and Navy Departments, both deeply interested in the right type of athletic programs for servicemen, joined in the informal discussions. Out of this meeting developed the NAAF in 1922 with Col. Henry Breckinridge (1886–   ), a New York City attorney who was President of U.S. Navy League, as President and Mrs. Herbert Hoover (1878–1944), whose husband was at the time United States Secretary of Commerce and who, herself, was President of the Girl Scouts of America, as one Vice President and Dr. George J. Fisher, Executive Director of the Boy Scouts of America, as the other Vice President. Its stated aim was "to create and maintain in the United States a permanent organization representative of amateur athletics and organizations devoted thereto; to establish and maintain the highest ideals of amateur sport; to promote the development of physical education; to encourage the standardization of rules of all amateur athletic games and competitions, and to encourage the participation of men of this country in the International Olympic games." All leading organizations in the United States interested in sane sports for American youth joined the Federation which lasted until 1930. In that year it dissolved, having accomplished its main purpose—to raise the standards of American sports and to break the hold of certain sports promoters who had seized substantial control of American sports and American athletes.

Women's Division of the NAAF. In April, 1923, Mrs. Hoover called a meeting in Washington attended by over 200 women who were interested in the promotion of sports for women, and they set up a Women's Division within the newly organized NAAF. Mrs. Hoover was elected Chairman of the Board, which position she gave up in 1928, when her husband became President of the United States. The groundwork of the organization was laid by the following recognized leaders among women physical educators of the country who were elected to membership on the Executive Committee: Helen McKinstry (1878–1949) of the Central School of Physical Education; Dr. J. Anna Norris (1874–   ) of the University of Minnesota; Ethel Perrin, Executive Secretary of the American Child Health Association; Blanche Trilling, of the University of Wisconsin; and Agnes R. Wayman of Barnard College. Within five months the new organization had 250 members made up of institutions, organizations, and individuals. At its first annual conference held at the University of Chicago in April, 1924, the organization adopted a platform for the formation of sane and wholesome athletics for girls and women of the United States, and they worked to get acceptance of this platform in schools, in industry, in fact, in all segments of life promoting physical activities for girls and women. Miss Perrin served as the first Chairman of the Executive Committee, and Dr. Norris served as Chairman of the Resolutions Committee which drew up the first NAAF standards for the conduct of sports for girls and women.

State Leagues of High School Girls' Athletic Associations. In the early 1920's the first State League of Girls' Athletic Associations was established in Illinois. Its purpose was to promote programs of athletics for all girls to offset the undesirable program of interschool athletics maintained in many schools for the favored few. Shortly after this leagues were set up in Colorado and Nebraska. These three state leagues advised local girls' athletic associations in high schools and helped them set up intramural programs for all girls. They established state point systems leading to local and state awards for athletic participation and achievement. The Illinois League became the most highly organized of all such girls' leagues, maintaining an executive secretary and central office in Chicago and sponsoring summer camps for its member schools.

LEADERS OF PHYSICAL EDUCATION

With the greatly increased size of the profession at the opening of the twentieth century there naturally arose a larger group of leaders than in the earlier era. Among these were many recognized above others for their foresight, wisdom, and enthusiasm which advanced the profession to a higher place in education and community life. Of these mention can be given here to only a pre-eminent few.

Time has given prominence to four leaders of physical education of this period to whom comes acclaim far beyond the confines of the profession itself, namely Luther Halsey Gulick, who brought the profession to the notice of the lay public; Thomas D. Wood, who called the profession to the attention of health education; R. Tait McKenzie, who brought recognition of the profession to the medical and art worlds; and Clark W. Hetherington, who sold physical education to general education. They are discussed chronologically.

Luther Halsey Gulick (1865–1918). Luther Gulick was born in Honolulu of missionary parents and as a child lived in several foreign countries, in Europe as well as in the Orient. At Oberlin College he came under the influence of Dr. Delphine Hanna, who aroused his interest in physical education. Wood was his roommate, and together they worked out a philosophy of physical education which in later years brought strength and advancement to the profession. After receiving his medical degree from the Medical College of New York University he went to the Springfield YMCA Training School to start its "gymnasium department."

From YMCA work he went to New York City in 1900 to organize the Department of Physical Education of Greater New York City, leaving that work in 1907 to join the staff of the Russell Sage Foundation to work full-time for the Playground Association of America which he had founded. During this period he built his camp at Lake Sebago in Maine which developed into the famous Gulick Camps which gave birth to the Camp Fire Girls of America. In 1913 he left the Russell Sage Foundation to take up full-time work for the Camp Fire Girls, leaving that work in 1918 to devote himself fully to the War Board of the YMCA. In this last work he went to France early in 1918, heading up the foreign war work of the YMCA. After a six-week stay, he left Dr. James H. McCurdy in charge of affairs for the Board in France with six helpers— all that were then available instead of the 300 urgently needed—and returned to the United States to conduct a recruitment campaign for the YMCA overseas workers. And it was in his Lake Sebago Camp that he loved where he died in his sleep on August 13, 1918, having gone there for a brief rest from his arduous war-work duties.

Fig. 16. Luther Halsey Gulick. (Courtesy of *Journal of Health—Physical Education—Recreation.*)

Foremost Contributions. His many important contributions to physical education, recreation, education in general, and to the enrichment of American life are unmatched in number by any other leader in the profession. He was the founder of many important movements such as the establishment of physical education in the YMCA's of America, the first public school athletic league in America, the Playground Association of America, New York University Summer School of Physical Education, the Department of School Hygiene of the New York Academy of Medicine, the position of Secretary of the International Committee of YMCA's (he being the first to hold the position), and Camp Fire Girls of America. Besides this he was one of the founders of the American School Hygiene Association, the Boy Scouts of America, American Folk Dance Society, and American Camping Association.

Literary Productions. He served as editor of five different magazines, four of which he founded: *The Triangle*, 1891–92; *Physical Education*, 1892–96; *American Physical Education Review*, 1900–02; *Physical Training*, the organ of YMCA, 1901–03; and *Wahelo*, organ of the Camp Fire Girls, 1914–18. Besides his editorial work he published 217 articles on both popular and professional topics in fifty different periodicals and eight handbooks, nine pamphlets, and fourteen books. Perhaps his two best known books are *Physical Education* of 1904 and *The Efficient Life* of 1907.

Honors and Important Offices. The honors conferred upon Gulick and the high offices he held in important organizations are legion. To mention but a few he was a member of the International YMCA committee, President of AAAPE for five years, a member of the American Olympic Committee, the first President of the Playground Association of America, President of American School Hygiene Association, and the first President of the Camp Fire Girls of America. Three medals are awarded in his honor: (1) The Gulick Award of the American Association for Health, Physical Education and Recreation, (2) the Roberts-Gulick Award of the Society of Physical Directors of the YMCA's of North America, and (3) the Gulick Medal of the Camp Fire Association of America. New York City operates a playground named in his honor. He is a Fellow in Memoriam of the American Academy of Physical Education.

Appraisal of the Man. Gulick had educational ideas in advance of his time. Before John Dewey came upon the educational scene as the exponent of a new education Gulick was informing all his teachers that he was hiring them to teach boys and girls rather than subject matter, and as early as 1891 he introduced the use of photography to analyze movement.

When he first began his career the YMCA physical activity teachers were ex-pugilists, old soldiers, and ex-circus performers—most were non-Christian and not interested in educational ideals. He started the movement to have none but men of Christian character to teach in the YMCA's for which he was criticized as expecting too much.

He was a great individualist, essentially different from others, quick to take up new ideas and also quick to drop them, the executive type not interested in details. He had an enormous capacity for work, and his interests were wide. He had unusual drive, unusual leadership ability, unusual vision—hence he accomplished a prodigious amount of worthwhile work in the fifty-three years of his life.

Thomas Dennison Wood (1865–1951). Thomas D. Wood was born in Sycamore, Illinois. As a student at Oberlin College he, along with Gulick, his roommate, came under the influence of Dr. Hanna who interested him in taking up the study of physical education. After graduation from Oberlin in 1888 he procured his medical degree at Columbia University. His first position was that of Director of Physical Education and College Physician at Stanford University where he organized the department of physical education. Trying out his own theories, Wood set up the first Stanford Program around games, sports, tumbling, and outdoor living, thus establishing the first so-called "natural program" in the United States.

Fig. 17. Thomas D. Wood. (Courtesy of *Journal of Health – Physical Education–Recreation*.)

From 1901 to 1917 he was Professor and Director of Hygiene and Physical Education and College Physician at Columbia University; then served as Professor of Health Education of the same university until his retirement in 1932.

Foremost Contributions. Wood established the first professorship of health education, the first outlines for a school health program, the first graduate work in both physical education and health education in the United States and was the originator of the movement to replace foreign systems of gymnastics with natural gymnastics of American origins. He was an advocate of the study of child development and he fought to bring the attention of educators to the fact that physical education could help in the social, emotional, and intellectual development of the child as well as in its physical development. He also championed the education of the child for democratic living.

Honors and Important Offices. Wood was a Fellow of the American Association for the Advancement of Science, of the New York Academy of Medicine, and of the American Academy of Physical Education. He was the second person to receive the Gulick Award of APEA. He served the profession through many important positions in many related organizations. He organized the Joint Committee on Health Problems in Education of the American Medical Association and the National Education Association and served as chairman of the committee for over twenty-five years. He also helped develop the American Child Health Association and was a great crusader to make the schools accept their responsibility for protecting the health of school children. As Chairman of the Committee on the School and the Child of the White House Conference of 1930 on Child Health and Protection called by President Hoover, he put twenty-eight subcommittees to work under his direction and turned out a prodigious report.

Appraisal of the Man. As co-author of many books and contributor of major sections of various yearbooks on health and physical education, his writings have greatly enriched the profession. He was a great leader. His earnest seeking after a better life for all children and his educational philosophy advanced the professions of both physical education and health education to a marked degree.

Robert Tait McKenzie (1867–1938). R. Tait McKenzie, (the form of his name which he preferred) was born in Almonte, Ontario, Canada. He achieved international fame as a sculptor, but no less noteworthy were his achievements in the fields of medicine, writing, and physical education. A delicate boy, he took up gymnastics to strengthen his physique, and he continued this training at McGill University.

Becoming interested in physical education, he studied at the Springfield YMCA School and the Harvard Summer School before completing his medical studies at McGill University. In 1893 he became the Director of the Department of Physical Training at McGill and at the same time House Physician at the General Hospital in Montreal. He remained at McGill University for ten years serving also one year as House Physician to the Governor General of Canada. In

Fig. 18. R. Tait McKenzie. (From a painting by Maurice Molarsky. Courtesy of the University of Pennsylvania, Philadelphia, Pennsylvania.)

1904 he became Director of Physical Education at the University of Pennsylvania, which position he held until his retirement in 1931. In 1915 he offered his services to help the British in their war effort, becoming Temporary Major in the Medical Corps of the Royal Air Force of England and later Inspector of Physical Training for Kitchener's Armies.

Literary and Artistic Productions. The best known of McKenzie's several books are: *Exercise in Education and Medicine* (1909), *The Treatment of Convalescent Soldiers by Physical Means,* and *Reclaiming the Maimed* (1918). A sculptor of international repute, several of his sculptured pieces are world famous. The King of Sweden conferred upon him the King's Medal for distinguished service as a sculptor. His Olympic Shield of athletes is the only one ever attempted by a sculptor. The famous Greek sculptor, Phidias, made the famous shield of Athena Parthenos, and the Italian sculptor, Benvenuto Cellini made three shields, but neither attempted to make one depicting athletes, although, through the ages, the athlete has been a popular subject for sculptors. A copy of McKenzie's "Blighty" was a favorite desk ornament of King George V of England. Reproductions of many of his statues adorn the magnificent Payne Whitney gymnasium at Yale.

McKenzie achieved international reputation for his British war memorials, notably the one in Edinburgh in Prince's Street Gardens entitled "The Call" and one in Cambridge, England, entitled "The Homecoming" and one in his birthplace at Almonte, Canada. Other well-known pieces of sculpture are his monuments at Harvard University and the University of Pennsylvania. He became famous in art circles as the first sculptor since the days of the Greek ascendency to use the athletic ideal as his subject. His biography, *R. Tait McKenzie: Sculptor of Youth,* contains illustrations of all of his chief sculptured pieces. As early as 1904 his art work was exhibited in London at the Royal Academy. He held a one-man exhibit of his sculpturing in London in 1920 and in New York City in the 1930's.

Honors and Important Offices. In 1904 McKenzie was selected as lecturer in artistic anatomy for the Olympic games held in connection with the St. Louis World Fair. He served the APEA as President for four years and was one of the founders and the first President of The American Academy of Physical Education, serving from 1930 until his death in 1938. Three colleges conferred honorary degrees upon him.

The American Academy has created the R. Tait McKenzie Memorial Lectureship which is given at the annual convention of the AAHPER. The full issue of the *Journal of Health and Physical Education*, February, 1944, is devoted to his memory, containing biographical material and tributes from his vast circle of admirers. The AAHPER purchased from his estate the original of his "Column of Youth" and placed it in the national headquarters building of the National Education Association in Washington as a memorial to him.

Appraisal of the Man. Time alone can determine R. Tait McKenzie's proper niche among the pre-eminent leaders of the profession. No one of modern times has bound the profession to the glories of its ancient heritage as did he through his art work. In this alone his contribution is unique. He was a gentleman of the old school, a man of great cultural background and of unusual personal magnetism.

Clark W. Hetherington (1870–1942). Clark Hetherington was born at Lanesborough, Minnesota. A graduate of Stanford University and trained in psychology, he became an assistant in psychology at Clark University (1899–1900) and organized their laboratory in animal psychology. From 1900 to 1910 he was Professor of Physical Education and Director of Gymnastics and Athletics at the University of Missouri; from 1911 to 1918, Lecturer and Professor at the University of Wisconsin; from 1918 to 1921, Supervisor of Physical Education of the State of California; from 1921 to 1922, Professor of Physical Education at Columbia University and special lecturer at Wellesley College; from 1922 to 1928, Professor of Physical Education at New York University; from 1929 to 1933, Professor of Physical Education at Stanford University; and for the last five years before his retirement in 1938 he was Consultant in Hygiene and Physical Education at Stanford.

Fig. 19. Clark W. Hetherington

Foremost Contributions. Hetherington was one of the founders of the Athletic Research Society, the Joint Committee of NEA and the AMA on Health Problems in Education, the Midwest Physical Education Society, the Pacific Coast Society of Physical Education (today's South West District of AAHPER), and the American Academy of Physical Education. He was one of the chief promoters of the natural gymnastics movement. He produced several books and articles, chief among which was his book, *The School Program of Physical Education.*

Honors and Important Offices. He served as a member of the Board of Directors of the PAA, President of the Athletic Research Society, President of the Department of Physical Education of the NEA, President of the Midwest Physical Education Association, and in the four years of its organizational period he served as Chairman of the American Academy of Physical Education.

He was the recipient of the Posse Medal for distinguished service in the field of health and the Gulick Award of AAHPER for distinguished service to physical education. The University of Southern California conferred upon him the honorary degree of Doctor of Pedagogy. The American Academy of Physical Education has established the Hetherington Award in his honor.

Appraisal of the Man. Clark Hetherington was recognized as the foremost scholar and philosopher of physical education of his day. In the words of Charles H. McCloy (1886–), of the University of Iowa, upon receiving the first Academy Hetherington Award: "Clark Hetherington's thinking laid the base, not only for an integrated philosophy of physical education, but also pointed the way for much scientific research which was to follow, to establish facts upon which to base further constructive philosophizing."

Others. It is not possible in a short history to give space to biographical sketches of all the leaders whose fine work notably advanced the profession of physical education in the early decades of the twentieth century. Many have been mentioned throughout this book in connection with specific activities and movements in which they played an important part. Brief biographical sketches follow for five leaders whose work was of special significance to the profession— Jessie H. Bancroft, Elizabeth Burchenal, James H. McCurdy, Clelia Mosher, and Ethel Perrin.

Jessie H. Bancroft (1867–1952). Jessie Bancroft was born in Winona, Minnesota. After one year at Winona Normal School and one at Iowa Medical College she took a few gymnastic courses in Minneapolis from a former pupil of Sargent who was located there. She then opened a school of her own and conducted "parlor classes" throughout Minnesota, Iowa, and Illinois before attending the Harvard Summer School in 1891. In 1893 she was appointed Director of Physical Training of the Brooklyn Public Schools at a salary of $1200 per year. Ten years later she became Assistant Director of Physical Education of the schools of Greater New York City under Gulick which position she held until she retired in 1928. She produced many books and carried on much research, particularly in the field of posture. As a result of her measurements of school children she procured adjustments in school seats and desks, an unheard-of innovation for those days. She was a founder and President of the American Posture League, the first person to receive the Gulick Award of the American Physical Education Association, the first woman to be taken into membership in the American Academy of Physical Education, the first woman in the profession to produce a considerable body of professional literature, writing on posture, games, and anthropometry, and the first woman to head a large public school department of physical education. During World War I she was Chairman of the Government Commission on Training Camp Activities and President of the War Camp Community Service. Also she established the American Cooked Food Services for the American Expeditionary Forces.

Elizabeth Burchenal. Elizabeth Burchenal was born in Richmond, Indiana. She graduated from Earlham College and the Sargent School of Physical Education. Her first position was at Columbia University where she taught from 1902 until 1905 when she organized and became Executive Director of the Girls' Branch of the Public School Athletic League of New York City. Four years later she became Inspector of Girls' Athletics for the New York City public schools, which position she held until she founded and became Executive Director of the American Folk Arts Society in 1916. In 1929 she became President and permanent Director in charge of the Folk Arts Center in New York City. Her professional contributions have been chiefly in the fields of athletics for girls and women and folk dance. In the former she served as the first chairman of the Women's Athletic Committee of APEA. This organization is today the National Division of Women's Athletics. As its first chairman she started the work in the United States of establishing national standards for girls' and women's sports.

In the field of folk dance Miss Burchenal travelled widely in Europe from 1904 on, collecting and publishing dances of the people of many lands and conducting dance research. For many years she lectured and conducted institutes of folk dance throughout the United States, Canada, England, Scotland, Ireland, and Germany. For many years she was Chairman of the USA Committee on Folk Arts and a member of the International Committee on Folk Arts. She was the official delegate of the United States to the Fine Arts Section meetings of the League of Nations and, later, UNESCO of the United Nations at Geneva, Prague, London and Paris.

Miss Burchenal has been a resident Fellow of Carl Schurz Memorial Foundation and a Research Fellow of the Oberlaender Trust. During World War I she was Assistant State Inspector of N.Y. Military Training Commission and National Representative of U.S. War and Navy Departments Commission Training Camp Activities and also a member of the War Workers Committee of the U.S. Department of Labor.

Miss Burchenal was one of four women who were charter members of the American Academy of Physical Education, a recipient of both the Honor Award (1931) and Gulick Award (1953) of AAHPER. Boston University conferred upon her the honorary degree of Doctor of Science in Physical Education and she has long been listed in *Who's Who In America*.

James Huff McCurdy (1866–1940). Graduating from the International YMCA School of Springfield, James H. McCurdy went to New York University where he procured the medical doctor's degree in 1893. In 1895 he returned to the school in Springfield as Director of the Physical Department which position he held for thirty-five years. From 1930 until his retirement in 1934 he was head of the Division of Health and Physical Education of Pratt Institute in Brooklyn. During World War I he was on leave to serve as head of athletics, medical and social services of the YMCA in France. Always deeply interested in physiological research he devoted his years of retirement to studies of organic efficiency, particularly for men past middle age, war veterans, and Army and Navy fliers. Throughout his teaching career he made significant contributions to the profession in the field of physiology of exercise and published much material of value to the profession. His book on the physiology of exercise was one of the earliest in America on that subject. Indeed, he devoted his adult life to the establishment of sound scientific procedures for the profession. He was a charter member of the American Academy of Physical Education. As Executive Secretary of APEA and Editor of its magazine, *The American Physical Education Review,* for twenty-four years (1906–30) he gave the national professional association the best of his talents and the best years of his life.

Clelia D. Mosher (1863–1940). Born in Albany, New York, Dr. Clelia Mosher was educated at Wellesley College and at Cornell, Johns Hopkins, and Stanford Universities. She was deeply interested in research and early in her medical career she challenged the all too prevalent ideas about the physical incapacities of women. As an assistant in hygiene at Stanford University she developed her studies that exploded the idea that women breathe costally. Out of this study grew her deep interest in dress reform for women. From 1894 on she waged battle for abandonment of stiff corsets and the adoption of sensible shoes and lightweight clothing, and encouraged women's participation in sports. She organized girls' basketball teams and arranged game schedules for them. When she became physical examiner of women at Stanford University she developed her research in functional periodicity in women and exploded the fallacious theory that menstruation is an infirmity that must be suffered by women. Later she devised exercises for the relief of painful menstruation, known as the "Mosher exercises," which have been used for fifty years in Europe as well as in America. Following this she was a co-inventor at Stanford of the schematograph as an aid in posture training. During World War I she went to France with the American Red Cross to work with refugee children and later became Medical Director of the Bureau of Refugees and Relief. All women owe Clelia Mosher a great debt for, through her studies, she set them free physiologically.

Ethel Perrin (1871–   ). Born in Wellesley, Massachusetts, Ethel Perrin graduated in the second class of the Boston Normal School of Gymnastics in 1892. She remained at the school and taught there for fourteen years. From there she went to Smith College and the University of Michigan before the Superintendent of Schools of Detroit persuaded her to join his staff and organize a department of physical education for girls in one of his high schools. Up to that time their program consisted merely of basketball played by a few girls. She organized such a good program of a variety of activities interesting large groups of girls that the following year the superintendent urged her to take over the directorship of physical education for both boys and girls for all the schools of Detroit. Accepting the offer she became the second woman in the United States to head a department of physical education in a city public school system. In her first year in that position (1909–10) she had three men and three women on her staff who supervised all classwork which was carried on by the regular classroom teachers. In a few years she was able to appoint all professionally trained persons to do the teaching. Then she added health

education work to her program and soon had forty specialists in that field on her staff. By 1923 when she left the
Detroit position she had built up a staff of 350 physical
and health educators and 15 supervisors. Her department
soon came to be considered the model public school department of all in the United States.

Miss Perrin left the field of physical education in 1923
to become Associate Director of the American Child Health
Association with her office in New York City. She held this
position for fifteen years until her retirement in 1936 when
she joined a friend in a farming venture near New York City.
She was recognized as one of the most ardent champions of
correct standards of physical education and athletics for
both boys and girls. As one of the founders of the Women's
Division of the NAAF she served as the first chairman of the
Executive Committee. She also served as one of the early
presidents of the Midwest Physical Education Association.
A recipient of the Honor Award of APEA (1931) she later
received the Gulick Award (1946) for her distinguished
services to the profession.

24

PHYSICAL ACTIVITIES OF THE
MID-TWENTIETH CENTURY

The great mechanization of life at mid-twentieth century has brought much leisure to the people. The fourteen-to-sixteen-hour work day of the 1880's has changed to the six-to-eight-hour work day of today on a forty-hour a week basis with talk of even a six-hour work day for four days a week. Children as well as adults have greatly increased leisure. Except in rural areas there is little opportunity for children and adults to do hard physical labor together. Outside of school hours many children spend much time at movies, poring over "funnies," or watching television, so that physical education in the schools has an increased responsibility for giving them a rich program to meet physical development needs to make up for the breakdown of this responsibility in the home. Outside the schools, physical education plays an increasingly important role in the life of adults, also, who have come to realize that they should devote much of their recreational hours to physical activities.

In the fall of 1956 an estimated 41,381,000 pupils were enrolled in our schools with 7,919,000 of them in high schools (an estimated 4,751,400 will finish); 3,232,000 in colleges (an estimated 387,840 will finish); and 3,500,000 starting to school for the first time. In 1930 there were but 971,584 students enrolled in our 1,078 colleges. These figures reflect population increases largely, although some of the advance can be accounted for by increased percentages in school attendance. For example the draftees of World War I had an average of seven years of schooling as against ten for the draftees of World War II; 20 per cent of the former had completed high school as against 47 per cent of the latter group; and but 5 per cent of the former group had one year of college as against 16 per cent for the World War II draftees. These figures, reflecting not only an increase in population but also an increase in interest in education, give physical education a greatly increased horizon for action and service.

ACTIVITIES OF PHYSICAL EDUCATION

Dance and Rhythms. The new developments in dance of this era have been the establishment of the so-called "modern dance" and the revival of square dance. In the early thirties a Dance Section was added to the AAHPE, and the Bennington School of Dance opened at Burlington, Vermont, as a summer school which functioned from 1934 to 1942 and served splendidly in presenting modern dance as one of the best tools in both motor and creative education. By 1947, there were seventeen colleges offering a dance major. Since then the Summer School of Dance of Connecticut College has opened, also the Dance Department of the Juilliard School of Music.

Modern or Contemporary Dance. Modern dance came to America when Mary Wigman (1886–   ), an exponent of this form of dance and a leading teacher of Germany, first came to the United States in 1925. She was a pupil of Rudolph Laban (1879–   ), a famous European dance teacher, and was an exponent of "absolute" dance to the extent of discarding all musical accompaniment. Later she accepted the use of percussion instruments and primitive flutes and still later restored the piano to the dance studio provided the music used was composed for the dance—not the dance for the music. This form of dance offers no set forms. It requires merely that the movements of the dance express something. Fundamental techniques are concerned not with form as in the ballet form of dance but with putting the body under the control of the dancer.

American students of Miss Wigman brought this form of dance to a high stage of development in the United States, modifying the European form to suit America's own interpretation. At mid-century this form of dance is used in all schools and colleges where teachers trained in this activity can be procured.

Square Dance. In the 1930's there arose an awakened interest in the dances of our pioneers. By the late 1940's and early 1950's the revival was moving forward enthusiastically. The Nebraska revival is typical of that in many other states. Lincoln, a city of a little over 100,000 population, had twenty-three square dance clubs in 1956; Omaha, twenty-nine; and other local groups supported thirty-one other clubs. All are united in the Nebraska Folk and Square Dance Association, which, organized in the 1940's, holds an annual festival in Lincoln each spring with as many as 800 dancers on the floor at a time. It maintains a youth section which sponsors square dancing for young boys and girls throughout the state. Each year at its festival it features some one nationality represented among the citizenry of the state and invites this group to put on an exhibition of its Old-Country folk dancing. This has brought much pleasure to these groups in the way of friendly recognition of their Old-World culture and much of educational value to all others.

While Henry Ford's efforts of the 1920's and 1930's were directed towards a revival of the dignified New England form of the dance, Lloyd Shaw (1890–　), a school superintendent of Colorado Springs, and many others of the South and West have brought back the cowboy and southern mountain forms which were in common use in frontier days. Along with this revival has come renewed interest in the old-time round dances, also, the polka, schottisch, mazurka, and Varsovienne.

Gymnastics. A marked trend away from the use of gymnastics in school programs had developed by 1930. Formal activities were in use then in but 12 per cent of the schools— a marked contrast to the 100 per cent use at the opening of the century. Although the great array of educators and physical education leaders of this period charged that gymnastics was too subjective to meet the needs of education and did not carry over into life situations, there still were many who felt that, insofar as gymnastics serve for body-building in children's growth periods, they do have a place in the schools. These exponents of physical fitness have persisted in maintaining some gymnastics in the program. Gymnastics have held a firmer place in girls' programs than in boys', no doubt because of boys' more intense preoccupation with sports. However, as recently as 1956 a strong case for gymnastics for boys has developed as a sound educational venture in self-realization and creativity, built not on the free-standing exercises of gymnastics but on the apparatus work, using it for projects in stunts. Some men's departments in colleges support gymnastic teams and have supported them for many years. These teams compete in intercollegiate sports programs specializing in apparatus work, stunts, and tumbling. Practically none uses the old-time free-standing exercises done to a leader's commands. As to apparatus, the parallel bars, horizontal bars, side and long horse, and flying rings are used, plus the new and popular trampoline.

Corrective or Individual Gymnastics. A survey made for the United States Office of Education in 1931 brought out a criticism of the schools in that they were not offering corrective work for the children needing this individual attention. Out of the 460 schools investigated only 50 per cent were offering such work. An estimate of 1926, that 80 per cent of college men and women in the United States showed the lack of corrective work that should have been given them in high school, did arouse many schools and perhaps accounted for some of the 50 per cent of the schools that were offering this work by 1931. After World War II there was an awakening, and many schools have now established corrective work. Hospitals have also added specialized gymnastics to their rehabilitation programs. Most of these use calisthenics and apparatus work of various types. However, when the same end can be reached, many teachers use the games and sports skills instead of gymnastics.

Danish Gymnastics. This system of gymnastics has largely replaced the old German and Swedish forms. Designed for the Folk Arts Schools of rural areas of Denmark, it stresses flexibility to relieve the musclebound condition found in the Danish youth. In the early 1930's Helen McKinstry, then Head of the Central School of Physical Education, and later President of Russell Sage College, was the representative in America of Niels Bukh, its chief exponent. She promoted several summer sessions for American teachers who went to Ollerup, Denmark, to take instruction from Bukh. These teachers brought back this activity to the school and college programs. There has been much enthusiasm for this form of gymnastics, and it has been used widely. During World War II it was used in the women's physical fitness programs for both civilians and the Armed Services. After the war, popularity for this form of gymnastics gradually died out to be revived temporarily here and there after touring Danish gymnastics teams aroused enthusiasm afresh.

Sports and Athletics. Without question, the sports and games program, which developed slowly during the nineteenth century, had literally pushed the traditional and formal required physical education program into the background by the middle of the twentieth century. Despite efforts by many leaders to broaden the base of athletic sports in schools and colleges, football, basketball, track, and baseball remain as the standard and important athletic games for boys and men throughout the country. Of these four, football holds the number one position, but in the world outside the colleges the situation is different. In 1934, the ten fastest growing sports were reported to be the following in the order listed: softball, badminton, basketball, squash, football, table tennis, lawn tennis, handball, paddle tennis, and horseshoes. But by 1940, the order was: skiing, fishing, bowling, softball, badminton, skating, bicycling, basketball, table tennis, and paddle tennis. A government report shows that sales of boats, bicycles, water craft, and golf clubs went up 137 per cent from 1940 to 1955 and that participation in bowling, skating, and golf was up 34 per cent and spectator sports had fallen off 19 per cent.

This era opened with the first radio broadcasts of important games, which caused much discussion "pro and con." Time proved that the broadcasts did hurt attendance as predicted but not enough to discontinue them. The same thing happened again in 1940 when television first came upon the competitive sports contest scene, but TV won out just as had radio before it.

Baseball. The earlier era saw the marked rise of professional baseball with its great following of fans completely overshadowing the amateur game. In this new era the North American Baseball Association has been making an effort to revive and encourage small-town teams and to restore the rural baseball diamond to its old-time popularity. In 1930 the first night baseball game was played in Des Moines, Iowa, and five years later the first night game was played in the major league. The techniques for night lighting have brought baseball to the amateurs of summer evenings.

Basketball. Basketball, the first team sport of purely American origin, had, by the 1950's, spread throughout the world. Teams of many nations now compete in the sport in the Olympic games. When it was first used in international competition in the Olympics in Berlin in 1936, Dr. James A. Naismith, its originator, was the guest of the Olympic Committee and was honored at the games. An estimated twenty million people play this sport throughout the world. The National Collegiate Athletic Association eliminations contest, the National Intercollegiate championship, and the National Invitation tournaments represent the major college play-offs held near the end of each basketball season. Crowds of 15,000 people or more often attend college basketball games in various cities throughout the country. Gambling has reached down to involve college basketball players on occasion, but even with accompanying poor publicity the game continues to grow in its appeal. Basketball seems destined to remain the most popular winter sport in colleges and high schools.

Today's game is changed considerably from its early days when the tallest men were the height we consider today but average. In all "pro" basketball teams of today the centers range from 6 feet, 9 inches, to 7 feet tall, the forwards from 6 feet, 6 inches to 6 feet, 9 inches, and the guards from 6 feet, 1 inch to 6 feet, 7 inches.

In college basketball the University of Nebraska varsity team of 1957 ranged in height from 5 feet, 10 inches to 6 feet, 8 inches. This was, no doubt, typical of most college teams. However, Nebraska and Kansas State each had a player a few years ago who was 6 feet, 10 inches tall. The University of Kansas claimed in 1957 the tallest man of all basketball history in their player who was 7 feet, 2 inches tall. Today's high school players average 5 feet, 5 inches.

Because of this great increase in the stature of athletes over that of the early 1900's, the height of the basket, which has remained unchanged through the years, is in an altogether different ratio with the height of the average player. Some have advocated, although as yet in vain, that the basket be raised. However, there have been of late years several rules changes aimed at the extra tall man such as widening the lane to twelve feet and prohibiting a player from guiding the ball to the basket.

Bowling. In 1940 more people engaged in bowling in the United States than in any other sport. Fifteen million people were bowling at that time with the sport holding its greatest popularity in the Midwest. By that date there were in the United States 25,000 bowling alleys with an average of eight lanes each.

While the first tournament in 1901 brought out 215 entrants, the 1940 International World's Championship tournament brought out 30,000 entrants on 6,000 teams from 731 cities with 100,000 spectators during the eight-week contest.

The American Bowling Congress (ABC) and the Women's International Bowling Congress (WIBC) were attacked by many individuals and groups in the 1940's for the racial discrimination clauses in their constitutions. Industrial recreation groups particularly felt this injustice. The Director of the UAW-CIO Recreation Department spoke out in 1950 in the UAW-CIO Recreation Bulletin, *The Round-up:*

How about bowling? The UAW likes bowling. The union wants to see plenty of lanes jammed with UAW keglers this year. But this union doesn't spell b-o-w-l-i-n-g A.B.C. So jot this down in your book and underline it. The American Bowling Congress is still singing the white supremacy song. The "Caucasian Only" sign is tacked on their door. . . . Maybe it doesn't seem too important to you, this bowling battle. But if you'll sit down and think about it a while, you'll figure how this business of everybody's right to knock down tenpins fits into the whole big pattern of democracy.

The attacks paid off, for in May, 1950, the ABC at its annual convention with 518 members present voted overwhelmingly to remove the word "white" from their constitution and thereby opened their "supposed-to-be" national tournaments to all the American people. Previous to this a judge of the Superior Court of Cook County, Illinois, found the ABC guilty of racial discrimination and fined the organization $2500 on the ground that its conduct was "violative of the provision of the Illinois Civil Rights Act." This opened the door, and the American Bowling Congress "saw the light." Immediately the women's group voted racial discrimination out of its constitution also.

Football. The popularity of American football in colleges is tremendous—crowds of between 90,000 and 100,000 people at a single contest are no longer rarities. The first Rose Bowl game (post-season and intersectional) occurred in 1902, and more than 20 other bowl games have been promoted in a single season in various sections of the United States.

The budget, the efforts to lure athletes to schools or colleges, the commercialization of football surpass that of any other sport. More coaches, in high schools and colleges, are enployed for football than any other sport. Despite occasional mild scandals concerning the conduct of football, it continues to grow in importance, and it is the "wealthy uncle" who supports practically all the other sports in colleges and high schools and builds the magnificent stadiums and gymnasiums.

Night football like night baseball took on importance early in this era. Touch football has now become popular in boys' and men's intramural programs. A modification of the game—six-man football—was devised in 1934 by Stephen E. Epler (1909–   ) then physical director and coach at the high school in Hebron, Nebraska. It took the small high schools of the country by storm, and most high schools of America are small schools. Within two years, 1,233 schools were playing this form of the game. Epler later received from the American Academy of Physical Education a citation for this creative service to the profession.

Softball. The Amateur Softball Association was organized in 1932. In 1934 a Rules Committe made up of representatives of NRA, YMCA, NCAA and APEA drew up official rules. The game has become tremendously popular in industry, in intramural programs in the schools and small towns, and with all ages and both sexes.

Swimming. This era opened with 25 per cent of all high schools and 1.2 per cent of elementary schools in cities of over 100,000 population equipped with swimming pools. Cities of population from 30,000 to 100,000 had pools in 23.9

per cent of high schools and 1 per cent of elementary
schools; towns of 10,000 to 30,000 population had pools in
14.8 per cent of their high schools; and cities of population
below 10,000 had no school pools. By 1937 there were 700
YMCA's in the United States that had swimming pools with
98 per cent of them built since 1900 and the other 2 per cent
built between 1885 and 1900 and still in use in 1937. By
1940 there were in the United States 8,000 pools, half of
them outdoor and half indoor with 50 per cent of them built
since 1925. Building was at a standstill in most of the 1930's
because of the depression and in the 1940's because of
World War II, so that only in the 1950's are new pools being
built. By mid-century pools are considered a "must" for all
gymnasiums in large cities. Small towns that never would
have dreamed of having a municipal pool a generation ago
are installing them today.

Other Sports. Badminton came to the United States by
way of Canada around 1936 and enjoys its greatest popularity in the large cities. The 1930's brought a craze for midget
golf and golf-driving ranges which proved a great boon to
schools wishing to teach golfing skills but without facilities.
Sports equipment firms reported sales of golf equipment of
twenty-nine million dollars at that time compared to a
twelve-million-dollar sale five years earlier. Between 1936
and 1940, the WPA constructed 207 municipal golf courses in
the United States. At the present time every large city
numbers thousands of golf enthusiasts who find valuable
recreation in the game. An estimate places the number of
golf links in United States today at more than two thousand.

Paddle tennis became popular in the 1930's. NRA reported that by 1939 there were an estimated 64,000 players
using the ninety-two courts at Manhattan Beach alone.
There has been an American Paddle Tennis Association
since 1934.

In 1930 Sonja Henie (1913–   ), the famous skating star,
made her debut in the United States, starting a wave of enthusiasm for skating. Skating had existed for years in the

northern climates but now the development of artificial ice rinks brought it to all parts of the country all seasons of the year. Ice hockey, too, now came into prominence, and before long professional ice hockey leagues were established. The WPA built 691 ice-skating rinks throughout the United States in the 1940's, and, by 1950, no city considered building a municipal auditorium without provision for an artificial ice-rink. The year 1931 brought the United States of America the first "ski" train or rather "snow" train as it was then called. Since then skiing has become one of the great participation sports of the nation. Hundreds of thousands of skiers fill the ski trails of the White Mountains area, and the Utah, Oregon, Colorado, and Washington forests and mountains.

ATHLETIC COMPETITION FOR BOYS AND MEN

Interest in sports has become so keen that more publicity is given to them in the daily papers than is given to any other single activity. The tendency of sports to attract many fans gives rise to considerable concern by many who desire to see people actively engaged. However, those so concerned should gain satisfaction from the numbers who participate in bowling, fishing and hunting, tennis, softball, swimming, and various other sports and games.

Intercollegiate Athletics. Some physical educators believe that the emphasis on winning which pervades athletic competition in many schools and colleges will lead to the eventual disintegration of athletic competition if not curbed. There is, also, much concern in education circles over the subsidization of athletes and a growing desire that all colleges follow the example set by the Ivy League schools.

In the college Ivy League (Brown, Columbia, Cornell, Dartmouth, Harvard, Pennsylvania, Princeton, and Yale) with a range of enrollment from 2,400 to 7,900 undergraduates, the members of the football teams are students in every sense of the word—not men brought in to play football.

Strictly amateur, these teams nonetheless draw large crowds and hold student, as well as public, interest.

These Ivy League colleges play round-robin schedules with each other, completely under the control of the academic authorities. There are no athletic scholarships. No student who was subsidized as a high school player is eligible to play on these college teams. Each player must be working in earnest toward a college degree, and there are no snap courses for athletes. Players receive the same consideration for scholarships as do all other students. The amount of scholarship granted to each student, athlete or non-athlete, is determined by educational authorities and not by coaches or athletic directors. All gate receipts from games go into the college treasury.

The NCAA has increased its sports coverage in national tournaments in this era bringing in boxing (1932), gymnastics, tennis, and cross country (1938), basketball (1939), golf (1940), fencing (1941), baseball (1947), and ice hockey (1948) so that today there is wide sports coverage in intercollegiate contests.

Interscholastic Athletics. Early in this era there developed interschool competition for elementary schools which called forth protests from the medical profession, many school administrators, and physical educators. At its convention in 1947, AAHPER adopted resolutions advocating the abolition of interschool competitive athletics for elementary school children. In spite of this open opposition, little league football and baseball is sponsored by private organizations for the benefit of boys twelve years of age and under. In the summer of 1951, little league baseball was being played in thirty-seven states. The national championship games attracted over 10,000 people. Thousands of boys participate in these sports each year, and the number competing is increasing, although educational guidance is sadly lacking in the conduct of these programs.

Competition at high school level is controlled by the State Leagues of High School Athletic Associations as discussed earlier. Communities throughout the nation have become interested in having their high schools sponsor winning football, basketball, baseball, and track teams. This condition has made it possible to erect large gymnasiums, playing fields, and stadiums in which public school students participate. Support for such ventures has come from public taxation, school bonds, or donations from businessmen.

Intramurals. Although intramural athletics have grown tremendously at both the college and high school levels, it was reported in 1949 in the proceedings of the 54th Annual Convention of AAHPER that, of 113 elementary schools surveyed, only 46 per cent provided intramural sports programs for the elementary school children. So there is much room for growth in the years ahead. Practically all colleges, large high schools, and a high percentage of smaller high schools now offer a varied intramural program of sports. Today most students in college find some opportunity to satisfy their desire to engage in athletic contests of a recreative nature.

Nonschool Athletic Competition. The AAU is the main promoter in the United States of tournaments of amateur sports outside the school realm, although today it is crowded by the YMCA national sports program which reaches thousands of boys. Baseball and football leagues cover the professional players. These leagues are playing an important role in the racial desegregation problem. Players of a variety of races and nationalities are on their teams: Negroes, Mexicans, and Cubans, as well as others whose names suggest every European country imaginable. Several Negro players in both football and baseball leagues have won the coveted "Most Valuable Player" and "All-American" awards.

From an inauspicious beginning at Latrobe, Pennsylvania, in 1895, major professional football has grown into big business. Major football teams are located in the East, Midwest, and Far West. Each summer since 1934 the winning professional team has played a football game against a team of all-stars selected from the graduating classes of the various colleges throughout the United States. This classic has attracted as many as 101,000 spectators.

Professional basketball has not yet achieved the success of "pro" baseball and football. However, the Harlem Globe Trotters, who have played exhibition games around the world, have promoted much enthusiasm for the sport. The State Department of the United States has, since World War II, used athletes such as these Globe Trotters as goodwill ambassadors in various parts of the world, and the investment in them has paid good dividends.

Olympic Games. The Olympic games of this era have engaged U.S.A. teams as follows: 1932 in Los Angeles, 1936 in Berlin, 1948 in London, 1952 in Helsinki, and 1956 in Melbourne. In these modern Olympics, U.S.A. teams have been the acknowledged victors until 1956 when the Russian team out-scored the Americans in team points and totals. These team points and totals are, however, unofficial. Olympic winners are determined only event by event. There is no official point system by which totals may be decided. However, newspaper reporters have, through the years, devised their own unofficial point system, for these games, particularly for the track and field events, and it is because of their own unofficial pronouncement that a claim is made that any country has won the Olympics. Such claims are without official sanction.

Be that as it may, in the 1956 Olympics, the Americans defeated the Russians in track and field, basketball, swimming and diving, and weight-lifting, but the Russians defeated the Americans in boxing, gymnastics, Greco-Roman wrestling, shooting, and soccer. The Soviet government subsidizes all its athletes. They are civil-servant athletes under the control and in the pay of the government. But, at that, they make a splendid showing in athletic ability.

SPORTS FOR GIRLS AND WOMEN

This era has been one of great activity in sports for girls and women. With the National Section for Girls and

Women's Sports of AAHPER, State High School Leagues, Women's Division of NAAF, and Athletic Federation of College Women all working for sports for all and play for play's sake, intramurals have become the organized form of sports for the great mass of American school girls and women. Since only an infinitesimal number of girls and women go out for the sports that involve gate receipts and "spectatoritis" with their resultant objective of winning at all costs and the settling of important championships, girls' sports do not make sensational news and so are not played up in the papers. Only a very few girls and women are of public interest in the sports world, and few girls' teams achieve even local, let alone state-wide or national, interest as do boys' and men's teams. A few states stir up some interest in girl's sports in the small towns, chiefly over girls' basketball, but this interest is, for the most part, spasmodic and of little consequence except in a few small communities.

This does not mean that American girls and women are not interested in sports. Intramural records from schools and colleges, youth centers, and community centers belie that thought. In all these organizations much in the way of girls' sports goes on constantly—mostly dual and individual sports since American girls and women on the whole prefer them to team sports.

The mottoes of the first group of women who organized and promoted sports for girls and women of America were, "A game for every girl and every girl in a game" and "Play for play's sake." These mottoes of the 1920's and 1930's are seldom heard in the 1950's although a check with the leaders will show that they still have them in mind.

Intercollegiate Competition. There is today practically no intercollegiate competition in sports for women in this country. American college girls do not care to go in for the intensive training and practice it would entail. A survey of intercollegiate athletics for women made in 1923 was repeated in 1930 at the request of the Women's Division of NAAF. One hundred fifty-four colleges and universities were included in this second survey. The 22 per cent of colleges reporting participation in intercollegiate athletics in 1923 had dropped to 12 per cent by 1930 with only 7 per cent using the varsity-team type of competition, the other 5 per cent using only the inter-class type. Fifty-three per cent of the colleges took part in play days with other schools in which the girls were mixed together in temporary teams with no team representing any one college.

Following that survey, play days took on importance and flourished for a while. Then with the coming of World War II they gave way, as did everything else, to the demands of the times and since then have not been revived to any appreciable extent. The intramural programs seem to take their place satisfactorily.

Interscholastic Competition. In the early part of this era, basketball as played by many high school girls was causing "headaches" for physical education teachers and girls' leaders more than any other sport. Through it the girls were frequently exploited for the publicity of many small towns and a few groups of men. These groups used boys' rules for girls and men coaches in most situations, and where women coaches were used, they were as a rule women who were not trained in the educational aspects of sports and in the care of girls in their sports play.

At mid-century nine states (Georgia, Iowa, Louisiana, North Carolina, North Dakota, Oklahoma, South Carolina, Tennessee, and Texas) maintain state tournaments for high school girls in basketball which are supported by the small towns of the state. No towns of population above 10,000 take part in these tournaments, no doubt because these larger schools maintain physical education programs for their girls with professionally trained women in charge. Nine states, through their State High School Athletics Associations, prohibit all interschool athletics for girls: Alabama, Colorado, Illinois, Nebraska, New York, Oregon, Utah, Wisconsin, and Wyoming. Nine other states prohibit interschool basketball for girls, and several others, while not prohibiting, do discourage such activities.

Nonschool Competition. YWCA's and like organizations and recreation centers offer women varied sports programs; yet little is known generally of these activities. Of all sports, basketball played by women causes the most controversy between physical educators (both men and women) who would keep sports for women purely in the realm of education and recreation and those sports promoters and Chambers of Commerce who would push women into spectator sports with their accompanying gate receipts, win-at-all-costs atmosphere, and championships at stake. Such sports activities for girls and women in the United States are almost 100 per cent promoted and organized by men.

Women educators trained in physical education have waged constant war throughout this century in favor of sports for all instead of intense participation for the few. In this battle they have been supported by noted men leaders who have given them courage to stand up against groups of other men who wish to exploit girls and women through sports.

Olympic Games. Since women first entered the modern Oympics as contestants in 1928 at Amsterdam, they have taken part in all Olympic games, but never have they achieved genuine public acclaim except in the 1932 games in Los Angeles. It was then that Babe Didrickson (1914–1956) started her career; she eventually was acclaimed the world's greatest woman athlete before her death in 1956 at the age of forty-two. No American sportswoman has achieved any particular fame in any succeeding Olympic games.

The women entering the Olympic games in 1956 were younger than in previous years. Australia's star woman athlete was but eighteen years old. Also, for the first time in the Olympic games the majority of the United States Olympic women contestants came from the college field rather than from industry as had been the case in all previous games. The United States women athletes, however, made no particular showing in any field. Only a few months after the 1956 games had ended it seemed doubtful if the name of any United States woman athlete would be remembered long by the public in general. But this did not seem to distress the American public which, on the whole, looks to its men athletes rather than to its women to represent it in the Olympics. In other words, the spirit of mid-century United States is not one to publicize women in sports. Most women still prefer to pursue their sports without fanfare or publicity; and apparently the public in general prefers it that way also.

ORGANIZED PHYSICAL EDUCATION
OF THE MID-TWENTIETH CENTURY

The impact of the sports and games program on physical education during the first half of the twentieth century has caused many leading physical educators to analyze the potential role that physical education can play in the national life. This, in turn, tends to be the basis for a changing concept of physical education. In the first place, physical education is focusing on sharing in the development and carrying out the pattern of general education. In the second place, physical education is vitalizing its program to make it an integral phase of community living so that the recreational aspects of physical education assume a significant role in bringing the program before the community and in interesting everyone in its outcome. In the third place, physical education is coming to recognize again that it has a responsibility toward the school children of the nation—one that is peculiarly its own—a responsibility that no other department of education faces, namely the development of those aspects of physical fitness that depend upon physical activity for accomplishment.

EVENTS AFFECTING PHYSICAL EDUCATION

This era opened with the depression of the 1930's. The 1940's brought World War II, and the 1950's have presented the problem of physical fitness that looms large in the face of world-wide tensions. These events have materially affected physical education.

The Depression. In the economic stress of the depression of the 1930's, school boards, urged on by groups of citizens, ordered drastic cuts in education. The specialized subjects —music, art, home economics, and physical education— were labeled the "fads and frills" of education and came in for undue and sharp criticism and attacks. In many towns and cities these subjects were forced to bear the brunt of cuts in budgets and staffs. But thanks to the efforts of educators and citizen groups who recognized the aims of physical education and put up a fight in its behalf, physical education, on the whole, suffered no more than did the regular school subjects and was spared the drastic treatment meted out to music, art, and home economics.

World War II. Out of nine million registrants examined for the armed services of the United States in early 1943, almost three million (one third) were found to be unfit for any form of military duty. However, because of improved techniques of examinations and diagnosis since 1917, many were rejected who would have been accepted in World War I. Indeed more men were rejected for World War II than were accepted for World War I. But those who were accepted were soft and flabby and in need of conditioning. The chief of Athletics and Recreation of the Services Division of the United States Army had this to say at the War Fitness Conference in 1943:

Our physical programs in high schools have been a miserable failure. Physical education through play must be discarded and a more rugged program substituted. We must assume our share of the responsibility for the unnecessary loss of American lives. Many of our boys have perished because of the accumulation of fatigue, the lack of endurance, stamina, and certain abilities. You read about the men who struggled through swamps and jungles and over mountains for days and days before reaching safety, or survived in rubber boats for many days before being rescued. They had the strength and stamina to survive such ordeals, but you don't read about the hundreds that did not have such strength and stamina. They did not live to make a report.

By 1943 there were 232,000 women wearing the uniform of our Armed Services—the first women in United States history to be accepted for military duty. In September, 1944, the Surgeon General's office reported to the National Civilian Advisory Committee of the Women's Army Corps an unusually large number of rejections due to excessive weight, and a general lack of strength, flexibility, and endurance of those women who were accepted. Those who were accepted for the WAC were given a rigorous program of conditioning as outlined in the *WAC Field Manual of Physical Training*.

Following this, women enlisted in the WAVES, Marine Corps, American WAF, and the Medical Corps, and they, too, were found equally lacking in strength and endurance. Other women poured out of their homes by the thousands to work in industry, to help replace the men called to the armed services, and to do their bit for the war effort. Their softness and general lack of physical fitness showed up at once. The Labor Department reported that there were sixteen million women working in industry in the summer of 1943, working a ten-hour day for seven days a week. Some were working on night shifts, some were loading freight cars, others were driving heavy trucks or welding and walking cat walks in shipyards. American women in such staggering numbers had never before been called upon for such physically difficult tasks.

Physical Fitness Movements. John B. Kelley (1888–), a distinguished citizen of Philadelphia and a former University of Pennsylvania athlete, who had been intensely interested in fitness from his early youth and was deeply shocked at the draft information of World War II, appealed to President Roosevelt for immediate action to correct this situation among civilians as quickly as possible. The President set up a Division of Physical Fitness under the Office of Civilian Defense and appointed Mr. Kelley head of this new Division. District divisions were immediately set up along the lines of the various Army Service Commands with two co-directors, a man and a woman, appointed as District Directors in each Service Command. Several of the regional directors appointed were physical educators. Frank Lloyd (1897–1957) of New York University was appointed Chief of the Physical Fitness Division of the Federal Security Agency with headquarters in Washington, D.C., and William L. Hughes (1895–1957) of Columbia University was appointed Chief Consultant.

This movement brought about a change in attitude in regard to athletics in both the Armed Forces and the schools. The military called on physical educators and trained coaches to man the Armed Services' physical training and athletic programs, and in the schools eligibility rules were relaxed to permit college freshman and transfer students to participate at once; intensive participation of all students in sports was encouraged. The United States Office of Education organized the Victory Corps for school children with achievement tests and insignia for physical fitness activities and held regional institutes to promote the work.

With World War II at an end the enthusiasm for fitness died down. Then people were again startled in the early 1950's by the rejection figures of the new draftees. The head of Selective Service reported in 1952 that one and a half million of the 18½-to-26-year-olds were rejected for the draft. Then come the Kraus-Weber tests of minimum muscular fitness of school children, the results of which were first published in 1953. They showed the poor fitness records of American school children compared with European children. These tests consist of six tests of key muscle groups which show up the abilities required for healthy living. They were developed from a fifteen-year study of patients with low-back pain made by Dr. Hans Kraus (1905–   ), Associate Professor of Physical Medicine and Rehabilitation of New York University. Designed to measure one's ability to participate effectively in activities required for everyday living, these are not supposed to be tests of high levels of muscular fitness. The six tests are: (1) for strength of abdominal muscles working with the psoas muscle, (2) for strength of abdominal muscles working without help of the psoas, (3) for strength of lower abdominal muscles and the psoas without help of other abdominals, (4) for strength of upper back muscles, (5) for strength of lower back muscles, and (6) for length of back muscles and hamstrings. Given to 4,264 United States school children and 2,870 European children from comparable urban and suburban communities, 57.9 per cent of the United States children failed the tests compared to 8.7 per cent of the European children.

When the attention of the President of the United States was called to the report of this study he immediately called for a special White House Conference on the subject which was finally held in June, 1956. Following this the AAHPER held a Fitness Conference in Washington in September, 1956, and President Eisenhower established a President's Council on Youth Fitness and a President's Citizens Advisory Committee on the Fitness of American Youth.

Many states are now promoting state fitness programs, and among them Oregon's work is noteworthy. Through its State Department of Public Instruction it has maintained a motor-fitness program as a part of its physical education program since 1945. The program is optional in all elementary schools but required in all secondary schools.

State Legislation. By 1951, forty-four states had adopted legislation for physical education. Many school districts in the other four states have voluntarily initiated programs in recognition of the needs of children and youth. Thus, there is nearly complete legislative coverage for physical education throughout the United States today, and most states maintain state physical directors.

STATUS OF PHYSICAL EDUCATION

Lower Schools. In spite of the great increase in physical education in the schools of America over all preceding periods, less than 50 per cent of all secondary school boys and girls were receiving training in physical education in 1956. Ninety-one per cent of the 150,000 elementary schools had no gymnasiums, and 90 per cent had less than the five acres for playing area as recommended in 1930. Also, only 1,200 out of 17,000 communities had full-time recreation leadership, and less than 5 per cent of the children were getting camping experience.

Facilities. As early as 1930 many school boards were following the lead of Providence, Rhode Island, and had established the standard of two gymnasiums for every new building, each 40 by 60 feet for elementary schools, 45 to 55 feet wide by 65 to 70 feet long for junior high schools, and 60 by 90 feet for senior high schools with two auxilliary smaller gymnasiums for corrective work in the larger schools.

In 1937 the College Physical Education Association recommended a gymnasium 65 by 90 feet for all average-sized schools. This same year brought the first of many high school stadiums with facilities for night lighting.

Programs. The College Physical Education Association spent nine years on the study of a national curriculum for all grades through college and from this study set up an approved program for the elementary grades which has been accepted as a national pattern. It consists of the following: athletic games, 25 per cent of program; rhythms, 20 per cent; hunting games, 15 per cent; and 10 per cent each of self-testing activities, mimetics, free exercises, and relays combined with stunts and tumbling. Mid-twentieth century programs of physical education are considered excellent only if they contain a wide variety of activities chosen from aquatics, camping, combat activities, body mechanics, equitation, dancing in various forms, festivals and pageantry, free play, games, hiking, stunts, and sports of all kinds—group, individual and dual. Many schools now also maintain programs of recreation for the student body. The usual plan is to place the responsibility for administering the recreation program in the physical education department.

Closely allied to recreation is school camping. The gains in school camping in the past two decades have been tremendous. In 1951 there were approximately ninety school districts including nearly two hundred schools which sponsored some type of school-camp program. Physical educators have taken great interest and much responsibility in this movement.

Requirements. A 1932 survey showed that 80 per cent of the three-year high schools required physical education for all three years and 70 per cent of the four-year schools required it all four years. This survey covered schools in forty-six leading cities in twenty-two states. No doubt, with the great increase in facilities and teachers, the percentages would run even higher if the survey were repeated in the 1950's.

At mid-twentieth century the most common weekly requirement is that of three periods per week, although many schools hold to a daily requirement. River Forest Township High School at Oak Park, Illinois, with its separate gymnasiums for boys and girls, sets the standard of five hours per week for all four years, which standard is maintained by many of the best high schools.

Staffs. By 1931 Alabama, California, and Virginia were maintaining county directors of physical education as well as state directors. Indicative of the progress throughout the country are the following figures: Indiana schools from 802 physical education teachers in 1930 to 1,037 in 1932; Massachusetts schools from 211 physical education teachers and 60 school gymnasiums in 1920 to 1,100 teachers in 700 gymnasiums in 1932; and Pennsylvania schools from 153 physical education teachers in 1921 to 2,200 in 1935. Indiana schools in 1932 required all coaches of interscholastic sports in high schools to hold certificates of training in the field of physical education.

Colleges. For the past twenty-five or more years most colleges have required physical education of all undergraduate students except in the schools where military training may be substituted. As to programs there has been a constant increase in sports offerings although women's programs have taken on an emphasis on body mechanics. A survey of 1930 made in connection with research on women's athletics covering 120 colleges in all sections of the country showed that the most commonly used athletic activities were the following: basketball used in 96 per cent of the colleges; softball, in 90 per cent; field hockey, in 87 per cent; swimming, in 80 per cent; archery, in 70 per cent; track and field, in 60 per cent; and soccer, in 58 per cent. In the 1930's and 1940's, fieldball and speedball, badminton, deck tennis, and handball were added to the women's programs.

Facilities. Some magnificent gymnasiums both for men and for women have been built since 1930, and a few fine ones have been built for the joint use of both men and women. Two of the latest in this last group are the two-million-dollar gymnasium at New York State University Teachers College at Cortland, dedicated in 1954, and the million-dollar gymnasium completed in the early 1950's for the new Riverside Branch of the University of California. The University of Southern California built a coeducational gymnasium in 1925 which is still an excellent building, but it did not at that time establish a trend. Whether the two modern coeducational buildings will now start a trend remains to be seen.

The novelty of electrically controlled doors to divide gymnasium floors came as early as 1930. One of the first was in the women's gymnasium at St. Catherine's School in St. Paul, Minnesota.

In the early 1930's several splendid gymnasiums were constructed for the women students such as those at the Universities of Texas and California (Los Angeles branch), Stanford University, and Wellesley and Oberlin Colleges. These buildings, representing Spanish Renaissance, Lombardian Italian Romanesque, Tudor Gothic, and modern types of architecture, set a new style of beauty with utility for women's gymnasiums in the United States.

A late addition to these women's gymnasiums is the Mary Channing Coleman Gymnasium of the Women's College of the University of North Carolina, which was built in 1950–52. This gymnasium is named after Mary Channing Coleman (1883–1947), who was the second woman to be elected to the presidency of AAHPER. As Director of the Department of Physical Education at the Women's College for many years, she organized and developed a department that not only has set high standards for the South but also has achieved national recognition.

The most magnificent gymnasium in the United States, no doubt in the entire world, is the ten-million-dollar Payne Whitney Gymnasium at Yale University, which was completed in 1932. Five stories high with an additional four stories in the large tower, each level represents some one phase of activities of the physical education program. Its beautiful entrance hall is decorated with reproductions of R. Tait McKenzie's sculptures of athletes. In its spacious quarters it can accommodate 1,200 students participating in activities per hour. A splendid men's gymnasium, built in the 1950's, is that at the University of Florida at Gainesville.

Many fine stadiums also have been built in colleges and universities since 1930. As of 1956 the Ivy League schools have stadiums with the following capacities: Brown, 19,900 with accommodations for 2,350 undergraduates; Cornell, 34,000 with 7,900 undergraduates; Dartmouth, 14,620 with 2,800 undergraduates; Harvard, 40,000 with 4,400 undergraduates; Pennsylvania, 65,667 with 4,100 undergraduates; Princeton, 46,000 with 2,900 undergraduates; and Yale, 70,896 with 4,100 undergraduates.

Academic Degrees of Staffs. Graduate degrees are the rule today for practically all physical education teachers in colleges. For top degree the M.D. of the early days of the profession has almost completely given way to today's Ph.D. and Ed.D. Before and shortly after World War I a master's degree or its equivalent was the usual requirement for the director of a department. Gradually the doctor's degree became a requirement for the directors, and then it became obligatory for all staff members to hold the master's degree. Today on some of the larger staffs there are several who hold the doctor's degree.

Costumes for Women. Not until the 1930's were swimming suits of other than gray cotton permissible for school use. By this date special treatment of materials had been devised to protect against the shedding of lint and the running of dyes. Thus swimming costumes at last became attractive to women students. For girls' gymnasium suits, this period brought into use the short cotton, knicker-type, scant bloomer with sleeveless blouse, or shorts with tailored blouse. For dance, the leotards came into use—knitted material like that used in swimming suits—some with short sleeves, some long, some short-legged and some long. Boys' costumes, too, took on a "new look" with trunks greatly abbreviated over those of earlier eras.

Research. Interest in testing and research, aimed at improvement of the profession in all of its aspects, had grown so remarkably by the opening of this era (1930) that 25 per cent of the schools of a national survey were found to be using a testing program of some kind whereas practically none had testing programs at the opening of the century. Written tests of knowledge came into popular use in the early 1930's, also, and have now become a recognized part of all testing programs. Also, beginning in 1930 the American Association for Health, Physical Education and Recreation has maintained a periodical on the subject, *The Research Quarterly.*

Today there is a large number of research workers in the field of physical education. Particularly productive in this work have been Frederick W. Cozens (1891–1954), of the University of California (Berkeley), who received the Ling Foundation Medal, the Medal of Merit of the Ministry of Social Welfare of Czechoslovakia, and the Gulick Award of AAHPER in recognition of his services to the profession; and Charles H. McCloy (1886–   ), of the University of Iowa, who as special consultant to both the U.S. Army and Navy during World War II carried on much research work for them. As a prolific worker and writer in the field of research, McCloy has been recognized by three honorary doctor's degrees and the Gulick Award of AAHPER. He has, also, received from the American Academy of Physical Education, besides their Hetherington Award, a special citation for his productivity in research. His writings include a dozen books in English and a great number of articles in periodicals published in nine different languages.

The national professional association maintains both a Research Section and a Research Council, the latter coordinating its work with that of various other organizations. All this activity in research is a far cry from the lonely efforts of Edward Hitchcock at Amherst College in those days of long ago when he came to recognize that physical education must stand or fall on the research work that furnishes its foundation.

Teacher Preparation. By 1930 the demand for trained teachers in the field of physical education had increased markedly. Not only schools and colleges were asking for trained personnel but also playgrounds, recreation centers, boys' and girls' clubs, YMCA's, YWCA's, all manner of youth-saving groups, hospitals, rehabilitation centers, and all branches of the Armed Services. This demand brought about greatly increased teacher training offerings. But the day of the private noncollegiate school of physical education is over. All teacher training in the field of physical education is at the present time established in the colleges and universities.

At the time of the Civil War the only schools in the United States preparing teachers of physical education were those of Dio Lewis and the North American Turnerbund. Only the latter survived. In 1941 that college (the Normal School of the North American Gymnastic Union) affiliated with the University of Indiana but remained in Indianapolis, thus completing the old private school affiliations with colleges. However one of the oldest of the private schools of physical education, the one that first made collegiate affiliation, the Boston Normal School of Gymnastics which affiliated with Wellesley College in 1909, closed in 1953 when Wellesley College decided to return to the status of a pure liberal arts college and therefore could no longer maintain a graduate professional department. So after sixty-four years of service to the profession (1889–1953) the school came to the end of its long and distinguished career.

At the opening of this period ninety-three institutions of collegiate rank were offering teacher preparation in physical education, but there was such a continuously increasing growth of the profession with its multiplying demands for trained teachers that by 1953 there were 532 colleges offering undergraduate majors in physical education, in health and physical education combined, or in recreation. They were located in every state in the Union and in the District of Columbia, Alaska, Hawaii, and Puerto Rico as well. One hundred fifty-eight of these colleges and universities were offering graduate majors at the master's level and thirty-five, at the doctor's level.

At the close of World War I there were approximately 10,000 men and women in the United States professionally trained in physical education but by 1950 the figure had risen to 76,000. These figures represent a total growth of physical education that was scarcely envisaged by the most forward-looking dreams of a hundred years ago.

Since 1930 a struggle has developed in the colleges within the fields of physical education, health education, and recreation for the control of teacher preparation in these fields. The heavy requirement of "education courses" demanded by the teachers colleges on the false assumption that all students expect to go into the public schools to teach allows but little time for courses in allied fields, hence handicapping professional training. Under the professional school form of organization, professional preparation in physical education can readily combine with preparation in the fields of athletics, health education, safety education, and recreation.

Several universities have established this form of organization, some setting up this teacher-training work in a school and others in a college. Schools of health and physical education are maintained at Stanford University (the first one, established in 1924), the Universities of Connecticut, Indiana, Oregon, and Washington, Springfield College, and Boston University. Colleges of health and physical education are now functioning at the Universities of Florida, Illinois, Maryland, and West Virginia, and at Brigham Young University, Pennsylvania State University, and Washington State College.

Nonschool Organizations. At mid-twentieth century the old stand-by groups that have, through the years, carried on physical education activities outside the schools are still functioning—the programs of the YMCA and YWCA increasing in importance with the years but those of the turners and Sokols gradually becoming absorbed into national life with other groups and losing their Old World identities.

Young Men's Christian Association. This era, as the preceding one, has seen great advances in physical activity in the YMCA. Notable achievements through 1955 have been the following: the first national YMCA aquatic conference held in Chicago in 1937, first postwar national YMCA handball tournament held in St. Louis in 1944, learn-to-swim campaigns launched in 1940, first postwar national YMCA volleyball tournament, held in Chicago in 1946, and 7,500 athletes registered for national YMCA amateur sports competition in 1952. In 1955 their Research Committee assigned $18,000 for special research in physical education.

The National Office reported the following growth figures from 1928 to 1953: swim classes enrollment from 162,000 per year to 450,000; gym class attendance from eight million to thirty million; money spent on physical activities from two million dollars to six million. Only the number of trained physical directors dropped—from 820 to 537—showing the shortage of teachers of physical education which is universal in the 1950's. By 1953 over 178,000 persons had passed the national YMCA aquatics tests with 368 certified aquatics instructors at work, and 556 learn-to-swim campaigns were carried on in that year.

The YMCA has materially increased its service to women and girls, particularly in communities where there are no YWCA programs. Membership of women and girls more than doubled in the 1940's. About 70 per cent of all newly established associations have made provision for them in their sports and recreational offerings. An estimated 300,000 women were enrolled in YMCA physical activities classes in 1953.

The outstanding contributions of the YMCA during both World Wars I and II deserve special mention. The aid that various associations gave the armed forces, not only developing fitness programs for the men in service but also maintaining morale among soldiers at home and abroad, was an outstanding contribution to the nation. In peacetime, as well as wartime, the promotion of athletic games in foreign countries has tended to bring people of different countries together in informal situations so that they understood each other better.

Here at home the YMCA is one of the most powerful forces working for racial integration. Its physical education program offers unusual opportunities in this direction.

Young Women's Christian Association. The rapid growth of the YWCA physical education program has been accompanied by a broadening of the activities to include recreation and social activities. In the mid-fifties activities in canteens, lounges, swimming pools, and gymnasiums attracted over 380,000 participants. The YWCA camps play host to many others who seek pleasure in the out of doors. In 1955, the YWCA maintained 450 associations in the United States with between 150 and 160 swimming pools in the association buildings. In early 1957 there were 350 trained physical education teachers in charge of the activity programs.

Turners and Sokols. The turner and Sokol groups in the United States are mostly third, fourth, and even fifth generation Americans thoroughly assimilated into American culture. These people have turned their attention to the American recreation movement and athletic clubs and are their ardent supporters. In only a few places are groups of Old-World descendants banded together still practicing the Old-World gymnastics. American Sokols still hold a slet (Sokol Olympics) every six years. The IXth American Slet was held in Chicago, June 30, 1957. Gymnasts and athletes of the United States and Canada of Sokol descent came together, as they said, "to reaffirm their faith in a free and democratic way of life."

Movements Related to Physical Education. The camping and recreation movements have shown remarkable growth in this era. Added to these two movements in the 1930's was the American Youth Hostel movement.

Recreation Movement. Recreation in the United States today is sponsored by many agencies as listed below.

1. Public agencies that sponsor recreation include the separate municipal departments of recreation, the municipal park boards, and the public schools. At times a combination of efforts of two of these public agencies occurs. By 1946 there were 1,488 cities maintaining playgrounds. Philadelphia alone has constructed thirty-six new ones since 1954.

   The immediate effect of the depression in the early 1930's resulted in cutting paid recreation leaders in community recreation to a bare minimum—some municipal agencies ceased to function. The Federal Works Progress Administration, National Youth Administration, Civil Works Administration, and others contributed to the movement by constructing and maintaining areas and facilities and providing leadership in the programs. The end result was expansion in some cities and the establishment of new programs in other cities. By 1941, as a consequence of all the events during the depression, municipal departments had made definite increases in the number of programs and leaders.

   In the 1930's, the WPA came into existence to relieve the unemployment problem. It covered projects for recreation in every state but Maine. It built 13,700 parks, 22,000 playing fields, 670 golf courses, 1,510 swimming pools, and built or repaired 7,930 recreation buildings besides employing, in 1938, 38,000 people per month to carry on recreation programs.

2. Voluntary agencies that offer recreation as part or all of their program are the Boy Scouts, Girl Scouts, Camp Fire Girls, youth centers, church recreation, and the like.

3. Private agencies sponsoring recreation are sports clubs and commercial recreation establishments.

4. Industrial recreation agencies are those such as the UAW-CIO Recreation Department, which was established in 1937 with a trained physical educator at its head who has the status of International Representative of the Union. By 1957 there were 200 full-time industrial recreation directors in the United States.

5. The Navy Welfare and Recreation Department and the Army Special Services Department sponsor recreation programs for service men and women.

The Playground Association of America (PAA) of 1906 became the Playground and Recreation Association of America (PRA) in 1911, and in 1930 changed its name once more —this time to the National Recreation Association (NRA). Since 1949 the affairs of the Association are managed by an Executive Director and a Headquarters Staff of thirty-six.

The National Recreation Association has come to mean or to stand for many things to the communities spread throughout the United States. Some of the services provided include: personnel service to serve private, voluntary, and governmental agencies; special consultant services for all phases of areas and facilities; service to industrial concerns engaged in recreation; consultant and correspondence services to agencies and individuals; special publications about problems concerning recreation; publication of the *Recreation* magazine; annual convention or congress for the professional leaders in the field; and research on various aspects of recreation.

Camping Movement. By 1930 the camping movement had moved into the stage of orientation and responsibility.

Physicians, nurses, and dieticians were added to the camp staffs. Camp life became less highly organized than in the 1920's.

By 1950, ten thousand camps of many kinds in the United States and Canada served from three to five million boys and girls and adults each summer. Today camping has become big business in the summer. There has developed a wide variety of camps in America such as: (1) organization camps, (2) school camps, (3) public camps, (4) private camps, (5) labor-union camps, (6) specialized camps, (7) day camps, and (8) CCC camps. This last type, the Civilian Conservation Corps camp, was established during the depression of the 1930's by the federal government so that young boys could be housed, fed, and given employment in areas where they could, under supervision, help construct camps, state and federal parks, mountain trails, and recreation areas. It was a life-saver for thousands of boys who would otherwise have been thrown onto the streets unemployed during those difficult years.

The American Camping Association was organized in the 1930's and was made up of owners, directors, and leaders of various camps. By 1949 it had 2,000 camp members and over 4,000 individual members.

American Youth Hostels. This European movement for inexpensive outings came to the United States in 1934, but it was confined mostly to the New England states and localized areas surrounding a few metropolitan centers where several hostels were established in communities easily accessible to each other by foot or bicycle. A few physical educators threw their influence and enthusiasm into this movement because of its possibilities of bringing aroused interest for hiking and biking to American youth and adults. Because of the great distances in the United States and the hazards of the highways from automobile traffic, the movement has never flourished here as in Europe.

Professional Literature. By the opening of this era the profession was receiving great impetus from the many publications that were coming off the press in this field. A perusal of publisher's notices given in each issue of the *Journal of Health and Physical Education,* year by year, from 1930 to date gives an idea of the great wealth of material that has become available.

Films and Microcards. A new development of this era has been the production of films and microcards. In 1957 there were available through the Athletic Institute over 2,000 16-millimeter sports films. The AAHPER has films for loan or purchase at its national office. Many schools produce their own film strips.

The School of Health and Physical Education of the University of Oregon carries on a microfilm publication project as a nonprofit service to the profession. The productions are, for the most part, unpublished research materials and doctoral dissertations, scholarly books that are now out of print, and periodicals of historical value which are no longer available. The school furnishes, on request, a catalog of all their microcards with prices.

Periodicals. In 1930 *The Journal of Health and Physical Education* replaced the *American Physical Education Review* that had been published in thirty-four volumes from 1896 through 1929. Elmer D. Mitchell, the Editor of the *Pentathlon* (the official organ of the Midwest Physical Education Association, which had been established in 1929 and had been produced in five issues) succeeded to the office of Secretary-Treasurer-Editor of the APEA in 1930. Thereupon the Midwest group gave up its own five-month venture, throwing its influence and support back of the new national magazine. At the same time the APEA began publication of the *Research Quarterly.* The YMCA continues the publication of its magazine, *The Journal of Physical Education,* which started in 1901 under the title, *Physical Training.* Also, the NAGU continued until 1935 its publication of *Mind and Body,* which had been started in 1894. With the January, 1949, issue of the *Journal of Health and Physical Education* the word *Recreation* was added to its official title.

26

ORGANIZATIONS AND LEADERS
OF THE MID-TWENTIETH CENTURY

Each succeeding era brings new problems and new horizons. Out of these grow the reorganization of old groups and the establishment of new ones. For the new problems, the new horizons, the day always produces its leaders. The stories of these organizations and leaders make up the heart of mid-century history of physical education.

PROFESSIONAL ORGANIZATIONS

American Association for Health, Physical Education and Recreation. The original American Association for the Advancement of Physical Education (AAAPE) of 1885 changed its name in 1903 to the American Physical Education Association (APEA), in 1937 to the American Association for Health and Physical Education (AAHPE), and in 1938, to give recognition to its actual scope of many years past, it adopted its present long name which is abbreviated to AAHPER.

In 1937, it affiliated with the National Education Association and is now that organization's largest department. Since that date it has maintained its official offices in the NEA building in Washington, D.C. The latest copy of its constitution and bylaws is available in the November, 1954, issue of its official magazine, and its history is in the April, 1954, issue.

After 1930 three new districts came into the mother organization, two new ones carrying states not heretofore represented and a third resulting from a redistricting of the earlier large Midwest group. The Northwest states joined APEA in 1931 and the Southwest states in 1934, thus bringing all of the United States into the organization. In 1934 the old Midwest group, extending from Pittsburgh to Denver, split into two groups, the portion east of the Mississippi retaining the old name and the states west of the Mississippi taking the name of Central District. Within each district the states maintain state associations, and each has representation on the national council, thus reaching down to the very grass roots of the profession.

Its interest groups, starting in 1904 with three sections, grew so numerous that in the 1940's they were combined into divisions: physical education, health education, and recreation, and each section was assigned to some one division with each division head recognized as a vice president of the organization. By 1957 the divisions had grown to five and the sections under them to forty-one. This is a marked extension of the horizons of the profession since 1930 when the Association maintained but eleven sections. (Today's forty-one sections within the five divisions are listed in Part II of the October, 1956, issue of the *Journal of Health— Physical Education—Recreation.*)

Many organizations are affiliated with the Association. As of January, 1957, they numbered sixteen. This, also, is a far cry from the five such organizations of 1930. Besides the promotional work carried on by the district and state societies and by the forty-one sections of the five divisions and the sixteen affiliated organizations, the AAHPER does a great deal of work through its many committees.

The membership in 1885 was 49; it rose to 1,089 by 1905; to 3,022 by 1925; to 6,479 by 1935; to 10,193 by 1945; and to 20,000 by 1954.

The original objectives of the Association stated in 1886 hold good today: "To disseminate knowledge concerning physical education, to improve the methods . . . to bring those interested in the subject into closer relation with each other." But today it has added the interests of health education and recreation to its main concerns.

College Physical Education Association. The Society of College Gymnasium Directors of 1897 became the Society of Directors of Physical Education in Colleges in 1908 and in 1935 became the College Physical Education Association. Exclusively a man's organization its membership in 1957 numbered 675 representing 45 states and 320 institutions. Thirteen per cent of the members hold only the bachelor's degree; 47 per cent, the master's degree as top degree; 35 per cent the Ph.D. or Ed.D. degree; and the remaining 5 per cent hold the M.D. or Doctor of Public Health degree, an honorary doctorate, or the title "Director" without degree.

(The names of those who have held the presidency of this organization are given in the Appendix. It is, indeed, a roster of the foremost men leaders through the years.)

National Association of Physical Education for College Women. From the small group of sixteen women directors who were present when this organization was formed in 1924 it has grown to a membership of 639 as of May, 1956, representing 212 colleges and universities from all sections of the country with membership open to all college women staff members. It has developed into a working organization with over 10 per cent of the members actively at work on committees promoting improved physical education for women in colleges. For the past several years the organization has sponsored workshops which have been held biennially. (For a list of women who have served as president throughout the years see the Appendix. Like its counterpart organization, its roster of presidents is also a list of foremost women leaders of the profession.)

American Academy of Physical Education. From the group of charter members of 1930 this organization grew quietly and moderately until by 1957 it had achieved an additional one hundred members. (The lists of charter members and presidents of this organization are given in the Appendix.) Through the years the organization has served as a liaison group between physical educators of America and those of the rest of the world. Its "steadfast belief in the integrity of physical education as a significant attribute to the perpetuation of American culture" is the keystone of its functioning.

Conferences on Physical Education. This era has brought forth a great number of important conferences related to physical education which have been called by special groups for special purposes quite aside from the conventions held regularly by the various professional organizations. A few of the more important special conferences have been as follows: the White House Conference on Child Health and Protection (1930); the International Recreation Congress in connection with the Olympics at Los Angeles (1932); the National Facilities Conference (1946); the National Conference on Undergraduate Professional Preparation and the International Congress on Physical Education, Recreation and Rehabilitation (1948); the National Conference on Graduate Study (1950); the National Mobilization Conference on Physical Fitness and Youth (1951); the National Workshop on Recreation and the AAHPER Conference on Physical Education for College Men and Women (1953); the International Congress on Essentials of Physical Education for Youth (1954); the National Conference on Intramural Sports for College Men and Women (1955); and the National Conference for Education for Leisure and the National Conference of City Directors of Physical Education, Health, and Recreation (1956). Several of these conferences were financed by the Athletic Institute. (See p. 382.)

ATHLETIC ORGANIZATIONS

There are today countless athletic organizations in the United States, most existing merely for the promotion of various sports. But many are not for promotion alone but also for proper control of sports at both local and national levels. The mid-century history of the more notable of these is given in the material that follows. The organizations are listed in the order of their founding.

Amateur Athletic Union. Since this organization's founding in 1888 it has become powerful in the athletic world. Today it claims jurisdiction over basketball, boxing, gymnastics, handball, running, jumping, walking, weight-putting, hurdles, pole vault, swimming, tug-of-war, wrestling, weight-lifting, and volleyball. District and national championship meets and tournaments are held under its rules and management. Its attempts to take over the management of girls' and women's competitive sports, after World War I, aroused the women leaders of physical education and many prominent lay women, as well, who attempted to counter its influence by the organization of the Women's Division of the NAAF. Although this organization did accomplish much in awaking the lay public to the desirability of sane and wholesome standards for sports for women, it never succeeded in breaking the AAU's hold completely for the AAU continued to control women's competition in several fields, particularly the participation of those women in industry who are not reached by the school and college programs nor by the YWCA's. In the 1930's the AAU was very active in this field and staged many district and national championships for women in basketball, swimming, and track and field. These tournaments were given great publicity and were quite popular with certain segments of the public. They brought in large gate receipts for their promoters. It was in this setting that Babe Didrickson got her start toward athletic fame. Interesting are the stories of how the Women's Division forced the AAU to accept certain standards for women's sports, to place women chaperons and nurses in women's dressing rooms at championship tournaments, replacing men trainers and "rubbers," and to give up its pre-game bathing-suit parades of contestants on the streets of the tournament city. Since the days of the hectic 1920's and 1930's a second world war has brought a sobering aftermath, and the AAU, although still promoting some sports for women, does it less rambunctiously and less arrogantly, and for the most part confines itself to activities for out-of-school boys and men.

National Collegiate Athletic Association. Over the years, the National Collegiate Athletic Association has endeavored to develop the rules of various sports and to control the eligibility of the players. To combat many malpractices, in 1947 this association effected certain organizational changes which permitted it to act as an inspection and accrediting body which could force institutions to conform to a code of action (sanity code). This code covered such matters as: amateurism, institutional control, academic standards, financial aid, and recruiting. Its power to enforce such issues, however, has not proved too successful.

Division of Girls and Women's Sports of AAHPER. The National Women's Basketball Committee, which was established in 1905, paved the way for the organization of a larger group in 1917 which was founded under the auspices of APEA as the National Committee on Women's Sports. In 1927 this committee became the Women's Athletic Section (WAS) of APEA. In the early 1930's it changed its name to the National Section on Women's Athletics and was known for the next twenty years as the NSWA. In 1953 it again changed its name, this time to the National Section for Girls and Women's Sports (NSGWS). But this name soon gave way to another as the organization in 1957 took on the status of a Division of AAHPER with ever-increasing responsibilities in behalf of girls' and women's sports in the United States. This group, that started out in such a small way over fifty years ago to set standards and make rules for one sport for women, has advanced through its several stages to the responsibility of setting standards and making rules for all sports for girls and women. The group is today familiarly known as DGWS.

Although there are other groups in the United States that make rules for various women's sports, mostly men's groups interested in exploiting girls and women in their sports activities, the profession of physical education looks upon the Division of Girls and Women's Sports of AAHPER as the official rules-making body for all sports for girls and women.

As of 1957 this group had an estimated 10,000 members, all working for correct standards and for rules of sports made for women by women. Through its many committees it publishes official rules for sports and works for the promotion of sports that are educational in nature rather than highly competitive for championships. (Its chairmen through the years are listed in the Appendix.)

Athletic and Recreation Federation of College Women. The organization which started in 1917 as the Athletic Conference of American College Women (ACACW) took on a new name in 1933 and functioned for twenty-four years as the Athletic Federation of College Women (AFCW). At its April, 1957, conference it changed its name to the one given above, which better reflects its true purpose, namely "to further athletic interests and activities for girls and women according to the highest and soundest standards of sports and recreation." In its platform it states that it aims "to uphold the Standard of Athletics for Girls and Women as set forth by the National Section for Girls and Women's Sports."

Since 1947 the organization has held conferences biennially instead of triennially as in its earlier years. From the twenty-three schools which were represented in the charter membership the organization has grown to a membership of 295 colleges and universities including junior colleges.

National Federation of High School Athletic Associations. This organization grew from its 1920 start until by 1940 it had established a national office with a full-time executive staff.

Today the State High School Athletic Associations of all states in the union except Texas belong to this Federation including groups in Alaska and four Canadian provinces. As of 1957, 20,000 high schools belong to the state groups that make up this organization. It checks on close adherence of all state groups to eligibility rules for interstate contests. It opposes athletic competition on the national level but does sanction sectional events provided they are held in strict observance of Federation rules on distance to be traveled, type of sponsor, and extent to which the event might interfere with smaller events that will include greater participation. The Federation, among many notable achievements, has brought about a reduction in the size of footballs and basketballs for high school use, shortened the low-hurdle race, set up less expensive equipment as standard, standardized officiating in high school contests, and materially raised the coaching and playing ethics. One of its chief objectives is to protect high school boys from exploitation by noneducation projects.

March is tournament month all over the United States for high school boys' basketball. According to the NFHSAA *Handbook of 1956–1957*, as many as 4,000 tournaments were held in 1956 with 20,000 players taking part representing three million students and with over fifteen million admissions to the tournaments.

Women's Division of NAAF. Organized in 1923 this group was well set up and hard at work by 1930. By 1938 it had 768 organization members. At its seventh annual meeting, held in Detroit in April, 1931, it adopted a platform for women's athletics and took a determined stand against women's participation in the approaching Olympics and in state tournaments for girls. At this time the National Board of the YWCA, the National Association for Physical Education of College Women, the Women's Athletic Section of APEA, and the Athletic Conference of American College Women joined the Women's Division to procure abandonment of all state basketball tournaments for girls.

Feeling as did the Men's Division of the NAAF before it, that now its purpose had been accomplished and other existing organizations could carry on, it merged its interest in 1940 in the NSWA of AAHPER. In its sixteen years of battling for correct standards of sports for American women it had distributed over $106,000 donated by individuals, foundations, and trusts for their work and had spent an additional $12,000 for three years in maintenance of a Field Secretary to travel to trouble spots to help correct unfavorable conditions in women's sports. Whereas the National Section on Women's Athletics had been mainly a rules- and policy-making body, the Women's Division had set itself up as a standard-maker and a liaison group between physical educators and the lay public. Now the NSWA took over these added functions.

State Leagues of High School Girls' Athletic Associations. By the late 1930's there were eight states supporting state leagues for girls' athletics: Illinois, Colorado, Nebraska, Alabama, North Carolina, Kansas, Iowa, and Oklahoma, founded in the order listed. Illinois, the originator of the league idea, has the most effective organization, maintaining an executive secretary and a central office in Chicago and sponsoring summer camps for its member groups. The Alabama and Oklahoma Leagues are closely related to their state departments of education, the others are coordinated with the boys' state leagues of their states.

Most of these state organizations are opposed to interscholastic competition for girls but work instead for large-scale participation of girls in their home-school intramural programs. The state organization assists local groups with program plans, advises on local GAA affairs, and offers state awards for unusual achievement in physical education and sports activities.

Athletic Institute. The Athletic Institute is an organization of sporting goods companies which was set up in 1946 as a nonprofit group for the advancement of athletics, physical education, and recreation. In an eleven-year period (1946 through 1956) the Institute accomplished the following: promoted Living War Memorials in the form of recreational facilities; secured an allocation of raw materials for physical education and sports equipment during the war; aided the young National Industrial Recreation Association; financed research and testing in physical fitness at the University of Illinois; financed the joint committee meeting of AAHPER and the Society of Recreation Workers; distributed to mayors of all cities in the United States 20,000 copies of the book, *Essentials for Developing Community Recreation;* financed three professional workshops; and produced many films for professional advancement.

LEADERS OF PHYSICAL EDUCATION

The number of leaders in the field of physical education has grown tremendously since 1930. All parts of the country are now covered by well-trained and effective men and women who are working in its service.

The American Association for Health, Physical Education and Recreation confers three types of awards in recognition of leadership in the profession: (1) the Gulick Award, established in the 1920's to the memory of Luther Halsey Gulick and conferred upon one physical educator a year for unusually significant leadership to the profession; (2) the Anderson Award, established in 1949 in memory of William G. Anderson, and conferred upon from four to six persons a year who work in the field of physical education or allied fields for distinguished service to physical education; and (3) the Honor Award, established in 1931 and conferred upon several persons each year in recognition of notable leadership in behalf of the profession.

Since the inauguration of its Honor Awards in 1931, the American Association for Health, Physical Education and Recreation had through 1956 honored 252 leaders. From 1923 through 1956 it conferred the Gulick Award on twenty persons and from 1949 through 1956, the Anderson Award on eleven other physical education leaders. (Lists of the recipients of the Gulick and Anderson Awards are given in the Appendix. Information on, and photographs of, Award

Fellows are found in the volume of the *Journal of Health and Physical Education* for the year of the award. Also biographical material on the more notable of these leaders appears in *Who's Who in America, Who's Who of American Women,* and other biographical publications in their various editions, particularly in those issues just preceding a person's retirement. Special "In Memoriam" articles, also, are carried in the professional magazine following the death of many.)

Time alone will sort out the pre-eminent few of today for listing in the short histories of tomorrow. In the meantime the interested inquirer about today's leaders will do well to make his own investigations from the references suggested above.

Appendix

SOME IMPORTANT PUBLICATIONS

The references which follow, chapter by chapter, include some of the more important ones used in the writing of this history of physical education. In the preparation of the first edition, published in 1926, Emmett A. Rice consulted books and periodicals of European countries, many of which at that time were available in libraries in the United States and some of which were among the special collections at the Stockholm Central Institute of Gymnastics and the Berlin Turnleher-bildungsanstalt. The documentations of a majority of the old publications are incomplete, and the works themselves are practically impossible to obtain now; however, they are retained in this fourth edition because of their historical significance. Thus the books and magazine articles below should not be viewed as a bibliography or considered as suggestions for further reading—they merely indicate and acknowledge the sources which the authors have used, in this and earlier editions of the book, in developing the story of physical education.

CHAPTER 1

Physical Education in Ancient Oriental Nations

BILBY, JULIAN W. *Among Unknown Eskimo.* Philadelphia, 1923. Chap. xvii deals with sport and hunting.

BOGENY and OTHERS. *Die Geschichte Des Sports Aller Völker und Zeiten.* Leipzig: Seemann, 1925.

BUREAU OF AMERICAN ETHNOLOGY. *21st Annual Report, 1899–1900.*
————. *24th Annual Report, 1902–03.*
BUTTERWORTH, HORACE. "Physical Training of the Japanese," *Mind and Body* (August, 1904), 153–57.
————. "The Japanese National Sport," *Mind and Body* (October, 1904), 196–200.
ELLIS, WILLIAM. *Polynesian Researches.* London, 1859. Vol. I, chaps. vii–ix.
GRACE and OTHERS. *History of Dancing.* (The Badminton Library.) Chap. iii, "The Dances of the Savages."
GRAVES, FRANK P. *History of Education Before the Middle Ages.* New York: The Macmillan Co., 1909.
HERODOTUS. (Loeb Classical Library.) New York, 1914. Book I, arts. 136–38.
LAURIE, SIMON. *Historical Survey of Pre-Christian Education.* London: Longmans, 1895.
MONROE, PAUL. *A Text-book in the History of Education.* New York: The Macmillan Co., 1905.
O'BRIEN, FREDERICK. *Mystic Isles of the South Seas.* New York: The Century Co., 1921.
RAWLINSON, GEORGE. *Five Great Monarchies.* New York, 1870. Vol. III, "Persia."
VUILLIER, GASTON. *History of Dancing from Earliest Ages to Our Own Times.* New York: D. Appleton & Co., 1897. Chap. i.
WOLLASTON, A. F. R. *Pigmies and Papuans.* New York, 1912.
XENOPHON. *Cyropædia.* Book I, art. 2; Book II, art. 20–30. *Anabasis.* I, ix, 6. London: University Tutorial Services [B. J. HAYES, (ed.)] n.d. Both references are on Persia.

CHAPTER 2

Physical Education in Greece

ALEXANDER, CHRISTINE. *Greek Athletics.* New York: Metropolitan Museum of Art, 1925. Excellent for pictures.
ARISTOTLE. *Politics.* Book VII, sec. 17; Book VIII, secs. 4–5.
BOTSFORD, G. W. and SIHLER, E. G. *Hellenic Civilization.* New York: Columbia University Press, 1915.
CUBBERLEY, ELLWOOD P. *The History of Education.* Boston: Houghton Mifflin Co., 1920. Chaps. i–ii.
DEPPING, GUILLAUME. *Wunder der Körperkraft und Geschicklichkeit des Menschen.* Berlin, 1870. Historical for all periods and many sports.
Die Leibensübungen, Heft 16 (August, 1925), 377–82. Excellent article on swimming among the Greeks and Romans.
DIEHL, CHARLES. *Excursions in Greece.* London, 1893. Chap. vii.
Encyclopædia Britannica and *Encyclopedia Americana.* See Olympia and Olympian games.

EULER, KARL. *Die Geschichte des Turnunterrichtes.* Berlin, 1881.

FORBES, CLARENCE A. *Greek Physical Education.* New York: The Century Co., 1929.

GRAVES, FRANK P. *History of Education Before the Middle Ages.* New York: The Macmillan Co., 1909.

GROTE, GEORGE. *History of Greece.* London, 1888.

GULICK, CHARLES B. *The Life of the Ancient Greeks.* New York: Twentieth Century Textbooks, 1902. A. F. NIGHTENGALE (ed.). Chaps. vi, vii, viii, and xiii.

HALLE, JENNIE. *Buried Cities.* New York: The Macmillan Co., 1922. See Olympia.

Harper's Dictionary of Classical Literature and Antiquities. New York, 1896. See Palæstra, Gymnasium Olympia.

HIRTH, GEORG. *Das Gesamte Turnwesen.* Leipzig, 1893. Band I, pp. 5–230. Includes "Die Wissenschaft der Gymnastik," by Flavius Philostratus.

HOMER. *Iliad,* 23rd book; *Odyssey.* (Loeb Classical Library.) New York, 1925.

HYDE, WALTER WOODBURN. "Athletic Reliefs from the Themistoclean Wall at Athens," *Art and Archeology* (Jan.-Dec., 1923), 117, 124.

KRAUSE, JOHANN H. *Die Gymnastik und Agonistik der Hellenen.* Leipzig, 1841.

———. *Theagenes: Oder Wissenschaftliche Darstellung der Gymnastik, Agonistik und Festspiele der Hellenen.* Hall, 1835.

LUCIAN. *Anacharsis or Athletics.* (Loeb Classical Library, Lucian Vol. iv.) New York, 1925. Very interesting dialogue on Greek athletics.

McCLEES, HELEN. *The Daily Life of the Greeks and Romans as Illustrated in the Classical Collections of the Metropolitan Museum of Art.* New York, 1925. Chaps. vii–xi.

MONROE, PAUL. *Source Book in the History of Education for the Greek and Roman Period.* New York: The Macmillan Co., 1901.

PINDAR. *Odes of Pindar.* (Loeb Classical Library.) New York, 1925.

PLUMMER, EDWARD M. "Toys and Games for Children Among Ancient Hellenes," *Mind and Body* (Aug., 1900), 124–32.

PLUTARCH. *Lives.* (Loeb Classical Library.) New York, 1914. See Lycurgus, sec. xii to xvii on Sparta.

ROBINSON, CYRIL E. *Days of Alcibiades.* Oxford: The Clarendon Press, 1933. Chap xi.

ST. JOHN, JAMES A. *The History of the Manners and Customs of Ancient Greece.* London, 1842. Vol. I, Bk. II, chaps. i, iii, iv, v, viii; Bk. III, chap. ii.

STOBART, JOHN CLARK. *The Glory That Was Greece.* London: Sidgwick and Jackson, Ltd., 1911.

TUCKER, THOMAS GEORGE. *Life in Ancient Athens.* New York: The Macmillan Co., 1906.

VAN HOOK, LARUE. *Greek Life and Thought.* New York: Columbia University Press, 1937.

WHIBLEY, LEONARD. *A Companion to Greek Studies.* London: Cambridge University Press, 1905.

CHAPTER 3

Physical Education among the Romans

CUBBERLEY, ELLWOOD P. *The History of Education.* Boston: Houghton Mifflin Co., 1920.

FOWLER, WILLIAM WARDE. *Social Life at Rome in the Age of Cicero.* New York: The Macmillan Co., 1909. Chap. x.

GIBBON, EDWARD. *The History of the Decline and Fall of the Roman Empire.* New York, 1845. Vol. I.

GRAVES, FRANK P. *History of Education Before the Middle Ages.* New York: The Macmillan Co., 1909.

HALL, JENNIE. *Buried Cities.* New York: The Macmillan Co., 1922.

HIRTH, GEORG. *Das Gesamte Turnwesen.* Leipzig, 1893. Band I, pp. 5–230.

JOHNSTON, HAROLD W. *Private Life of the Romans.* Chicago, 1903.

MONROE, PAUL. *Source Book in the History of Education for the Greek and Roman Period.* New York: The Macmillan Co., 1901.

SANDYS, SIR JOHN E. *A Companion to Latin Studies.* London: Cambridge University Press, 1921. Articles on Education, Public Games, and Medicine.

SCHRADER, CARL L. "The Baths of Old," *Mind and Body* (May, 1916), 97–103.

SUETONIUS. *Lives of the Cæsars.* Boston: Allyn & Bacon, 1903. Book VI, art. 12, on Nero's games.

TACITUS, CORNELIUS. *Annals.* Art. xiv, secs. 20–21. Contains note on the introduction of Greek games to Rome.

THOMAS, EMILE. *Roman Life Under the Cæsars.* New York, 1899. Chap. iv.

VIRGIL. *Æneid.* Book V. Account of funeral games.

CHAPTER 4

Physical Education in the Dark Ages

ADAMS, GEORGE B. *Civilization During the Middle Ages.* New York: Charles Scribner's Sons, 1922.

BINTZ, JULIUS. *Die Leibesübungen des Mittelalters.* Gütersloh, 1880.

GRAVES, FRANK, P. *History of Education During the Middle Ages and the Transition to Modern Times.* New York: The Macmillan Co., 1910.

KINGSLEY, CHARLES. *The Roman and the Teuton.* London, 1901.

MONROE, PAUL. *A Text-Book in the History of Education.* New York: The Macmillan Co., 1920.

MUNRO, DANA C. *The Middle Ages.* New York: The Century Co., 1926. Chap. iii.

MUNRO, DANA C. and WHITCOMB, M. *The Middle Ages and Modern Europe.* New York: The Century Co., 1903. Chaps. xii and xv.

TACITUS, CORNELIUS. *Germania.* (Loeb Classical Library.) London, 1920. Treats of the lives of the early Germans.

THATCHER, O. J. and McNEAL, E. H. *Source Book for Medieval History.* New York, 1907. Chap. viii.

WORKMAN, HERBERT B. *Evolution of the Monastic Ideal From the Earliest Times Down to the Coming of the Friars.* London, 1913.

CHAPTER 5

Physical Education in the Age of Chivalry

ADAMS, GEORGE B. *Civilization During the Middle Ages.* New York: Charles Scribner's Sons, 1922.

BINTZ, JULIUS. *Die Liebesübungen des Mittelalters.* Gütersloh, 1880. This work includes all popular sports.

CORNISH, F. WARRE. *Chivalry.* New York: The Macmillan Co., 1901.

DORAN, JOHN. *Knights and Their Days.* New York, 1856.

MONROE, PAUL. *A Text-Book in the History of Education.* New York: The Macmillan Co., 1920.

MUNRO, DANA C. *The Middle Ages.* New York: The Century Co., 1926. Chap. xii.

MUNRO, DANA C. and WHITCOMB, M. *The Middle Ages and Modern Europe.* New York: The Century Co., 1903. Chaps. xiii and xiv.

STRUTT, JOSEPH. *The Sports and Pastimes of the People of England.* (Reprint.) London, 1898.

TAPPAN, EVA MARCH. *When Knights Were Bold.* Boston: Houghton Mifflin Co., 1911. Elementary.

THATCHER, O. J. and McNEAL, E. H. *Source Book for Medieval History.* New York, 1907. Chap. vi.

CHAPTER 6

Physical Education during the Renaissance

ASCHAM, ROGER. *The Scholemaster.* Edited by EDWARD ARBER. (Heath's Pedagogical Library.) Boston, 1898. Vol. XXXII.

BOGENY and OTHERS. *Die Geschichte des Sports Aller Völker und Zeiten.* Lieferung 3. Leipzig: Seemann, 1925.

COMPAYRE, JULES GABRIEL. *The History of Pedagogy.* Boston: D. C. Heath & Co., 1892. Chap. v.

ELYOT, SIR THOMAS. *The Boke Named the Gouvernour.* (Everyman's Library.) London, 1885. Book I, Secs. 16–20, on exercise and dancing. Book III, Sec. 22, on diet.

EULER, KARL. *Die Geschichte des Turnunterrichtes.* Berlin, 1881.

GRAVES, FRANK P. *History of Education During the Middle Ages and the Transition to Modern Times.* New York: The Macmillan Co., 1910.

LAURIE, SIMON S. *Studies in the History of Educational Opinion From the Renaissance.* London: Cambridge University Press, 1903.

LEONARD, FRED EUGENE and AFFLECK, GEORGE B. *A Guide to the History of Physical Education.* Philadelphia: Lea & Febiger, Publishers, 1947.

QUICK, R. H. *Essays on Educational Reformers.* New York: D. Appleton Co., 1898. Chaps. i, ii.

WOODWARD, W. H. *Vittorino Da Feltre and Other Humanist Educators.* London: Cambridge University Press, 1921.

CHAPTER 7

Physical Education and Realism

BOYKIN, JAMES C. "Physical Training," *Report of the U.S. Commissioner of Education, 1891–92.* I.

COMPAYRE, JULES GABRIEL. *The History of Pedagogy.* Boston: D. C. Heath & Co., 1892. Chap. vi.

GRAVES, FRANK P. *A Student's History of Education.* New York: The Macmillan Co., 1915. Chaps. xiv and xv.

LOCKE, JOHN. *Some Thoughts Concerning Education.* London: Cambridge University Press, 1902.

MILTON, JOHN. *Tractate on Education.* (Harvard Classics, Vol. 13.) New Haven: Yale University Press, 1928.

MONTAIGNE, MICHEL DE. *The Education of Children.* (Harvard Classics, Vol. 32.) New York: G. P. Putnam's Sons, Inc., 1910.

QUICK, R. H. *Essays on Educational Reformers.* New York: D. Appleton Co., 1912. Chaps. v, vi, viii, x.

WATSON, FOSTER. *On Mulcaster.* (Report of U.S. Commissioner of Education, 1904, Vol. I.)

CHAPTER 8

Physical Education in the Age of Enlightenment

BARNARD, HENRY. *Memoirs of Eminent Teachers and Educators in Germany.* Hartford, Conn., 1878. See article on Basedow.

DAVIDSON, THOMAS. *Rousseau and Education According to Nature.* New York, 1898. Chaps. iv–vii.

EULER, KARL. *Die Geschichte des Turnunterrichtes.* Berlin, 1881. See article on GutsMuths.

HIRTH, GEORG. *Das Gesamte Turnwesen.* Leipzig, 1893. Band I, pp. 330–62 and 519–23; Band III, pp. 534–45.

LEONARD, FRED EUGENE and AFFLECK, GEORGE B. *A Guide to the History of Physical Education.* Philadelphia: Lea & Febiger, Publishers, 1947.

LEONARD, FRED E. "Johann C. F. GutsMuths," *Mind and Body* (Jan., 1911), 321–26.

QUICK, R. H. *Essays on Educational Reformers.* New York: D. Appleton Co., 1912. Chaps. xiv, xv.

ROUSSEAU, J. J. *Émile; or, Treatise on Education.* Translated by W. H. PAYNE. New York: D. Appleton Co., 1892.

SIEBERT, ALBERT. "The Development of Physical Education in Germany," *Mind and Body* (Nov., 1909), 249–53. Brief historical survey to 1909.

CHAPTER 9

Physical Education in Germany since 1800

AYRES, L. P. *Open Air Schools.* Rev. New York: Sage Foundation, 1910. Chaps. i, ii.

BOYKIN, JAMES C. "Physical Training," *Report of the U.S. Commissioner of Education, 1891–92.* I.

DIEM, C. "Development and Aims of Physical Education in Germany," *Journal of Health and Physical Education,* XIX (June, 1948), 390.

EULER, KARL. *Die Geschichte des Turnunterrichtes.* 1881. Contains complete account of German physical education to 1880.

GARDINER, ROLF. "Rhythmic Gymnastics in Germany," *Mind and Body* (Dec., 1925), 776–80.

GASCH, RUDLOPH. *Geschichte der Turnkunst.* Leipzig, 1910.

———. *Handbuch des Gesamten Turnwesens und der Verwandten Leibesübungen.* Leipzig, 1928. 918 pages.

HARTWELL, EDWARD M. "Physical Training in American Colleges and Universities." Bureau of Education; Circular of Information, No. 5, 1885. Pp. 157–85.

———. "On Physical Training," *Report of the U.S. Commissioner of Education, 1898.* 523–39.

HIRTH, GEORG. *Das Gesamte Turnwesen.* Leipzig, 1893. Contains writings of Jahn, Spiess, and their contemporaries.

JAHN, FRIEDRICH L. *Die Deutsche Turnkunst.* Berlin, 1847.

LEONARD, FRED EUGENE and AFFLECK, GEORGE B. *A Guide to the History of Physical Education.* Philadelphia: Lea & Febiger, Publishers, 1947.

LEONARD, FRED. *Pioneers of Modern Physical Training.* New York: Association Press, 1915. Chaps. i, iv, vii.

MCKENZIE, R. TAIT. *Exercise in Education and Medicine.* Philadelphia: W. B. Saunders Co., 1923. Chap. vii.

METZNER, HENRY. *A Brief History of the American Turnerbund.* Pittsburgh, 1924.

PROHLE, HEINRICH. *Friedrich Ludwig Jahn's Leben.* Berlin, 1872.

RATH, EMIL. "Physical Education in Germany," *Mind and Body* (Feb., 1923), 389–94.

RUHL, HUGO. *Entwicklungsgeschichte des Turnens.* Leipzig, 1912.

SPIESS, ADOLPH. *Turnbuch für Schulen.* Basel, 1847.

ZWARG, LEOPOLD. "The Play and Sport Movement in Germany," *Mind and Body* (Feb., 1915), 485–88.

CHAPTER 10

Physical Education in Scandinavia since 1800

BUKH, NIELS. *Fundamental Gymnastics.* Translated by EMILY ANDREWS and KAREN VESTERDAL. New York, 1928.

HARTWELL, EDWARD M. *The Principal Types of Physical Training Compared.* Boston: Damrell and Upham, 1892.

———. "On Physical Training," *Report of the U.S. Commissioner of Education, 1898.* I, 539–48.

KNUDSEN, K. A. *A Textbook of Gymnastics.* Translated by RUTH HERBERT and H. G. JUNKER. Philadelphia, 1923.

LEONARD, FRED E. *Pioneers in Modern Physical Training.* New York: Association Press, 1915. Chaps. ii, iii, and viii.

McDOWELL, HILDA. "Ollerup Gymnastik Folkhojskile," *Mind and Body* (July, 1921), 668–70.

McKENZIE, R. TAIT. *Exercise in Education and Medicine.* Philadelphia: W. B. Saunders Co., 1923. Chap. viii.

"Physical Education in Scandinavia," *School and Society,* XLIII (April 18, 1936), 548–49.

"Physical Education in Schools," *Bulletin of the International Bureau of Education,* No. 88, 3d quarter (1948), p. 118.

POSSE, BARON NILS. *Handbook of School Gymnastics of the Swedish System.* Boston, 1902.

STECHER, W. A. "Niels Bukh and His Danish Team," *Mind and Body* (Dec., 1923), 303–4.

SUMPTION, DOROTHY. *Fundamental Danish Gymnastics.* New York: A. S. Barnes & Co., Inc., 1927.

CHAPTER 11

Physical Education in Great Britain, Australia, New Zealand, and Canada

BESANT, W. *London in the Nineteenth Century.* London: A. & C. Black, Ltd., 1909.

BROWN, H. A. "Physical Training in English Schools," *Mind and Body* (October, 1900), 176–79.

———. "French National Gymnastic Festival, Bordeaux," *Mind and Body* (August, 1905), 178–79.

COLGAN, KATHERINE. "Open Air Schools in London," *Mind and Body* (September, 1909), 179–81.

CORBIN, JOHN. *School Boy Life in England.* New York: Harper & Bros., 1898.

CURTIS, HENRY S. "Play in the English Schools," *Mind and Body* (May, 1911), 127–30.

GEM, A. H. "Physical Education in School and After," *Journal of Education* (London), LXXX (1948), 608–09.

GLOSS, GEORGE M. "Our Australian Neighbors," *Journal of Health and Physical Education* (June, 1947), 380.

GRAVES, JOHN. *Policy and Progress in Secondary Education (1902–1942).* London: Thomas Nelson & Sons, Ltd., 1943.

JACOB, A. GERTRUDE. "Health Work in London," *Mind and Body* (September–October, 1926), 204–12.

LOCKART, A. D. "Teachers and Teacher Training in Australia," *School and Society* (June, 1947), 695–98.

MACLAREN, ARCHIBALD. *A System of Physical Education.* Oxford: Clarendon Press, 1885.

PLEWES, DORIS W. "Affiliated Organization: The Canadian Physical Education Association," *Journal of Health and Physical Education* (May, 1946), 273.

SAVAGE, H. J. *Games and Sports in British Schools and Universities.* New York: Carnegie Foundation, 1927.

SHANN, F. *Canberra System of School Athletics.* Victoria, Australia: Melbourne University Press, 1948.

"Training in Leisure Time Standards, Standards to Aim At," *The Times Educational Supplement* (London), August 10, 1940, p. 313.

CHAPTER 12

Physical Education in Other European Countries

BELBENOIT, G. "Sports and Physical Education," *Journal of Health and Physical Education* (April, 1948), 251–52.

BROWN, M. C. "Gymnastic Reunion in Prague," *Journal of Health and Physical Education* (May, 1939), 270.

EDGERTON, N. B. "Soviet Education Today," *Institute of International Education News Bulletin* (March, 1956), 6–10.

KINLOCH, J. L. "Education in the U.S.S.R.," *Educational Digest* (October, 1955), 4–6.

"International Conference on Physical Education," *Journal of Health and Physical Education* (November, 1932), 15–64.

MALLINSON, V. "Education in Belgium Today," *Journal of Education* (London), August, 1954, 361–63.

———. "Education in France Today," *Journal of Education* (London), April, 1954, 161–63.

"Physical Education in the Schools of Belgium," *School and Society* (December 25, 1937), 818–19.

PURVIS, W. A. "School System in France," *The Times Educational Supplement* (London), March 4, 1955, p. 232.

Report of the International Congress, Physical Education, Recreation, and Rehabilitation. London: Ministry of Education, 1948.

REISS, L. W. "Physical Education in Czechoslavakia," *Journal of Health and Physical Education* (February, 1932), 42.

ROUCEK, J. S. "Education in Bulgaria," *School and Society* (December 8, 1934), 775–78.

SCHROEDER, L. C. "Physical Education and Sports in Europe," *American Physical Education Review* (November, 1929), 516–21.

STALEY, S. C. "Sports in Europe," *Journal of Health and Physical Education* (October, 1931), 3.

WOODY, THOMAS "Sokols; 1948," *Journal of Health and Physical Education* (June, 1948), 342–43, 393.

CHAPTER 13

Physical Education in Japan, China, India, and South Africa

BAUER, LUCILLE. "Japanese Dances for Children," *Journal of Health and Physical Education* (May, 1935), 17.

BHOUDE, R. B. "Indian Sports in Olden Days in Madras," *Mind and Body* (October, 1935), 100–104.

JOKL, ERNST. "A Scientific Syllabus of Physical Education for Small Children," *South African Journal of Science* (December, 1938), 407–11.

———. "Medical Research in Physical Education in South Africa," *Research Quarterly* (March, 1949), 88–109.

LEWIS, TEDFORD P. "Health, Physical Education, and Recreation in Lebanon and the Near East," *Journal of the American Association of Health, Physical Education, and Recreation* (March, 1949), 159–61, 210–13.

McCLOY, C. H. "Physical Education Around the World, What We Can Learn from Other Nations," *Journal of Health and Physical Education* (February, 1947), 69.

WEGTHMAN, RUTH. "Relay Races from Japan," *Journal of Health and Physical Education* (October, 1935), 34.

CHAPTER 14

Physical Education in South America and Mexico

BRICKMAN, W. W. "Education in Latin America," *School and Society* (June 26, 1948), 479–87.

CASTILLON, O. F. "Physical Education in Mexico," *Journal of Health and Physical Education* (May, 1943), 11.

CHOPLIN, R. I. "Education in Paraguay," *Journal of Secondary Education* (May, 1948), 300–303.

"Colombia Physical Education," *World Education* (January, 1941), 67.

EBAUGH, C. D. "Education Among Our Latin American Neighbors," *American School Board Journal* (August, 1947), 33–35, (September, 1947), 35–37.

———. "Education in Chile," (U.S. Office of Education, Bulletin 1945, Number 10.) Washington, D.C.: U.S. Government Printing Office, 1945.

———. "Education in Ecuador," (U.S. Office of Education, Bulletin 1947, Number 2.) Washington, D.C.: U.S. Government Printing Office, 1947.

———. "Education in Peru," (U.S. Office of Education, Bulletin 1946, Number 3.) Washington, D.C.: U.S. Government Printing Office, 1946.

FURBAY, JOHN H. "Education in Colombia," (U.S. Office of Education, Bulletin 1946, Number 6.) Washington, D.C.: U.S. Government Printing Office, 1946.

GOYOSE, LAMBERTO A. "Physical Education for Pan-American Cooperation," *Journal of Health and Physical Education* (June, 1942), 356.

SALAS, ROSARIO and BRAVO, JORGE. "Physical Education in Chile," *Journal of Health and Physical Education* (September, 1949), 478–79.

CHAPTER 15

Physical Education in the Colonial Period

BROWN, ELMER. *The Making of Our Middle Schools.* 3d ed. New York: Longmans, Green & Co., Inc., 1907.

COLLINS, VARNUM LANSING. *Princeton.* New York: Oxford University Press, 1914. P. 208.

DUNNING, EDGAR D. "The Oldest Boarding School in America," *Nation's Schools,* XVI (Dec., 1935), 14–18.

EARLE, ALICE. *Child Life in Colonial Days.* London: Macmillan & Co., Ltd., 1926.

FRANKLIN, BENJAMIN. "Proposals Relating to the Education of Youth," *Report of U.S. Commissioner of Education,* I (1902), 182–85.

GOODSELL, WILLYSTINE. *The Education of Women.* New York: The Macmillan Co., 1923.

MCKENZIE, R. TAIT. "Benjamin Franklin—Illustrious Pioneer in Physical Education," *Journal of Health and Physical Education,* VII (1936).

SEYBOLT, R. F. *Source Studies in Colonial Education: The Private School.* (Bulletin no. 28.) Urbana: Bureau of Educational Research, College of Education, University of Illinois, 1925.

SHARF, J. THOMAS and WESTCOTT, THOMPSON. *History of Philadelphia, 1609–1884.* I & II. Philadelphia: L. H. Everts & Co., 1884.

WITTKE, CARL. *We Who Built America.* New York: Prentice-Hall, Inc., 1939.

WOOD, THOMAS D. and BROWNELL, CLIFFORD. "Discipline of the Methodist Episcopal Church," *Source Book in Physical Education.* New York: The Macmillan Co., 1925. P. 352.

WOODY, THOMAS. *A History of Women's Education in the United States.* II. New York: Science Press, 1929.

———. *Educational Views of Benjamin Franklin.* New York: McGraw-Hill Book Co., Inc., 1931.

CHAPTER 16

Physical Activities of the Early Nineteenth Century

BEECHER, CATHERINE. *Educational Reminiscences and Suggestions.* New York: J. B. Ford & Co., 1874.

BELL, JOHN. *A Treatise on Baths.* Philadelphia: Barrington & Haswell, 1850.

BROWN, ELMER E. *The Making of Our Middle Schools.* 3d. ed. New York: Longmans, Green & Co., Inc., 1907.

GOODSELL, WILLYSTINE. *Pioneers of Women's Education in the United States.* New York: McGraw-Hill Book Co., Inc., 1931. Discusses educational theories of Emma Willard, Mary Lyon, and Catherine Beecher.

HENDERSON, ROBERT W. *Early American Sports.* New York: A. S. Barnes & Co., Inc., 1953.

LEWIS, DIO. "The New Gymnastics," *Atlantic Monthly* (Aug., 1862), 129–48.

MCKENZIE, R. TAIT. "Physical Education at Girard College," *Mind and Body* (Sept., 1923), 197–203.

SPALDING, A. G. *America's National Game.* New York: American Sports Publishing Co., 1911.

WATSON, JOHN F. *Annals of Philadelphia and Pennsylvania in the Olden Times.* Philadelphia: Leary, Stuart & Co., 1900. Vol. III.

WINSHIP, GEORGE. "Autobiographical Sketches of a Strength-Seeker," *Atlantic Monthly* (Jan., 1862), 102–15.

WITTKE, CARL. *We Who Built America.* New York: Prentice-Hall, Inc., 1939.

CHAPTER 17

Organized Physical Education in the Early Nineteenth Century

Amherst College. Springfield: Association Press, 1919.

BENNET, CHARLES A. *A History of Manual and Industrial Education to 1870.* Peoria: Peoria Press, 1926.

BRUCE, H. A. *Women in the Making of America.* Boston: Little, Brown & Co., 1912.

DEGROOT, DUDLEY S. "A History of Physical Education in California— 1848–1939." Doctoral Dissertation. Stanford University, 1940.

EASTMAN, MARY F. and LEWIS, CEILIA CLARK. *The Biography of Dio Lewis.* New York: Fowler & Wells Co., 1891.

EDDY, SHERWOOD. *A Century With Youth.* New York: Association Press, 1904. A history of the YMCA from 1844 to 1904.

FOLLEN, E. L. *Life of Charles Follen.* Boston: Thomas H. Webb & Co., 1844.

KINDERVATER, A. G. "Early History of Physical Education in The Public Schools of America," *Mind and Body*, XXXIII (Jan., 1926), 97–105.

MILLER, KENNETH D. "Stearns, Hitchcock, and Amherst College," *Journal of Health and Physical Education*, XXV (May-June, 1957), 29–30.

MORSE, RICHARD C. *The History of the North American Young Men's Christian Association*. New York: Association Press, 1918.

NEW YORK STATE DEPARTMENT OF EDUCATION. "Back in 1859," *Physical Education Bulletin*. No. 39 (May, 1935).

PERRY, THOMAS S. *Life and Letters of Francis Lieber*. Boston: James R. Osgood & Co., 1882.

WARREN, JOHN C. *The Importance of Physical Education*. Lecture No. 1, 1831.

WOODY, THOMAS. *A History of Women's Education in the United States*. II. New York: Science Press, 1929.

CHAPTER 18

Physical Activities of the Latter Nineteenth Century

BARROWS, ISABEL. *Conference on Physical Training—1889*. Boston: George Ellis Press, 1899.

DAVIS, PARKE H. *Football, the American Intercollegiate Game*. New York: Charles Scribner's Sons, 1911.

DURIVAGE, F. A. "A Visit to François Delsarte," *Atlantic Monthly*, XXVII (1871), 613.

ENEBUSKE, CLAËS. *Progressive Gymnastics Day's Orders*. New York: Silver Burdette & Co., 1890.

HANGAR, G. W. *Public Baths in The United States*. U.S. Bureau of Labor Bulletin No. 54, Sept., 1904.

LEONARD, FRED EUGENE and AFFLECK, GEORGE B. *A Guide to the History of Physical Education*. Philadelphia: Lea & Febiger, Publishers, 1947.

SCHWINN, FRANK W. *The Story of the Bicycle and Its Contribution to Our Way of Life*. Chicago: Arnold Schwinn & Co., 1945.

SCHMIDT, F. A. "Physiological Treatise of The German System of Gymnastics," *Supplement to Mind and Body*, I (May, 1894), chart between pp. 10 and 11.

STEBBINS, GENEVIEVE. *Delsarte System of Expression*. 6th ed. New York: E. S. Werner, 1902.

Supplement to Research Quarterly of APEA, XII (Oct, 1941). Contains biographical material on Senda Berenson and Anne Barr.

CHAPTER 19

Organized Physical Education in the Latter Nineteenth Century

AINSWORTH, DOROTHY. *History of Physical Education in Women's Colleges*. New York: Columbia University Press, 1927.

BEECHER, CATHERINE. *Educational Reminiscences and Suggestions.* New York: J. B. Ford & Co., 1874.

BOSTON PUBLIC SCHOOL TEACHERS. *Memorial Services In Honor of Mary Hemenway.* Boston: George Ellis Press, 1899. Contains material on the founding of the Boston Normal School of Gymnastics.

BOYKIN, JAMES C. "Physical Training," *Report of U.S. Commissioner of Education,* Washington, D.C.: Government Printing Office, 1891-92.

CALIFORNIA STATE SUPERINTENDENT OF PUBLIC INSTRUCTION. *Second Biennial Report* (Appendix E) Revised School Law, March 24, 1866, Sec. 55.

ELLIOTT, RUTH. *The Organization of Professional Training in Physical Education in State Universities.* New York: Teachers College, Bureau of Publications, Columbia University, 1927.

GOODSELL, WILLYSTINE. *Pioneers of Women's Education in the United States.* New York: McGraw-Hill Book Co., Inc., 1931.

GULICK, LUTHER H. "Physical Education in the YMCA," *Proceedings, AAAPE,* 1891.

HARTWELL, EDWARD M. *Physical Training in American Colleges and Universities.* Washington, D.C.: U.S. Bureau of Education, Circular No. 5, 1885.

————. *The Rise of College Gymnastics in the USA.* Washington, D.C.: Government Printing Office, 1886. Special report of U.S. Bureau of Education given at World's Industrial and Cotton Centennial Exposition in New Orleans, 1884 & 1885.

HITCHCOCK, EDWARD and SEELYE, H. H. *An Anthropometric Manual.* Amherst: Press of Carpenter and Morehouse, 1893.

McCURDY, MRS. PERSIS. "Physical Training at Mt. Holyoke," *American Physical Education Review,* XIV (March, 1900), 139.

MUELLER, GROVER. "A Hundred Years of Health and Physical Education in Philadelphia," National Physical Education Service, *News Letter,* No. 114, Nov., 1938.

"Ohio State Law on Physical Education," *Mind and Body,* VII (March, 1900), 12-15.

SEELYE, L. CLARK. *The Early History of Smith College, 1871-1910.* New York: Houghton Mifflin Co., 1923.

Wellesley College, *Calendar for 1878-79.*

WILSON, ELIZABETH. *Fifty Years of Association Work Among YWCA's.* New York: National Board of YWCA of U.S.A., 1916.

YMCA. *Brief Review of Background and Progress in National YMCA Physical Education.* Exhibit E, March 31, 1955. Mimeographed material sent out from national office.

CHAPTER 20

Organizations and Leaders of the Latter Nineteenth Century

ANDERSON, W. G. "The American Association for the Advancement of Physical Education," *American Physical Education Review,* XXV (Nov., 1920), 312.

BARROWS, ISABEL. *Conference on Physical Training—1889.* Boston: George Ellis Press, 1899. For Sargent quotations see pp. 66–68. The addresses reported in this book carry great significance for today's student.

BRINK, B. DEANE. *The Body Builder, Robert J. Roberts.* New York: Association Press, 1916.

"Edward Mussey Hartwell," *National Cyclopedia of American Biography.* New York: James J. White & Co., 1929. XX, 132–33.

FINGELS, M. *"Biography of William Stecher,"* Master's Thesis, Temple University, 1934.

KERR, A. M. "Dr. W. G. Anderson," *Journal of Health and Physical Education,* VI (April, 1935), 31.

LEONARD, FRED EUGENE. *Pioneers of Modern Physical Training.* New York: Association Press, 1915.

"Organization of Ohio State Physical Education Association," *Mind and Body* VII (April, 1895), 38.

PHILLIPS, PAUL C. "Dr. Edward Hitchcock," *American Physical Education Review,* XVI (March, 1911), 217.

Proceedings. AAAPE Conventions, 1885–95.

SARGENT, DUDLEY A. *Autobiography.* Philadelphia: Lea & Febiger, Publishers, 1927.

SCOTT, HARRY A. "The Society of Directors of Physical Education in Colleges," *Journal of Health and Physical Education,* III (April, 1932), 3.

Supplement to Research Quarterly of APEA, XII (Oct., 1941). This issue carries biographies of Delphine Hanna, Amy Morris Homans, and Eliza Mosher.

"Tributes to Dudley A. Sargent," *American Physical Education Review,* XXIX (1924). This issue of the magazine carries several tributes by many different people under the one title.

CHAPTER 21

Physical Activities of the Early Twentieth Century

GULICK, LUTHER. *Physical Education.* Philadelphia: Blakiston's Sons & Co., 1907.

HETHERINGTON, CLARK W. "Fundamental Education," *Journal of Proceedings and Addresses of the National Education Association,* XLVIII. (1910).

LEE, MABEL. "The Case For and Against Intercollegiate Athletics for Women and the Situation As It Stands Today," *Mind and Body* (Nov., 1923) and *American Physical Education Review,* XXIX (Jan., 1924). This article was reprinted in whole or in part in four bulletins and two books, and hundreds of reprints were distributed throughout the United States by the Women's Division of NAAF.

TUNIS, JOHN. "The Great Sports Myth," *$ports: Heroics and Hysterics.* New York: John Day Co., Inc., 1928. Pp. 16–35.

WILLIAMS, JESSE F. *Physical Education.* Philadelphia: W. B. Saunders Co., 1922.

WOOD, THOMAS D. and CASSIDY, ROSALIND E. *The New Physical Education.* New York: The Macmillan Co., 1927.

CHAPTER 22

Organized Physical Education of the Early Twentieth Century

CLARKE, H. HARRISON. "The Extent of Graduate Study in Physical Education in the U.S.A.," *Journal of Health and Physical Education,* V (April, 1934), 33.

COOPER, FRANK IRVING. "Report of Committee," *School House Planning.* Washington, D.C.: NEA, 1925. P. 144.

DINSMORE, AVIS and GATES, EDITH. "The National Association of Employed Officers of the YWCA," *Journal of Health and Physical Education,* IV (Jan., 1933).

ELLIOTT, RUTH. *Organization of Professional Training in Physical Education in State Universities.* New York: Teachers College, Bureau of Publications, Columbia University, 1927.

HETHERINGTON, CLARK W. *School Program in Physical Education.* Yonkers, New York: World Book Co., 1922.

YMCA. *Centennial Report.* New York: National Office YMCA, 1916.

CHAPTER 23

Organizations and Leaders of the Early Twentieth Century

AMERICAN ACADEMY OF PHYSICAL EDUCATION. *Archives.* Mimeographed material.

CARKIN, JANICE. *Biographies of Five Women Gulick Award Recipients.* Doctoral thesis, Stanford University, 1952. Gives biographies of Jessie Bancroft, Elizabeth Burchenal, Mabel Lee, Ethel Perrin, and Blanche Trilling.

DORGAN, ETHEL. *Luther Halsey Gulick.* New York: Teachers College, Bureau of Publications, Columbia University, 1934.

GRIFFITH, JOHN L. "Annual Report of NAAF," *American Physical Education Review,* XXXIV (March, 1929), 156.

GULICK, LUTHER H. "The Academy of Physical Education," *American Physical Education Review,* XV (May, 1919), 342.

HAZELTON, HELEN. "Seventeen Years of Progress—Women's Rules and Editorial Committee of APEA," *Journal of Health and Physical Education,* V (April, 1934), 11.

HOWARD, GLENN W. "The College Physical Education Association," *Journal of Health and Physical Education,* XVII (Sept., 1946), 19.

HUSSEY, CHRISTOPER. R. *Tait McKenzie—Sculptor of Youth.* London: Country Life, Ltd., 1929.

LASALLE, DOROTHY. "Thomas D. Wood, M.D.—A Great Leader," *Journal of Health–Physical Education–Recreation,* XXII (Nov., 1951), 28–30.

"James Huff McCurdy," *Journal of Health and Physical Education,* XI (Oct. & Dec., 1940), 476, 619.

"R. Tait McKenzie," *Journal of Health and Physical Education,* XV (Feb., 1944). The entire issue of the magazine is devoted to articles about the man.

NATIONAL FEDERATION OF HIGH SCHOOL ATHLETIC ASSOCIATIONS. *Handbook—1956–1957.* Chicago: NFHSAA, 1956. Gives history of development of the organization.

SAVAGE, HOWARD J., et al. *Current Developments in American College Sports.* Bulletin No. 26, Carnegie Foundation for the Advancement of Teaching, 1951.

SCHWARTZ, MARGUERITE. "The Athletic Conference of American College Women," *Journal of Health and Physical Education,* VII (May, 1936), 297.

SEFTON, ALICE. *The Women's Division of NAAF.* Stanford: Stanford University Press, 1941.

STAGG, PAUL. *The Development of NCAA and Its Relation to Intercollegiate Athletics in the U.S.A.* Doctoral dissertation, New York University, 1946.

Supplement to Research Quarterly of APEA, XII (Oct., 1941). Contains biographies of Jessie H. Bancroft, Clelia Mosher, and Ethel Perrin.

"Twentieth Anniversary of the National Physical Education Service," *Journal of Health and Physical Education,* IX (Sept., 1938), 424.

"Tributes to Luther Halsey Gulick," *American Physical Education Review,* XXVIII (1923). This issue contains tributes by many different persons.

WAYMAN, AGNES. "The Women's Division of NAAF," *Journal of Health and Physical Education,* III (March, 1932), 3.

CHAPTER 24

Physical Activities of the Mid-Twentieth Century

AAHPER. *Proceedings—54th Annual Convention.* 1949.

BRAMMEL, P. ROY. *Health Work and Physical Education.* U.S. Office of Education, Bulletin No. 19, Monograph No. 28, 1932.

LEE, MABEL. "The Case For and Against Intercollegiate Athletics for Women and the Situation Since 1923," *Research Quarterly of APEA,* II (May, 1931), 93–127. This study was made at request of Women's Division of NAAF as a follow-up of earlier one.

MADAR, OLGA. "How About Bowling," *The Roundup.* Detroit: UAW-CIO, Jan.-Feb., 1950. P. 3. (Bulletin of Recreation Department of UAW-CIO.)

NATIONAL FEDERATION OF HIGH SCHOOL ATHLETIC ASSOCIATIONS. *Handbook—1956–1957.*

TUNIS, JOHN. *Sport for the Fun of It.* Rev. ed. New York: The Ronald Press Co., 1950.

VALENTE, PHYLLIS PIER. "The Dance in American Colleges," *Journal of Health and Physical Education,* XX (May, 1949), 312.

CHAPTER 25

Organized Physical Education of the Mid-Twentieth Century

BANK, THEODORE P. "Physical Fitness From the Standpoint of The Army," *Proceedings, National War Fitness Conference,* 1943. P. 29.

HERSEY, MAJOR GENERAL LEWIS B. "Inside Story of the Rejection Rates," *Journal of Health and Physical Education,* XXIV (Jan., 1953), 9.

KRAUS, HANS and PRUDDEN, BONNIE. "Minimum Muscular Fitness Tests In School Children," *The Research Quarterly,* 25:2 (May, 1954), 178–88.

LAPORTE, WILLIAM R. *The Physical Education Curriculum.* College Physical Education Association, 1937.

HOUSTON, RUTH ELLIOTT. *Modern Trends in Physical Education Facilities for College Women.* New York: A. S. Barnes & Co., Inc., 1939.

LUEHRING, FREDERICK. *Swimming Pool Standards.* New York: A. S. Barnes & Co., Inc., 1939.

STITT, LOUISE. "Problems of Women in Industry," *Proceedings of Victory through Fitness Workshop.* NAPECW, June, 1943. P. 21.

ROWNTREE, LEONARD. "Education, Health, and Physical Fitness," *Journal of Health and Physical Education,* XIV (Sept., 1943), 370.

U.S. OFFICE OF EDUCATION. *Preparation in Health Education, Physical Education, and Recreation, Year 1952–1953.* Washington, D.C.: Government Printing Office, 1954.

WORKS PROGRESS ADMINISTRATION. *A Study of WPA Recreation Projects.* Washington, D.C.: Federal Works Agency, 1940.

CHAPTER 26

Organizations and Leaders of the Mid-Twentieth Century

"AAHPER: Yesterday, Today, Tomorrow," *Journal of Health and Physical Education,* XXV (April, 1954), 29.

FISHER, GEORGE and NASH, JAY B. "The Luther Gulick Award," *Journal of Health and Physical Education,* XVII (June, 1946), 302.

NATIONAL FEDERATION OF HIGH SCHOOL ATHLETIC ASSOCIATIONS. *Handbook for 1956–1957.* Chicago: NFHSAA, 1956.

WASHKE, PAUL R. *The Development of The American Association for Health, Physical Education, and Recreation and its Relationship to Physical Education in the United States.* Doctoral dissertation, New York University, 1943.

ASSOCIATIONS, OFFICERS, AND AWARDS

AMERICAN ASSOCIATION FOR HEALTH, PHYSICAL EDUCATION AND RECREATION

Presidents

Under name: American Association for the Advancement of Physical Education

1885, '86 .... Edward Hitchcock	1894 .... Dudley A. Sargent
1887, '88, '89 ... William Blaikie	1895, '96 .... Jay W. Seaver
1890 .... Dudley A. Sargent	1897, '98, '99
1891 ..... Edward M. Hartwell	Edward M. Hartwell
1892 .... Dudley A. Sargent	1900, '01, '02. Dudley A. Sargent
1893 ..... Edward M. Hartwell	

Under name: American Physical Education Association

1903 .... Watson L. Savage	1923, '24, '25 .. Carl L. Schrader
1904 through 1908	1926, '27, '28 Charles W. Savage
Luther H. Gulick	1929, '30.. Frederick W. Maroney
1909 through 1911	1931, (Jan.–April) '32 Mabel Lee
George L. Meylan	1932–33 ..... Jesse F. Williams
1912 through 1915	1933–34 ..... Mary C. Coleman
R. Tait McKenzie	1934–35 .... Strong Hinman
1916 .... Earnest H. Arnold	1935–36 .... Agnes R. Wayman
1917, '18, '19 William H. Burdick	1936–37 .. William G. Moorhead
1920, '21, '22 .. Dudley B. Reed	

Under present name given above

1937–38 ... Charles H. McCloy
1938 (April–Sept.)
                    Neils P. Neilson
1938–39 .. Frederick W. Cozens
1939–40 .... Margaret Bell
1940–41 .... Hiram A. Jones
1941–42 .. Anne Schley Duggan
1942–43 .... Jay B. Nash
1943–44 .... August H. Pritzlaff
1944–46 .... William L. Hughes

1946–47 .... Helen Manley
1947–48.. Vaughan B. Blanchard
1948–49 .... Ruth Evans
1949–50 ...... Carl L. Nordly
1950–51 .. Dorothy S. Ainsworth
1951 (2–3 days) Frank S. Stafford
1951–52 ..... Bernice R. Moss
1952–54 ... Clifford L. Brownell
1954–56 ...... Ruth Abernathy
1956–58 .... Ray O. Duncan

Executive Secretaries

1908 through 1929
                James H. McCurdy
1930 through Sept., 1938
                Elmer D. Mitchell

Sept., 1938–April, 1943
                Neils P. Neilson
1943–48 .... Ben W. Miller
1948 to date Carl A. Troester, Jr.

Recipients of Gulick Awards

1923 .... Luther H. Gulick
                (Posthumous award)
1924 .... Jessie H. Bancroft
1925 .... Thomas D. Wood
1926 .... Thomas A. Storey
1928 ... Clark W. Hetherington
1929 .... George J. Fisher
1939 .... Jesse F. Williams
1940 .... Jay B. Nash
1944 .... Charles H. McCloy
1945 ..... William G. Anderson
1946 .... Ethel Perrin

1947 ...... Blanche M. Trilling
1948 .... Mabel Lee
1949 ...... Elmer D. Mitchell
1950 ..... Elizabeth Burchenal
1951 ... William Ralph LaPorte
1952 .... Charles W. Savage
1953 ..... Frederick W. Cozens
1954 .... William L. Hughes
1955 .... Carl L. Nordly
1956 ..... Rosalind E. Cassidy
1957 .... Clair V. Langton

Recipients of Anderson Awards to Physical Educators

1949 .... Mazie V. Scanlon
1951...... { Helen Manley
            Seward C. Staley
            Arthur H. Steinhaus
1952......... { Bernice R. Moss
              Agnes R. Wayman

1953 ... { Margaret C. Brown
          Thomas E. McDonough
1954......... { Elwood C. Davis
              Clair V. Langton
              James E. Rogers

Recipients of Honor Awards

The 252 recipients from 1931 through 1956 are listed in the *Journal of Health and Physical Education*, October, 1954, (pp. 38–39) for recipients 1931 through 1954 and Oct., 1956, (p. 23) for 1956 recipients. Photographs and biographical sketches appear in the *Journal* of the year of the award.

AMERICAN ACADEMY OF PHYSICAL EDUCATION

Charter Members

Clark W. Hetherington
R. Tait McKenzie
William H. Burdick
Thomas A. Storey
Jay B. Nash
Carl L. Schrader
James H. McCurdy
Jessie H. Bancroft
Wilbur P. Bowen
Dudley B. Reed
Howard S. Braucher
Amy Morris Homans
William A. Stecher
Earnest H. Arnold

George L. Meylan
William Ralph LaPorte
Charles W. Savage
John F. Bovard
Paul C. Phillips
Arthur S. Lamb
John Brown, Jr.
J. Anna Norris
E. C. Schneider
Elmer D. Mitchell
Charles H. McCloy
Elizabeth Burchenal
Arthur H. Steinhaus

Presidents

1926–30 . (organizing chairman) Clark W. Hetherington
1930–38 ..... R. Tait McKenzie
1938–39 ..... (Acting President) Mabel Lee
1939–41 .... John Brown, Jr.
1941–43 .... Mabel Lee
1943–45 ... Arthur H. Steinhaus
1945–47 .... Jay B. Nash
1947–49 ... Charles H. McCloy

1949–50 .. Frederick W. Cozens
1950–51 ... Rosalind E. Cassidy
1951–52 ..... Seward C. Staley
1952–53 .... David K. Brace
1953–54 ...... Neils P. Neilson
1954–55 .....Elmer D. Mitchell
1955–56 .. Anna S. Espenschade
1956–57 .... Harry A. Scott
1957–58 .... Charles C. Cowell

PRESIDENTS OF
THE COLLEGE PHYSICAL EDUCATION ASSOCIATION

(1898 to date.) Dates before 1951 not available.

Edward Hitchcock
Jay W. Seaver
Dudley A. Sargent
William G. Anderson
R. Tait McKenzie
Paul C. Phillips
Watson L. Savage
George L. Meylan
Thomas A. Storey
Amos Alonzo Stagg
Frederick E. Leonard
W. A. Lambeth
James A. Naismith
Charles W. Savage
C. V. Young
Joseph M. Raycroft
Edwin Fauer
Frederick W. Luehring
James H. McCurdy
J. H. Nicols
William H. Geer
Dudley B. Reed
A. W. Marsh
Jesse F. Williams
A. I. Prettyman
William Ralph LaPorte

T. N. Metcalf
O. F. Cutts
George E. Little
William L. Hughes
C. L. Brewer
E. L. Mercer
W. J. Livingston
Harold S. Wood
L. C. Boles
Harry A. Scott
Oliver K. Cornwell
Elwood C. Davis
Carl P. Schott
Delbert Oberteuffer
A. W. Marsh
Carl L. Nordly
Lloyd M. Jones
Louis F. Keller
Glenn W. Howard
Thomas E. McDonough ('51)
F. J. Hoeter ('52)
Elmer D. Mitchell ('53)
William F. Meredith ('54)
Seward C. Staley ('55)
E. B. Smith ('56)
Arthur S. Daniels ('57)

PRESIDENTS OF THE NATIONAL ASSOCIATION OF
PHYSICAL EDUCATION FOR COLLEGE WOMEN

1924–25 .... Lydia Clark
1925–26 .... Alice Belding
1926–27 .... Mabel Lee
1927–29 .... Mary E. Gross
1929–32 .. Gertrude E. Moulton
1932–34 .... Ruth Elliott
1934–37 ... Rosalind E. Cassidy
1937–41 .. Dorothy S. Ainsworth
1941–43 .... Elizabeth Kelly

1943–45 ..... Elizabeth Halsey
1945–47 .. Gertrude Manchester
1947–49 ... Helen W. Hazelton
1949–51 ...... Irene A. Clayton
1951–53 ..... Pauline Hodgson
1953–55 ..... Laura J. Hueslter
1955–57 ...... Ruth M. Wilson
1957–59 ... Lucille H. Verhulst

PRESIDENTS OF THE SOCIETY OF STATE DIRECTORS OF HEALTH, PHYSICAL EDUCATION AND RECREATION

1926–27 ...... Carl L. Schrader	1943–44 .... Harold K. Jack
1927–28 ... William H. Burdick	1944–45 ..... Frank S. Stafford
1928–29 ..... Allen G. Ireland	1945–46 ..... George W. Ayars
1929–30 .... E. W. Everts	1946–47 .. Thomas C. Ferguson
1930–31 ..... Elliott V. Graves	1947–48 .... Charles E. Spencer
1931–33..William G. Moorehead	1948–49 .... Paul E. Landis
1933–34 ...... Neils P. Neilson	1949–50 ...... Ray O. Duncan
1934–35 .... C. J. Prohaska	1950–51 ...... Julian W. Smith
1935–36 ...... G. K. Hendricks	1951–52 .... Verne S. Landreth
1936–37 ..... Jessie R. Garrison	1952–53 .... Ellis H. Champlin
1937–38 .... W. H. Orion	1953–54 .... Robert Yoho
1938–39 .... Hiram A. Jones	1954–55 .... Harley Robertson
1939–40 .... Harry Edwards	1955–56 ..... Elmer B. Cottrell
1940–41 .... Jess W. Hair	1956–57 ...... George J. Sirnio
1941–42 ..... Bernice R. Moss	1957–58 .... Vaughn Hall
1942–43 ..... Alice G. Aldrich	

CHAIRMEN OF NATIONAL SECTION FOR GIRLS AND WOMEN'S SPORTS

1917–21 ... Elizabeth Burchenal	1943–46 .. Anna S. Espenschade
1921–25 ... Blanche M. Trilling	1946–48 ..... Alfreda Mosscrop
1925–27 ..... Katherine Sibley	1948–49 ..... Martha A. Gable
1927–30 ... Florence A. Somers	1949–52 ..... Laurie Campbell
1930–31 .... Helen W. Hazelton	1952–54 ...... Josephine Fiske
1931–32 .... Grace Jones	1954 (June–Dec.)
1932–34 ..... Grace B. Davies	Aileene Lockhart
1934–36 .... Eline Von Borries	1954 (Dec.)–56 .... Grace I. Fox
1936–38 .... Elinor Schroeder	1956–58 .... Mabel Locke
1938–40 .... Jane Shurmer	1958 (A Division of AAHPER)
1940–42 .... Ruth D. Atwell	Jane A. Mott, Vice-President
1942–43 .... Alice Shriver	

PRESIDENTS OF EASTERN DISTRICT ASSOCIATION OF AAHPER

1895–1924..Names not available	1931–33 .... Marjorie Bouvé
1923–25 ...... William H. Geer	1933–35 .... Jay B. Nash
1925–27 .... Charles H. Keene	1935–37 .... Franklin Gray
1927–29 .... Name not available	1937–39 .... Hiram A. Jones
1929–31 ..... Jesse F. Williams	1939–40 ...... Alice C. Aldrich

1940–41 .... William L. Hughes
1941–42 .. William F. Meredith
1942–44 .... Ruth Evans
1944–46 ..... George W. Ayars
1946–47 ..... Mazie V. Scanlon
1947–48 ... Clifford L. Brownell
1948–49 . Dorothy S. Ainsworth
1949–50 .. Thomas C. Ferguson

1950–51 ...... Minnie L. Lynn
1951–52 .... John W. Shaw
1952–53 ..... Ethel T. Kloberg
1953–55 .... Lloyd M. Jones
1955–56 .. Karl C. H. Oermann
1956–57 .... Marion E. Purbeck
1957–58 . William M. Grimshaw

PRESIDENTS OF
MIDWEST DISTRICT ASSOCIATION OF AAHPER

The Old Midwest—(When the present Midwest and Central Districts were one)

1912–13 Clark W. Hetherington
1913–17 ...... Dudley R. Reed
1917–18 .... Ethel Perrin
1918–19 .... Wilbur P. Bowen
1919–20 .... Martin I. Foss
1920–21 ... Charles W. Savage
1921–23 .... W. J. Monilaw
1923–26 ...... J. Anna Norris

1926–27 ... Margaret R. McKee
1927–28 ...... E. C. Delaporte
1928–Feb., 29 ... Loren M. Post
Feb.–Apr., 29
      Mabel Lee (Acting President)
1929–30 .... Mabel Lee
1930–32 .... Emil Rath
1932–33 .... Strong Hinman

The Present Midwest

1933–34 .... Margaret Bell
1934–35 ...... Guy S. Lowman
1935–36 .... Helen N. Smith
1936–37 ..... John McCollough
1937–38 .. Laurentine B. Collins
1938–39 .... William K. Streit
1939–40 ... Helen W. Hazelton
1940–41 .... August H. Pritzlaff
1941–42 .... Grace M. Griffen
1942–43 .... Ben W. Miller
1943–44 .... Iris Boulton
1944–46 .... Robert Nohr

1946–47 .. Gertrude E. Moulton
1947–48 ...... Leon G. Kranz
1948–49 .... Edwina Jones
1949–50 ...... Lou H. Hollway
1950–51 .... Anne Finlayson
1951–52 ... Clarence Biedenweg
1952–53 ... Carolyn Bookwalter
1953–54 .... Paul E. Landis
1954–55 ... Margaret A. Bourne
1955–56 ... Arthur H. Steinhaus
1956–57 ...... Hester B. Bland
1957–58 ...... King McCristol

PRESIDENTS OF
CENTRAL DISTRICT ASSOCIATION OF AAHPER

1933–34 .... Charles H. McCloy
1934–35 .... Clare H. Small
1935–36 .... Louis E. Hutto

1936–37 .... Edna McCullough
1937–38 ... Alfred O. Anderson
1938–39 .... Elizabeth Halsey

1939–40	..... Willard N. Greim	1949–50	..... M. Gladys Scott
1940–41	.... Helen Manley	1950–51	.... Merle Henre
1941–42	.... James H. Morrison	1951–52	..... Mabel J. Shirley
1942–43	.... Gertrude M. Baker	1952–53	.... Leonard R. Marti
1943–44	.... Carl L. Nordly	1953–54	.... Wilma Gimmestad
1944–46	... Germaine G. Guiot	1954–55	.... R. B. Frost
1946–47	.... Louis F. Keller	1955–56	.... Jean Bontz
1947–48	... Elizabeth Graybeal	1956–57	...... Edwin R. Elbel
1948–49	..... L. P. Washburn	1957–58	.. A. Gwendolyn Drew

PRESIDENTS OF
SOUTHERN DISTRICT ASSOCIATION OF AAHPER

1927–29	.... A. D. Browne	1943–44	.... Katherine W.
1929–30	... Jackson R. Sharman		Montgomery
1930–31	..... Elliott V. Graves	1944–46	.... Oliver K. Cornwell
1931–32	.... Mary C. Coleman	1946–47	...... Mary Ella Soule
1932–33	...... David K. Brace	1947–48	.... Joy W. Kistler
1933–34	..... Caswell M. Miles	1948–49	...... Helen Corrubia
1934–35	.... Jessie R. Garrison	1949–50	..... Solon B. Sudduth
1935–36	.... Harry A. Scott	1950–51	..... Margaret McCall
1936–37	..... Harold T. Taylor	1951–52	... Charles E. Spencer
1937–38	..... Alfreda Mosscrop	1952–53	..... Elizabeth Moore
1938–39	Thomas E. McDonough	1953–54	.. Gilbert L. Hermance
1939–40	.. Anne Schley Duggan	1954–55	..... Caroline Sinclair
1940–41	...... Lynn B. Sherril	1955–56	.... C. J. Alderson
1941–42	...... Ethel J. Saxman	1956–57	..... Elizabeth Autrey
1942–43	.. Name not available	1957–58	...... Guy W. Nesom

PRESIDENTS OF
NORTHWEST DISTRICT ASSOCIATION OF AAHPER

1930–31	.... J. Fred Bohler	1944–45	.... Lestle Sparks
1931–32	..... Henry M. Foster	1945–46	.... Eva M. Seen
1932–33	...... Paul R. Washke	1946–47	..... Edwina Graham
1933–34	...... Henry H. House	1947–48	...Dorothea M. Lensch
1934–35	..... Ruth Weythman	1948–49	.... G. Spencer Reeves
1935–36	...... John F. Bovard	1949–50	.... Grace Houghton
1936–37	...... Eva Jurgensohn	1950–51	.... Leon Green
1937–38	.... Madeline Larson	1951–53	... Agnes L. Stoodley
1938–39	..... Earl E. Boushey	1953–54	...... George J. Sirnio
1939–40	..... Helen G. Smith	1954–55	...... Mabel Locke
1940–41	.... A. C. Pelton	1955–56	..... Glen E. Galligan
1941–42	..... Virginia L. Shaw	1956–57	.... Harold Alterowitz
1942–43	..... Clair V. Langton	1957–58	.. Robert W. Bergstrom
1943–44	Mary Gross Hutchinson		

PRESIDENTS OF
SOUTHWEST DISTRICT ASSOCIATION OF AAHPER

1934–36 ... William R. LaPorte	1947–48 .... Verne S. Landreth
1936–38 .... Charles Davis	1948–49 .. Luell Weed Guthrie
1938–39 ..... Louise S. Cobb	1949–50 .... Frank R. Williams
1939–40 .... Catherine A. Worthingham	1950–51 .... J. E. Marti
	1951–52 ..... Elwood C. Davis
1940–41 ...... Bernice R. Moss	1952–53 ... Dudley S. DeGroot
1941–42 ...... James Coleman	1953–54 Catherine A. Wilkinson
1942–43 ..... Mrs. Leo Cleaves	1954–55 ..... H. B. Hunsaker
1943–44 ...... John F. Bovard	1955–56 .... Glenn Arnett
1944–45 .... Glen Worthington	1956–57 .... Ruth I. Russell
1945–46 .... Hazel J. Cubberly	1957–58 ...... John M. Cooper
1946–47 .. Alice Oakes Bronson	1958–59 .... Lois Downs

HONORARY DOCTOR'S DEGREES CONFERRED UPON
PHYSICAL EDUCATORS

1851–M.D. to Dio Lewis by The Medical School of Cleveland

1898–LL.D. to Edward M. Hartwell by Amherst College

1921–LL.D. to R. Tait McKenzie by McGill University

1928–D.F.A. to R. Tait McKenzie by the University of Pennsylvania

1930–Pd.D. (Doctor of Pedagogy) to Amy Morris Homans by Russell Sage College

1933–LL.D. to Amos Alonzo Stagg by the College of Wooster

1935–Pd.D. to Clark W. Hetherington by the University of Southern California

1939–LL.D. to Mabel Lee by Coe College

1942–Pd.D. to Agnes R. Wayman by Russell Sage College

1943–D. Sc. in P.E. to Elizabeth Burchenal by Boston University

1944–LL.D. to Helen McKinstry by Skidmore College

1947–D. Sc. to Charles H. McCloy by Marietta College

1949–D. Sc. in P.E. to Anna Hiss, Ruth Evans, Francis M. Greene, William L. Hughes, and F. R. Aquino by Boston University

1949–D. Sc. to Catherine A. Worthingham by Boston University

1950–L.H.D. (Doctor of Humane Letters) to Rosalind E. Cassidy by Mills College

1954–LL.D. to William Ralph LaPorte by Pepperdine College

1954–LL.D. to G. Ott Romney by Montana State College

1955–D. Sc. to Charles H. McCloy by Grinnell College

1955–D. Sc. to William L. Hughes by Springfield College

1956–D.P.E. to Mabel Lee by George Williams College

1957–Lit. D. to Charles H. McCloy by George Williams College

EARLY STATE DIRECTORS OF PHYSICAL EDUCATION

1916—New York
　　　　Thomas A. Storey
1918—California
　　　　Clark W. Hetherington
1922—Connecticut
　　　　Allen G. Ireland
1922—Massachusetts
　　　　Carl L. Schrader
1925—Virginia
　　　　Elliott V. Graves
1926—New Jersey
　　　　Frederick W. Maroney

1926—Missouri
　　　　Henry S. Curtis
1926—Alabama
　　　　Jackson R. Sharman
1926—Maryland
　　　　William H. Burdick
1926—Michigan
　　　　Alden O. Thompson
1926—Ohio
　　　　Clifford L. Brownell
1926—Pennsylvania
　　　　Charles H. Keene

In 1931 Jessie R. Garrison was appointed State Physical Director of Alabama to succeed Jackson R. Sharman—the first woman in the United States to hold such a position.

NAME INDEX

SUBJECT INDEX

Academies, 177, 181, 183, 186, 198, 250
Greek, 24, 26
Albania, physical education in, 142
Amateur Athletic Union, 227, 228, 286, 291, 350, 378–79
Amateur sports, 195, 349, 350, 368
American Academy of Physical Education, 316–17, 330, 332, 376–77, 407
American Association for Advancement of Physical Education (AAAPE), 261–63, 405
American Association for Health, Physical Education and Recreation, 339, 349, 360, 373, 374–76, 383, 405–12
American Physical Education Association (APEA), 259, 291, 304–5, 312, 314–15, 346, 373, 405
Amherst College, 189–90, 196, 201, 202–3, 204
Archery, 10, 62, 63, 65, 83, 122
Argentina, physical education in, 159–60
Asceticism, 51–52, 67
Assyria, physical activities in, 6
Athens; see Greece
Athletes, stature and muscularity of, 282, 344
Athletic clubs and organizations, 194, 227, 230, 318–23, 377–83; see also Sports, clubs and associations
Athletic coaches, 298, 346, 362, 381
Athletic competition for boys and men, 348–51
Athletic Conference (Federation) of American College Women (AFACW), 320, 352, 380, 381

Athletic Institute, 373, 377, 382–83
Athletic League of North America, 320
Athletic leagues, 224, 248, 255, 289, 318–19, 320, 348, 349, 350; see also Sports, leagues; State leagues
Athletic Research Society, 289, 319, 331, 332
Athletics for girls in industry, 291, 292, 354
Australia, physical education in, 130–32
Awards, 323, 350, 382, 383, 406–7

Babylonia, physical activities in, 6
Badminton, 227, 343, 347, 363
Ball games in ancient civilizations, 4, 7, 8, 10, 33, 38, 44, 49
Baseball, 135, 152–53, 172, 183, 193–94, 195, 209, 222–23, 285, 342, 343, 349, 350, 351; see also Rounders
Basketball, 132, 135, 172, 223, 255, 342, 343–44, 349, 350, 381
for girls, 227, 230, 256, 290, 291, 351, 353, 354, 363, 378
Belgium, physical education in, 148
Bicycling, 99, 132, 213, 223–24, 230, 343
Body building and mechanics, 138, 166, 167, 293, 341, 357, 361, 363
Bolivia, physical education in, 161
Boston Normal School of Gymnastics, 247, 252–53, 266, 306, 367
Bowdoin College, 201, 234, 240, 241, 243, 268
Bowling, 123, 224, 343, 344–45; see also Ninepins

419